The Acoustics of Crime

**The New Science of
Forensic Phonetics**

APPLIED PSYCHOLINGUISTICS AND COMMUNICATION DISORDERS

A Continuation Order Plan is available for this series. A continuation order will bring delivery of each new volume immediately upon publication. Volumes are billed only upon actual shipment. For further information please contact the publisher.

The Acoustics of Crime
The New Science of Forensic Phonetics

Harry Hollien
University of Florida
Gainesville, Florida

Plenum Press • New York and London

Library of Congress Cataloging-in-Publication Data

Hollien, Harry Francis, 1926-
    The acoustics of crime : the new science of forensic phonetics /
Harry Hollien.
        p.   cm. -- (Applied psycholinguistics and communication
disorders)
    Includes bibliographical references and index.
    ISBN 0-306-43467-9
    1. Criminal investigation. 2. Phonetics.   I. Title. II. Series.
HV8073.H624 1990
363.2'58--dc20   90-7448
                                                           CIP

©1990 Plenum Press, New York
A Division of Plenum Publishing Corporation
233 Spring Street, New York, N.Y. 10013

Printed in the United States of America

To Patti

My wife   my colleague

my friend

Preface

There are many reasons for writing a book; this one was conceived and developed mainly for two. First, a new area has emerged from within the forensic sciences—that of forensic phonetics. As with all new specialties, it is necessary to define it, identify its boundaries, justify its importance and compile a list of the elements it encompasses. This book attempts to outline these several relationships. Second, over the past decade I have become fascinated with forensics in general and the rapidly expanded subarea of forensic phonetics in particular. Admittedly, the latter field is one that is not as yet sufficiently appreciated—and much more needs to be known about its nature and extent. Yet, I have found it to be a most enjoyable area of study and my attempts to describe its domains were quite informative. It was especially interesting to struggle with the interfaces between forensic phonetics and related fields, and discover how they overlap.

Only a few comments will be made about the book's contents here in the preface. For one thing, they are described in some detail in the first chapter. Moreover, a detailed table of contents is provided; hence, information about the main divisions (i.e., "The Basics," "Problems with Tape Recordings," "Speaker Identification," "Stress in Voice," and "Related Areas"), as well as the primary sections within each of the individual chapters, can be found there. As the reader will discover very early, I believe forensic phonetics to include such topics as the enhancement of speech on tape recordings, the accurate decoding of recorded speech, the authentication of tape recordings, speaker identification, the detection of stress in voice and the identification of acoustic/recorded signatures of many types. Perhaps the territory should encompass yet other issues; in any event, this book should serve as a first approximation of the field.

The second point I wish to make concerns my approach to the task of presenting materials on the topics just cited. Since I recognize that the reader often will be interested in only one or two of the several areas presented, I have tried to write each chapter in a way that permits it to stand on its own. Thus, after the four chapters that comprise "The Basics," I wrote each chapter (or at least each section) as an independent element—and only later wove them into a sequence by means of a single writing style, cross-referencing and interfacing among the elements. This approach has led to a little redundancy in some places (see, for example, that between the "Basic Equipment" and "Electronic Surveillance" chapters; that among the chapters on the "Authentication of Tape Recordings," "Machine/Computer Approaches," and "Signatures: Machine and Acoustic"). So be it. I have found that whereas some readers can be briefed on a specific area without reference to the rest of the book, others report that—when they read the chapters in sequence—the occasional repetition simply serves to underscore the point being made. Please also note that certain chapters are organized in a different fashion than others. The reason for this is a practical one; some of the concepts presented are applied in nature and are based on practice rather than research, whereas others are strongly theoretical with a great deal of data but few techniques available to the practitioner. Hence, the approach used in writing the chapter on "Noisy Tapes" will be seen as different from that employed for "Psychological Stress."

Third, I should like to emphasize here as well as later (see Chapter 1) that this book is not an expose of any type. It is of little consequence to me which "side" requests that I carry out certain tasks. If the data that result from my investigations "aids" them, fine. If it does not, so be it. One must remember that nearly every attorney and/or law enforcement agent is an advocate. Hence, behaviors that might appear to constitute misconduct or marginal ethics usually are the result of their enthusiasms or conviction that they are "in the right." In short, most people in all the professions addressed by this book appear to be both sincere and ethical.

Finally, I would like to recognize the assistance and support of a number of agencies and people. Indeed, whatever contributions I have been able to make have resulted from the support I have received and the things—ordinarily good, occasionally bad, and sometimes profound—that I have learned from other people. The individuals to whom I am referring number in the hundreds; a few are listed below. Moreover, the agencies that have provided me with research support range from the National Institute of Justice to the Veterans Administration, from the Office of Naval Research to the Army Research Office, from the National Institutes of Health to the National Science Foundation, from the International Research Exchanges Board to the Fulbright Commission, and from the Dreyfus to the Gould and the Voice Foundations. I thank all of them for their kind consideration and support.

But, the interface with my colleagues has been even more important to me. From James F. Curtis, I learned that precision in research is a must and how to resist scientific fads; from Gordon Peterson, I learned the importance of being scientifically thorough and always ethical; and from Joseph Wepman, how to be honest and outspoken but not "play politics." The other dozen or so people who have had the greatest impact on my work—and especially on this book—are W. S. Brown, Jr., E. Thomas Doherty, Marylou P. Gelfer, W. J. Gould, J. W. Hicks, Jr., Ruth Huntley, Martin Kloster-Jensen, Jens-Peter Köster, Wojceich Majewski, Robert E. McGlone, William A. Sakow, Thomas Shipp, Gilbert C. Tolhurst, R. W. Wendahl, Jürgen Wendler—and my wife Patricia A. Hollien, who really should be coauthor. Special thanks go to her, Kay Ervin and Kevin Hollien who assisted mightily with the manuscript and figures, and to Robert Rieber for his patience. Finally, there are my children—Brian and Kevin, Christine and Stephanie, Keith and Karen; they contributed in many ways.

Contents

PART I

The Basics

CHAPTER 1

Introduction

Late in the 1970s, I was asked by a lawyer to evaluate a pair of tape recordings for authenticity. Specifically, he requested that I try to determine if either (or both) of the recordings had been altered, modified or tampered with in any manner. I call this case, and the resulting litigation, "Of Racehorses and Secretaries." It involved a pair of politicians who had been cronies for years. However, they now were no longer pals; in fact, they had become enemies over a racehorse. One of them, let's call him Jim, had purchased a thoroughbred, carefully raced it out of the money a number of times, and then "let her loose!" Needless to say, he won a bundle. When his partner (let's call him Bill) heard about Jim's financial success at the track, he was irate. Bill simply could not understand why he had been left out of the deal after years of friendship and collaboration. In any event, he vowed revenge. Knowing where all of the "skeletons" were hidden, Bill simply called in several law enforcement groups and told them of Jim's many crimes. As you would expect, he requested and received immunity. Unfortunately, there was a lack of firm evidence supporting Bill's statements and, hence, the relevant agents suggested that he "become concerned" about one of their illegal operations and get Jim to reveal his part in the affair while they discussed the problem over the telephone—a phone which, incidentally, had been tapped. The first tape recording, made by trained FBI agents, was technically very good. The conversation itself, however, while tantalizing, apparently did not provide grounds for indictment. The agents then suggested that Bill try again on his own—and from his house. He did so and managed to obtain the desired recorded evidence; at least it seemed so, for Jim was indicted. However, when Jim was confronted with the second tape, his recollection of the actual telephone conversations with Bill were in variance with those he heard played to him. Of course, many defendants claim that tape recordings made of their criminal activities have been falsified. It usually is wishful thinking on their part but, once in a while, they are justified in their belief. In any case, Bill stood fast, saying that he knew that the second of the two tape recordings had been altered in some manner. I was the expert on tape authentication called in to evaluate the recordings and make recommendations.

When you work for the prosecution in this or related areas, the tape recordings in question—and the relevant equipment—ordinarily are sent directly to your laboratory (or your home) by some secure method (registered mail, for example). Your responsibility is to treat such evidence with great respect, insuring that it is not damaged in any way, that the chain of custody is maintained and that the materials are returned in exactly the same pristine condition in which they were sent to you.

On the other hand, this rather pleasant relationship ordinarily does not occur when you are employed by the defense. Exceptions do happen occasionally—especially if you are known personally to the court or the prosecutor. However, if you are a defense expert, you either have to travel to where the tape recordings and equipment are kept or a law enforcement agent carries them to your laboratory. The second of these two procedures was used in this instance. The FBI agent arrived promptly at my office at the appointed time and had in his possession the two relevant tape recorders plus the two disputed tape recordings. First, I physically examined these items and made test tapes of the equipment; these physical examinations proved unremarkable. At this juncture, I made copies of the two tapes for further analysis (see Chapter 8). While doing so, the agent and I listened to the two tapes together in my office. The first of the two—the one made by the agents themselves—appeared to meet all of the criteria for authenticity with the few questionable instances appearing either trivial or easily explained (ultimately they proved to be so). The tape made by Bill was altogether a different matter. Here, there were several places where modifications could have occurred and these events would have to be carefully examined at a later time. After I finished copying the second tape, the agent got up to leave. I said that although I had carried out all of the tests possible while he was present and obtained all of the material necessary for a full examination, there was yet one procedure that had to be carried out. I had to listen to the reverse side of Bill's tape to make sure it was blank. The agent said that he would miss his plane if I did so. I responded that I had to follow through as I was required to be both fair and thorough in my work. To his consternation, I proceeded to play the "reverse" side of the tape recording.

In the beginning it, indeed, was blank, and the two of us sat there listening to hiss. Needless to say, the agent was pretty unhappy. However, after about a third of the tape recording had been run, someone apparently turned on the recorder, and a person, who proved to be Bill's daughter, was heard practicing for a piano recital. Apparently she did not listen to her performance, but rather simply left the room after completing this chore. The important thing was that the tape recorder was left on. For a while, all that could be heard were typical household sounds. But then, in the distance (apparently from another room) we heard Bill and his wife fighting over an affair he was having with his secretary. The argument proved to be pretty exciting, especially when the participants drifted into the room where the tape recorder was situated and we could hear them clearly. At this juncture Mrs. Bill, quite graphically and at some length, described what she would do to him (physically) if he did not terminate his affair. She then proceeded to relate how she also would go to the authorities, the defense lawyers or even the newspapers, and tell them why he was angry and how he actually had "set Jim up" for prosecution. Needless to say, my evaluation of the authenticity of this particular tape recording became quite secondary and the trial itself took on a markedly different character. I do not know how it all came out (the expert witness rarely does); I suspect, however, that the entire case pretty much fell apart.

I learned a great deal from this experience. First, it instilled in me the need to (1) be thorough in all examinations, (2) study as many facets of a project as is possible, (3) use all analysis approaches available, and (4) be as scientifically rigorous in forensic examinations as I would be when conducting laboratory research. I also learned that the emerging specialty of forensic phonetics can provide experiences that are funny as well as serious and important, that the cases nearly always are interesting and that some are downright fascinating. These observations have led me to write this book.

THE FOCUS OF THE BOOK

The book is written primarily for three groups of people: (1) scientists, engineers, and technicians who possess reasonably relevant (and basic) backgrounds in the areas covered, specialized knowledge in at least some of the areas discussed, and an interest in this type of work; (2) attorneys—both criminal and civil, trial and corporate—who have a need to know about the problems and issues to be covered; and (3) law enforcement personnel of all types and at all levels (as well as individuals involved in intelligence and security work) who have an interest in these issues and/or a need to know about them. Combined, these groups make up a fairly heterogeneous population. However, they are involved in a forensic area which, while relatively new, is becoming quite important. The problems and issues associated with forensic phonetics are increasing at an accelerating rate. It is an area that soon may become as important as others within the forensic sciences. Indeed, less than 20 years ago, there were but a few hundred cases a year (in the entire country) that involved tape-recorded evidence, authenticity of tape recordings, speech decoding from tape recordings, stress in voice, speaker identification, and so on. Currently that number of cases appears to be occurring nearly every week. The future? With new technological developments taking place almost daily, with new techniques and novel approaches being introduced at virtually as fast a rate, the challenge we face appears to be almost explosive in nature. Thus, it would appear useful to meet this challenge before it overwhelms us.

The problem I face in writing this book is to somehow make the text technical enough to satisfy the scientists and engineers, yet straightforward enough so that attorneys and agents will not be put off by a lot of unnecessary jargon. And, of course, my major goal is to be accurate.

It is tempting to take one of the several easy paths available to me. For example, I could make the text very technical; most scientists would be quite comfortable with this approach. Or I could construct a "how-to" cookbook that would permit agents and technicians to follow recipes to the practical solutions of specific (if somewhat limited) problems.

To me, the first approach would not be helpful to anyone. If interested in the area, scientists and engineers can educate themselves (basically, that is) simply by reading the relevant technical publications and research reports. Moreover, a book exclusively on the scientific/technical level would be of little use to attorneys and law enforcement personnel. Finally, while cookbooks are fine for the kitchen, this area is too large and complex for such a simplistic technique. In my judgment, the best approach is to attempt to provide those who are interested with an introduction to the area, the issues involved and some of the problems to be faced. To do so, I will review those basic processes relevant to forensic phonetics and attempt to define its boundaries.

To be specific, I have chosen to structure this book so that it will provide (1) an overview of, and relevant perspectives about, the field of forensic phonetics; (2) basic information about the field and the science upon which its approaches are based; (3) reasonable descriptions of the techniques employed to solve many of the problems encountered; (4) perspectives about some of the pseudoscientific or questionable approaches (such as "voiceprints" and "voice stress" evaluators) proposed for use by law enforcement agencies and the courts; and (5) some information about how scientists and engineers function relative to their problem-solving activities.

Some Perspectives

First, I expect that some scientists who read this book will grumble about the "popular" style of writing employed. So be it. I have long been vexed by the unnecessarily obscure presentations often found in scientific reports. For my part, I wish to communicate the relevant information and opinions as best I can—at least, in such a way that they can be followed by any reasonably educated person. Thus, the remarks and materials that follow are based both on personal experience and on those scientific principles and experimental results I believe to be sound. Illustrative examples involving actual cases in which I have participated will be woven into the text, and references will be provided when necessary (they are listed at the end of the last chapter). Please note that the reference section contains two types of references: (1) those that are cited in the text and (2) supplemental references which may be useful for additional study. Naturally, I will not attempt to include all of the sources I have used or all that are available. Nevertheless, you should find those listed to be both representative and reasonably comprehensive.

Second, please note also that some attorneys and/or law enforcement agents may feel that parts of this book are too "detailed" or too "scientific" in nature. Perhaps so. However, if these individuals are motivated to learn more about this area (or find it necessary to do so), they are urged to at least skim over the materials included so that they can better understand (1) what can and cannot be accomplished by specialists in the forensic phonetics area and (2) the time and effort it takes to accomplish some of the tasks described. "The Case of the Disappearing Dialogue" should serve to illustrate this issue. (Indeed, it provides a rather good example of the type of challenge I have faced over and over again during the 30 or more years I have been engaged in these activities— mostly as an aside to my primary job as a university professor/scientist.)

A number of years ago, a local detective, whom I will call Bob, appeared in my office clutching a cassette tape recording. It seems that he had been given (court) permission to install a surveillance microphone/transmitter under the house of an individual whom he—but, apparently, very few of his fellow agents—believed to be a drug dealer. After several sleepless nights (mostly on his own time), he finally was able to record his target who, it turned out, was in bed telling his girlfriend how, where and to whom she was to transport some heroin. The agent assured me that he had heard this exchange firsthand and, later on, the conversation "repeated" on the tape recording. But now "it is gone," he lamented. I played the tape, and after a few minutes of recorded (and titillating) conversation, moans, and bed-squeaks, the tape went quiet; it did so, according to Bob, just before the incriminating dialogue occurred. It took only a little additional examination to discover that this section somehow had been erased. "Yes," said Agent Bob, "I thought so too. What I want you to do is get down into the tape and bring out what's left of that speech. Then I can get a search warrant." No amount of explanation appeared to convince Bob that the dialogue he so very much wanted to hear again was irretrievably lost, at least on that tape recording. For nearly a year after that, I received telephone calls from Bob asking me what I thought about some new technique (he had heard about) which was purported to reconstruct the "residue" from a tape recording that had been erased. He was sure that "those people who erased that section of the Watergate tape all those times knew what they were doing." He was, of course, referring to the famous (or infamous) multiple erasures of the 18-minute section of the so-called "Rosemary Wood" White House tape recording. Had he only understood how a tape recorder actually works (see Chapter 4), he would have been a great deal more careful with his tape-recorded evidence. Perhaps this is the best reason of all for those of you who are law enforcement agents to plow through some of the technical discussions—that is, if you are interested in, or assigned to, activities such as those described in this book. Incidentally, I never did find out how Bob's tape was erased in the first place.

Third, I had better specify exactly how I intend to use my personal experiences to illustrate the various topics to be covered. As you might expect, I have participated in a number of actual cases that will prove useful as examples. In all they number well over 300. My 60-70 court appearances have been for the prosecution, the defense and the court itself; they have included criminal and civil cases in state and federal (and Canadian) courts as well as inquiry/ethics boards and the Florida legislature. I will use examples only as appropriate, and avoid identifying any of the persons involved. Thus, most cases used as examples will be somewhat disguised, primarily in order to avoid embarrassing any of the people involved. Indeed, I wish to emphasize that this book is not intended to be an expose of any event or any person. I have no wish to embarrass anyone; hence, none of the judges, experts, prosecutors, defense lawyers, witnesses, agents, investigators, defendants, or anyone else, will be named. I believe it is necessary to conceal the actual identity of the people involved since the examples that follow occasionally demonstrate that some of them have made serious mistakes, used poor judgment or guessed wrong. Sometimes these errors were made quite innocently or resulted from the fact that not enough good information was available at the time. However, I suspect that occasionally the "error" was made with malice aforethought, for personal gain/protection or because of intellectual inadequacy. On these occasions, I feel less charitable, of course, but I am still not willing to be specific. The only exception is when an individual expresses an opinion, takes a position, or releases data in some form (i.e., via the press, books, scientific journals, etc.) or testifies under oath. In these instances, I feel quite justified in taking issue with those opinions/actions with which I disagree, for once a person testifies under oath or signs his or her name to a work, that person is fair game—that is, if he or she has been inaccurate or sloppy.

To summarize, while you may be sure that the examples I use are factual and accurate, they have been disguised to protect the participants. Moreover, I reserve the right to include my personal opinions or analyses when relevant.

Finally, let me insert one additional perspective. Forensic phonetics is beginning to be recognized as an important specialty here in the United States, and a number of legal and law enforcement groups are beginning to understand that they can obtain certain types of assistance from phonetics laboratories. For example, our institute (IASCP) at the University of Florida was so inundated with requests for assistance that we simply had to refuse them, referring all inquires to Forensic Communication Associates—a local firm of consultants specializing in this area. After all, the mission of a university is teaching and research. A little applied work is fine, but large service units such as shops, clinics and so forth belong out in the community—or, in this case, directly in crime laboratories or consulting agencies.

To the best of my knowledge, there is only one country that is substantially more enlightened than we are—and that country is West Germany. As would be expected, their Bundeskriminalamt (BKA), or National Police, is much concerned with the issues reviewed in this book. Accordingly, they have established a special laboratory to respond to these problems. It is headed by Herman Kuenzel, a doctoral-level phonetic scientist, and employs both phoneticians as well as support engineers and technicians. Small wonder at the incredible success rate exhibited by the BKA group. It is so swamped by requests from Germany and by other European countries that it finds it necessary to transfer many of the peripheral cases to other phonetics laboratories throughout that country. Quite clearly, this group is far ahead of virtually all other crime laboratories around the world. In all fairness, however, the British Home Office also is developing a specialized crime laboratory of this type; however, it tends to employ engineers, using phoneticians on a contract basis.

Please note that I in no way intend to disparage engineers or physicists (especially those at an advanced level), especially if they receive special training in phonetics and speech. My point is simply that the average engineer or audioengineer is hampered by a lack of knowledge about the physiology, structuring and perception of speech, and often is not able to operate as effectively in this area as can the phonetician with some engineering background. Of course, engineers and other classes of scientists bring many useful skills to the processes to be described. However, their lack of background in human behavior and phonetics sometimes impedes them from operating effectively in the cited areas.

The worst case, of course, is the practice of taking agents from the field (as occurs so often in our country) and attempting to train them with a few 2-week courses and seminars in the relevant areas. This practice is a dangerous one. These agents actually are policemen and policewomen; undoubtedly they are good ones, as they often have advanced degrees in criminal justice and extensive field experience. Nevertheless, they simply are out of their depth if they attempt to become scientists or engage in unsupervised forensic phonetics. In any event, if the U.S. law enforcement sector is going to effectively handle the activities described in the succeeding chapters, they would do well to consider the success of the BKA. But now, let me review the contents of this book.

WHAT THE BOOK IS ALL ABOUT

This book is about forensic phonetics. In turn, forensic phonetics can best be understood by consideration of Figure 1-1; it will help to keep these relationships in mind as you read the rest of this chapter. I have divided the book into five

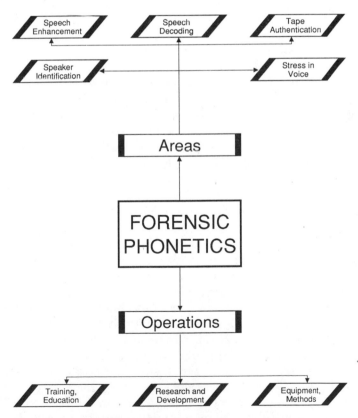

Figure 1-1. A model of the nature and scope of forensic phonetics. The five content areas most basic to the specialty are listed in the upper third of the figure; the three major activities at the bottom.

parts of 2 to 4 chapters each. The first section—"The Basics" — provides a foundation for all of the other parts. Indeed, it will be a little difficult (but not impossible) to follow the text relative to the other topics if you have little to no understanding of (1) simple acoustics, (2) how speech is produced, coded and perceived, or (3) the nature of such simple instruments as microphones, earphones and tape recorders. If you already have a grounding in these areas, or wish only a quick overview of the main issues, this entire section can be skipped. On the other hand, if you are interested in becoming a specialist in forensic phonetics or an allied area (consulting, active career), the four chapters that make up Part I are but an introduction. A great deal of additional, and advanced, study in each of the several specialties would be required before you would be competent to operate effectively.

In Part II, I consider the sources of forensic problems on tape recordings and what to do about them; it consists of four chapters (Chapters 5-8). Basically, they deal with tape recordings of all types—and from all sources. However, each chapter is focused on a particular issue. For example, Chapter 5 involves a discussion of the various forms of electronic surveillance and the tape recording of evidence. Included are descriptions of body bugs, miniature tape recorders and transmitters, fixed position microphones, wire taps—and the problems that can occur in these and related situations. The next chapter involves describing the characteristics of distortion and noise—especially as they occur on tape recordings—and what can be done about them. Both analog and digital filtering are discussed and some advanced technologies are introduced. Next, in Chapter 7, the decoding process/techniques and problems with courtroom transcripts will be reviewed. The final chapter in the second section will focus on the authentication of tape recordings. Suggested rules/procedures will be presented; included will be those that were developed for the sometimes federally mandated "minimization process." A systematic review of the steps that must be taken before a tape recording can be considered valid are described.

The next grouping (Part III) involves the identification of speakers from their voice alone (usually from tape-recorded samples). Chapter 9 initiates these discussions with definitions and briefly covers the general history of the speaker recognition problem. However, the main focus of this chapter is on voice identification by aural-perceptual means. Included are those procedures carried out in the courtroom and the "voice lineup" process which sometimes is used in criminal investigations. The review includes information about the weaknesses of the lineup technique, oft-made errors, and some of the ways to insure that it is employed with reasonable fairness to all involved, if it is employed at all. Chapter 9 also includes discussions of research and using human listeners to make aural-perceptual judgments of a talker's identity (it extends the section on the voice lineup into more complex areas). Chapters 10 and 11 are designed to cover the other approaches to speaker identification (as well as much of the research that has been carried out on each) and their strengths and weaknesses. In Chapter 10, I review the so-called voiceprint, or voicegram, approach to speaker identification and its limitations. The final chapter in this section will focus on the currently proposed, or used, machine and/or computer-assisted approaches.

This chapter also provides a brief discussion of, and references for, some of the approaches to speaker verification.

Part IV addresses the general problem of detecting stress in the human voice; it consists of two chapters. There are many groups of people who would like to, or need to, determine if or when a speaker is suffering from stress states. Illustrations include control tower operators talking to pilots in trouble; crisis center personnel talking to callers threatening suicide; people who are monitoring aquanauts or astronauts, and law enforcement personnel in a variety of situations. It also may be important to know if the speaker is suffering from psychosis—or is drunk or on drugs. As will be seen from a reading of Chapter 12, some information is available in these areas, and certain predictions about what "stressed" speech sounds like are possible. Chapter 13, on the other hand, discusses the use of currently marketed voice stress monitors—often referred to as "psychological stress evaluators." These systems, which most often are used as a kind of "voice lie detector," are described and contrasted to the polygraph, and the research evaluating their validity is discussed. The so-called lie factor, and the possibility of its existence, is also reviewed.

Finally, I would like to discuss the very last part in the book or, to be more accurate, justify it. It is the shortest of the five and contains three chapters. These include discussions of several topics which, while related to forensic phonetics, possibly are not included within this discipline. They are reviewed for two reasons: (1) phoneticians often find themselves working in these areas and (2) the topics discussed often interact with those fundamental to our field.

Chapter 14 is focused upon an area that can be referred to as analysis of "machine signatures." This term can be defined as the idiosyncratic (and repeatable) acoustic or electronic noises created when some machine, system or device is operated. There are many reasons to study these events and catalog them. For example, knowledge about machine and electronic signatures is of vital importance to the tape recording authentication process; it is important also in and of itself. To be specific, I have been involved in a number of cases where the issue of interest was acoustic or electronic signatures of gunshots, aircraft engine "noise," clicks made by solenoids located in a telephone rack room, telephone hang-up pulses and the activation signatures of tape recorders. Hence, this book would not be complete without a consideration of "machine" signatures.

The next to last chapter contains a review of several areas which are ancillary to forensic phonetics. Brief introductions of four areas will be provided; they include language evaluation for forensic purposes, forensic psychoacoustics, the pirating of tape recordings and crimes involving computers that are relevant to our area of interest. A few examples should suffice as an introduction to this chapter. Language and/or linguistic analysis can be employed for forensic purposes. Included among these approaches are: (1) cross-language analyses (was the pilot speaking English or Farsi just before the crash?; could the Spanish-speaking defendant understand the "Miranda" warning when spoken in English?); (2) analysis of dialects (did the rapist speak with a Spanish or Brooklyn accent?; did the funny way the extortionist pronounced "bottle" mean he was from New England—or Pakistan?), and (3) quantitative analysis of spoken speech (did Patty Hearst say those terrible things of her own free will or was she forced to repeat prepared statements?; can you tell if the person who calls the crisis center and threatens suicide really means it?). Another discipline that interfaces with forensic phonetics is audition or psychoacoustics. Hearing loss and its cause constitutes a large part of this area. One such issue revolves around normal auditory sensitivity (could the tugboat captain have heard a foghorn warning before he took out a section of the bridge?) and noise (how loud does the music/noise at a lakeside bar have to be before the resident neighbors have a valid complaint?; does "mating activity" carried out in a parking lot constitute "noise"?). In short, forensic phonetics as a discipline impinges on, or interfaces with, such fields as linguistics, psychology, computer science, and engineering. While these relationships may not be at issue, the experimental phonetician often is a psychologist also and has background in engineering. Hence, he or she sometimes is in the best position to form the investigational team—or, at least, contribute to its activities.

Finally, Chapter 16 will include a discussion of expert testimony, its nature and some of the problems associated with it. Perhaps it is a little unusual to incorporate a chapter on expert testimony in a book of this type. It is included not because the forensic phonetician will face special problems here, but rather to provide insight into the special ways his or her product often will be used. Again, the chapter is not written in "how-to" style. Instead it deals with principles upon which expert testimony is based and the legitimate concerns of anyone who must face the adversarial situation in a courtroom. It is easy to sum up your findings relative to any analyses or evaluation you might make in a written report. It is not as simple to present them within the very special environment of a courtroom. Thus, this chapter will include a few points about ethics and the different roles (e.g., consulting, expert witness) forensic phoneticians typically have to carry out. It also will include a few illustrations of how data should be presented in the courtroom, as well as a listing of some problems to be avoided if possible. Case law will not be included in this chapter as a pamphlet on this subject already is available (4).

In short, this book progresses from the substrata, or "basics," needed to understand forensic phonetics, to speech enhancement and decoding, to the authentication of recordings, and then to speaker identification and the detection of stress/psychosis from analysis of voice. It winds up with some remarks about corollary areas and suggestions (at least implied) about how this new field may develop further. I hope that you will find it useful and interesting.

CHAPTER 2

Simple Acoustics

INTRODUCTION

Much of the material contained in this book involves the use, analysis and/or understanding of sound. For example, if we were to analyze the speech contained on a tape recording resulting from an electronic surveillance, the "material" we would process is the acoustic signal of that conversation which was captured on magnetic tape. How did it get there? Or to be more specific: what is its nature; what are its features; what are the actual codes it contains? Yet another example: let us say that we are attempting to evaluate a tape recording to see if it is authentic or has been modified in some manner. All of the sounds we can hear when the tape is played have been created by either some sort of acoustic event or electronic disturbance; we must understand their nature if we are to make valid judgments of authenticity. Another example can be found in the case I will call "Watch Out For Your Relatives." A caller attempted to extort money from a wealthy women. She recorded the second of several calls, which she believed was made by one of her nephews. The stored acoustic signals (the telephone call) and the exemplars later made of the nephews' voices (as well as those of foils, or controls) became the basis of a speaker identification task. The outcome was that one of the nephews was identified as the extortionist. All of these examples relate in some manner to basic acoustics; indeed, the list that could be provided is a very long one. The items cited simply illustrate the fact that an individual must have a basic understanding of acoustics if he or she is going to comprehend and/or carry out the many different processes and procedures described in this book.

Another practical example of this relationship can be found in "The Case of Overheard Murder." Late one night, a young, female deputy sheriff was sitting alone at a switchboard fielding "911" calls. It was a quiet night, that is until she answered a particular call and heard a woman scream, "He's killing me, he's killing my children!" At this juncture it appeared that the assailant grabbed the telephone and ripped it from the wall. What he did not know, however, was that he had not broken the line and the phone was still operative. If law enforcement officials did not give that young deputy a medal they should have, because she:

(1) stopped talking once she realized what had happened (if the assailant had heard her, he really would have severed the connection), (2) kept recording what was happening, (3) called her superior, and (4) asked the telephone company to trace the call. Unbelievably, the telephone company official she reached refused to do so. The reasons for this decision apparently were that (1) it would take too long, (2) they probably would not be successful and (3) anyway, everyone who could trace a call was in bed. The deputy's supervisor arrived quickly; however, the murders were almost over before he could provide assistance. Many hours later, when they found out where the murders had taken place, a team of detectives (already assembled) descended upon the scene and within a few days identified a man they thought was the killer. However, a problem developed. While the detectives were quite sure that the suspect acted alone, there was a very puzzling "utterance" on the tape recording. At one point, the murdered woman had screamed, "God damn you Mike!" But the suspect's name was not Mike. Who was this Mike? None of the other possible suspects were named Mike either, and the suspect was not thought even to know a "Mike."

We were asked to analyze the speech on the tape recording. First, we noted that the dialect employed by the victim, when producing the utterance in question, was not consistent with that of her other speech. At that juncture, we began to segment the acoustic signal into its component parts and discovered that only the first three words of the phrase actually were spoken. What appeared to be "Mike" actually consisted of several nonspeech sounds. Apparently the victim gasped from a blow to the abdomen just as a crashing noise occurred in the background (perhaps a piece of furniture fell over). In short, there was no "Mike"—or at least the victim did not speak that word—as the sound clearly was made up of two different acoustic events emanating from two different sources. Could we have been wrong? I think not. The detectives could not find even the slightest trace of a second suspect (or one named Mike) and, since the physical evidence was overwhelming, the principal suspect was indicted, tried and convicted.

There are many other examples that could be given as to the necessity of knowing at least basic acoustics if you are to work in, or even understand, the field of forensic phonetics. However, if your knowledge in this area is extensive, you can skip this chapter. If it is not, please plow through the concepts that follow. They really are not very difficult to understand.

SOUND

The Nature of Sound

No matter what kind of sound we hear or study, its source is a vibrating body of some kind. That is, the sound in question must have been produced by some type of oscillator or the operation of a system capable of initiating acoustic signals. Further, the source signal must have been converted into some type of oscillations which are transmitted to us so that we can hear and/or measure them. It follows, then, that acoustic signals also require a medium through which they can be transmitted and, in the case of any sound we hear in our normal living environment, the primary medium for such transmission is air. As an aside, however, it should be pointed out that when you listen to your own voice, you hear it as it travels both through air (two ways: sidetone, or around the side of your head, and reflected off any walls or surfaces you may be near) and through the bones and flesh of your neck and head. As a matter of fact, sound can be transmitted through any substance (even water) as long as the medium has minimal elastic properties. However, since air is the primary transmitter of the sounds we will deal with in this book, it is the medium which will be considered in all our discussions of acoustics.

Sound Transmission

Whether at rest or in motion, air is an elastic commodity which transmits sound in somewhat the same way that the water in a pool carries ripples away from the point of impact of a dropped pebble. That is, when some sort of vibrating source sets up a disturbance, the sound is carried from it (and to you) in a series of waves. In air, vibrations are acoustic in nature. They radiate in all directions and not just along a plane, as in the case of a pebble dropped in water. An understanding of sound transmission can be aided by examination of the characteristics of air itself; it is composed of many tiny particles which individually (or as a group) are capable of movement. When some force moves these air particles, a chain reaction occurs. Specifically, a particle will be distorted (i.e., squeezed) and pushed from its rest position in a direction that is away from the force. When doing so, it will move into the space occupied by the next particle. In turn, this second particle will be forced away from the first; i.e., it will move from its rest position and impinge upon the space of still a third particle—and so on. Each particle which is displaced, or set into motion, will eventually resume its original position, but before it does, several events will occur. First, as the particle moves away from its rest, or "home," position, the effect of the vibrating force decreases and, conversely, the countereffect of the particle's complex elasticity (movement, compression) will be increased. At some point, this counterforce will overcome the initiating push and the particle will start moving back toward its "home position." Actually, it will overshoot this position, but if the sound source is producing a periodic vibration, it also will be moving in the other direction at this point in time. Hence, not only will the particle move back as a function of its own elasticity but, in a sense, it also will be "pulled back" by the action of the energy source. The net result is that the particle will overshoot its neutral position and do so to a greater extent than it would if only a single "push" were made. The particle will continue on in the other direction much as the pendulum of a clock overshoots its resting state after you have set it into motion. This relationship is diagrammed in Figure 2-1. Although any periodic movement could be portrayed, to simplify things I am using simple harmonic motion, or a sinusoid (see Figure 2-2), in this example. In any case, assume that the ball is a particle or molecule of air. If it is pushed to the right (i.e., from position 1 to position 2), it will return past position 1 to position 3; it will then swing back and forth until it eventually comes to rest—at least it will if no more

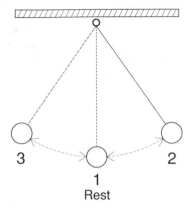

Figure 2-1. The ball or pendulum seen in this figure is activated when a force is applied to it at position 1. It then swings to position 2, back to 1, on to 3, and so on—in a movement referred to as simple harmonic motion—at least if the driving force is constant. If it is removed, the decreasing energy permits it to stop at the neutral position (1).

energy is added to the original "push." The molecules which bump together constitute a compression in the air, while the molecules bouncing apart constitute a rarefaction. It is these compressions and rarefactions moving outward through air as pressure waves which we ultimately hear as sound. They can be best understood by consideration of Figure 2-2. In this figure, a tuning fork can be seen as the sound source; it is vibrating. The groups of small dots represent molecules or particles of air emanating from it in one direction only. As the arm of the tuning fork moves toward this particular string of molecules, they bunch up (compression), and a wave is sent out. As the arm of the tuning fork "moves"

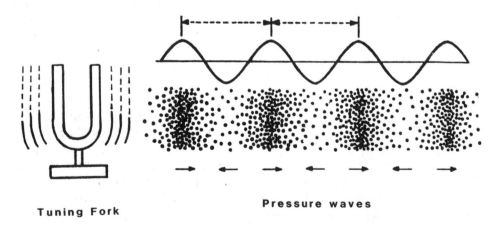

Figure 2-2. Another view of sinusoidal activity. Here, a force is applied to a tuning fork; it overcomes inertia. As the fork's arms move right and then left, it sends out a series of compressions followed by rarefactions—not just laterally but in all directions. The curves at the top show the positive/negative relationships of these compressions/rarefactions, as well as the period length (i.e., time).

away from them, this counterforce (coupled with their elastic recoil) causes them to string out as rarefaction follows compression. As may be seen in the figure, if the tuning fork keeps vibrating, these waves continue to move outward as alternating areas of compression and rarefaction. It is these *bands* of positive and negative pressure—not the molecules themselves—that move out through air and radiate in all directions from the source, not just in the single line shown in Figure 2-2. Moreover, no particular molecule travels very far; it swings back and forth, away from and toward the disturbance within a relatively small segment of space. Finally, it is necessary to keep in mind that the pattern in which the sound source vibrates determines the form of the molecular movement and, as stated, a "source" may produce all sorts of complex arrays—i.e., not just the simple ones seen in Figures 2-1, 2-2 and the top half of 2-3, but also the one found in the bottom half of Figure 2-3.

Frequency

While we will start by discussing periodicity or frequency, it should be recognized that sound is an entity; a gestalt, if you accept that concept of totality. As such, it actually is a little difficult to divide it into its component parts. Thus, I have chosen to structure this chapter into four segments which will provide discussions of frequency, intensity, psychophysics (including scaling) and speech. Naturally, the reviews in each section will overlap with the others—and sometimes

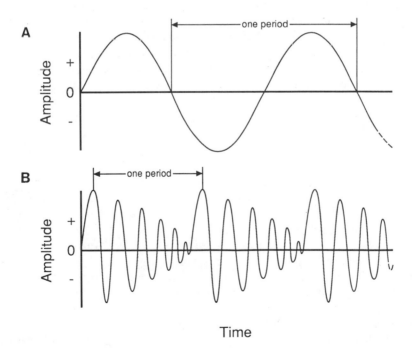

Figure 2-3. Two periodic waves with different fundamentals. The top one is a sine wave (one frequency); the bottom a complex wave made up of a number of partials.

extensively so—but I believe the redundancy among the points I will make will serve to clarify rather than confuse. I certainly hope so.

Periodic Sounds: The Sine Wave

As you are well aware, there are all kinds of sounds: speech, noise, music, thunder, and so on. However, all sounds can be divided roughly into two classes of disturbance: periodic, or "musical," sounds and aperiodic sounds, or noise. While it is difficult to separate the overlap that occurs between these two types of signals, noise can be thought to result from a source that vibrates in an irregular or aperiodic fashion. Hence, let me define noise before proceeding. When you hear a noise, it will tend to be perceived as rough or even unpleasant. It is a type of sound to which it is difficult to assign a musical pitch (primarily because it has little to no periodicity). As you will see, the sounds in which we will be most interested are periodic or quasi-periodic in nature. Hence, our interest in noise will relate mostly to how it can be avoided, removed or mitigated. For purposes of this book, noise will be presented as a kind of second-level sound source or as a distortion. Finally, for forensic determinations anyway, noise can have yet a second definition. Specifically, it is any kind of acoustic energy that interferes with the target sound. Hence, I will be rather specific when discussing "noise," as I can be referring to either ordinary acoustic noise or "forensic noise."

But back to the basic concept of periodicity. The term *periodic* does not refer to how long a sound lasts or if it can be repeated at some other time. Rather, it refers to whether or not the individual waves produced by the sound source keep repeating themselves. As you can see, they do so in Figure 2-2. That is, the tuning fork illustrated there keeps vibrating, and the disturbance it creates travels outward through the air away from it. As has been pointed out, most periodic sounds are not as simple as the sine wave seen in Figure 2-2. Rather, most are complex (see B of Figure 2-3), and some are very complex. However, we will initiate the discussion on periodicity by the consideration of simple harmonic motion or sine waves. In one sense, the concept of simple harmonic motion was described (in the preceding section) when sound transmission was explained as the movement of particles resulting from the application of a simple physical force. Figures 2-3A (a sinusoid portrayed as a function of time) and 2-4 (two sinusoids of the same frequency, different amplitudes) illustrate this type of vibration—just as do Figures 2-1 and 2-2. Basically, a sine wave is produced by an oscillator moving in a very simple, pendulum-like manner. A single frequency is produced; hence, all of the following descriptive terms are synonyms: simple harmonic motion, sine wave, sinusoid, pure tone.

Sinusoids have three main characteristics: frequency, intensity (amplitude) and duration (we will defer discussion of wave composition or spectra until later). These features are common to most sound waves and are related to the perceptual (i.e., heard) attributes of pitch, loudness, and length (of the tone), respectively. When you listen to a voice, for example, you hear a higher pitch if the person raises his or her fundamental frequency; the vocalization seems louder if they increase the intensity of their phonation, and when the duration of

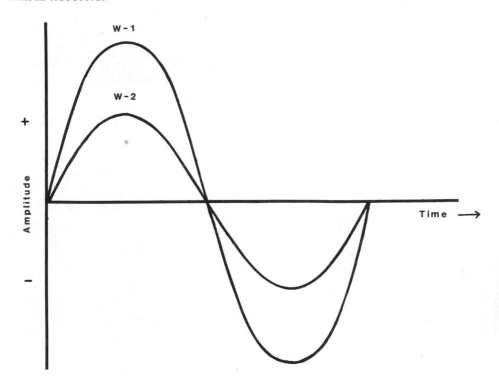

Figure 2-4. A pair of sine waves of the same frequency but with differing amplitudes. They are heard as a single tone.

a tone is increased, it is heard for a longer period of time. Please note, yet again, that most of the examples to follow will relate to speech, as speech constitutes the primary acoustic domain within which we will be working. Of course, other types of acoustic signals are of interest too—for example, noise, clicks, pulses, gunshots and so on. Fortunately, the acoustical concepts we are discussing will apply equally well to them.

As was pointed out, a sine wave is shown in the top part of Figure 2-3. Think of it as a single air molecule being displaced over time. In this figure, time is plotted along the horizontal plane, and amplitude (extent of particle displacement) along the vertical axis. As was stated, when a molecule is displaced (and inertia is overcome), it begins to move away from its point of rest. However, in this case "away from the rest position" is up, the center line is the neutral position, or "zero," and negative pressure is below this center line. Thus, compression (+) is above the horizontal and rarefaction (–) is below it. Depending on the force applied to the molecule, it will reach a maximum amplitude and then, as a result of its elasticity and the activity of the vibrator, will attempt to return to its original place of rest. At this juncture, and due to momentum, it will travel past the neutral or zero position and reach a place of maximum amplitude in an opposite (negative) direction—one which will be approximately equal to the positive displacement. The molecule again will attempt to return to the rest position, in this case by movement in the positive direction, but will bypass it—

and so on. This process will continue for as long as the source energy is applied. Potentially it could continue indefinitely. However, if the vibrating force ceases, each of these positive (+) and negative (−) swings will systematically decrease in amplitude until movement eventually stops and the particle rests in its original position.

From this description of the sinusoidal activity of but a single molecule, we now can demonstrate the three basic acoustic characteristics of frequency, intensity and duration. Specifically, the number of times the sinusoid repeats itself within a set period of time creates its *fundamental frequency.* Said another way, *frequency* is the number of repetitions of a periodic wave (of any type actually) during the time unit of one second. If a sine wave is repeated 100 times a second, its frequency is 100 Hertz (Hz). (Incidentally, the term *Hertz* has replaced the older expression "cycles per second." Both refer to frequency or frequency level, but the new term is used to honor a German acoustician of the last century, just as the Bel in deciBel is used to honor Alexander Graham Bell.) Since the period (or time) of a wave is the inverse of frequency, it is possible to calculate the frequency of any sine wave simply by determining its period. In this example, the time of the period is 0.01 sec., hence the frequency of the sinusoid is 100 Hz; if the period were 0.1 sec., the frequency would be 10 Hz. Conversely, if the frequency of a signal is known, it also is possible to calculate the time and/or length of its wave. The formula is ft = 1, or frequency times time is equal to one. Thus, if you know either the period of the wave or its frequency, you can find the other value by dividing the one you have into one (i.e., f = 1/t and t = 1/f).

The second characteristic of any acoustic signal is amplitude, or intensity. Intensity, in and of itself, is a rather complex concept; it will be discussed at length in a subsequent section. However, it is necessary to introduce it here— and in relationship to the sinusoids seen portrayed in the first four figures. *Intensity* refers to the amount of energy in the sound wave. In Figure 2-3 it is represented by the extent of the positive (+) and negative (−) swings of the molecules as they are disturbed by the sound source. Thus, intensity can be thought of as the amplitude of maximum particle displacement; the greater its amplitude (or displacement), the greater the energy in the sound source. In Figure 2-4 we have superimposed two sine waves of the same frequency, one on top of the other. It can be seen that although the frequency of the two waves is identical, the amplitude of W-1 is greater than that of W-2. Thus, W-1 is more "intense" than W-2. Incidentally, if these two waves actually occurred simultaneously, they would combine into a single wave, as their frequencies are the same; however, the amplitude of the new wave would be the sum of both their energies.

It should be noted also that frequency and intensity can vary independently. That is, sound waves can be of the same frequency but of different intensities, or of different frequencies and the same intensity; further, any combination of these two acoustic features can occur in time and result in any number of different sound waves. As you will see, this concept is of some importance relative to many of the processes and tasks that will discussed in this book.

The third dimension of sound is that of duration. *Duration* is a simple concept and refers only to the amount of time the sound lasts. In short, any sound can last for any length of time—for a second, for a fraction of a second, for a minute, and so on.

Periodic Sounds: The Complex Wave

A great deal of space was used to introduce the concept of frequency, to describe simple harmonic motion, and to place it in relationship to time and energy. This approach was necessary because a good understanding of these acoustic elements is fundamental to all of the other relationships and concepts to be presented. For example, when the properties of sine waves are understood, the concepts of frequency, intensity and duration also should become meaningful to you. However, most acoustic sources generate tones that are far more complex than simple sinusoids. For example, you have only to listen to the human voice to know that it produces all sorts of complex tones. Moreover, as we will see, the sounds of speech could not be produced if the larynx and vocal tract operated in a manner that created only sinusoids.

By now you surely realize that sine waves serve as the building blocks for complex, periodic sounds. These relationships were known for some time, but it was not until the last century that Fourier developed a mathematical technique to reduce a sound wave into its component series of sine waves. A complex (but periodic) tone, then, is made up of a group of sinusoids, all being generated at the same time, in a set relationship to each other. To return to the sinusoid for a moment, Figure 2-5 shows that it constitutes but a single frequency. A figure of

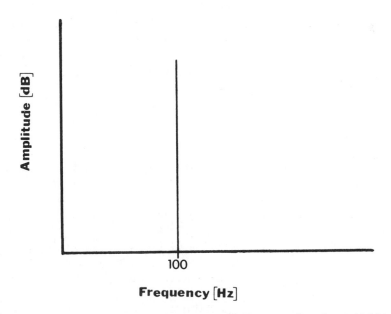

Figure 2-5. An "instantaneous" spectrogram of a sinusoid. Frequency (from low to high) is along the horizontal plane, or abscissa, and the level of sound energy—or amplitude (also from low to high)—along the vertical, or ordinate. A single frequency or series of frequencies can be plotted on a spectrogram of this type.

this type is often referred to as an instantaneous spectrogram, primarily because time is not represented. As can be seen, frequency, from low to high, is represented from left to right along the horizontal axis (or abscissa) and amplitude or intensity, from low (bottom) to high (top) along the vertical axis (or ordinate). Each sinusoid (one or more) is placed appropriately along the frequency continuum. Since the sound source creates this wave, it naturally produces it at a specific energy level—and this energy level can be measured and plotted along the "intensity axis" in deciBels (dB). Thus, it can be seen that this type of graph, or spectrogram, provides a two-dimensional version of any sine wave; time is ignored and only the frequency and intensity features of that wave are included.

Before proceeding, it should be indicated that, when several sine waves are produced at once, they combine into a single tone (especially if all are the integral multiples of the lowest) and they do so according to sign (or direction of displacement). Hence, in Figure 2-6 you can see, first, two waves of equal amplitude. As can be seen also, one sinusoid (A) has a specific period (frequency) and the bottom one (B), is double that frequency. These two waves combine into a tone with a fundamental and one harmonic overtone. They do so by the process of summing the two amplitudes according to sign. Thus (as in C) they combine first by adding their positive energy, then as the second wave goes negative they begin to cancel each other. Finally, the two waves sum in a negative direction. In any event, the third waveform is created by this process; it will appear as C unless phase changes occur between the two original waves (i.e., if they start at different times). Please note that, although phase is an important element in acoustics, it will not be discussed at any length in this chapter—primarily because the actual times that waves (internal to a complex sound) stop and start in relationship to each other has little effect on the tasks we will want to carry out.

A yet more complex wave can be found plotted in Figure 2-7. This signal consists of a fundamental frequency (100 Hz) plus eight other sinusoids—all being produced simultaneously. As you now are aware, Figure 2-7 can be referred to as a spectrum. It is "periodic" because all of the frequencies produced are whole number (or integral) multiples of the fundamental frequency. Therein lies the rule governing complex but periodic sounds; i.e., all of the partials, or overtones, present must be some multiple of the fundamental frequency. To reiterate this relationship, the fundamental frequency is the lowest frequency produced in an ordinary periodic wave and, as you can see, it is the common denominator specifying the relationships among all of the other frequencies. To be periodic or "musical," these other frequencies must be multiples of the fundamental frequency. If the fundamental is 200 Hz, then the other frequencies must be its multiples; i.e., 400, 600, 800 Hz, and so on. In the case of a fundamental frequency of 100 Hz, values of 200, 300, 400, 500, Hz, and so on, would define the tone. Incidentally, one or more frequencies in a series can be missing; however, those that remain must be whole number multiples of the fundamental— that is, if the tone is to be periodic.

Perhaps you already have heard of the terms overtone, partial, and harmonic. They apply to spectrum plots such as the ones seen in Figures 2-7 and especially 2-8. Musicians use a system specifying a fundamental frequency and overtones; physicists tend to refer to these same units as partials. Since these are

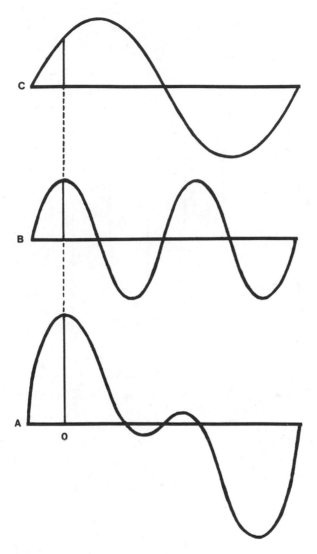

Figure 2-6. Diagram demonstrating how two frequencies (waves A and B) are combined into a single but complex tone (wave C).

parallel systems, they sometimes are confused. The musician will refer to the fundamental frequency (100 Hz in Figure 2-8) in precisely those terms. Through convention, this value is often written as f_0 or F0 (and spoken as "f sub zero"); the subsequent sinusoids then are *overtones*, with the overtone which is double F0 designated as 0_1, or the first overtone. All subsequent harmonic overtones are numbered serially in the sequence—and each one is numbered in specific relationship to the fundamental, even if some are missing. For an example of this relationship, please refer again to Figure 2-8. If 500 Hz were not present in this spectrum, 400 Hz would remain 0_3, and 600 Hz still would be 0_5.

The notational system for physical acoustics utilizes the term *partial*. In this

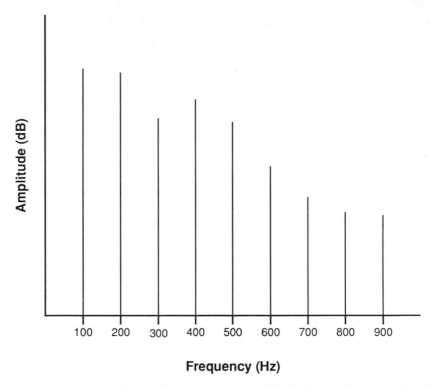

Figure 2-7. A spectrogram of a complex tone consisting of a fundamental (at 100 Hz) and eight harmonic overtones of varying amplitude.

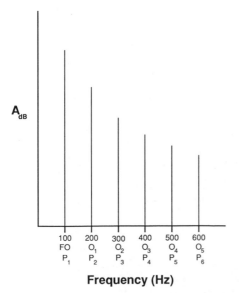

Figure 2-8. A spectrogram denoting the two systems of frequency nomenclature. The first is the musician's approach of a fundamental frequency (F0) and overtones (O); the second an approach used by physicists, whereby the entire tone is divided into its partials (P).

system, the fundamental frequency is the first partial (P_1), and all frequencies that are the multiples of P_1 are numbered serially; thus, $F0 = P_1$, $0_1 = P_2$, . . . $0_6 = P_7$, and so on.

All of the overtones and partials (beyond F0 or P_1) seen in Figure 2-8 are harmonic overtones or partials. The term *harmonic* means that the overtone or partial is an integral multiple of the fundamental frequency; if it were not, it would be called an *inharmonic* partial or overtone. Many individuals simplify their writing and speaking by referring to harmonic partials and harmonic overtones simply as harmonics. To do so is incorrect, and, while I am personally uncomfortable with this approach, there is little I can do about it. Moreover, in this book you will find that I sometimes use the terms partial and overtone interchangeably; I can do so because they *are* interchangeable, and this switching does no violence to the concepts involved. However, when specific partials or overtones within the spectrum are calculated and numbers assigned, one or the other of the two systems will be employed on an exclusive basis.

Aperiodic Sounds (Noise)

For our purposes, noise may be defined in two ways, acoustically and forensically. *Acoustic noise* is a complex sound consisting of a group of inharmonic partials. There are many types of noise; for example, it can be continuous, intermittent or impact; white or thermal (all frequencies and all intensities at random); pink (similar to thermal but within a specific passband) (see Figure 2-9B); sawtooth (regular but rough); and so on. The main characteristic shared by noises is that they are essentially nonperiodic (even though they can occur over time). Further, *forensic noise* is *any* sound—periodic or aperiodic—that interferes with the signal of interest. For example, music and speech can qualify as "forensic" noise if they mask the speech you are trying to hear and decode. A single instance can serve to illustrate both the nature of forensic noise and how an understanding of the acoustics of speech can be useful to the forensic phonetician. In "The Case of the Anxious Killer," a young man followed an older, divorced woman home apparently believing that she lived alone. He broke into the house and attempted to rape her. When she resisted, he took a knife and stabbed her to death. As he was doing so, the woman's daughter came home. He stabbed her too and then fled. While sure that he had killed both women and, hence, they could not identify him, he nonetheless became quite anxious about having left evidence of his presence at the scene of the crime. Hence, he returned to the apartment. In the meantime, the daughter, who was still alive, attempted to call the police; not receiving a response when she dialed "0," she finally remembered to dial 911. The assailant returned just as she did so; frightened, she crawled under a bed. Apparently the assailant heard her attempting to give the 911 operator her address, found her, threw the bed against the wall, and said something. The noise of the bed hitting the wall plus her voice (also "noise" in this case) partially obscured what he said. He did not molest her further but rather quickly exited the apartment. Apparently he believed that the police were on the way (they were). The problem: for some reason it was important for the detectives to know what the assailant said (it was recorded by the 911 operator). With the two types of noise present (speech and the impact noise), part of his utterance was obscured. Not so once an acoustic analysis was carried out. With our knowledge of speech and the spectra we developed, we were able to give the police nearly all the information they requested.

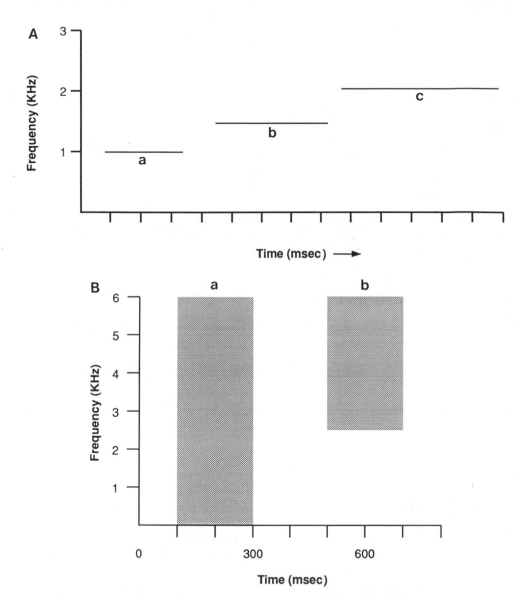

Figure 2-9. A pair of simplified time-by-frequency-by-amplitude (t-f-a) spectrograms. Time is from left to right, the ordinate is frequency and the darkness of the markings portrays the amplitude of the signal. Three sine waves of varying frequency and duration are portrayed in A; two noise bands of the same duration, but different frequency ranges, are seen in B.

It is without question that sound spectra displays can often be used to permit speech to be "pictured." Indeed, such displays can materially help you in understanding the nature of acoustics and especially difficult-to-identify speech sounds. You already have seen some of these displays (especially useful are those seen in Figures 2-7 and 2-8). Other approaches also can be employed. For example, another type of spectrogram (an older approach) can be seen in Figure 2-9; it provides a rough three-dimensional display of sound. Here, time is shown plotted on the horizontal axis, frequency on the vertical axis, and an estimate of amplitude or sound energy plotted as gradations in the darkness of the trace. As you will recall, simple harmonic motion (the sinusoid) is the most basic of the acoustic events, since all energy is confined to a single frequency. Figure 2-9A provides an idealized time-frequency-amplitude spectrogram of three sinusoids of three durations. As can be seen, the energies for all three are confined to single frequencies, but different ones. The first is the shortest (250 ms) and has the lowest frequency (1 kHz); the second is longer (400 ms) and higher (1.5 kHz); and the third is of both the longest duration and highest frequency (500 ms and 2 kHz). The three sounds are roughly of the same amplitude. Figure 2-9B provides similar representations, but of thermal and bandpass noise.

Now, please compare Figure 2-10 with Figure 2-7. In Figure 2-10 an utterance is portrayed by a time-frequency-amplitude (t-f-a) spectrogram; while far more complex, it bears a relationship to the instantaneous spectrogram of Figure 2-7. As you can see, energy displays are horizontal (and extend over time) on the t-f-a spectrogram. Here, frequency is only approximated, and amplitude is almost a matter of conjecture. On the other hand, in Figure 2-7, both the frequency and energy level of the individual partials can be seen to be quite accurate; however, in this case, they are portrayed only for a brief moment in time and can change dramatically almost immediately. These two (plus other types of spectrograms) can be used effectively in conjunction with each other. Note, for example, yet another type of display in Figure 2-11. This one is a computer-generated portrayal of a digitized signal and provides approximate energy levels, as a function of frequency, over time (these often are referred to as *waterfall* spectra.)

Resonance

The concept of resonance is one to which we will refer many times. It will be introduced here and discussed again in the section on speech near the end of the chapter. In its simplest form, *resonance* is the selective amplification of frequencies within a spectrum. What forces cause these changes to occur? Basically they result from the complex sound being transmitted into a cavity or through a tube. Structures such as these will have natural frequencies which are related primarily to their volume and shape as well as the size of their openings and the density of their walls. Hence, those partials that are in the region of the cavity's natural frequency (or frequencies) will be amplified at the expense of those (other) frequencies where the cavity is not resonant. The overall energy level of

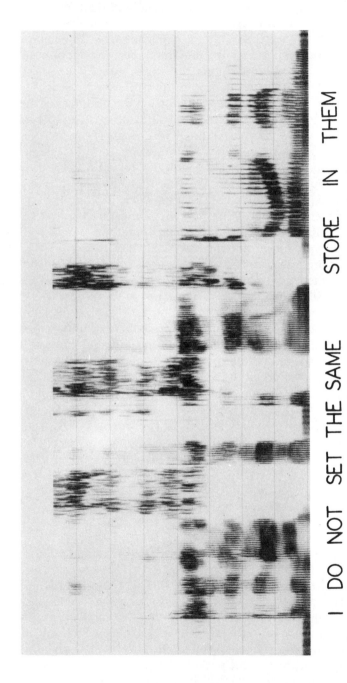

Figure 2-10. A t-f-a spectrogram of a spoken passage. As can be seen, individual frequencies are lost, but the noise bands for consonants and the resonance bars of the vowel formats are prominent. The vertical striations are caused by the vocal folds opening and closing during phonation.

I DO NOT SET THE SAME STORE IN THEM

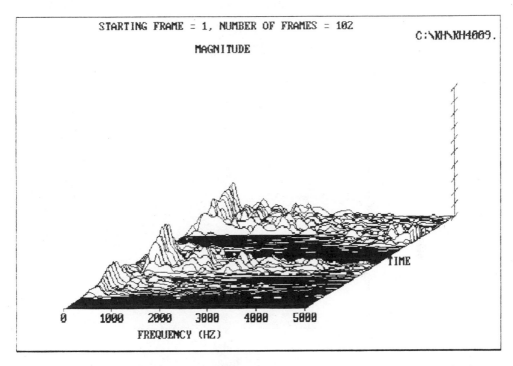

STARTING FRAME = 1, NUMBER OF FRAMES = 102

MAGNITUDE

C:\XH\XH4889.

TIME

0   1000   2000   3000   4000   5000

FREQUENCY (HZ)

Figure 2-11. A "three-dimensional" spectrogram. Frequency is along the horizontal; time, the diagonal. Signal levels or amplitudes (at any frequency-time intersect) are portrayed by the height of the curve. The spectrogram is of a three-word utterance.

the spectrum will not be reduced a great deal, but the energy pattern will change to reflect the resonance characteristics of the cavity. Figure 2-12 is a simple illustration of the effect of resonance. If the flat energy level seen in spectrum envelope A encounters a cavity with a broad natural frequency focused at about 1 kHz, it will be modified to appear somewhat like line B. Note how the energy level is damped in the highs and lows and amplified in the region of 1kHz. This concept, which provides the basis for the creation of vowels, for general voice quality and many other acoustic phenomena, will be referred to again and again.

Scaling Frequency

Ordinarily, frequency scaling falls within the rubric of psychoacoustics. However, for our purposes, it appears to be best placed here. When we refer to the frequency or the intensity of a sound, we are alluding to that attribute relative to some base level. Consequently, when we refer to frequency or intensity changes and/or give their absolute levels in numbers, these values must be based on some sort of scale—one which must be anchored to a reference.

Furthermore, it may be said that almost any dimension of sound production or perception (except time) is related to some sort of a ratio scale. That is, the

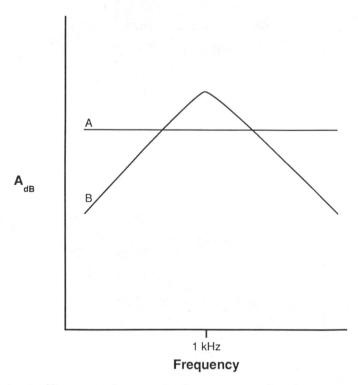

Figure 2-12. A pair of line spectra demonstrating how resonance affects frequency response. If the frequencies represented by curve A are transmitted through a cavity with a natural resonance centered at 1000 Hz, curve B will result.

frequency of one sound may be half as high as that of another—or twice as high—and these differences may vary in absolute terms (i.e., Hertz) at different parts of the frequency scale. Thus, while nearly everyone is acquainted with linear scales (a ruler, for example), geometric, ratio or logarithmic scales are a little more difficult to conceptualize. Yet, in most psychophysical relationships, it is necessary to operate on the basis of ratio units rather than with equal intervals. Consider most of the measurements we make in our everyday lives; we utilize interval units such as those measuring length (feet) or weight (pounds), wherein every unit or interval is equal to every other unit or interval. For example, in measuring length, the unit of an inch is always of the same absolute dimension. Ratio scales are a little different. Here, the ratio is always the same even though the absolute (or linear) size of the unit will vary.

First, let us consider fundamental frequency (F0) and its perceptual correlate—pitch. Even in the ancient studies of music, it was well established that ratio relationships underlie pitch differences. Much later these operations were formalized. Indeed, one of the ratios most fundamental to acoustics is the octave, a unit which is defined as a 2 to 1 ratio. Perceptually, we can reliably detect a tone (pretty much so anyway) that is either half, or twice, the frequency of another tone, regardless of the level of the reference signal. Thus, this 2 to 1 relationship is basic to our perception of pitch; it turns out to be just as relevant to the physical structure of sound.

The most commonly accepted scale for relating the pitch of one tone to another is the *equal-tempered music scale* (based on A = 440 Hz). This scale, expressed in terms of frequency level, may be seen portrayed as a single octave (i.e., C4 to C5) of the piano keyboard in Figure 2-13. As may be seen, the equal-tempered music scale requires that middle C (also called C4) be equal to 261.6 Hz. The C which is an octave above middle C is twice that frequency (i.e., 523.2 Hz), and the C which lies an octave below middle C is half that frequency (i.e., 130.8 Hz). Zero frequency level is 16.35 Hz. Each octave (difference) starting and ending anywhere on the scale is a ratio of 2 to 1. Thus, to our ears, a one-octave difference, is equal to any other one-octave difference no matter where it lies on the frequency scale. Hence, the octave has a psychological reality, as well as one in the acoustical domain.

Obviously, we have to deal with, and can perceive, differences in frequency that are smaller than an octave. Accordingly, this ratio is subdivided into six tones, and each tone can be further subdivided into semitones (there are 12

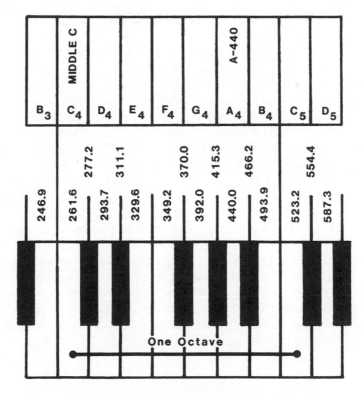

Figure 2-13. A section of a piano keyboard illustrating the equal tempered music scale. As can be seen, the scale is based on a 2:1 ratio with 12 parts or semitones (all notes from C4 to C5 for example). However, as also can be seen, there are eight notes (i.e., white keys) in each octave. Since, two semitones make a tone, some white notes are separated by a full tone while others (E–F, B–C) by only a semitone.

semitones in an octave). Like the octave, tones and semitones also are ratios; specifically, a tone is a ratio of 1.122 to 1, and a semitone is a ratio of 1.059 to 1. Although the use of such fractional numbers may seem burdensome, they are required in order to maintain the ratio scale which best relates to frequency. Technically speaking, while the tone ratio equals the sixth root of two (or that number which when multiplied by itself six times equals two), and the semitone the twelfth root of two (or the number which when multiplied by itself twelve times equals two), it is the basic 2 to 1 frequency ratio which is important—and it is so because it is both controlling and useful. That is, if you go up an octave you have doubled frequency (no matter where you started), and if you go down an octave you have halved it. To illustrate, if you raise a frequency from 50 to 100 Hz, you have traveled upward an octave; conversely, if you go from 3000 Hz to 1500 Hz, you have reduced the signal by an octave. Thus, the 50 Hz between 50 and 100 Hz is a frequency change of the same magnitude as the 1500 Hz between 3000 and 1500 Hz. This relationship can be very useful if understood; conversely, it can seriously mislead the acoustically uninitiated. Let me illustrate this point by describing a case I call "Rich Boys Make Nice Targets." A law enforcement agent believed that he had identified a telephone extortionist by means of application of the "voiceprint" technique (see Chapter 10). Using a t-f-a spectrograph, he identified a wealthy young man as the "unknown" talker in question, partly because t-f-a spectrograms of both voices showed a frequency pattern that was quite similar. What the agent did not realize was that the pattern of one of the events was several hundred Hertz above the other (similar) pattern. Hence, the two frequency arrays (while equal arithmetically and looking alike) actually were in two different frequency domains and extended over different frequency ranges—just as 50 and 1500 Hz are equal in the above illustration; a shift from 150 to 185 Hz (i.e., 35 Hz) is *different* from the 35-Hz shift from 1315 to 1350 Hz.

Other confusions can exist when the equal-tempered music scale is used. One can result from the way the notes on the musical scale are organized; they are commonly designated as A, B, C, D, E, F, and G. There are eight notes in an octave, and, by this notation, the interval between some of them is equal to a tone, whereas that difference between the others is only a semitone (see again Figure 2-13). Those of you who have had musical training will recognize that if sharps and flats are included along with the whole notes (i.e., both black and white notes on a piano), there are a total of twelve steps—or semitones—within an octave. On the other hand, the eight notes of the equal tempered scale dictate that the difference between B and C, and E and F is only a semitone, but all others are a tone in extent. Of course, it is not necessary to keep all of these relationships in mind (unless you are a forensic phonetician, that is); it is sufficient to know where you can find the information.

Intensity

Up until now we have been discussing little but frequency phenomena, i.e., (1) sinusoids, with some introduction to the psychophysical correlate of pitch, (2) spectra and a little about their psychophysical correlates to tone quality, and (3) noise. It was inferred that there are such things as energy levels by the references made to amplitude and intensity. You will remember that the term amplitude serves as a kind of "catch-all" which says: The greater the amplitude, the greater the sound energy—or sound intensity—or sound pressure level—or loudness. Unfortunately, sound energy and its levels are more difficult concepts to understand than are those in the frequency domain. For one thing, the fundamental relationships in this area are based on sound power, yet most of the measurements made are of sound pressure. Worse yet, when you try to estimate the loudness level of a signal when you hear it, you will find that the interface between sound energy/pressure and human hearing is a little tricky to assess. For one thing, intensity shifts are somewhat frequency dependent and, hence, the concepts I am going to describe for intensity are not as neat and stable as were those for frequency. But first, a review of some of the basic correlates of sound energy.

If we were to use watts as a measure of power (because this is a relatively common unit), we would find that even the most powerful sounds contain relatively little energy. For example, a 100-watt bulb provides only local (and limited) illumination, yet, it has been estimated that if everyone in the world spoke at the same time, they would generate barely enough energy (electricity in this case) to light a bulb of that size. In fact, to express sound intensity, we must utilize the microwatt, a unit equal to one one-millionth of a watt. Even so, a sound loud enough to elicit pain in the ear is only equal to 10,000 microwatts per unit area—i.e., per square centimeter—or one one-hundredth of a watt. On the other hand, in the most sensitive frequency range, a person with a healthy ear can detect the presence of sound which has an energy of only one ten-billionth of a microwatt per square centimeter. This unit of energy is small enough to be approaching that of simple molecular activity in air. In any case, the range of sound energy from the least to most intense level is a tremendous one. In order to conveniently express intervals within this range, we cannot deal with the linear units but, as with frequency, we must turn to a ratio scale.

Now, back to acoustics. The basic unit for the expression of the intensity level is the deciBel. There are 10 deciBels in a Bel, and a Bel is equal to a 10 to 1 ratio. Similarly, the deciBel is a ratio equal to the tenth root of 10—or that number which multiplied by itself 10 times will equal 10—this number is 1.214. To express intensity level, a reference point (which is called 0 deciBels), has been arbitrarily chosen as that intensity which is below the normal threshold of hearing. This reference is equal to one ten-billionth of a microwatt per square centimeter. The relation between deciBels and intensity level is shown in Table 2-1. As may be seen, the use of a ratio scale allows us to treat an extraordinarily large range of intensities with a relatively compressed scale. Moreover, and most importantly, the Bel and deciBel units are appropriate because human hearing tends to operate on this 10 to 1 basis.

Sound Pressure Level

It is necessary to provide definitions before any attempt is made to discuss sound pressure level (SPL) and its relationship to intensity. First, *sound intensity* is defined as the rate of radiation of sound energy through a unit area (a square

TABLE 2-1. The Relation of Intensity Level (in deciBels) to
Intensity (in microwatts per square centimeter)

Intensity level (dB)	Intensity (mw/cm²)
160	100,000 (10^5)
140	10,000 (10^4)
130	1,000 (10^3)
120	100 (10^2)
110	10 (10^1)
100	1 (10^0)
90	0.1 (10^{-1})
80	0.01 (10^{-2})
70	0.001 (10^{-3})
60	0.0001 (10^{-4})
50	0.00001 (10^{-5})
40	0.000001 (10^{-6})
30	0.0000001 (10^{-7})
20	0.00000001 (10^{-8})
10	0.000000001 (10^{-9})
0	0.0000000001 (10^{-10})

centimeter). Rate of radiation is a measurable event, but one not easily accomplished even today; it certainly was not in the early days of acoustical investigation. *Sound pressure level*, on the other hand, can be defined as the force of sound energy as it strikes the surface of a unit area. Moreover, pressure relates to intensity in a known way; i.e., sound pressure squared is approximately equal to intensity. The "approximately equal" is used because such everyday occurrences or constants as temperature and atmospheric pressure affect the intensity-pressure relationship. These effects are small and, hence, pressure essentially can be considered the square of intensity. Because of this relationship, the pressure ratio of one Bel is 20 to 1 and a (pressure) deciBel is a ratio of 1.244 to 1. It is measured in units called dynes, and the SPL ratio scale can be seen in Table 2-2. This table perhaps is not quite as impressive as that for intensity (see again Table 2-1), but it must be remembered that the pressure level at 160 dB is still

TABLE 2-2. The Relationship of Sound Pressure Level (in dB)
to Pressure (in dynes per square centimeter)

Pressure level (dB)	Pressure (0.0002 dynes/cm²)
160	20,000.0
140	2,000.0
120	200.0
100	20.0
80	2.0
60	0.2
40	0.02
20	0.002
0	0.0002

100,000,000 times greater than that at 0 dB. Figure 2-14 provides rough estimates of the mean pressure levels of some sounds commonly heard.

Perhaps the following discussion will make the relationships among the tables a little easier to understand. What we are doing is converting very large numerical relationships into values that reflect function. Thus, we are scaling sound energy or pressure just as we did frequency. To be specific, each scale has

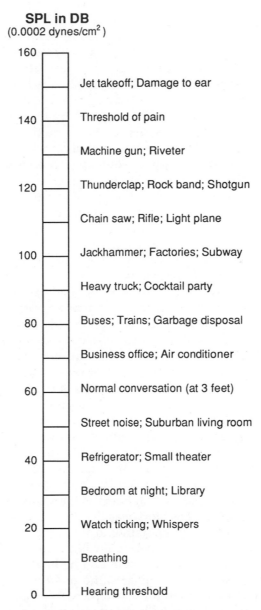

SPL in DB
(0.0002 dynes/cm^2)

160	
	Jet takeoff; Damage to ear
140	Threshold of pain
	Machine gun; Riveter
120	Thunderclap; Rock band; Shotgun
	Chain saw; Rifle; Light plane
100	Jackhammer; Factories; Subway
	Heavy truck; Cocktail party
80	Buses; Trains; Garbage disposal
	Business office; Air conditioner
60	Normal conversation (at 3 feet)
	Street noise; Suburban living room
40	Refrigerator; Small theater
	Bedroom at night; Library
20	Watch ticking; Whispers
	Breathing
0	Hearing threshold

Figure 2-14. The approximate pressure levels (in dB re: 0 SPL) of a number of common sound sources.

a multiplying unit called the *base*. Any system consisting of specific units which are multiplied by a specific base is called a logarithmic or exponential scale. Each time a unit is multiplied by the base, then, it has been varied by a power. In the case of the frequency scale described above (i.e., the octave), the base was 2. For energy (not frequency), the base is 10, and, hence 10^6 has a numerical value of 1,000,000 because it means 10 is multiplied by itself six times. And, as you are aware, the sound power or intensity scale has a base of 10, and sound pressure a corresponding base of 20.

As with frequency, these systems provide a valuable means by which to discuss or refer to change. For example, the intensity ratio of the loudest to the faintest tone can be represented logarithmically by determining the power to which 10 must be raised in order to equal 10,000,000; it turns out to be 10^7. In this case, the 10 does not carry any information, so just the logarithm of the ratio is used (you will remember that it is expressed in Bels). So, our ratio of 10^7 to 1 may be expressed as 70 dB. Moreover, since pressure is approximately the square of intensity (or double its ratio), this value in SPL would be 140 deciBels. These relationships also should aid you in understanding why one-tenth of a Bel is used as the actual ratio. Since nearly all sound produced is in the range of 10-11 Bels (intensity), and the range for human hearing (probably) is slightly less than 14 Bels (pressure), this unit (i.e., the Bel) simply is too gross. On the other hand, a unit of one-tenth of a Bel is one which is quite convenient. It permits us to avoid struggling either with huge sums or those not specific enough to permit useful calculations. Thus, it turns out that the deciBel is quite helpful in the assessment of all sound and, as we will see, for the description and measurement of human hearing (see Chapter 3).

An illustration of how useful basic acoustic analysis can be is found in "The Case of the Recorded Shootout." While this type of research is not typical of forensic phonetics, it is of a kind that many phoneticians, with their particularly extensive background in acoustics, are able to handle (of course, many engineers and physicists can do so too). In any event, an employment counselor was interviewing a job applicant in a ground floor office and, for efficiency's sake, was tape recording the entire meeting. The wall of her office connected to that of an adjoining jewelry store. About halfway through the interview both women became aware of the sounds of gunfire and cries for help emanating from the store next door. To everyones amazement, it was later discovered that these shots and calls had been recorded on the tape. The detectives who investigated the shooting found both the jeweler and his young assailant dead, plus evidence that the assailant had been accompanied by another youth. The name of this other young man surfaced and, within hours of the crime, he was arrested and charged with felony murder. His story was that he had accompanied his friend to the jewelry store, not to rob it but rather to aid in recovering some items that the jeweler was repairing (at an unrealistically high rate). He admitted knowing that his friend was carrying a revolver, but said he had no intention of using it and that it was the jeweler who initiated the quarrel. Although I am not a lawyer, it was obvious to me that, if the youth's story was true, he was facing a much less serious charge than if he had accompanied his friend to the jewelry store with the intention of robbing it—and a murder resulted. In an effort to discover the truth, the police took the tape recording to a "voiceprint examiner" (see Chapter 10 for more about voiceprints). This person made some t-f-a spectrograms and, after study, indicated he knew the sequence of firing that occurred among the guns. Still more important, he assured the state's attorney that the sequence was one which supported the prosecution—i.e., the youth's gun was fired first, and the sequence was one of "robbery and murder."

I was retained by the court (via the public defender) to assess these claims. I indicated that I could not do so unless I carried out an experiment to see if the firing of handguns actually resulted in individual "signatures." To make a long story short, the court underwrote a modest experiment (details can be found in Chapter 14) through which I was able to demonstrate that, while each handgun appears to exhibit its own signature, variations in type of bullet, load, person firing and especially "room acoustics" (i.e., the position fired and the relevant acoustic environment) overrides—and markedly so—this basic pattern. Hence, the "voiceprinter's" conclusion appeared invalid primarily because there was no way to determine the position of the guns when they were fired. Moreover, a replication of the shooting was out of the question. Since other evidence confirmed the defendant's story, the public defender suggested he plead guilty to the lesser charge (i.e., to the crime he actually committed); the prosecutor and judge agreed. The relevant relationship here is that, since all firings were of an impulsive nature, it was the analysis of the sound pressure patterns that proved valuable to the project.

Special Problems

As you can see, "intensity" is less easily assessed than frequency even when the actual measurements are of sound pressure. Nevertheless, the behavior of sound energy is lawful, and the alert individual often can use such information to assist him or her with relevant investigations/evaluations. There are, however, two cautions that must be reviewed here. They involve errors that can occur when an attempt is made to measure absolute intensity or SPL (sound pressure level) as a function of distance. First, it often would be useful if you could make measurements of the absolute energy level of a sound. The basic problem here is that even minor shifts in the relationship of the pickup transducer (usually a microphone) and sound source will substantially vary the recorded or measured sound pressure level; so will a change in the gain or volume control of the system used. As would be expected, uncontrolled variation in the input level will degrade measurement accuracy. Occasionally, however, this problem can be overcome; an example is found in "The Case of the Commie-Klan Shootout." This case is quite complicated and will be referred to again. However, at one point in the shootout, two shots were recorded in rapid succession via the same audio system—and the two guns were spatially quite close together. Here, absolute intensity (actually SPL) measurements aided in establishing the fact that one gun was a shotgun and the other a revolver. Such determination might not have been possible if the guns and shots were not so close together and there simply was insufficient time to shift the position of the microphone.

The second problem cited involves the inverse square law relative to sound energy. This law specifies that sound decays at a rate which is a function of the square of the distance from the source. Hence, and as you all know, it is almost impossible to shout loud enough to be heard a block or two away; your voice certainly will not carry for a mile. The inverse square law becomes understandable when considering how sound waves are transmitted to a person's ear. Let us say that two people are standing directly in front of a third person who is the speaker. However, one is standing 100 feet from the speaker, whereas the other one is standing at a distance of 200 feet. As the speaker produces a normal utterance, only the individual standing 100 feet away will hear it. This is because the spread of molecule displacement extends outward in all directions from the talker for approximately 100 feet or, at best, a little more. Thus, the wave does not reach the person at 200 feet, as the fixed level of sound energy has decayed—i.e, it has not just traveled double the distance, it also has been disbursed over a sphere with a radius twice that of the first. To reach 200 feet, the energy level actually must be a great many times more intense than the one which only needed to reach 100 feet. As will be seen, relationships such as this one are quite important when electronic surveillance and other forensic phonetic issues are considered.

A Note on Psychoacoustics

So far, the psychophysics of sound has been considered only with respect to how frequency and intensity are scaled. Basically, we have stressed the physical properties of sound, specifically those of frequency, spectra, intensity and duration. Only a passing reference has been made to the psychological counterparts of these dimensions; those of pitch, quality, loudness and time (or duration), respectively. While I will not go into details about, or the theoretical implications of, these physical-psychological differences, I wish to make at least one point: often the terms F0-pitch, intensity-loudness and so on are used interchangeably. Such usage is incorrect. When considering the sound associated with the number of times the vocal folds open and close, it is best to use the term fundamental frequency, as this event is a physical one. On the other hand, if the description is of what a person has perceived auditorily, then pitch is the proper concept. Thus, F0 describes the physical happening and pitch the psychological (or subjective) evaluation of the heard tone. The same relationship applies to intensity and loudness. The actual work carried out, or pressure level within the medium, is a physical occurrence and can be referred to as pressure or intensity, whereas the psychological response to the physical events is that of loudness. The same relationships occur when wave composition (or spectra) and quality are considered. The use of these terms interchangeably can only lead to confusion; such will be avoided in this book.

SPEECH

Even though this chapter is primarily about basic acoustics, it should be remembered that most of the subareas and techniques within forensic phonetics involve the processing of human speech. Hence, it is necessary to include some discussion of the properties that relate to this specific class of sounds. That is, there are some features and patterns in speech that are fairly unique to this behavior. Thus, a reasonably good understanding of these relationships is necessary for a correspondingly acceptable grasp of the methods and processes described in the specialized sections of this book.

As you might expect, the measurement and analysis of speech signals can be a fairly complex process. To be specific, voiced speech consists of a number of related sinusoids produced simultaneously at a number of SPLs. Of course, this array is heard as a single tone—and one of either relatively steady-state or varying nature. Thus, while the physical scaling of speech is not much more complex than is the calculation of multiple ratios, we do have the addition of an integrated spectra dimension (or the percept: quality) to consider. Accordingly, the relationship of wave composition to perceived quality will be reviewed. Please note that, while the discussions below focus on periodic sounds, noise also can be created to structure some speech elements.

Voice Quality

As noted earlier, when we attempt to study complex sounds (including speech), we are concerned to a great extent with spectral variations over time. In turn, both the spectra and their temporal alterations are important cues for our perception of quality. Because this expression includes such a large number of events and dimensions, it often has been considered a kind of "wastebasket" term (i.e., a name which is used when no other seems appropriate). Yet, we can identify many qualitative attributes of voice and speech; to name but a few: vowel quality, nasality, breathiness, roughness, general voice quality, and so on. Most of the characteristics of these signals can be related directly to the specific energy-frequency distributions produced (over time) by the talker. Others can be expressed best in terms of a target spectrum which is only approximated, while still others are best characterized by specific temporal variations in the energy levels within the frequency range produced (e.g., the quality of certain speech sounds as produced by shifts in energy over time). To be yet more specific, the quality of a complex sound, be it speech, voice or noise is determined by: (1) the nature of its source and (2) how it is modified by the resonant characteristics of the sound system. Thus, it would appear necessary to discuss that concept prior to completion of this chapter.

The heard sound quality and changes in quality result from the periodicity of the tone (or lack of it), the complexity of the tone (its partials) and the envelope or shape of the spectrum. In turn, the spectral characteristics of a sound are due to the effects of some set of resonators, such as those in the vocal tract, or the source pattern. As has been explained above, a resonator is frequency selective; that is, when excited by a sound source, it will transmit some frequencies better than others due to its natural resonance (cavity size, shape, etc.). A nonresonant system, on the other hand, will transmit all frequencies equally. Essentially, air is such a system and tends to serve well for the transmission of nearly any sound within the range of human hearing. On the other hand, resonance is especially relevant to speech production. For example, assume that the unmodified source,

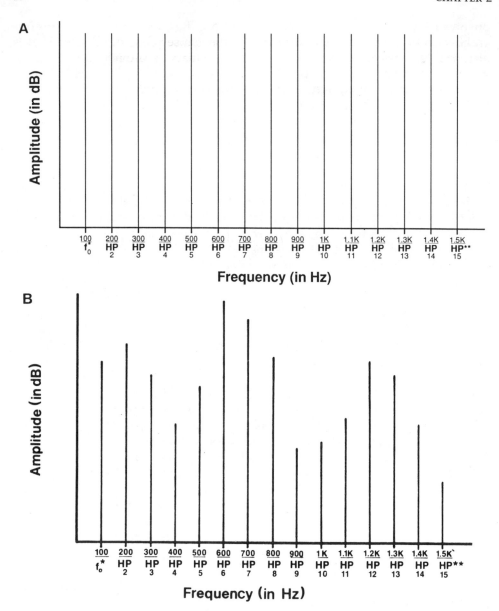

Figure 2-15. Two spectra of 15 partials each. If plot A was the spectrum of a laryngeal tone (which it is not), spectrum B would demonstrate the differential affects of a system (such as the vocal tract) consisting of a series of cavities with three or more natural frequencies. * = (P-1), or the first partial; ** = HP, harmonic partials.

or laryngeal tone, resembles the spectrum found in part A of Figure 2-15. As you can see, it is an "instantaneous spectrum" of a complex tone consisting of a number of harmonic partials. Here the fundamental frequency (F0) and all harmonic overtones are of about equal amplitude. In reality, they would vary. What would happen to this complex tone if we were to send it through a system with three natural frequencies (resonances)? The second part (B) of Figure 2-15 demonstrates the effect of a resonator of this type. The frequencies at and around each resonant frequency are enhanced, whereas those at other frequencies are in fact damped (or filtered). These general resonances provide the basis for voice/speech quality. They are the reason why two different instruments or talkers will sound dissimilar, even though they are producing sounds that have the same F0 and overall SPL.

Vowel Quality

The vocal tract, or articulatory mechanism, by no means consists of a simple resonating system tuned to one frequency. Rather, it is a complex system which includes variable resonant cavities and constrictions. The resulting multiple resonances are formed by the configuration of the pharynx, the varying shapes within the mouth (due to action of the tongue and jaw), changes in lip shape, and the coupling and decoupling of the nasal passages. The best analogy to the vocal tract would be a tube exhibiting several diameters and several constrictions. The result would be a series of cavities coupled together which serially modify the source tone. Essentially, the resonant frequencies of such tubes can be determined largely by their length (the longer the tube the lower the frequency), their diameter and by where the constrictions are placed. As these constrictions and cavities are varied, so are the resonances and, hence, the vowel or speech sound being produced. Indeed, each perceptually identifiable vowel is associated with its own particular set of cavities and constrictions—and, hence,

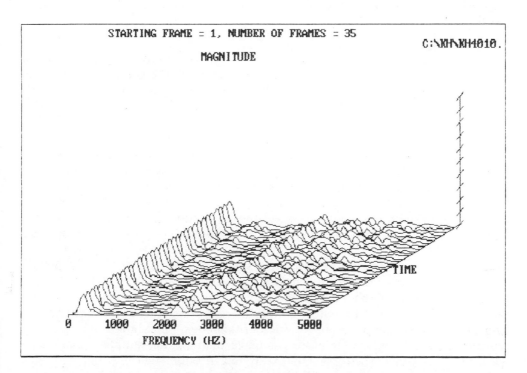

Figure 2-16. A three-dimensional digital spectrum of the phonated vowel /i/. This type of spectrum is sometimes referred to as a "waterfall."

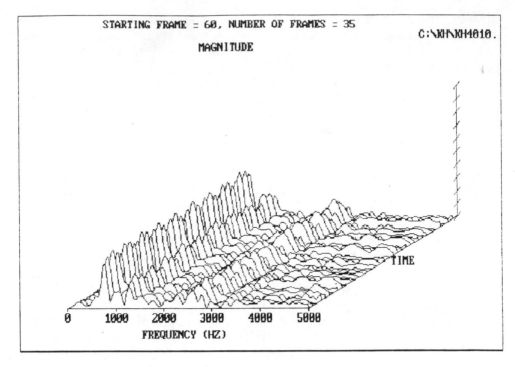

Figure 2-17. A similar spectrum of the vowel /a/. Note that the first two formats (or resonance regions) are close together here—and border on 1000 Hz—rather than wide apart, as was the case for /i/.

with particular resonances and anti-resonances. For example, the tone heard when a male produces the sustained vowel /i/ ordinarily will have five vowel formants, or resonance regions; the three lowest and most important will be around 265, 2100 and 3000 Hz (see Figure 2-16.) As can be seen in Figure 2-17, the formants for the vowel /a/ are different from those for /i/—as are those for each of the other vowels. The consonants also are created by a series of articulatory gestures both voiced and unvoiced; they will be described in some detail in Chapter 3. In any case, during articulation, the changing vocal tract configurations will vary the resonant characteristics of the tube and different acoustic patterns will result. These signals will be heard as the various speech sounds which comprise an utterance. In short, it is the acoustic signal (resonant peaks, friction/plosive gestures) that permits a talker to produce speech and a listener to decode the heard message. The next chapter will deal with the ways these acoustic patterns are developed and how speech is produced. It also will include discussions of how we hear and how speech sounds are organized.

A final note. This chapter is but a very brief introduction to speech acoustics and related subjects. While these concepts are fundamental to the understanding of the topics that make up the bulk of this book, you should not be overly concerned that they are far more extensive than are the simple explanations presented. If you wish to take the next step in understanding this area, you might consult the books found in the reference section for this chapter. I found them helpful when writing it.

CHAPTER 3

Speech Characteristics

INTRODUCTION

The last chapter was organized in such a way as to provide you with a basic introduction to the physical properties of sound. As I explained, a fundamental knowledge of acoustics is very important if you are to understand what has happened to the signal when (1) it is distorted (surveillance), (2) several electronic signatures from the same machine prove inconsistent (tape authentication), (3) a pair of spectra appear to match when in actuality they do not (speaker identification), and so on. In short, acoustic analysis can be employed to explain how messages and other speech information are produced/transmitted, and what can go wrong. Moreover, the electronic transfer of similar types of information tends to parallel these acoustic processes; hence, they are easier to understand if you have some appreciation of acoustics and sound transmission.

These same arguments can be made in defense of a basic understanding of the physiology of speech production and coding, as well as of perception and decoding. That is, it is necessary to know something about the structure of speech if you also are to understand what can go wrong when a person produces a particular utterance or how speech can be decoded even when it is distorted. It also is important to know how messages are organized (or coded) as a link among speech production, (acoustic) transmission and perception. Additionally, you should be aware of the capabilities of the human ear in order to understand how speech and nonspeech sounds are received and utilized. Is the ear (in concert with the cortex) so sensitive that a person can tell which of two dogs is the one barking, the specific type of a gun that was fired, why a baby is crying? To meet these challenges, this chapter is divided into three parts: (1) How Speech is Produced, (2) How the Ear Works and (3) How Speech is Coded.

HOW SPEECH IS PRODUCED

The flowchart seen in Figure 3-1 will provide some insight into how speech is produced. First off, there is a control system (i.e., the nervous system), as it is necessary to: (1) generate something to say, (2) organize the message and (3)

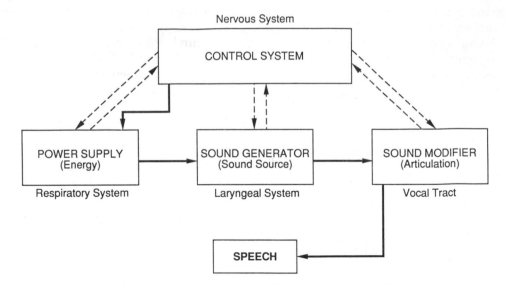

Figure 3-1. A block diagram of the elements that comprise the human speech-producing mechanism.

instruct your "speech mechanism" to produce the desired utterance. Your brain receives, processes, stores and reprocesses information for a lot of reasons; included among them is speech. In that case, your skeletal-muscular system—especially your speech-producing mechanism—is commanded to operate in a manner that will create the message you wish. While there is no reason to review the cognitive properties of the brain, or the receptive and motor functions of the autonomic and central nervous systems, it is important to realize that these mechanisms support or direct almost every human function. Accordingly, we must assume that intelligence and neural control exist; it is only then that we can proceed to discuss the speech mechanism itself. However, if you wish further information about these issues, you can consult any number of appropriate references (see, for example, 5, 9, 15, 17).

Figure 3-1 also provides a flowchart of the three systems which—in addition to the neural system—permit speech to be produced. The power for all this activity is provided by the respiratory mechanism, whereas most of the sound necessary for speech is generated by the larynx—a system which is activated by muscle activity and subglottic air pressures. Finally, the speech itself is created by the organized manipulation of the throat, nose, mouth, tongue and lips; this complex mechanism often is referred to as the vocal tract. These three systems will be discussed below. However, anyone desiring a more thorough orientation to speech physiology can consult the appropriate references (see especially 1, 2, 11, 13, 17).

The Power Supply

Almost everyone is aware of how the respiratory system works. All you have to do is sit quietly and place a hand on your chest in order to feel the rib cage rising with inhalation and lowering during exhalation. If you shift your hand to the abdomen you will observe a roughly similar motion (out with inhalation, in with exhalation). This mechanism, which is contained in the upper half of your body, is subject to two types of neural control. When breathing for life support occurs, the autonomic nervous system activates mechanisms which expand the thoracic cage slightly (the air pressure then becomes greater on the outside and air flows into the lungs); at this juncture, innervation to the inhalatory system is reduced and you simply "relax" to let the air flow out of your lungs. Second, you also have volitional control over the respiratory mechanism by means of the central nervous system. For example, you can take a deep breath and hold it—or exhale very slowly. Indeed, a control process of this type is applied when you wish to produce speech—i.e., a quick, deep inhalation, and then a slow controlled exhalation. The breathing process is so routine for either purpose, you probably are not consciously aware of it.

Basically, there are four main components to your respiratory system (see Figure 3-2 for details). The lungs, including the trachea (or windpipe) and bronchi, consist of a series of branching tubes connected to numerous small balloon-like sacs. This system is simply one for holding air (to a great extent for the physiological purpose of oxygen and carbon dioxide exchange); in any case, the lungs are passive in nature. They will fill with air when the thoracic cavity is

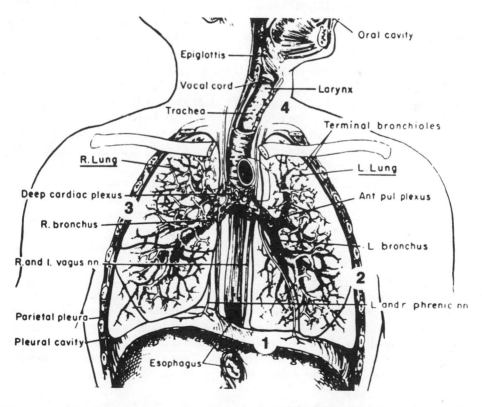

Figure 3-2. The pulmonary system. This system is sealed within the thorax and consists of a trachea, bronchi and lung sacs. The lower border, or diaphram, is identified by 1, the ribs in cross section by 2, the intercostal muscles (i.e., between the ribs) by 3 and the superior muscles (that aid in lifting the ribcage) by 4.

expanded and deliver it when the chest is reduced in size. The second system consists of the ribs and the muscles (the intercostals) situated between them. Simply put, when these muscles contract, in concert with other upper chest muscles, they tend to pull the rib cage upward and out thereby increasing the volume of the sealed cavity containing the lungs. Third, just below the lungs is a dome-shaped structure, the diaphragm, made up of muscle and connective fibers. It extends across the entire girth of your body from front to back and side to side. When the muscle fibers of the diaphragm contract, they flatten the dome, which increases the volume of the chest area. Thus, the lungs are structured to store air, and operation of the thoracic muscles and diaphragm are designed to increase the size of the cavity within which the lungs reside. In turn, these gestures will lower the internal pressure of the thorax and (assuming an open airway) let air flow into the sacs (inspiration). The fourth major system involved in respiration consists of the trunk muscles—the rectus abdominus in the front of your body and the girdle muscles coming from back to front (the obliques and transverse muscles). When these (and associated muscles) are contracted, they tend to push the viscera (bowels, etc.) up into the chest area and pull the rib cage in and down. The process here, coupled to the controlled relaxation of the inhalatory muscles, tends to increase the pressure in the lungs and create an outward airflow (exhalation).

The respiratory process is far more complex than this description, which is simply a rough outline. In summary, activation of the chest and upper chest muscles plus the diaphragm, coupled with some relaxation of the abdominal muscles, tends to increase the internal thoracic area—and, hence, the area in which the lungs reside. Pressure is reduced and inhalation results. Alternately, the effects of gravity plus relaxation of the diaphragm and chest muscles, coupled with some contraction of the abdominals, tend to reduce the volume inside the chest, and exhalation results. In short, this is the process by which we breathe for purposes of life support. With certain minor changes, it also is the process that supports speech.

When breathing for speech, inhalation (now under the control of the central nervous system) is accomplished quickly, and the amount of air taken in is greater than that for life support. On exhalation, the reduction in thoracic space increases pressure and, hence, the excess air is forced out through the trachea and larynx in a relatively steady flow; i.e., the flow rate for speech is fairly slow and controlled. Of course, little to no sound is made when we breathe normally—either for vegetative purposes or when the rate is controlled. A sound source is needed; in this case, it is the larynx. The slow, highly controlled exhalation described above is the operation which provides the steady pressure at the level of the vocal folds (when they are adducted), allowing them to vibrate. As you will see, they are part of the larynx, a structure which "sits" on top of the trachea or windpipe. Since, in turn, it can control the flow of exhalation, this structure creates the signal that supports most speech sounds.

The Sound Source

The proper name for the sound-making system in your throat is not the Adam's apple or even the voice box; rather, it is the larynx. In a sense, this structure is seemingly accessible. For example, it can be felt simply by placing your hand on the front of your throat and humming, then coughing, then swallowing. A partial view of the vocal folds can be found at the bottom of the drawing seen in Figure 3-3A (neither the chest/lungs nor the vocal tract are shown in this figure).

The larynx is not very large, but it is rather complex. Its primary purposes are to protect the respiratory airway from invasion or blockage and to permit heavy work to be accomplished. A reasonably good way to understand the first

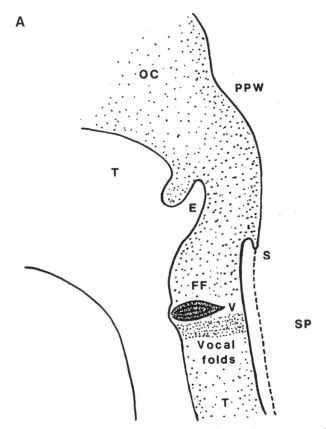

Figure 3-3. A four-part view of the larynx. View A is a midsaggital (side) view of this structure—with the vocal folds represented by the shaded portion just below the horizontal dark area, which is the ventrical (V). From top to bottom, OC is the oral cavity; T, the tongue; E, the epiglottis; PPW, the posterior pharyngeal wall; FF, the false folds; S, the esophagus; SP, the spinal cord; T, the trachea. Scene B shows the larynx and laryngeal cartilages from the front with the skin peeled off. Here, H is the hyoid bone; T, the thyroid cartilage; C, the cricoid cartilage; R, the tracheal rings. These structures are joined together by muscle and connective tissue; they house the larynx and vocal folds. View C shows how the vocal folds would look if you saw them from above. The front of the body is at the top of the picture, with the vocal folds identified by V, the false folds by F, the epiglottis by E and the tubercles of the arythenoids by T. The vibratory portion of the vocal folds extends primarily from A to B. Finally, in D, the vocal folds are seen in coronal cross section (i.e., from the front with the laryngeal cartilages removed). Here, T is the trachea, and the vocal folds are V—they protrude into the airway. So do the false folds (F), which are separated from the true folds by the ventrical.

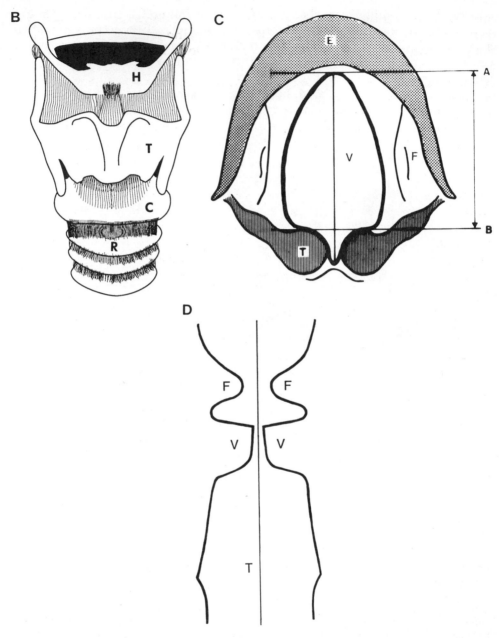

Figure 3-3. (Continued)

of these two processes is to describe how food is swallowed (see again Figure 3-3A). First, the back of the tongue (T) is lowered, an action that both opens the area superior to the larynx and esophagus, and tilts the epiglottis (E) so it projects rearward (and somewhat downward) over the opening at the top of the larynx. This action also causes the top of the esophagus (S) to open and form a cup. The food, moving backward and downward, is deflected into this cup; it is then moved on down into the stomach by gravity and serial muscle movement along the esophagus. Moreover, both the true vocal folds (the darkened area below V, or ventricle) and the fatty "false" vocal folds (FF) just above them close during swallowing. It is in this manner that they generally assist in protection of the airway. However, their operation is much more important if some of the food accidentally is deflected into the larynx. First, the vocal folds can close powerfully in order to keep this material from progressing further down the trachea and, second, the many sensory nerve endings in the area trigger the coughing reflex, an action designed to expel foreign matter. One of my favorite TV commercials touts a particular cough medicine. The sequence shows a drawing similar to the lower half of Figure 3-3A but with a feather tickling the vocal folds. Suddenly a spoonful of cough syrup comes crashing down on top of the feather and "removes the source of the cough." Presumably the cough medicine then zips on down into the lungs and drowns the person—but, of course, this consequence is not shown. In an odd way, observation of that commercial might assist you in understanding the actual protective functions of the larynx and vocal folds.

The second function of the larynx (and vocal folds) is to permit you to fix your chest or torso in order to provide a foundation for the muscle activity associated with lifting or other hard work. Here, inhalation of a large amount of air is followed by contraction of the muscles of the vocal folds in order to close off the airway; such action fixes the chest in a rigid position and permits the cited activities.

It is the third function of the vocal folds that is of greatest interest to us here. Basically, they provide the sound source that supports nearly all speech (frictiontype noise or turbulence in the vocal tract provides the rest). The structure in question—the larynx—is made up of a group of cartilages (rubbery structures that are not as hard as bone), muscles, ligaments and "skin." As you would expect, it is operated by the neural system and allows the vocal folds (wedges of muscle and tissue) to project into the airway and close it off. This system is best understood by looking at Figures 3-3A to 3-3D. Figure 3-3A shows where the larynx is positioned within your body. Figure 3-3B shows the larynx from the front—and generally the outside (but with the skin removed). Here you can see from top to bottom, the hyoid bone (H), which is a free-floating horseshoeshaped bone just at the top of your throat. Moving downward, you see a sheath made up primarily of ligament, then the thyroid cartilage (T), which is the laryngeal shield. Yet further downward is the cricoid cartilage (C), which articulates with the thyroid and below it, the trachea, or windpipe (R), with its rings. Figure 3-3C is a drawing of the vocal folds from above; the front of the larynx is at the top of the picture, and back is at the bottom. The oval structures in the middle are the true vocal folds (V); as you can see, they are closed. The epiglottis (E) can be seen situated anteriorly to the folds (top of picture), the mounds made of the tops of the arytenoids (T) are to the back and the false folds (FF) are the structures seen projecting from the sides of the figure. Figure 3-3D demonstrates how both the true (V) and false (F) vocal folds project into the airway. The top of the picture shows the pharynx (throat) as it extends upward into the mouth. The tube at the bottom is the trachea (T), which progresses down into the lungs. This set of figures should aid you in picturing the laryngeal system as it is operated to make sound.

Now for some laryngeal physiology (anatomy deals with structure; physiology relates to function). Basically, the flow of exhaled air reaches the larynx as it comes up through the trachea. It would flow on through unimpeded except that the laryngeal muscles are innervated and move the vocal folds to the midline (Figures 3-3C and 3-3D), closing them and holding them in that position. Of course, nothing at all would happen if the increasing pressure of the air from the lungs eventually did not overcome the resistance of the folds and blow them apart. Subsequently, they return to the closed position by the combined action of their elastic recoil and the aerodynamic characteristics of the glottis (the space between the vocal folds). That is, when the folds are blown apart, the muscles which forced them to the middle of the larynx in the first place continue to be active and operate to return them to that position by elastic recoil. The aerodynamic contribution to this activity is based on a different principle. It is well known that a steady-flowing fluid or gas moving through a pipe will increase in velocity and be reduced in pressure if a partial obstruction is introduced (the Bernoulli effect). In the larynx, the Bernoulli effect tends to suck the two folds toward each other—especially when they near the midline. It is by this combined mechanism that the folds are returned to their original position and the airway closed.

Since this vibratory process is repeated many hundreds of times each second, the result is a buzzing sound which travels upward and then forward through the vocal tract where it is modified into speech. Variation in the intensity of your speech is accomplished primarily through increases or decreases in subglottal pressure (i.e., pressure below the vocal folds) and the dynamic changes in the resistance of the vocal folds. Of course, the process is not quite this simple but, if physiological subtleties are ignored, the description above pretty much tells the story. Please note, however, that the process is even more complex when changes are made in voice quality, voice register, vocal intensity and/or fundamental frequency. To illustrate, changes in the fundamental frequency of voice (or heard pitch) are accomplished (essentially) by variation in vocal fold length and per-unit mass (i.e., to control stiffness), vocal intensity by variations in subglottic pressure, and voice quality by various adjustments to the shape, texture, position and/or functioning of the vocal folds and larynx.

In short, the larynx produces the many and varied sounds that permit speech to be carried out. For forensic purposes, it should be remembered that the speech features of vocal pitch (F0), voice quality (source spectra) and intensity ("vocal" loudness) are controlled at this level. These paralinguistic characteristics of speaking are of critical importance to your understanding of the relationships in speaker identification, speech decoding and stress in voice. However, it should be remembered also that speech may contribute as much or more to these processes as does the voice itself. That is, the way we articulate particular sounds, the dialects we use, the linguistic emphasis in speech, our prosody (speech melody), articulatory precision, and so on, are all important to most of the issues/processes found in subsequent chapters.

The Articulatory System

The vocal tract is a complex structure, but an understanding of how it works can be critical to many of the issues we have to face in forensic phonetics. Let me provide you with an example. Dialect plus speech precision and mode of articulation became rather important issues in "The Case of the Reluctant Union Steward." To be specific, a telephoned bomb threat was received by one of the telephone companies in the western part of the United States. The particular telephone line used was one that was pretty much reserved for company repairmen (however, it turned out that many other people used it also). The linemen became the prime suspects and they were asked to provide the police with a voice exemplar so "voiceprint" identification could be attempted. All of them did so except the union steward who maintained that such activity was prohibited by contract, and that by refusing he simply was conforming to his principles (guess who then became the main suspect?). He eventually made a recording, however, and almost immediately was identified as the unknown caller. Identification was made even though all the speech transmitted through that system was somewhat distorted due to the fact that partial machine processing was used on the line. Several scientists (including me) were asked to testify at the trial; hence, we were able to hear the tape of the unknown caller plus the exemplars. To my surprise, a number of rather unique articulatory and dialect features showed up on the bomb threat call—but did not appear in the defendant's speech (or that of any of the other linemen whose tapes we were permitted to hear). Indeed, due to particular articulatory features (such as the retroflexive /l/), it began to appear that the unknown caller was an individual who spoke English as a second language—possibly a person from Pakistan. At this juncture, the judge grew suspicious and had the "voiceprint examiner" redo the test; however, this time all the foils were produced by the assistant district attorneys from that city. The "voiceprint" examiner picked one of the attorneys as the caller in question and, as would be expected, the case was dismissed. Now, I do not *know* beyond all possible doubt if the defendant was guilty or innocent (he appeared innocent). However, it can be said that speech analysis certainly aided him in receiving a fair trial.

But how does the articulatory system work? Once the basic sound for speech is created by operation of the respiratory system and larynx (see again Figure 3-1), the sound radiates through the entire vocal tract (see Figure 3-4) wherein the talker modifies it in ways that result in the acoustic production of speech. As can be seen, there are three main chambers within the vocal tract. One is the pharynx (or throat); it is found just above the larynx. The second is the nasal cavity (above the mouth) and the third is the mouth itself—including the tongue, teeth and lips.

The pharynx is a vertical tube that connects the larynx with the oral cavity or mouth—and, to some extent, with the nasal cavity. Pharyngeal size and shape vary relatively little and mostly for nonspeech activities such as swallowing, coughing and singing. It does contribute to voice quality and to many speech sounds by its more or less fixed resonance. For example, it can be speculated that this resonance is associated with what we would recognize as the naturalness of

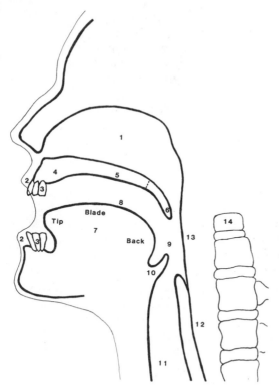

Figure 3-4. A midsaggital cross section of the head showing the articulatory mechanism, or vocal tract. The nomenclature is as follows: 1, the nasal cavity; 2, the lips; 3, the teeth; 4, the alveolar ridge; 5, the hard palate; 6, the soft palate or velum; 7, the tongue; 8, the oral cavity; 9, the upper pharynx; 10, the epiglottis; 11, the larynx; 12, the esophagus; 13, the posterior pharyngeal wall; 14, the spinal column.

speech. Also, certain nonvoiced sounds are created by combined action of the pharynx and tongue. So are some friction sounds which are created by turbulence within this part of the vocal tract. In sum, the pharynx plays a somewhat minor, yet definite, role in the production of speech.

As may be seen in Figure 3-4, the nasal cavity lies above the mouth; it extends from the nostrils (anterior) in two parts (separated in the midline by the septum) all the way back to the pharynx. It is divided from the mouth by the lips and teeth in the front, the hard palate in the middle and the soft palate in the back. The sides are irregular but fixed, and the three nasal consonants are created by opening this cavity to the airstream and closing off the mouth or oral cavity. The way in which the nasal cavity may be opened or closed (as it is for most sounds) is by the raising or lowering the soft palate (or velum). If it is raised, nearly all speech energy radiates out through the mouth; if it is lowered, the energy radiates pretty much through the nose. Evaluation of nasality (especially if excessive) can be useful in the speaker identification task; the speech quality that results from excessive growth of adenoidal tissue also can be an identification cue. To be more specific, there is a tube at the top rear of the nasal cavity that connects this space to the middle ear (it is called the eustachian tube). Sometimes a tonsil-like growth develops around the nasal end of this tube and, if not removed, can impair the operation of the soft palate. If the adenoids are large, a rather distinctive quality results in that person's speech. In sum, the nasal cavity is important to speech, as the three nasal speech sounds are created by the coordinated action of the soft palate (opening the nasopharyngeal port) and the tongue (differential resonance).

The oral cavity, or mouth, is the single most important structure in the vocal tract relative to the creation of speech. It can be thought of as having one fixed part and three movable parts. The fixed elements are, of course, the teeth; they play a generally passive role in speech production but one that is important nonetheless. The three movable units include: (1) the jaw—which can increase or decrease the overall space or volume within the mouth, (2) the lips (and to some extent, the cheeks), which can influence the length and shape of the vocal tract; actions of the lips also can modify the particular speech sound being produced if they are closed, spread, rounded or placed in a neutral position, and (3) the tongue—the most important of all the articulators. Incidentally, the soft palate sometimes is considered part of the mouth—and, in that case, would become the fourth movable part.

Of course, the *general* contributions to speech made by the jaw, teeth, lips/cheeks and the palate should be pretty obvious. What probably is not so obvious is how they all work with the tongue to produce particular speech sounds. We now face a problem similar to the one encountered in the chapter on speech acoustics—but, in this case, it involves articulatory physiology. Specifically, it is a little awkward for me to attempt to describe the function of the tongue in speech unless you have some knowledge of the speech sounds, as well as their nature, function and classes. Since appropriate descriptions will come later in the chapter, these movements and relationships will be discussed only in general at this stage.

The tongue is a very complex and elegant mechanism. It is perhaps the single most flexible set of muscles in the human body, as it can change both its position and shape in a variety of ways—and it does so with impressive rapidity. Internally, the tongue contains several sets of muscle fibers which intermingle in all three dimensions; some fibers (the longitudinal muscles) run from the front to the back of the tongue, others (transverse muscles) from side to side, and still others (the verticalis) course upward and downward. When coordinated with extrinsic systems, this interconnecting network of muscles is responsible for the various tongue shapes you can create; these include humping the tongue, extending it, grooving it, curling it backwards, and so forth. In turn, these gestures permit you to structure a series of cavities and constrictions in your mouth and thereby radically and rapidly change those regions of resonance that result in vowel production. Please note also that these gestures are orderly. That is, specific positions result in specific speech sounds, and I am sure you understand that this orderliness is very important to our comprehension of many of the relationships within forensic phonetics.

The various and complex gestures and constrictions that can be made by the articulators also permit the many consonants we use to be created. The specific "placing" of the tongue and other articulators for this purpose will be reviewed in the very last section of this chapter. That is, the configurations and manner of both the vowels and consonants will be described in enough detail to suggest their importance to many of the tasks we carry out in the forensic phonetics area.

To summarize, coordinated action by the respiratory system, larynx and vocal tract permits all types of speech sounds to be created and then formed into utterances. A more comprehensive knowledge of these processes will be necessary if a person is to carry out the many and varied tasks (speech decoding, tape recording authentication, speaker identification, and so on) necessary for specialization in forensic phonetics/communication. However, the somewhat basic information contained in this chapter should be sufficient to provide an appreciation and understanding of what speech is all about and how it can be analyzed for forensic purposes. In this regard, it also is important to know how the hearing mechanism works—at least roughly—so you can understand what tasks can be carried out on an aural-perceptual basis. It is useful to be able to comprehend the limits of your perceptual talents, and some of the errors that can occur, if these limitations are not identified and observed. Thus, a short review of hearing will be provided before we continue on with descriptions of speech mechanics.

HUMAN HEARING

Like all human sensory processes, hearing is a fairly complicated one. On the other hand, the auditory mechanism has been quite thoroughly researched and is reasonably well understood. In this section, I will briefly review the structure of the hearing mechanism and then specify some of the characteristics of this sensory system. Please note first that individuals can vary greatly in their ability to detect and interpret sensations. Hence, the auditory process is, at once, one of great precision but also one which can be quite deceptive in function (especially from person to person). A lack of understanding certainly can result in errors relative to certain of the tasks associated with forensic phonetics. Several references (4, 12, 16, 17) are provided in case you wish to obtain a more comprehensive understanding of audition than the one which follows.

Anatomy of the Ear

The peripheral portion of our hearing mechanism is the ear. However, as a whole, this system includes much more than just the part seen on the outside of the head. In addition, there are internal portions and the neural pathways that course from the periphery to the higher neural centers in the brain stem and cortex. The ear is divided into two parts: (1) the "peripheral" ear with its outer, middle and inner ear segments and (2) the neural system with its sensory nerve and the temporal lobe of the brain. In its entirety, this system transforms acoustic vibrations into neural signals that are processed at the cortex. It is during this transformation process that the ear behaves somewhat like a filter. That is, certain acoustic features are faithfully transmitted, whereas some are distorted and yet others are blocked. In this section, we will follow the passage of sound as it progresses through the outer, middle and inner ears, and to the higher centers via the eighth (VIII) cranial nerve.

A schematic diagram of the ear is shown in Figure 3-5. The most external portion is called the auricle, with its cup, or pinna, and lobe; this section, of course, is the most peripheral part of the outer ear. It collects sound, amplifying it perhaps as much as 3 dB, and also assists in the sound localization process. However, the outer ear also includes the external auditory canal, through which the airborne sound collected by the pinna travels to the eardrum (or tympanic membrane). Since this canal is a tube, it amplifies and damps the received signal differentially (based on its resonances and antiresonances). The middle ear is separated from the outer ear by the eardrum. It is a semi-isolated air chamber connected to the nasal cavities via the eustachian tube. Since the eustachian tube is normally closed, the middle ear is sensitive to variations in pressure traveling through the external auditory meatus—with the eardrum responding to their pattern. Attached to the eardrum (and within the middle ear) are the three tiny bones called the ossicles (see again Figure 3-5). The middle ear also contains two

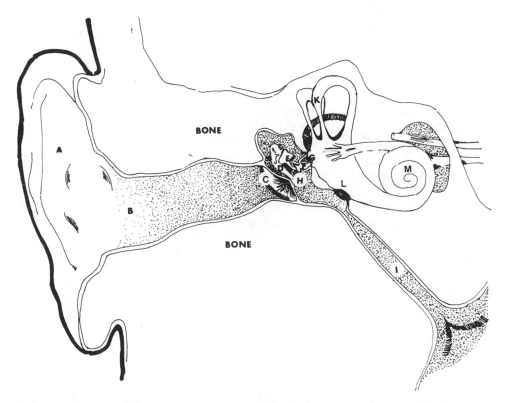

Figure 3-5. A drawing of the ear or peripheral auditory system. The outer ear consists of the concha (A) and the external auditory meatus (B). The middle ear (H) consists of the eardrum (C), the ossicular chain (D, malleus; E, incus; F, stapes)—with the eustachian tube (I) connecting it to the nose. The inner ear consists of the vestibular system, with the semicircular canals (K) for balance and cochlea (M) for hearing. The inner ear is connected to the middle ear by means of the oval (G) and round (L) windows.

small muscles that tend to contract in the presence of loud sounds and, to some extent anyway, protect the auditory mechanism from overload. Vibrations received by the eardrum are transmitted mechanically from one bone to another of the ossicular chain and, thence, to the oval window. This structure is a small opening into what is called the vestibular system; it is covered by a thin membrane and separates the middle from the inner ear. Now reconsider the ossicular chain. From a functional point of view, this bridge of three bones serves to match the impedance of the air at the eardrum with the fluid behind the oval window; it even provides some amplification. The entire peripheral hearing mechanism also serves to transform the high-amplitude, low-force sound energy transduced through air into a high-force, low-amplitude form that can be introduced into the heavy, viscous fluid of the cochlea. It should be noted also that the stapes bone (the third in the ossicular chain) does not push into the vestibule like a plunger but rather rocks; it is the rocking action of the stapes that permits the sound vibrations to be introduced into the dense fluid of the inner ear. It is by means of this process that a fairly accurate presentation of the acoustic energy arriving at the eardrum is transmitted by the middle ear system to the cochlea or inner ear. Some distortion of the signal occurs primarily in the form of varied and limited frequency response.

The inner ear is a spiral-shaped hole in the skull; it is completely filled with heavy fluids. As stated, these fluids are set into motion by the vibratory activity at the oval window and, in turn, the fluid motion is transformed to neural activity by the hair cells within the inner ear. Figure 3-6, is a cross-section of the part of the hearing mechanism called the cochlea, a cone-shaped structure of about two and one-half turns within which there are three roughly parallel "tubes": the scala vestibuli, the scala tympani and the cochlear duct. The scala vestibuli is separated from the cochlear duct by Reissner's membrane; the other division being Bassilar's membrane and the organ of Corti, which wall off the scala tympani. Rows of hair cells situated in the organ of Corti are systematically distributed from the base of the cochlea to its apex. The hair cells which lie closest to the oval window, at the base of the cochlea, respond to the highest-frequency signals; progressively lower frequencies are sensed at points further along the cochlea toward the apex of the spiral where, in turn, they respond to the lowest of the "heard" frequencies. Information about the intensity or strength of a signal probably is provided by the number of hair cells firing. The cochlea is contiguous with the semicircular canal system which is responsible for our sense of balance. Neural impulses from both our hearing and balance senses are transmitted through the eighth (VIII) cranial nerve to higher neural centers and the temporal lobe of the brain. Incidentally, the efficiency of the mechanical patterns introduced into the cochlea is increased to some extent by pressure compensations provided by the round window, a membrane covered hole that interfaces the scala tympani and the middle ear.

Hearing Acuity

The human ear exhibits a somewhat limited response to both frequency and intensity. The normal auditory range is displayed in Figure 3-7. As shown, most

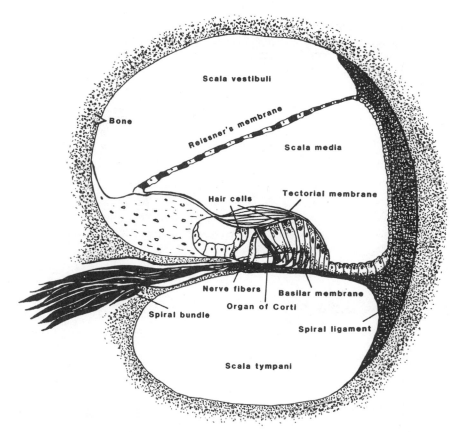

Figure 3-6. A cross section of the cochlea or inner ear. The oval window interfaces with the scala vestibuli (the round window with the scala tympani), but it is the sound wave traveling along the basilar membrane that results in the neural response—and the sensation of hearing.

adults are sensitive to frequencies ranging roughly between 16 and 16,000 Hz, with most young healthy people able to hear above 16,000 Hz—often to 20,000 Hz, or perhaps a little higher. While sound is heard below 16-20 Hz, it no longer takes on a "tonal" character; instead we are able to identify the individual pulses of sound energy. It should be noted also that older people tend to lose their high frequencies on a progressive basis, and some people have restricted ranges or sensitivity due to pathology. The intensity domain exhibits a dynamic range also. For example, when the energy level of a sound reaches about 120 dB SPL, it creates a sensation sometimes described as that of touch. But a few deciBels above this level comes the threshold of tickle and eventually the threshold of pain. As you might expect, the pain threshold has not been very thoroughly studied, but it is thought to occur somewhere around 140-150 dB SPL. Thus, we take the threshold of pain as the absolute upper limit of hearing. Moreover, it should be noted that this threshold is not particularly frequency selective (i.e., it tends to be relatively uniform for all frequencies).

By contrast, the threshold of detectability is frequency selective. As shown

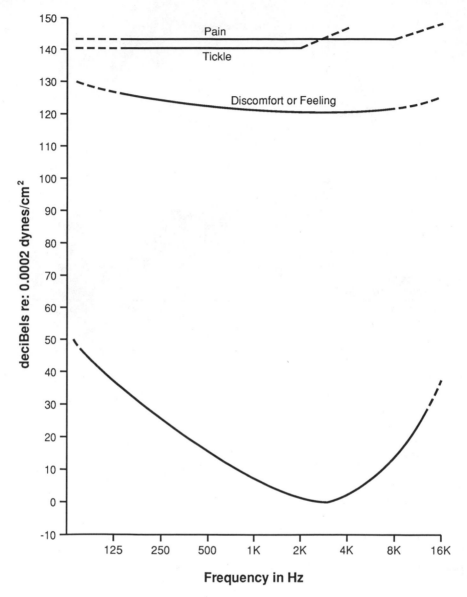

Figure 3-7. Thresholds of hearing. The lower curve is that related to the detection of the presence of sound; the three upper curves relate to a person's sensitivity to high-level sound fields.

in Figure 3-7, the middle frequencies (i.e., roughly from 1-3 kHz) can be detected much more readily than those that are either higher or lower. That is, more energy is required for an individual to become aware of the presence of sound in the extremes of our hearing range (especially 4000 Hz and above or 500 Hz and below) than in the middle frequencies. You will remember from Figure 2-14 that the pressure levels of commonly heard sounds can vary; perhaps it would be useful to glance back at this figure. Note also that I always reference my pressure levels (SPL) to 0.0002 dynes/cm^2, whereas some other authors employ systems based on microbars or micropascals. Figure 3-8 contrasts these three systems, so you will have a handy reference for conversions.

It also should be stressed that, within our hearing range, we can detect relatively small changes in either frequency or intensity. For example, changes in frequency as small as 2 or 3 cycles can be detected by most people for low frequencies. As you will remember from our discussion of the nonlinear aspects of acoustics, we are more sensitive to absolute changes in the low frequencies than in the high, even though the ratios are parallel in both regions. Moreover, intensity differences as small as 1 dB often can be discriminated. This degree of sensitivity is quite impressive, but it must be remembered that the values were obtained when an investigator varied a single parameter of a highly controlled signal under laboratory conditions. Thus, it cannot be expected that human sensitivity will be as precise when responding to complex sounds presented under field conditions.

I have given but short shrift to a sensory system as complicated as is hearing. There are many lawful but strange ways by which we hear and interpret auditory stimuli—including speech. If you will remember "The Case of The Overheard Murder" from Chapter 2, you also will remember that a series of relatively unrelated sounds (unrelated to speech that is) were falsely perceived as the integrated utterance "Mike." On the other hand, the nonlinearity of the ear can aid the listener in some instances. For example (see again Figure 3-7), if a person has a mean fundamental frequency of 95 Hz—and is talking over a telephone (with a bandpass of 250-4000 Hz at best)—his F0 should not be discernible. Yet it is! How so? In this case, the nonlinearity of the ear operates to provide information about that parameter. The ear senses the differences among all of the partials (integral multiples of F0) of the "heard" speech and assigns a "perceived" pitch to what it hears. Phantom tones also can plague the forensic phonetician and foster errors in aural-perceptual tasks.

In short, an understanding of how the human auditory system operates is quite important to the basic comprehension of the many processes and tasks described in this book. It should be remembered, however, that a substantially greater knowledge of hearing function is necessary if you are to carry out some of the tasks/processes that follow. Indeed, rather serious mistakes have been made by "workers" in this field simply because they were not aware of some of the illusions that can be created by the idiosyncracies of the auditory mechanism.

PHONETICS

The Science of Speech

In this section will be found an application or culmination of virtually all of the materials and relationships found in this chapter and in Chapter 2. That is, I will discuss the constituent parts, the nature and the classification of speech and speech sounds. The structure and understanding of these elements is at the

Decibel Equivalency Table

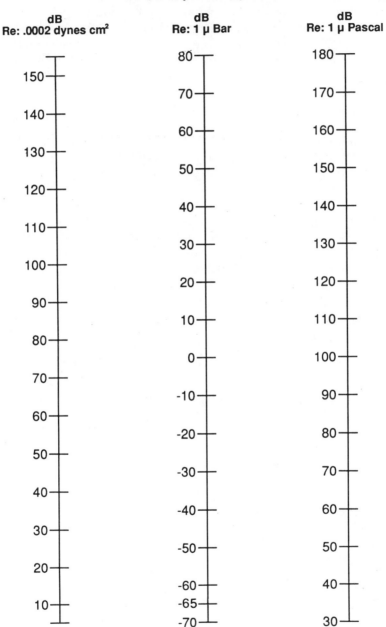

Figure 3-8. Sound can be scaled in many ways. This figure contrasts three systems for scaling sound pressure. That is, the three references are in dynes, microbars and micropascals (respectively) per unit area.

heart of the phonetic sciences—and, thereby, forensic phonetics. The other facets—acoustics, speech physiology, neurophysiology, linguistics, computer sciences, engineering, psychoacoustics, and so on—are only peripheral to the task. Indeed, any individual working in this area must have a good understanding of basic phonetics, or he or she simply will be unable to meet the challenges imposed by speech enhancement, speech decoding, tape authentication, speaker identification and related tasks. In short, phonetics is at the center of this field, just as the phonetician is the key person in the areas to be discussed in this book.

The Sounds of Speech

The English language is divided into two major classes of sounds: vowels (with the related diphthongs) and consonants (for references, see 1, 3, 8, 13, 14). Before we can analyze and use these speech elements, we need to know several of the ways/terms by which they are classified. Four definitions should suffice; they are as follows.

1. *Phones.* A phone is a specific speech sound, which usually can be produced in isolation and/or can be combined with other phones to make up syllables and words.
2. *Phoneme.* The term phoneme refers to classes or families of speech sounds which exhibit specific features distinguishing them from all other families, or phonemes.
3. *Allophones.* This concept can be very important when analyzing the speech sounds in a message. It refers to the fact that speech is dynamic and that individual phonemes vary in their acoustic composition and perception. Thus, the production of a certain speech sound by two different people can be somewhat different, yet both of the sounds recognized as a specific phoneme and, hence, with meaning not altered. Allophones, then, are variations in speech sounds that are not large enough to change them into other speech sounds.
4. *Distinctive Features.* This term refers to those modifiers used to describe a speech sound. If you examine the literature, you will find a number of different approaches in use. However, in each case, the author is attempting to describe the sound by referring to some aspect of its place or manner of production, whether or not it is voiced, and so on. Knowledge about distinctive features of phonemes can aid in speech decoding, tape authentication, speaker identification and several of the other subareas within forensic phonetics.

The Vowel

Depending upon which author you choose, you will be told that there are 15-19 vowels in the English language. I have no quarrel with any of them but simply will provide you with a structure which I believe includes the most useful/defensible set of vowels (and consonants too). You will find 14 listed—plus variations of yet two others—for a total of 16.

Although vowels can be whispered, they basically are characterized as voiced sounds. Since they are produced at relatively high energy levels, they are the sounds that "carry" speech. Further, vowels can be characterized by the resonance characteristics (i.e., cavities, constrictions) of the vocal tract. Indeed, they are perceived as individual entities because they modify the source spectra (the vocal signal) in ways that set up resonance regions—or vowel formants—unique to each one of them. To state this concept differently: vowels can be thought of as relatively "open," unobstructed sounds that are produced by changing the size and shape of the constrictions and cavities within the vocal tract in such ways that the distinctive resonance features for each of them are created.

Vowels are classified primarily by the place of articulation (or constriction of the vocal tract), tongue height (amount of constriction) and lip rounding/-spreading. They provide the nuclei of most syllables, are voiced and are continuants (they are sustained). As they relate closely to articulatory characteristics, voice quality and dialect, the way they are produced can be very important to a number of issues in forensic phonetics.

Perhaps vowels can be best understood by reference to Figures 3-9 and 3-10. Figure 3-9 shows the vowels as they are organized in terms of tongue height (from low to high) and place of constriction (from front to back), whereas Figure 3-10 reorganizes these same vowels into a relationship where they are contrasted with each other on the basis of the first two of their five formants, or resonance regions. The change in glottal source spectrum to vowel spectrum may be seen in the two parts of Figure 3-11 (see again Figures 2-15A and B). Here, the second of the two spectra (B) has been modified by the size and shape of the vocal tract to create the five formants necessary to produce the vowel /i/. Thus, as can be seen, the constrictions and cavities created by the tongue, jaw and lips draw energy from some frequencies and concentrate it in others (i.e., regions of energy concentration, resonance regions or vowel formants).

Entire books have been written on the vowel, and literally thousands of relevant experiments have been completed since the classic report authored by Peterson and Barney (10)—see top of Table 3-1. The greater the knowledge about vowels, the better the understanding of many of the processes that make up

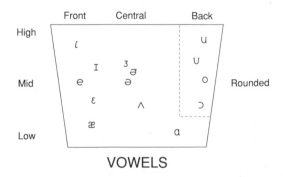

VOWELS

Figure 3-9. Basic tongue placement and height for the 14 most common English vowels.

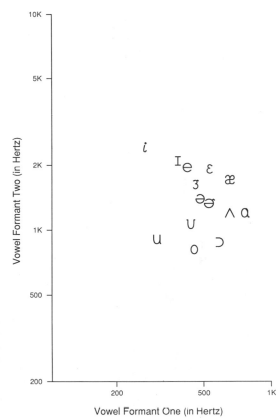

Figure 3-10. English vowels plotted in such a way that (resonance) Formant 1 is contrasted to Formant 2. Note that both scales are based on octave ratios (i.e., log to the base 2). i = peal; ɪ = pit; e = paint; ɛ = pet; æ = pan; ʌ = putt; ɑ = part; ɔ = pot; o = post; ʊ = put; u = pull; ɝ = pert; ə = unaccented; ɚ accented.

forensic phonetics. For example, it is known that the frequency of vowel formant F1 is lowered as tongue height is increased and the pharynx widens, whereas it is raised as the place of constriction is moved backwards in the vocal tract. The characteristics of F2 and the other vowel formants also are governed by the "laws" of acoustics and speech physiology, i.e., the shape of the resonant cavities and tubes. Hence, these values—plus those of the vowel transitions to and from various consonants (7)—can be used effectively to test the coarticulatory aspects of what may be a break in a tape recording (see below), or in accurately reconstructing speech in a difficult decoding process.

Diphthongs

There is a special group of vowel-like sounds that can be classified as multi-vowels or diphthongs. Most authors indicate that there are five or more but I will simplify them to three: /ɑɪ/ as in "ice", /ɑʊ/ as in "ouch," and /ɔɪ/ as in "boy." Some debate exists relative to two other possible diphthongs (they are /e/ and /o/), but I prefer to class them as vowels. In any case, a diphthong is described as the combination of two vowels into a "new" sound by a continuing or ongoing movement of the tongue, lips and mandible. What is created is a double, or

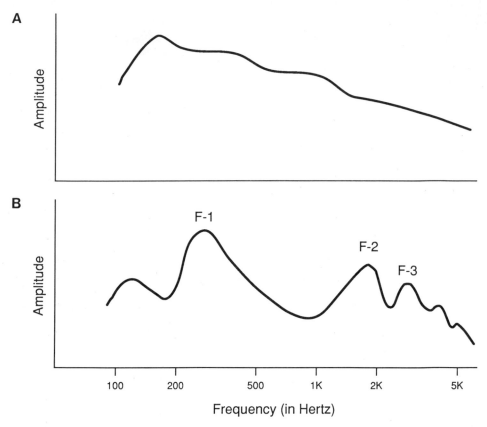

Figure 3-11. This figure demonstrates how the vocal tract functions to modify a source spectra into a speech sound. Given the spectrum seen in A, the vocal tract can be configured to selectively amplify and dampen the constituent frequencies so as to produce the vowel /i/ seen in B.

complex, vowel with one of the two being dominant. As you can see, if you utter a diphthong, you produce a somewhat shortened version of the first of the two constituent vowels (than were it uttered in isolation), then a transition, and finally a yet shorter version of the second vowel. As would be expected, diphthongs ordinarily take a longer time to produce than do simple vowels.

Transitions

The acoustic transition from one speech sound to another—especially from and to vowels—depends on where and how each of two or more adjacent sounds are produced in the vocal tract. While this discussion is best reserved for the review of coarticulation (below) and after consonants are described, the concept of transition is addressed here because it is important enough to forensic phonetics to deserve a double review. Basically, the steady-state portion of a vowel formant is modified by the sounds around it. As you know, the tongue, lips and jaw move rapidly from place to place as you produce the vowels and

TABLE 3-1. Summary Table of Measured Vowel Formants

Author	Formant	i	ɪ	e	ɛ	æ	ɑ	ɔ	ɝ	ʌ	ʊ	u	o
1. Peterson and Barney	F_1	270	390	—	530	660	730	570	490	640	440	300	—
	F_2	2290	1990	—	1840	1720	1090	840	1350	1190	1020	870	—
	F_3	3010	2550	—	2480	2410	2440	2410	1820	2390	2240	2240	—
2. Fairbanks and Grubb (approved)	F_1	267	426	—	530	660	680	612	—	599	419	276	—
	F_2	2251	1914	—	1691	1569	1096	788	—	1176	1136	840	—
	F_3	2974	2501	—	2520	2464	2614	2664	—	2576	2435	2517	—
(identified)	F_1	264	387	—	504	700	743	592	—	588	418	272	—
	F_2	2284	2038	—	1678	1686	1083	690	—	1187	1124	806	—
	F_3	2991	2591	—	2430	2468	2692	2615	—	2591	2388	2518	—
3. Wakita (not normalized)	F_1	324	444	—	567	723	798	—	464	677	462	363	—
	F_2	2450	2089	—	1964	1934	1233	—	1491	1452	1271	1102	—
	F_3	3149	2716	—	2654	2615	2594	—	1815	2613	2498	2430	—
(normalized)	F_1	299	425	—	521	650	767	—	499	641	495	379	—
	F_2	2246	2003	—	1833	1732	1187	—	1596	1380	1359	1153	—
	F_3	2888	2604	—	2448	2356	2502	—	1945	2501	2675	2544	—
4. Max-min (all sources)													
min	F_1	245	375	345	493	620	600	523	400	540	392	272	390
max	F_1	324	444	450	583	733	798	612	499	677	495	379	487
min	F_2	1950	1810	1800	1500	1490	975	690	1350	1176	720	575	690
max	F_2	2450	2087	2250	1964	1934	1281	1000	1596	1452	1359	1153	911
min	F_3	2750	2500	2480	2430	2250	2440	2410	1815	2390	2240	2240	2415
max	F_3	3150	2716	2850	2654	2615	2692	2692	2500	2675	2675	2550	2500

Note. Only mean data for men are included—and for the first three formants. The maximum/minimum data are a summary from nine sources. From Fairbanks, G., and Grubb, P. (1961) A Psychophysical Investigation of Vowels, *J. Speech Hear. Res.*, 4:203–219. See also references 10 and 16.

consonants of an utterance. These multiple gestures, then, have an effect on all sounds in the series, but in the case of vowels, they set up acoustic movements "toward" it (if the sound precedes the vowel) or from it (if a consonant succeeds a vowel. These gestures may be seen as the formant or resonance shifts identified by the arrows in Figure 3-12. Note the rapid shift in the formant frequency

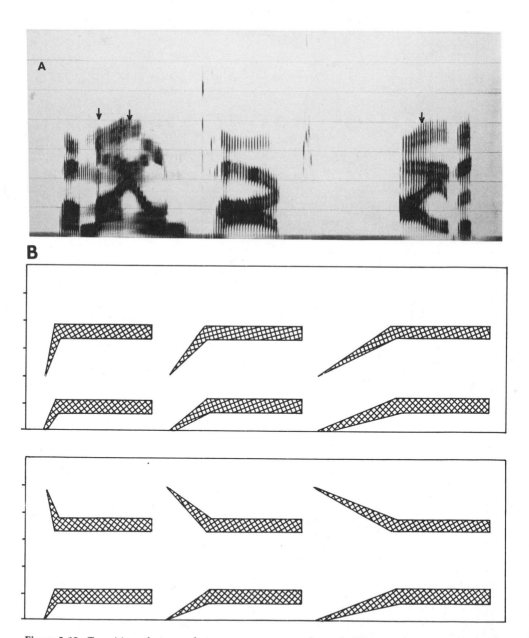

Figure 3-12. Transitions that occur between consonants and vowels. They may be seen at the arrows in part A; all of the F1/F2 shifts are from consonants to vowels in part B; vowel-to-consonant transitions also can occur.

bars at the beginning and/or the end of the steady-state portion of the vowel. These acoustic movements depend upon where the articulators were for one sound and where they are moving to for the second. Indeed, it is often possible to reconstruct an entire CVC (consonant-vowel-consonant) utterance simply from either hearing or analyzing the vowel and its two transitions. There can be little doubt, then, that knowledge of the nature and characteristics of vowel transitions (and speech transitions of other types) can aid the forensic phonetician in decoding distorted or masked speech, discovering if a tape recording has been modified, and so on. But more about these relationships later.

Consonants

While the number of consonants tends to vary as a function of language, most authors will agree that there are about 25 in English. Consonants are the elements within the speech wave that create the sound combinations which permit us to articulate a prodigious number of words. That is, they can be defined as those gestures within the vocal tract that control or modify the air stream to permit the creation of a variety of perceivable sounds. Consonants can be described with respect to what they sound like (manner) and/or where they are made (place). Consider Table 3-2; as can be seen, consonants are classed in a number of ways. If structured by manner, their classification includes (1) stop-plosives (the air stream is interrupted and then permitted to "explode"), (2) nasals (energy is passed through the nose), (3) fricatives (the consonant results from friction noise), (4) africates (stops followed by friction) and (5) continuants (or glides, semivowels, liquids); most consonants are voiced, some are not.

If structured by place of production, consonants can be classed by terms such as (1) bilabial (both lips), (2) labiodental (teeth against lip), (3) linguadental (tongue tip to teeth), (4) alveolar (tongue tip or blade to alveolar ridge), (5) palatal (tongue humps to palate), (6) velar (tongue humps to velum) and (7) pharyngeal, or glottal. Indication of what the consonants sound like also can be found listed on Table 3-2. The nature and production of consonants are far more intricate than are the descriptions provided by this short review. How they affect vowels and vowel transitions would take a chapter of its own to describe properly. Nevertheless, the above discussion should provide you with enough information to understand most, if not all, of the speech-related concepts to be found in the chapters that follow. For example, knowledge of consonants, how they are classed and produced will assist you in the decoding of proper names; the nuances of a dialect (in speaker identification, say) are better understood if you have a good knowledge of both vowels (substitutions) and consonants (variations) in your arsenal of analysis techniques.

Coarticulation

One of the concepts of extreme importance to forensic phonetics (especially in decoding and tape authentication) is a phenomenon called coarticulation. To be specific, no articulatory gesture is independent of those which precede and follow it. Rather, there is an overlapping between adjacent movements in any sequence of spoken sounds. This phenomenon—coarticulation—is the conse-

TABLE 3-2. Common English Consonants Structured by Means of Their Manner and Approximate Place of Production

Manner	Bilabial		Labiodental		Linguadental		Alveolar		Palatal		Velar		Pharyngeal	
	u	v	u	v	u	v	u	v	u	v	u	v	u	v
Stop-plosives	p	b					t	d			k	g		
Nasals		m						n				ŋ		
Fricatives	hw	w[1]	f	v	θ	ð	s	z	ʃ	z[2]			h	
Affricates									tʃ	dz₂				
Glides or semi-vowels								l	r[3]	j				

[1]Often classified as glides.
[2]Actually as much alveolar as palatal.
[3]Is postalveolar and voiced.
Note: u, unvoiced; v, voiced; most of the symbols are self-explanatory in that they sound just as they are written; however, the following are not.

ŋ as in going	ð as in *this*	tʃ as in *church*
hw as in *where*	ʃ as in *shoe*	dz as in *judge*
θ as in *thing*	z as in *azure*	j as in *young*

quence of at least two of the many characteristics of human speech production: (1) the rapidity with which we speak and (2) the interaction among the muscle networks used in this process. Consider the following: speech is just about the most rapid mode of face-to-face communication yet devised by humans. When speaking, we utter (on the average) about 150-180 words per minute or very nearly three words per second. Assuming that the average word consists of three to four sounds, it can be estimated that when a person speaks, he or she produces nine to twelve sounds per second. Thus, the adjustments of the articulators, as they shift from one sound to the next, must be very rapid. Indeed, they must occur within a fraction of a second (perhaps as little as 75-115 ms), even at normal rates of speaking.

When the speed of phoneme formation is considered, it is quite natural to expect that the articulation of one sound will bleed over into adjacent sounds and that this process will be quite variable. For example, some articulators (e.g., the tongue) are capable of very rapid adjustments, while others (e.g., the velum) move somewhat slower. Further, it is well known that when a vowel is produced between two nasal consonants, it also tends to be somewhat nasal, simply because there is insufficient time for the velopharyngeal port to open, close and then open as rapidly as this sequence would require. Similarly, it recently has been found that lip rounding sometimes begins as many as three or four phonemes before the sound requiring that gesture actually is produced. You should remember also that coarticulation spreads out in both directions. A given sound has the most influence on the sound which immediately follows it, the next most powerful effect on the one immediately preceding it and this effect generally continues for 2 to 3 phonemes in each direction.

The basis for coarticulation can best be understood when it is considered as the consequence of the interaction among the parts of the physical system used in speech production. The muscle networks which provide motive force for articulatory gestures are no more isolated from each other than are the individual muscles within any complex system. Indeed, contiguous muscle groups are quite dependent upon one another and, because these muscle networks are intertwined, we can expect movements in one group to effect all adjacent nets as well. Moreover, time is required for the contraction of muscle fibers, and once they contract (in order to move an articulator), inertial forces tend to maintain the movement until it is countered by an opposing contraction. To be specific, these relationships are reflected in the movements of the articulators: (1) in their adjustments from one phoneme to another and (2) in the brief time necessary to make these adjustments. In short, it is by these mechanisms that the production of one speech sound affects another and the coarticulatory process is created.

Knowledge about coarticulation and its nature is quite important to the forensic phonetician. Sometimes the only sign (initially anyway) that a tape recording has been modified may be a break in the normal coarticulation of a talker's speech. Moreover, coarticulatory events often can aid in the reconstruction of words obscured by noise. As such, this concept is an important one within the phonetic sciences and a robust tool for the forensic phonetician.

CHAPTER 4

Basic Equipment

INTRODUCTION

By now you should be fairly comfortable with many of the fundamental relationships among (1) speech production and encoding, (2) acoustic transmission, and (3) speech perception and decoding. Thus, at this juncture, it appears appropriate to provide information about some of the more basic equipment which will permit you to carry out the various processes and procedures outlined in the chapters that follow (i.e., electronic surveillance, speech decoding, speaker identification, voice analysis, and so on). A knowledge of the relevant equipment is especially important, since without it we could carry out but very few of the tasks relevant to forensic phonetics. Moreover, the apparatus we use sometimes is in and of itself the source of the problems we face (speech distortion, malfunctions). While it must be conceded that only elementary concepts will be reviewed in this chapter (and only certain types of equipment discussed), the material which is presented should be extensive enough to permit you to develop a reasonable understanding of the processes/procedures found in the succeeding chapters. Please note that specialized equipment used in support of a specific process ordinarily is discussed in the appropriate chapter. Therein lies the secondary purpose of this section, as understanding of the nature and operation of basic equipment should, in turn, permit a better comprehension of the characteristics and uses of the more specialized apparatus.

In this chapter I will review four types of equipment: (1) transducers (microphones, earphones, loud speakers), (2) tape recorders, (3) electroacoustic analysis equipment (a limited discussion primarily of spectrometers) and (4) computers (an introduction only). Since tape recorders are fundamental to nearly all of the sections to follow (both with respect to signal storage and as a source of problems), they will be discussed in somewhat greater detail than will any of the other systems.

TRANSDUCERS

A transducer is a device that converts one form of energy into another. In the present case, we will be concerned primarily with those that provide the interface between electrical and acoustical (mechanical) energy; they are of two basic types. The first class includes those which convert sound energy into electrical energy with the same frequencies and spectral patterns (microphones); the second class reverses this process (included here are loudspeakers and earphones).

Microphones

As you are aware, when speech is produced, an acoustic signal is introduced into the atmosphere. Since this acoustic signal is transient in nature, a problem arises if there is a reason to retain it for further use or analysis. The task, then, is to transform the acoustic signal into one that can be stored in a device such as a tape recorder—in this case, the first-stage transfer is from acoustic to electrical energy.

In order to better understand how such a transducer functions, you might reconsider the human ear. Remember that the external part of the peripheral system (i.e., the outer ear coupled to the middle ear) converts the acoustic energy received into a different type of mechanical energy. This system works as a unit, with the eardrum operating as the main element for detection. The rest of the middle ear (primarily the ossicular chain) then combines to transform the airborne acoustic energy into a form (still mechanical) that can be transmitted into the fluid of the inner ear or cochlea. There it again is transformed or transduced, but in this case into neural impulses which are passed on up to the cortex (for perception) via the auditory nerve. What transpired ultimately is stored in the memory centers of the brain. Note that there were two transfers associated with this process: one which converted one type of mechanical energy into another, and the second which involved a conversion from mechanical to neural form. It will become apparent that multiple transforms also will be necessary if we are to store acoustic energy such as speech on recording tape. Indeed, that process tends to roughly parallel the one just described. That is, the first stage of a tape recording system also involves an initial transformation of energy—viz., from an acoustic into an electrical signal which exactly replicates the mechanical pattern; the transducer in this case ordinarily is a microphone.

There are several types of microphones. All operate on the same basic principle; that is, they consist of an electrical-generating element facing the sound field (i.e., the atmosphere) with their output coupled to the circuitry of the tape recorder. The acoustic energy operates to move the microphone's receptor element which, in turn, creates an electrical disturbance within these circuits in exactly (or almost so) the pattern as the received wave. As would be expected, microphones range from inexpensive to expensive, from omnidirectional (acoustic energy coming from all directions equally affects the receiving element) to unidirectional (only acoustic energy coming directly onto the face of the microphone is transduced), from those with a relatively flat frequency response (input level is faithfully transduced) to others which have a variable frequency response. They also vary from limited-range units (responsive to energy present only in a specific frequency band, for instance, from 200 to 2000 Hz) to those exhibiting wide ranges (responsive to energy present at many frequencies, for example, from 20 to 12,000 Hz). If you are required to choose a microphone for a particular application, you should learn as much as you can about the nature/characteristics of those available; if you need to evaluate a microphone used in some procedure, you should examine it in terms of its type and operating characteristics.

Types of Microphones

As you might expect, there are several types of microphones. They usually are grouped into roughly five classes: (1) ceramic or crystal, (2) condenser, (3) electret, (4) ribbon and (5) dynamic, or moving coil. Carbon granule microphones will not be discussed, as they are outdated and rarely encountered anymore except in some telephones. Each microphone class has its specific characteristics and range of applications.

A very common type is the *crystal*, or *ceramic, microphone*. Most of these are inexpensive and sturdy but are somewhat limited in fidelity (at least in air). They are adequate for public-address or intercom systems, but in most cases are not the unit of choice for the recording and storing of signals for analysis. A typical microphone of this type will consist of a diaphragm of metal adhered to a small slab of crystal. The acoustic signal causes the metal to move, distorting the crystal; in turn, the piezoelectric crystal produces a voltage (the greater the bending the greater the voltage) which is passed on to other components within the electronic circuit. Since the crystal microphone is nondirectional (especially for low frequencies), virtually any acoustic signal moving the slab creates a voltage—for example, this type of microphone often will be excessively sensitive to room noise. It is a little difficult to generalize about crystal microphones since they vary so greatly in their quality; an additional feature is that very small ones can be made.

Condenser microphones are most often found in professional recording studios and phonetics laboratories. They consist of a highly machined, taut metal diaphragm placed behind a sock-type wind screen. A second plate is positioned to the rear of the first one, and they are separated by a tiny air gap. A high voltage (generated by an accompanying power supply) is placed across these two metal pieces. Any incoming acoustic signal vibrates the diaphragm (i.e., the first plate), and causes it to vary the space between the two slabs. As the air gap between the plates decreases, it reduces the resistance between them and permits a greater current flow. Conversely, as the gap is widened, the resistance is increased and the current reduced. This variation is passed on as an electrical signal (or pattern) to other components within the recording system. Condenser microphones exhibit very high fidelity but, due to their construction, they tend to be expensive, extremely fragile and susceptible to low-energy noise. For example, it is nearly always necessary to use a wind screen if the condenser microphone is used out-of-doors. Finally, these microphones tend to be omnidirectional.

An *electret microphone* is somewhat similar to a condenser microphone, with the exception that the capacitor is permanently charged; hence, an external power supply is not needed. Because the diaphragm is of reduced mass, an electret unit usually is quite sensitive; more so than most other microphones. Moreover, it is pretty much omnidirectional in its operation. Since this type of microphone tends to be less sensitive to physical, electrical and mechanical disturbances than other high-quality transducers (such as condenser microphones), it appears to be a unit of rather substantial potential for field use.

The fourth type of microphone is the *ribbon transducer*; it consists of a ribbon placed firmly between two magnetized poles or bars. This type of microphone is markedly bidirectional, being most sensitive to sound coming from its front or rear. Sounds arriving from the sides result in near zero response. Ribbon microphones are quite simple in construction and have reasonably good frequency response. If it was not for the fact that the ribbon itself is quite fragile and easily damaged, this type of microphone probably would enjoy greater use in the field—especially for applications which require directional operation.

The workhorse of the input-type transducers is the *dynamic microphone* — a system which employs a lightweight wire coil rigidly attached to a diaphragm. The coil, in turn, is suspended between two poles of a permanent magnet. When acoustic energy strikes the diaphragm, it vibrates, an action which moves the coil back and forth between the magnetic poles thus generating an alternating current. Variations in this electrical flow are in the same pattern as the original acoustic signal; they are passed on to other components within the system. Dynamic microphones are relatively inexpensive, rugged and widely used. Most provide reasonably good frequency response—for speech anyway— and can be used with both field-type and high-fidelity tape recorders. It is of interest that dynamic microphones can be designed to be sharply unidirectional; indeed, they can exhibit directivity over practically their entire frequency range.

Other Considerations

While most tape recordings encountered by the forensic phonetician will have been made with omnidirectional (or only partly directional) microphones, there are some transducers that employ cardioid features. A cardioid microphone tends to be quite responsive to sound coming from its front but is relatively unresponsive to that coming from the sides and rear; moreover, its sound response pattern tends to be somewhat heart-shaped. These microphones are fairly effective for some applications, and perhaps their use is not as extensive as it should be. They are employed to solve some surveillance problems—mainly those involving distance and certain types of noise fields. Incidentally, they are related to the noise-suppression-type microphones found in aircraft. In any case, directional microphones can be aimed and are quite useful in recording situations where moderate or even substantial noise conditions exist. However, it is important to be aware of the fact that even the best of these units are limited by the laws of acoustics—in this case, the inverse square law relative to the reduction of sound energy over distance. Even the most sensitive cardioid microphone cannot transduce sound that does not reach it.

In most cases, the user/examiner will be saddled with a microphone chosen by someone else or one that already is incorporated into the system. In the ideal situation, you would select the microphone to be used, specifying its size, frequency response, noise-canceling characteristics and directionality. However, you will not enjoy this luxury in most cases; indeed, many law enforcement agencies couple poor-quality microphones to high-quality tape recorders (or vice versa), apparently unaware of the "weakest link in a chain" theory. Conversely, the characteristics just discussed are those that you will want to know about relative to the microphone used when, for some reason, you are examining a system or the material stored in a tape recording. No matter what type of speech or signal processing you are carrying out for forensic purposes, no matter what type of acoustic/behavioral examination you are conducting, it is important that you learn all you can about the microphone that was employed.

Loudspeakers and Earphones

A loudspeaker is a device that reverses the transduction process typified by the microphone. (Please note that the word "loudspeaker," rather than just "speaker," will be used in this book in order to separate this concept from that involving a human speaker.) A loudspeaker is a system that turns electrical energy into acoustic/mechanical energy of the same pattern. Earphones essentially do the same thing. Some loudspeakers are separate from, but can be coupled to, any electronic system—including tape recorders; others (with their associated driving or power amplifiers) are incorporated into the system. Most loudspeakers are of the dynamic type. That is, they consist of a cone made of specially treated paper or plastic which is vibrated by an electromagnetic device, thereby re-creating the pattern which has been stored. To be specific, the movements of the cone are the mechanical analog of the amplified electrical signal fed to it (via electronic circuitry) from the reproduction head of a recording device—or some related system. In turn, the moving cone imparts the corresponding vibrations to the surrounding air and, in this manner, the loudspeaker reconverts the electrical signal into the same acoustic disturbance that was recorded earlier. If you are working in forensic phonetics, you again are often saddled with a "preselected" loudspeaker or the one that is part of the overall system. However, if you have any choice in its selection, the question always should be—does it reproduce the signal at a fidelity level that is at least as good as that of the system's other component parts? Of course, the loudspeaker's frequency response (and distortion) need be only as good as the associated recording equipment; however, if those systems have good frequency response characteristics, then the loudspeakers should also.

Another consideration with loudspeakers relates to impedance. Impedance can be defined as the complex resistance in a circuit to alternating current flow; it involves both resistance (as to direct current) and reactance (including phase differences). Thus, the impedance of a loudspeaker (or earphones, for that matter) must be matched to the characteristics of the output amplifier if efficient operation is to be expected. That is, if there is an impedance "mismatch" between the speaker and amplifier, the signal produced will be distorted in some manner. The relevant impedances can be found on the equipment, in the manuals provided by the manufacturer, or measured by a technician. There will be no problem if the speaker already is coupled to the recorder; in this case, the impedances are matched at the factory. However, under ordinary circumstances, it is important to check both the wattage and impedance interface between a loudspeaker and the amplifier used to drive it—or, for that matter, between any two pieces of equipment you may have to operate.

Headphones

In a sense headphones resemble a loudspeaker—but a small or very small one. They essentially consist of a permanent magnet, a coil, and a carefully designed and suitably suspended "cone" or vibrating plate. Ordinarily, earphones exhibit good frequency response—for speech anyway. However, they should be chosen or evaluated on the basis of the same frequency response and impedance-matching criteria as was applied to loudspeakers. It also should be remembered that, although you will only rarely have to evaluate a system that includes headphones (or a loudspeaker), if you do have to do so, you will need skills beyond those that will accrue from reading this book. The discussions provided here are simply designed to familiarize you with the nature and characteristics of a system or procedure rather than provide detailed information necessary at a level that would permit you to become a technician or a scientist (however, for additional reading, see 3, 4, 16).

TAPE RECORDERS

The modern tape recorder is at the core of almost all forensic phonetics activities. It is the device that, in most cases anyway, is utilized to store the signal or signals we wish to process. It is a very useful system. Yet it is one that actually is quite simple to both understand and use. You probably have seen tape recorders that appear to be very intricate and complex. They *look* complex but they really are not. Thus, in this section I will attempt to explain (1) how tape recorders work, (2) why they are not such difficult machines to understand and (3) how to operate almost any tape recorder you may happen to meet.

To reiterate, once the acoustic signal has been transformed by a microphone into an electrical signal, it can be further processed for storage on recording tape. This process is accomplished by the tape recorder circuitry, which essentially consists of four basic components: a recording amplifier, a bias/erase head, a magnetic transducer and a tape transport system. A schematic drawing of these circuits is found primarily on the left-hand side of Figure 4-1. As can be seen, the input (electrical) signal is passed to an amplifier—a device that increases the electrical energy level of the signal without distorting it appreciably—and then to a recording head which essentially is a magnetic transducer. The tape transport or drive system passes field-sensitive tape over the record head (see below), and the magnetic pattern is imprinted on it. Prior to this event, the tape is "erased" and a bias frequency placed on it. The reproduction procedure of a tape recorder (see the right portion of Figure 4-1) is not quite a mirror image of the recording process—primarily because there is no analog of the erase/bias function. The playback head simply operates as a transducer but functionally in a

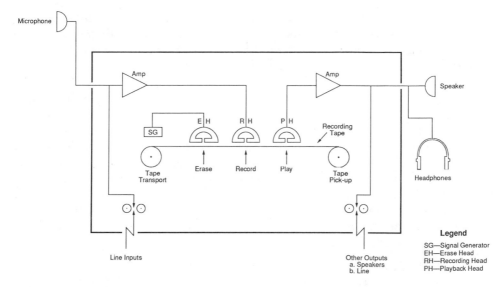

Figure 4-1. Diagram of the basic elements which comprise a tape recorder. The record section (inputs, erase/record heads) are on the left and the playback elements (magnetic head, amplifier, outputs) on the right. SG, signal generation; EH, erase head; RH, recording head; PH, playback head.

mode which is the reverse of that of the record head. That is, it picks up the varying magnetic patterns from the tape which is moved over it and converts them into an electrical signal. This electronic pattern is then passed on to the output amplifier and, ultimately, to a speaker, earphones or some measurement/analysis device. Now let us look at these functions in greater detail—in all cases referring to Figure 4-1.

The Recording Process

First, I would like to expand on my description of a record head. If you will examine this unit, as portrayed in Figure 4-1, you will see that it consists of a magnet (i.e., the core) which has wire (not shown) wound about it. The record head is activated by the electronic signal which passes through the wire. Please note that the circuit is not closed, because the permanent magnet is "interrupted" by a gap (usually filled with nonconductive material) which permits polarity to be maintained. What occurs is that the varying voltage causes the magnetic field to be modified in a pattern that mirrors the one traveling through the wire. The recording process is completed when the magnetic tape has passed over the recording head—in a sense, "completing" the circuit as the signal has been stored on the tape in a magnetic pattern.

The Recording Medium

It has been indicated that the pattern of the signal in question is stored on magnetic tape. But what is this material and how does it work? A recording tape essentially is made-up of two parts—a plastic base or strip on one side and a coating of iron oxide on the other. Look at a piece of recording tape. Ordinarily you will find that one side is dull and the other side shiny (that is, except for certain types of specialized tape). It is the dull side that is impregnated with the magnetic-sensitive iron oxide, and it is this side which is passed over the recording head to complete the circuit and store the signal. These iron-oxide particles can be thought of as being patterned in a random or nonsystematic manner. Actually, however, they are placed in a flux or bias pattern by the erase head (see below), one that is supersonic and cannot be heard if played to the listener. In short, before it is used as a recording medium, the tape has no audio signal on it. Then, when it is passed over the gap where there is magnetic flux, the relevant (bias aligned) particles are rearranged into the pattern created by the record head in response to the electronic flow. That pattern will stay on the tape until altered by another magnetic field.

The Playback Process

As stated, the record procedures essentially are reversed for playback purposes. In this case, a constant current flow is placed across the wires wound around the playback head—a unit which is very similar in nature to a record head (a single head is used for both purposes in some machines). As the tape passes across the head, the magnetic pattern it contains will increase or inhibit the electrical flow in the same pattern as is on the tape. Thus, the reproduction head can be seen to transduce the "stored" magnetic pattern to an electrical signal—which then is amplified and passed on to the output circuitry. Please remember also that the patterns on the tape are not removed by this process, so, once a recording is made, the tape can be played over and over again—at least until it is erased.

The Erase Process

But what about the third "head" — the erase head? In virtually all instances, it is activated only if the record head is operative. Its function is to "remove" — or actually, rearrange—any patterns that are on the tape being used, so that they will not interfere with the new recording, and place a "bias" frequency on the tape so its oxide particles are in a pattern conducive to the recording process. Actually the erase-bias process is a little more complex than that described (3), but my review is functionally accurate. In short, it is of little consequence if there is a prior recording on the tape being used, or if it is a fresh one straight from the manufacturer, because the erase head is automatically placed in operation when the unit's record circuits are activated. At the risk of being redundant, let me indicate once again that an erase head does not function as most people think it does—certainly not like the eraser on a pencil. Rather, it places a high-intensity, high-frequency recording on the tape. In this manner, the tape to be recorded on is saturated by a focused signal usually somewhere between 40 and 100 kHz. Thus, once a section of tape has been "erased" (whether a new recording has been placed on it or not), the old recording is removed irretrievably, unless the equipment is malfunctioning (and badly so). In the case, of malfunction, the "old" recording, or parts of it, might still remain. More than once I have had to disappoint a detective or attorney by telling him or her that their erased tape could not be processed in any manner that would recover the speech that once had been on it. Indeed, no audio signal at all could be recovered because it simply had ceased to exist. Once erased, the old signal is gone forever. All the tape contains is a powerful ultrasonic signal which was placed on it by the erase head.

Degaussers or Bulk Erasers

Now that the "basics" are in place, it is possible to review the simplicity of tape recorder operation. But before doing so, let me indicate that there are devices called bulk erasers or degaussers (see Figure 4-2). These units are either table-mounted or hand held and can be used to erase magnetic tape all at once. Equipment of this type produces strong alternating magnetic fields that reorder the iron oxide to the frequency being produced by the degausser. If used properly, all previously recorded magnetic patterns are "removed" — that is, rearranged. The frequencies of these degaussing fields may vary substantially, depending on the manufacturer, but they usually operate at low frequencies. Moreover, while any tape held close to the tabletop monsters is "wiped clean," it is more difficult to get the job done with a hand-held degausser. They must be held very close to the tape and rotated over it for up to a minute if a "clean" tape is to be the result. But back to the tape recorders and their nature.

Figure 4-2. A photograph of two tape degaussers. A hand-held model is on the left and a small table-mounted unit on the right.

Tape Recorders Simplified

As you have seen, it is possible to describe the theory and operation of a tape recorder in a relatively simple way—primarily since they actually are simple machines. Assuming that you now understand something about their basics, let us review the component parts of a tape recorder, how to run one, and, indeed, how *not* to be bemused by any tape recorder you may have to operate.

The Necessary Controls

First, note Figure 4-3. As you will see, there are only five or six functions you must identify if you are to successfully operate a tape recorder. All devices of this type have them and, while sometimes they are not so easy to find, you may be sure that they are there. First, a tape recorder must have a power supply: it will be either line voltage or batteries. Look for the power cord and plug it into a wall socket—or look for the batteries. If the tape recorder uses line voltage, it often will have a power light which will glow when it is plugged in and turned on. If battery powered, it may have a DC (direct current) indicator. In any case, it is your responsibility to find the power supply to the tape recorder and see that it is operative (do not assume that the batteries are charged even when found;

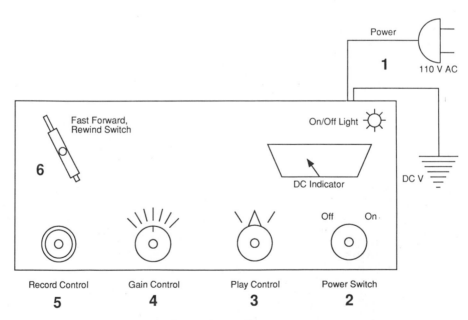

Figure 4-3. A schematic of those elements/controls essential to tape recorder operation. They include a power supply (1), power (2) and activation switches (3), a gain control (4) and an independent method of activating the record mode (5). A high-speed (forward/rewind) control (6) is quite useful.

check them). Second, find the power (or off/on) switch and turn it on. Most tape recorders will have one (it usually is identified by the word "power"); if it cannot be found, the recorder ordinarily will be turned on when you activate the tape transport—i.e., when you find and operate the switch that starts the tape reels turning. Thus, functions 2 and 3 in Figure 4-3 may be combined—or they may be separate.

The next control is the gain regulator (often called "volume"); it varies the strength of the input signal so it can be recorded at the proper level (not so intense that the input waves will be clipped, but high enough to make a recording). Sometimes the gain control will have a meter coupled to it (LED, lights or some type of signal strength indicator can be substituted). If so, it will provide useful information about the recording you are making. If you have an indicator, use it—keeping the needle (lights) peaking in the middle range; if you do not have one, make a test recording. Actually, when you turn on the tape transport, you will find that it only gives you playback (it usually is identified by the word "play"). To record you usually have to find and activate a separate switch—one that says record (it is often colored red). Thus, to make a recording, all you have to do is find and activate the power to the tape recorder and find and activate the two switches labeled play and record. You control the strength of the recording by the gain or volume switch. That is all there is to it! The process will not change very much even when the new digital audiotape (DAT) recorders become common.

Please note that the schematic in Figure 4-3 also includes a rewind plus fast-forward control. While technically these two functions are not necessary to permit either the recording or playback of a tape, they are mighty convenient and, hence, are included on virtually any tape recorder you will encounter.

Useful Controls

Figure 4-4 shows some of the other features that may be useful. While they are not absolutely necessary to the tape recording process, they usually prove to be a convenience. Moreover, they are found on many tape recorders and even on tape players or tape transports (these systems provide only the playback function). First, you may find several level indicators—they will be in pairs if the recorder has a stereo function. A second useful device is a monitor switch—a function which allows you to listen to either the signal that is coming in to be recorded or what actually is on the tape. Incidentally, it is wise to monitor the taped signal when making a recording. By this means, you will be sure to have the materials on the tape that you wish to be there. The pause control (3) simply permits you to interrupt the recording or playback without turning off the machine. A pause control ordinarily puts an electronic signature on a tape when it is activated during recording—but one which is different from that created by operation of the power switch. The reactivation wow and flutter usually are less for "pause" than for an "off-on" manipulation.

Many tape recorders have a counter; this device allows you to log the place where particular parts of the recording can be found and enables them to be

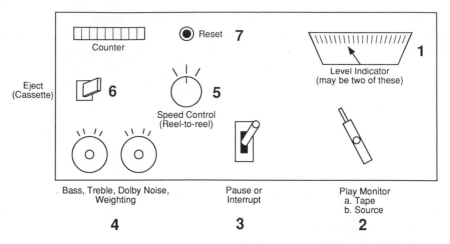

Figure 4-4. Features that are part of many tpe recorders. They permit a person to make good tape recordings—and do so efficiently.

easily identified and retrieved. Reel-to-reel tape recorders often can be operated at several speeds—hence, they sometimes will have a control switch that enables you to specify which speed you wish to employ. Most tape recorders can be played at $3^3/4$ inches per second (ips); others play at integral multiples of $3^3/4$ ips ($7^1/2$, 15, and even 30 or 60 ips) or at fractions of $3^3/4$ ($1^7/8$ or $^{15}/_{16}$ ips). It is important to remember that faster tape recorder speeds translate into better fidelity (especially with respect to frequency response), as there will be more space on which to record information. Please note also that if the tape recorder can accept any type of cassette, there may be a cassette ejection button.

Have you ever wondered why standard-size cassette tape recorders all run at the same speed, whereas there are several sizes/speeds among the reel-to-reel and micro/mini (cassette) recorders? As it turns out, when the Phillips Company invented (designed and fabricated) the first tape recorder of this type, they permitted other companies to make them also—and without paying anything but token royalties—provided these other companies built machines that all ran at exactly the same speed, and used the same size cassettes as did theirs. Thus, the largesse provided us by the Phillips Company is one of inestimable value. Just imagine the chaos that would have occurred if there were 6-8 speeds among this type of small tape recorder. On the other hand, the slow speed of a cassette tape recorder explains why these tapes have a restricted frequency response (usually not exceeding 10 kHz at best), but this is a minor problem relative to their positive features (e.g., conformity, size, cost, and so on).

Finally, the bass, treble, Dolby, noise, equalizer or weighting controls on the tape recorder all indicate similar functions. They are not just part of the "hype" included to help sell tape recorders or allow you to be charged more for them (they are that too, of course). Basically, all are filters which tend to reduce the response of the system within one or more frequency ranges. For example, since it is known that low-frequency noise is both distracting and tends to mask higher frequencies, the treble filter (or weighting network) can be activated to reduce this effect. All that happens here is that the low frequencies are reduced in strength and the entire signal is returned (roughly) to its overall level by internal amplification. The bass control operates to dampen the higher frequencies (and the distraction of hiss); thus when this process is initiated, and the signal is ampli- fied, the lower frequencies are emphasized and hiss is reduced. In any case, these filters or equalizers can aid you in making good tape recordings or improv- ing any recording you might have. It must be remembered, however, that vir- tually all of them are simply analog filters with very shallow slopes; hence, they cannot do more than slightly bias or equalize the frequencies on your recording. For instance, they are not robust enough to permit anything but a minor en- hancement of speech on a tape recording containing high noise levels.

Monophonic and Stereo

If you have studied human hearing, you will have learned that binaural hearing means to hear with both ears and that the location of sounds and other functions are aided by this process. On the other hand, the term "stereo" refers to a specific external process—one where two recordings of the same acoustic event are made simultaneously but with microphones in different positions. Thus, monophonic or sterophonic recordings can be made. It always is neces- sary to recognize which process is used and employ an appropriate tape record- er (see below).

Recording/Playback Head Configurations

A number of recording/playback configurations exist among different tape recorders (see Figure 4-5). First, a unit may be fabricated with two or three heads. There virtually always will be a separate erase head, but the record and playback functions can be combined, and they often are on inexpensive tape recorders.

The width of the head in relationship to the width of the tape also is very important. Actually, there are many tape widths, and each is used with the appropriate tape recorder. For our purposes, however, I will confine most of my descriptions to the most common width—that of the standard quarter-inch rec- ording tape. A full-track tape recorder head configuration can be seen in part A of Figure 4-5. Here, the recording must be monophonic, as there is no way in which two different recordings could be recorded simultaneously on the tape. However, more overall information can be recorded (higher fidelity) by this type of head for any given speed, as the entire width of the tape is used. The heads seen in section B are half-track heads that permit stereo recordings to be made— one recording (from one microphone) is made on track 1 and a simultaneous one from the other microphone on track 2. Dropping from B directly to D will aid you in better understanding the variations possible in recording heads. Here the system is monophonic (as in A), but the length of the recording will be double that of A; i.e., the tape may be played one way, then turned over and recorded (on the other track) in the other direction. Finally, configuration C shows a quarter-track head configuration that can be used to provide double-length ster-

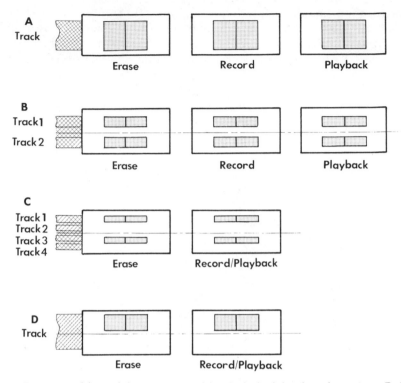

Figure 4-5. Drawings of four of the many record head/playback head configurations. Perhaps the most common is the quarter-track stereophonic unit (or monophonic, if there is only one recording section to the head) seen in drawing C.

eo recordings. First, quarter-tracks 1 and 3 are utilized; then the tape is "turned over" so a second stereo recording can be made on tracks 2 and 4 (which then become the new 1 and 3). Most stereo cassette tape recorders utilize this system. There can be other tape recorder head arrangements, but the four illustrated should be sufficient to permit an understanding of how they can be configured. Perhaps, even more important, Figure 4-5 should provide you with enough information to assist in the determination of the number and type of heads which exist on any tape recorder you may be examining.

Care of Tape Recordings

Information about how tape recordings can be protected will be found summarized in Table 4-1. As you can see, while tapes are generally rugged, they can be vulnerable to certain types of debilitating conditions. If you are making, analyzing and/or storing tape recordings, it would be helpful to review the points I have included in this list.

The ability of a modern magnetic tape recorder to store signals, such as voices, for later analysis is now well established. It is, perhaps, the key piece of instrumentation in this subarea of criminology. Best yet, modern technology and microelectronics permit easy access to truly portable tape recorders which, even

TABLE 4-1. Suggestions for Proper Maintenance and Storage of Tape Recordings

1. Tape recordings should be kept away from magnets, loudspeakers, transformers and power sources. For example, it is not wise to place a tape on an amplifier or other electronic equipment.
2. Recording tapes should be protected from heat and moisture; fire and water can damage or destroy them.
3. For permanent storage, tape recordings should be placed in an upright position and wound as evenly as possible. Smooth winding for storage can be achieved by using the playback mode as a slow rewind.
4. Tape recordings should be provided special shielding when they are transported. Metal boxes (such as those made by Advanced Magnetics Inc., Rochester, Indiana) will protect tapes from unexpected magnetic fields in transit.
5. Recording tape can shrink and stretch; these are conditions which can result in signal distortion. See items 2 and 3 for some of the causes; however, careless handling also can create this problem.
6. The bending or crimping of recording tape can prevent it from aligning properly with the record/playback heads. Tapes of critical import should be examined for this problem before and after use.
7. Should a recording tape become tangled or wedged in the reel or cassette, special care should be taken when straightening it. It can be stretched or crimped during this process and distortion often will result.
8. An operator should keep his or her hands clean and dry when working with tapes; they should not be handled any more than is absolutely necessary.
9. The proper labeling of recording tape boxes, cassettes and reels prevents confusion. Items should never be underidentified and they should be cross labeled in log books. Remember also that an incorrect label is as harmful as no label at all.
10. Certain procedures should be followed if it is necessary to splice magnetic tape. The operator should be certain that (a) the scissors or blade are not magnetized, (b) a diagonal cut is made and (c) there is no overhang of splicing tape.
11. If a recording tape is accidentally broken, it is wise to splice the two ends just as separated. A "clean" splice can debase the integrity or authenticity of that tape.
12. For good tape recordings, the operator should ensure that the recorder heads are demagnetized, clean and properly aligned. If these functions cannot be performed, the tape recorder should be taken to a technician.

though small to tiny, still meet at least minimal standards of fidelity. In the past, the components in small recorders often reduced the quality of the recordings to such an extent that they were unacceptable. Such is not the case any more. Today's technology permits even the smaller and less expensive tape recorders to reproduce human speech nearly as well as do many of the large, expensive, laboratory-type recorders. They simply wear out quicker; hence, their performance should be monitored closely and they should be repaired/calibrated whenever necessary. In sum, the descriptions/criteria above should provide reasonably useful information about the purchase, operation, care and/or analysis of tape recorders for forensic purposes (for additional readings see 1, 7, 27, 28).

ANALYSIS EQUIPMENT

There are all kinds of forensic phonetic evaluations/examinations that need the support of specialized equipment—plus many types of analysis equipment.

Indeed, there are far too many of these needs and equipment classes for them all to be considered in this short chapter. Then, too, specialized equipment often will be discussed within the chapter or area where it is most relevant. On the other hand, there are some general types of equipment that can be used for a number of different evaluations and yet other types that are rather basic to much of the work carried out in this field. For example: (1) wave analyzers can be used in speaker identification, tape recording authentication and electronic signature evaluations; (2) several types of spectrometers are relevant to these areas plus those of decoding and analysis of stress in voice; (3) electronic counters are used to time events of all types; (4) intensity/temporal analysis systems are used in a number of areas—speaker identification and vocal stress analysis among them. Moreover, most of the devices to be described in this section are used both in research and for field analyses.

I should like to emphasize that several terms will be used in the discussions that follow. Electroacoustical and electronic instruments sometimes will be referred to as "hardware;" an array of these devices often will be called a "system." If one or more units or systems are coupled to, or used in concert with, digital computers, the term "hybrid" will be used in describing the entire array. Finally, many of the analysis procedures utilized in this work are carried out exclusively by computers. For example, when I wish to analyze short-term or impact sounds, such as off-on tape recorder clicks or gunshots, I ordinarily will digitize the signal with a commercial program (ILS) and evaluate the results with our specially written DOER program (see below). These approaches will be referred to as "software" techniques.

Wave Composition—Spectrography

You will remember that the heard quality of a sound results primarily from the perception of its component frequencies; physically it is assessed by analysis of the spectrographic composition of the signal. The area of spectrography is a complex one. There are scores of spectrometers, most of which measure events other than acoustic waves/disturbances. But even in the acoustic domain, there are a variety of devices that are designed to measure the characteristics of a given simple or complex sound wave (6, 13, 17, 22). Problems facing the scientist who is interested in determining the wave composition of a signal can be understood by looking back at Figure 2-15. As you will remember, this figure shows an instantaneous spectrogram with a fundamental frequency of 100 Hz and 14 harmonic overtones. Inharmonic partials (i.e., energy at frequencies other than integral multiples of the fundamental) are not shown, for, as you will remember from Chapter 2, they would introduce noise into the signal or, if enough were present, change it into an aperiodic tone. This type of spectrogram provides information about the "instantaneous" composition of an acoustic wave. It identifies those frequencies that are present, the energy at each frequency, the resonance regions and the overall energy present in the wave. What cannot be determined from spectrograms of this type are the spectral changes that occur over time. Moreover, the signal must remain unchanged for periods of from 500 ms to as much as 4 sec (depending upon the particular device used) in order for a spectrum of this type to be computed. To obtain "instantaneous" spectra over time requires a yet more complex instrument or program (see again Figure 2-16). Even here, only a few milliseconds of the sound wave being analyzed are shown. Indeed, if spectra for large amounts of material are needed, the computing power at the disposal of the examiner must be quite extensive. It should be noted, however, that this type of spectrometry is particularly amenable to digital processing; it is particularly useful in the analysis of noise and vowel sounds.

A second type of spectrometry can be seen in Figure 4-6; these displays are referred to as long-term or power spectra. Here, a relatively long speech sample (20 sec to approximately 5 minutes) is analyzed for the frequency-by-intensity (actually, sound pressure) relationships in a speaker's voice—i.e., those that occur over time and independently of the specific words produced. While this spectrogram is shown as an "envelope," it actually consists of a series of points (as does the "instantaneous" spectrogram) which are connected together by some program or procedure. Among other things, this type of spectrogram is thought to be able to provide information of a person's general voice quality. Finally, although the envelope seen is analog in nature, power spectra equipment ordinarily are digital devices.

Among the oldest of all spectrographs are the time-frequency-amplitude (t-f-a) systems. This type of sound spectrography has been around for over 50 years and, until recently, was totally analog in nature. It provides (see Figure 4-7) a graphic display of a signal over time (usually about 2.4 sec), with the frequen-

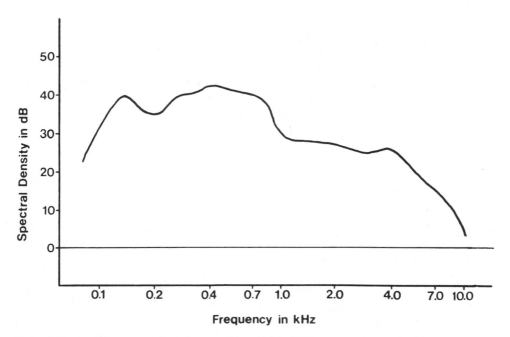

Figure 4-6. Output curve of a power spectrograph. Note that the spectral configuration does not relate to any particular phoneme. Patterns of this type are missing because a long-term spectrum consists of the combined energy (over time) of many phonemes.

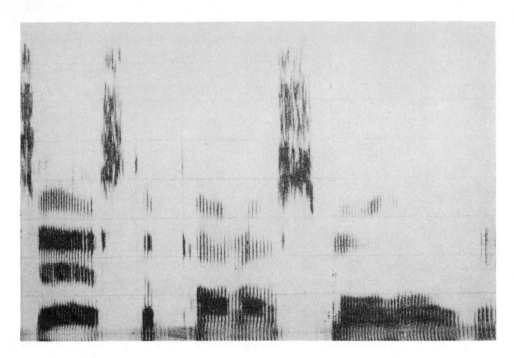

Figure 4-7. A typical time-frequency-amplitude spectrogram of the type also discussed in Chapter 2. These displays now can be generated either by hardware or software.

cies represented linearly (not geometrically) up the vertical scale and intensity roughly displayed by the darkness of the mark on the paper. This type of device actually distorts a signal both in the frequency and intensity domains but provides a rather nice picture of its general nature. The t-f-a spectrograph is a good teaching device; it is the favorite of the voiceprint adherents and can have some important and valid uses in forensic phonetics. Details of the three classes of sound spectrometers follow.

"Instantaneous" Spectrometers and Wave Analyzers

There are a number of different approaches to "instantaneous spectrometry." The following will review but a few of the devices that can be classed as this type of machine. The most basic type of spectrometer within this class is the wave analyzer; it can be typified by the General Radio unit, model 1900A. This particular unit has a maximum frequency response of 20-54,000 Hz and a choice of three filter bandwidths (3, 10, 50 Hz). It sweeps a continuously repeated signal and provides a spectrum (not precisely instantaneous, of course) that portrays the energy found within the entire period of the wave. Since, ordinarily, an individual cannot sustain phonation with an exact F0 and spectrum, the typical product of a wave analyzer usually will appear as in Figure 4-8. Nevertheless, reasonable calculations of steady-state tones (or at least, quasiperiodic phonation) can be analyzed by this method. More current units provide

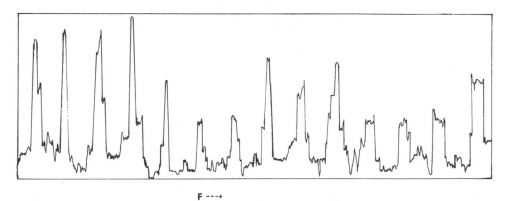

F ---→

Figure 4-8. A tracing of the output of a wave analyser. Twelve partials (or F0 + 11 H0) can be seen. Note the resonant effects of the vowel being produced and the possibility that the phonation contains vibrato; that is, some peaks are of greater amplitude than others (vowel formants) and the "width" of the higher partials is greater than the lower ones.

interface electronics so that the output of the wave analyzer can be fed directly to a digital computer and processed quantitatively. Of course, while simple observations of the graphic displays seen in the figure cited above can be interesting and lead to yet more sophisticated analysis, they are by nature subjective. Thus, if the observations made are not confirmed by external (quantitative) evidence, they sometimes can be misleading.

Somewhat more versatile units of the "instantaneous" spectrum class are the Bruel and Kjaer audio frequency spectrometers. For example, the B&K model 2110 has 30 one-third-octave filters with center frequencies ranging from 40 Hz to 3.15 kHz. By linking and time-aligning this unit to a graphic-level recorder, a display similar to that produced by the GR-1900A may be obtained. The B&K 2100 also has the capability (in modified configurations) to provide digital readout and long-term spectra.

The "real-time"spectrometers are a third type of device within this class. The Princeton Applied Research (PAR) model 4512 FFT Real-Time Spectrum Analyzer typifies this group and uses a Fast Fourier Transform (FFT) technique to determine the spectral content of a signal. As with many of the real-time class of analyzers, this unit has the capability of producing "line" (instantaneous) or long-term spectra, either for direct observation on the face of an oscilloscope or as hard copy. Perhaps the greatest advantage of these devices is that they can be interfaced easily with computers in a hardware/software (hybrid) configuration. Hence, they provide a method of carrying out a great deal of processing with a minimum expenditure of time. An analyzer such as the PAR 4512 is a little difficult to describe, since it has many capabilities and modes of operation. Basically, it has a frequency range of from 10 Hz to 41 kHz, with a real-time bandwidth of 15.5 kHz, a sampling frequency of up to nearly 82 kHz, and input windows varying from 0.0125-50 sec. Input signals are sampled by a 12-bit A/D converter and stored in input memory. The contents of the memory then are transferred to "calculate memory," where the spectral components are computed by means of the FFT algorithm. Since this processing can take as little as 33 ms, continuous spectral displays can be provided or fed into a computer for analysis.

Finally, it is now possible to carry out "instantaneous" spectrometry using computer software only. ILS and MACSPEECH are but two of the many programs available; we find that each of the software approaches we use has its individual strengths and weaknesses. In many cases, only relatively short samples can be analyzed; hence, you may find it necessary to evaluate your spectral analysis programs—and their adaptability to your computer and needs—before committing to this type of approach.

Long-Term Spectral Analysis (LTS)

This type of speech spectrum is a representation of the frequency-intensity relationships of the varying partials within the acoustic wave. In the preceding section, spectrometers were described that could be employed to provide information about the specific intensities of particular partials which occur at an "instant" in time; LTS is different. An understanding of this approach can best be gained by again referring to Figure 4-6, which provides information about this type of spectral display; an excellent description of LTS also can be found in Denes and Pinson (6). In the LTS process, the relative intensities of all frequencies occurring during the entire speech sample are measured and analyzed. Incidentally, the curve produced can provide either a profile for an individual or a composite profile for a group of talkers.

The old General Radio Spectrum Analyzer, model 1921, is a classic example of a device that produces power spectra. This device has a number of "channels," each consisting of a one-third-octave filter band, with 23 of these channels (a range of 80-12,500 Hz) commonly utilized for speech analysis. A tape-recorded speech sample can be fed into this unit and the amount of energy within each channel computed simultaneously for the entire duration of the sample. Since the maximum integration time for the GR 1921 analyzer is 32 sec. longer samples must be processed in segments and the several data sets averaged by a later operation. The output is an array of 23 measurements that can be fed into a digital computer for analysis. For example, Euclidean distances may be calculated to permit development of a vector useful in determining the identity of the speaker (13) or in contrasting languages (18). Of course, the GR 1921 is hardly the only averaging spectrum analyzer available; indeed, many others can be found that provide similar data. For example, the Princeton Applied Research model 4512 analyzer (previously discussed) has an LTS provision as do the several cited computer programs.

Time-Frequency-Amplitude Spectrometry

Without question the most commonly used type of sound spectrometry for speech/voice research (especially in the past) has been that involving time-frequency-amplitude (t-f-a) displays. First developed at Bell Telephone Laboratories over 50 years ago for aiding the deaf in learning to speak, these devices were described first by in-house publications and then later by Potter (23) and Potter, Kopp, and Green (24).

When the t-f-a spectrometer was first made commercially available by the Kay Company (now Kay Elemetrics), it provided phoneticians, linguists, speech scientists and engineers with a powerful tool for the acoustic analysis of connected speech. Joos (15), perhaps, was among the first to see its value; his work was followed closely by that of Potter and Steinberg (25) and Peterson and Barney (22) in their specification of vowel formants. The t-f-a sound spectrographic approach has been used as the basis of thousands of experiments on speech—most of which were useful, a few of which have been misleading.

Figure 4-9A shows a typical spectrometer: a Kay Elemetrics Corporation model 6061B Sona-Graph (and Figure 4-7 a typical t-f-a spectrogram). This system is but one of a class. Similar devices have been produced by Kay Elemetrics and other companies but, except for Kay Elemetrics' most recent units (see Figure 4-9B and their 7800 Digital Sonograph), they vary only in minor ways. The basic characteristics of this class of spectrometers are similar and can best be understood by reference to Figure 4-9. Specifically, the Kay 6061B has frequency ranges of 80-8000 Hz and 160-16,000 Hz. Operating procedures involve the input (recording) of a sample of speech 2.4 sec in length; the sample is stored and then continuously replayed while the filters "sweep" the entire frequency range for either its narrow or its wide filter band (i.e., 45 or 300 Hz). As with all of the systems described in this chapter, these units must be calibrated. Nevertheless, measurement accuracy varies somewhat as a function of parameter. The accuracy of the time measurement is best, accuracy of frequency reasonably accurate, except for the fact that the display is compacted (and is not consistant with the octave log scale), and amplitude accuracy is a distant third because the filter bandwidth causes the energy in the partials to be either blurred into bars or omitted altogether. Ordinarily, frequency measurements are made by hand or by means of digital data provided by auxiliary equipment; amplitude often can be estimated by an associated sectioner or similar auxiliary device.

The Kay Elemetric Company recently has introduced a digital t-f-a spectrometer (the model 7800), a device which quickly and efficiently provides all of the information available from traditional t-f-a spectrometers. Moreover, it also can provide several types of spectral information on a quantitative basis. It is useful for the usual t-f-a spectral analysis and many other procedures—including the analysis of pulse-like signals (for example, the electronic signatures of tape recorders).

As Fant pointed out as early as 1958 (8), hard-copy sonagraphs of an utterance provide the investigator with an array of interesting information about speech, some of which can be appreciated after only a short learning period. Indeed, these devices are excellent for teaching, for clinical evaluations, for picturing relative information/relationships and for viewing the dynamics of speech over time. They can be utilized to obtain rapid-pattern analysis of the type that can lead to the development of more precise evaluations. On the other hand, highly accurate quantitative data are difficult to extract by means of this technique. It has proved to be an almost disastrous approach when attempts

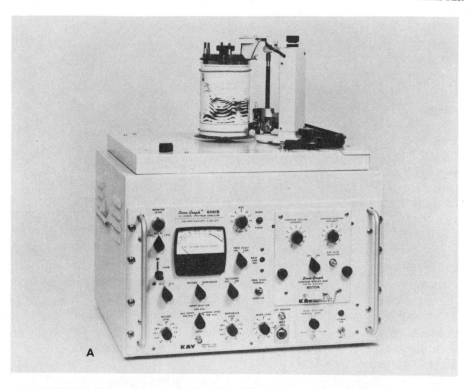

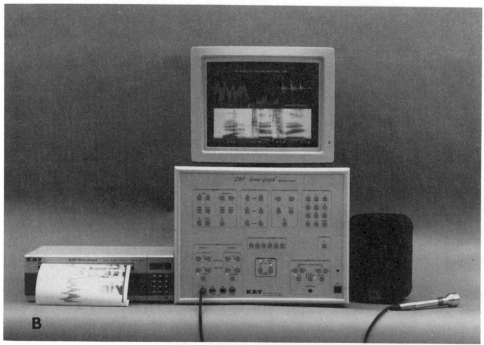

Figure 4-9. Photographs of the older and newer types of t-f-a spectrometers manufactured by Kay Elemetrics. The older unit (A) is a classic; it can be found worldwide in virtually any laboratory where the speech or communication of any species is studied.

have been made to use it for speaker identification (see Chapter 10, "The Voice-print Problem").

Fundamental Frequency Analysis

There have been a large number of F0 analysis schemes proposed and carried out; up until recently most did not work very well (21). Some individuals have attempted to use t-f-a spectrometry to estimate F0 (or speaking fundamental frequency, SFF). In this case, the differences between partials were measured and an average computed. However, this approach proved to be quite time-consuming, laborious and only marginally accurate. Other (older) approaches have included the use of oscillographs or oscilloscopes; a somewhat more up-to-date unit (the Visicorder) also has been employed, but not very successfully. Most of these devices utilize a focused light or electron beam, which is varied by circuitry in the same pattern as the acoustic signal and permanently traced on some type of sensitive paper. Many of them suffer from timing problems; in all cases data reduction is laborious and time-consuming in the extreme.

Somewhat more successful approaches include the Purdue Pitch Meter (5), the Boe and Rakotofiringa system, and those commercial devices produced by Kay Elemetrics (the Visipitch 6087; also a version for computer interface) and Frokjaer-Jensen (Fundamental Frequency Meter). Even though the latter two devices are easily obtained and have some digital capability, they are best used in teaching, clinical work and for preliminary viewing of SFF patterns. An additional approach to SFF/F0 processing involves the use of software. The techniques being developed here are quite sophisticated (9, 10, 19, 20, 26) and many relate in some manner to telephone communication systems or basic signal analysis. Most of these techniques require extensive processing time and can provide data only on very short speech samples; nearly all require extensive and powerful computing facilities.

Some years ago I developed (12) a hybrid SFF extraction system that analyzes large amounts of material in very short periods of time (nearly real-time). The system is called FFI-8 (or the eighth model of the Fundamental Frequency Indicator) and can be seen in block diagram form in Figure 4-10. FFI-8 is a system that continuously extracts SFF from tape-recorded speech input and performs statistical analysis of the resulting digital frequency data. It does not sample F0 but rather is designed to provide measures of all the individual waves in a sequence. Samples from 10 seconds to 10 minutes can be processed, but 1-minute samples tend to be optimal.

FFI operates as follows. The speech is played into a primary stage of eight very sharp low-pass filters (75 dB per octave) with roll-off frequencies fixed approximately 0.5 octave apart. Digital electronics, in the form of a parallel eight-channel analog-to-digital (A/D) converter, monitors the output of all eight filters and determines which filter contains only the fundamental frequency. This circuit is the only one coupled to the next stage (by high-speed electronic switches), where the signal is converted to a pulse by Schmitt triggers; hysteresis is employed to avoid "chatter." The period of each pulse is determined, digital information stored and a series of statistical processes carried out. These include various measures of central tendency (geometric means), data variability (SD),

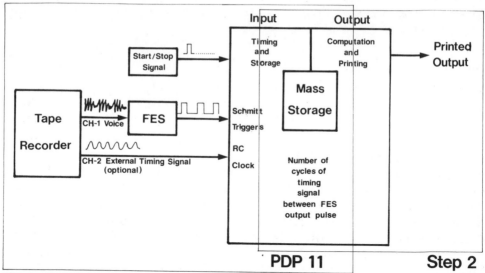

Figure 4-10. A schematic of the general nature of FFI-8. Basically, the complex speech wave is fed through the FES section where F0 appears in one of the dynamic filters. In turn, the high-speed switches permit only the energy from the lowest filter to be transmitted. The signal is then squared and stored in the computer for processing.

and patterns among the data; both digital information and graphic displays are available for further processing (see Figure 4-11). FFI-8 can be used whenever F0 information is needed; it is especially useful in speaker identification as it permits the parameters for an SFF vector to be generated.

Intensity Analysis

While speaking intensity level and variability are fruitful areas for certain types of forensic analyses, this acoustic event (and especially absolute intensity) is quite difficult to measure. In order to determine absolute-intensity levels accurately, extremely sophisticated equipment is required. Hence, the evaluation in this domain usually involves pressure measurements, which are easily made. On the other hand, the problems faced in the measurement of absolute pressure are about the same as are those for intensity. For example, the equipment utilized must be precisely calibrated, the exact characteristics of the input microphone must be known and, if absolute measurements are desired, the talker or signal source must be positioned in very specific relationship to the microphone or pickup transducer. This third variable is, perhaps, the most difficult of the three to control. If the microphone is to be kept a precise distance from the talker's lips (and at an exact angle to them), either a bulky apparatus must be worn on the head or the talker's head position must be severely restricted. Unfortunately, these are situations which simply do not occur in the forensic milieu and, since "absolute" data ordinarily are denied the investigator, only relative measures remain.

```
FFI REFERENCE FREQ. IS 16.35HZ AND CLOCK RATE IS 100000. CAST LIMIT= 6
2274. FFI CYCLES WERE VALIDATED IN 13 BUFFERS FOR 0.18343E+07 COUNTS
AVERAGE FREQUENCY IN SAMPLE IS 124.0 HZ
MEAN= 35.27  S.D.= 2.62  (SEMITONES)
```

	LOW RUN	HI RUN	CAST	GOOD	TOTAL	
# OF CYCLES	96.	168.	694.	2274.	3232.	
% OF CYCLES	2.97	5.20	21.47	70.36	1.00	
# SECONDS	8.95	0.39	5.52	18.34	33.20	SEC.
% OF TIME	26.97	1.16	16.63	55.24	1.00	

```
     DISTRIBUTION TABLE
ST      HZ        #       SECS      %
--------------------------------------
23     61.7      1.       0.0      0.1
24     65.4      0.       0.0      0.0
25     69.3      2.       0.0      0.2
26     73.4      1.       0.0      0.1
27     77.8     11.       0.1      0.7
28     82.4     26.       0.3      1.7
29     87.3     28        0.3      1.7
30     92.5     36.       0.4      2.1
31     98.0     74.       0.7      4.0
32    103.8    159        1.5      8.1
33    110.0    320        2.8     15.4
34    116.5    419.       3.5     19.0
35    123.5    400.       3.1     17.2
36    130.8    321.       2.4     13.0
37    138.6    201.       1.4      7.7
38    146.8    101.       0.7      3.6
39    155.6     57.       0.4      1.9
40    164.8     48.       0.3      1.5
41    174.6     34.       0.2      1.0
42    185.0     23.       0.1      0.7
43    196.0      9.       0.0      0.2
44    207.7      1.       0.0      0.0
45    220.0      2.       0.0      0.0
  % TIME          HISTOGRAM
   19                  *
   18                  *
   17                 **
   16                 **
   15                ***
   14                ***
   13               ****
   12               ****
   11               ****
   10               ****
    9               ****
    8              ******
    7              ******
    6              ******
    5              ******
    4             ********
    3             ********
    2          **************
    1          ****************
       +----+----+----+----+----+----+----+----+----+----+----+
ST 15    20   25   30   35   40   45   50   55   60   65   70
HZ 39    52   69   92  123  165  220  294  392  523  698  932
```

Figure 4-11. One of the many possible FFI readouts. Here the geometric mean of the distribution of those frequencies used by the talker is given in Hertz and semitones—as is the standard deviation of the distribution. Additional information is provided; included is a histogram of the distribution (both graphically and quantitatively). Numerous other displays (not shown) are provided/controlled by software programs.

A basic device used to provide data on pressure level is the sound-level meter. There are many such devices available, as numerous companies (including General Radio, Bruel and Kjaer, Tandy, Techtronix, etc.) manufacture and/or distribute them. Moreover, many can be hand held. Basically, they all operate in the same general fashion. A calibrated microphone is coupled to circuitry that permits sound pressure level (SPL, relative to 0.0002 dynes/cm² or some other reference; see again, Figure 3-8) to be obtained in (pressure) deciBels. Most often this information is read from the meter face, but some systems provide hard-copy readout and/or computer interface. Most of these devices incorporate controls that permit different ranges to be selected; the equipment can be operated in different modes (speed of response, for example) and with different weighting networks active. To illustrate, the C scale on most devices of this type involves an essentially flat frequency response network, whereas activation of the A-scale network results in a filtering of the input signal in a frequency/intensity pattern somewhat analogous to human hearing.

A second useful device in this area is the graphic-level recorder. One unit of this type is the GR 1521B; another is the Bruel and Kjaer model 2305. A graphic-level recorder can provide a running trace of the amplitude of a speech signal that will permit the measurement of durational periods or relative speech intensity (pressure). A typical hard copy can be seen in Figure 4-12. Here, the base, or ambient-noise level, can be seen extending across the bottom of the trace and emerging from it vertically are the speech bursts. If this system is properly calibrated, difference in level, extent of the slopes and other such features can

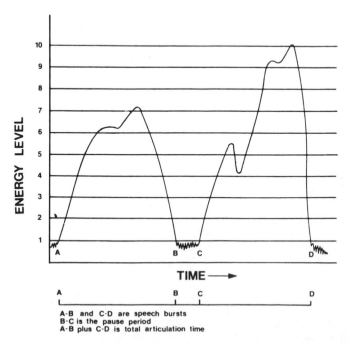

A-B and C-D are speech bursts
B-C is the pause period
A-B plus C-D is total articulation time

Figure 4-12. A tracing of the energy patterns of a series of speech bursts seen over time.

be calculated in deciBels. Finally, nearly all of the t-f-a spectrometers (especially the newer Kay Elemetrics models) have the capability of providing a graphic trace of the intensity (pressure) level of the stored speech. These displays are especially useful for the measurement of such features as consonant/vowel (time and/or energy) ratios, the number and extent of speech bursts in an utterance, and so on.

The procedures described usually are labor intensive and involve decisions that rely heavily on human judgment. Accordingly, a number of investigators have attempted to automate the intensity analysis process by developing computer-aided procedures. While there are several excellent schemes of this type, the one selected for discussion is that developed by Hicks (11) at our laboratory. This approach permits a large number of analyses to be made of a talker's intensity levels and patterns. One of the most useful displays here (whether visual, hard copy or digital) is that of the speaker's intensity distribution, in deciBel steps, with the levels calculated as proportions of his or her total energy produced. In turn, analysis of these distributions permits calculation of peak pressure, the range of pressures utilized, and pressure "configurations." In this procedure, the envelope of the speech signal is obtained by means of a rectifier/integrator circuit coupled, via an A/D converter, to a computer. Specially developed software controls the storage, processing and analysis of the energy dimensions of the recorded utterance. This software is designed to permit the investigator to preselect various parameters such as sampling rate and the length of the sample to be analyzed—and then measure the total pressure of the utterance, the intensity range utilized, pressure level, the standard deviation of the distribution and associated statistics. There is no question but that these are pretty sophisticated measures of a person's speech, and if you are to employ them, you must be well versed in phonetics and have a pretty good idea of exactly what information you are after. As you probably have determined by now, these measures can be useful for speaker identification, analysis of voice for stress, tape authentication and, sometimes, even for speech decoding.

Temporal Measures

The simple measure of "total time" elapsed has been applied to spoken utterances for many centuries and for many reasons. However, there also are other temporal, or time, measures that can be applied to speech samples for forensic purposes. Some of the more useful include: (1) sample duration, (2) speaking rate and rate patterns, (3) phonation-time (P/T) ratios and speech-time (S/T) ratios, (4) pauses—number/length/patterns, (5) speech bursts—number/length/patterns and (6) vectors of combined factors. In many instances, the parameters in question are measured with equipment as simple as a stopwatch, or on the time-elapsed readout of certain tape recorders or electronic counters. Information about speech pauses or bursts often is obtained from measurements of the traces provided by level recorders; P/T ratios can be obtained from SFF (speaking fundamental frequency) tracking devices, and there are several software routines that can provide information of these types.

Recently, a number of algorithms have been proposed that extract various temporal parameters from the speech signal, either directly or as a consequence of some related process. One such approach is the timing or "TED" vector developed at our laboratory by Johnson *et al.* (14). This approach is a relatively complex one and is based on sectional time-by-energy measurements. An R/C circuit is used to generate an energy envelope of the speech signal. In turn, the signal is converted to digitized form by an appropriate program. At this juncture, a special software package is applied to functionally partition the digital patterns into 10 linearly equal-energy levels initiating with the peak level (see discussion in Chapter 11). The number and durations of the speech bursts and pause periods, as well as the means and standard deviations for both, then can be calculated as a function of the 10 levels. The TED approach is just one of a number of temporal analysis schemes that currently are available. As will be seen, we are using it primarily for speaker identification; however, it also is included here because it has so many other uses in the forensic phonetics area.

COMPUTERS

Many references have been made to computers throughout this chapter. In some cases, the measurement techniques described have been supported totally by software, in other cases the system was hybrid in nature (hardware/software), and in yet other instances the desired processing was carried out on a specific piece of equipment—with computer analysis reserved only for data processing and statistical analysis. As a matter of fact, the two preceding discussions (ways to measure speech intensity and prosody by software approaches) were situated immediately prior to this section in order to serve as natural lead-ins to the limited remarks I have to make about computers. In short, it would be difficult to avoid their use, even if you would want to do so, as computers are incredibly helpful devices. However, they are advancing in technological sophistication at such a pace that it is a little difficult for most of us to maintain an adequate comprehension of their capabilities, structure and operation. Perhaps the comments that follow will assist you a little in keeping these systems in perspective.

First, you should remember that a digital computer is simply a tool. In its simplest form, it almost can be thought of as a large tape recorder that can store many, many events—at least those that can be converted to binary form—and then be made to quantitatively process them in unbelievably short periods of time. Computers are not magic or awesome devices, except with respect to their speed and the vast number of operations they can perform in a given period of time. Accordingly, you should not be intimidated by them. Moreover, the work we need to carry out should not be adjusted somehow to fit the nature of the computer; rather, computer capability and software should be developed to serve our analysis needs and the questions we wish answered.

Additionally, it should be remembered that digital computers are just becoming useful for most types of speech/voice research and analysis. For example, it has long been possible for scientists in the area of psychoacoustics to analyze human behavior in such a way that a computer controlled the presentation of stimuli and then processed the subject's or suspect's responses. In the case of many of the instrumental techniques described in this book, however, an approach of this type is not possible. Rather, you will rarely have the speech materials under your control when you wish to relate various speech/voice parameters to behavioral states or analyze the speech signal for specific features or relationships. Indeed, an investigation of these relationships may be the very reason an evaluation has to be performed. In any event, we are now just scratching the surface of computer support for forensic phonetics.

These reservations should not be construed to suggest that computers are not already powerful tools among the instrumental repertoire of the forensic phonetician. The modern digital computer permits the efficient storage and processing of data, as well as allowing an examiner to be privy to the results of the procedures carried out within a very short period of time. The general impact of computers already is substantial and continued development should intensify their effect. In short, an intelligent and judicious use of these devices should greatly enhance both the research and field evaluations described in this book.

Consideration of Figure 4-13 will provide at least an illustrative view of the structure of a modern computer. The computers shown here are among the several types I use; they consist of a pair of DEC PDP 11/23 minicomputers operated in tandem. Note first that each has a central processing unit (CPU). This element basically is the computer's brain; it contains the unit's operating system and can receive any of the software programs that are used to support

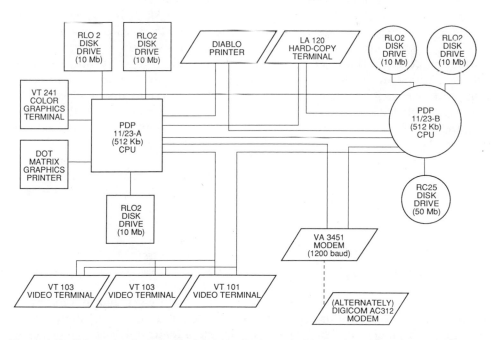

Figure 4-13. Schematic of a pair of mini-computers operated in tandem. Note the two CPUs, the several disc drives (RL02, RC-25) and the I/O's (terminals, modems, etc). Many programs must be available if a computer of this type is to function effectively. Moreover, it currently is possible to develop microcomputer systems that are just as powerful as this array.

the many specialized tasks it can perform. Each CPU has a group of secondary storage disc-drives that permit the accumulation and processing of data and the storing of these products and any other relevant materials. A CPU also may contain circuits (such as clocks, timers, interfaces, ports, digital I/O lines and so on) that permit other tasks to be performed. Access to the CPU is through terminals of all types, analog-to-digital channels (not shown), input modems, and so on. Output also is to terminals of all types, modems and printers. Basically, you "boot" your system, input your specialized programs as well as material and/or data, then process and receive the outcome in some usable form.

Of course, to fully describe computers and their uses would require a treatise at least as long as this book. A final example would appear useful, however. The microcomputers of today (often called PCs or personal computers) are fast becoming nearly as powerful and versatile as the minicomputers of just a few years ago; and the mini's of today would rival mainframes in use but a decade or two ago. For example, an IBM AT or a Zenith 386 equipped with digitization programs like the ILS or SIG (or our programs) and a Winchester 40-megabite memory or two already can perform some of the operations currently carried out by our DEC PDP 11/23s equipped with several RLO2 and RC-25 drives and specialized programing. To illustrate, Figure 4-14 provides a set of curves for the off-on electronic clicks produced by four different tape recorders. As can be seen, all four are different and each appears (under these controlled circumstances anyway) to exhibit a "signature" of its own. These data were processed on a PDP 11/23 using 20K digitization by ILS and then the DOER program we specifically developed to carry out such tasks. This type of analysis would have been either impossible to carry out a decade or so ago or would have required a major effort by a scientific team and the state-of-the-science mainframe computer. Perhaps more surprising, you now can carry out this same procedure on your PC. In any event, computers now can store so much information, and process it so quickly, that the progress being made in developing new and useful analysis techniques in the forensic phonetics area is little short of astounding. As a matter of fact, this particular section of this book will be obsolete before it even is published. If you do not believe me, consider the following. A colleague of mine made up a list of over 20 commercial speech analysis programs available at that time; he says he received announcements/advertisements of three new programs in the mail before his secretary finished typing the original set.

TO CONCLUDE

Nearly any discerning reader will recognize that I have sharply limited my discussion of equipment and probably have left out a number of items that it might have been useful to describe. For example, I made only casual mention of much of the specialized software currently available. Of course, many items of hardware/software are not relevant or useful for the work to be carried out in

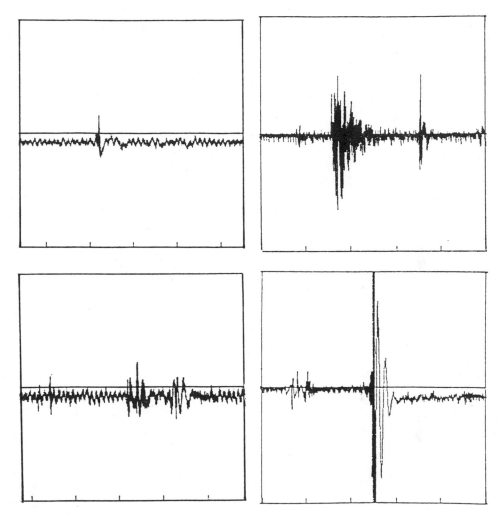

Figure 4-14. Traces of the "off-on" click configurations of four tape recorders. The signals they produced were fed to the computer, digitized and displayed as seen. The values on which these plots are based were also stored for mathematical analysis.

forensic phonetics. Moreover, descriptions of some equipment have been deferred, as they will be more meaningful when discussed in the context of the area/issues they serve. In short, this chapter is only intended to be an introduction to relevant equipment; however, a basic understanding of those items covered should aid in the comprehension of the issues to follow.

PART II

Problems with Tape Recordings

CHAPTER 5

Electronic Surveillance

INTRODUCTION

Perhaps I had better tell you first what this chapter is not about. It is not a "how-to" review of surveillance. Nor does it list all of the procedures and equipment that could be used in detecting and storing acoustic signals such as speech. What I will discuss are basic approaches to the process, common equipment and the types of problems that can—and very often do—occur.

As we all know, electronic surveillance can be pretty sophisticated and, indeed, more like science fiction than reality. As you might have suspected, the cocktail olive (containing a microphone, amplifier, radio transmitter, power pack and antenna) that can pick up every syllable spoken by everyone at a large banquet and transmit this dialogue across a city has yet to be invented. Nor can anyone carry out the remarkable processing of tape recordings seen in the movie "The Conversation." If you saw this film, you will remember that its hero used several microphones (one nearly a quarter mile away) to tape-record a conversation mixed with all kinds of truck, car, speech, music and wind noise. He then processed these tapes in such a way that the specific utterances were so clear and intelligible it was as though the two people were standing in a quiet studio only two feet away from him. Most of the events (of this type) seen in James Bond and similar movies can be compared to the Buck Rogers' cartoons of the 1930s. That is, none of what you saw was possible then, a little of it has come true, but most of it is still in the future. Even the scientist can be deluded by this type of science fiction—occasionally anyway—and sometimes even within his or her specialty area. For example, I remember a site visit made several years ago to my laboratory by a team of my peers who reviewed one of my projects on behalf of an agency from whom I was requesting research support. At one point in the discussion, I complained that one of the problems I was having was that I could not automatically detect and isolate vowels (in "cold running speech") for formant analysis. Two of the visitors were horrified: "Why," they said, "this type of processing has been going on for years." Not having been able to find anyone who had been successful in the area, I asked them for citations. "I do it all the time," each of them assured me. "It is a common scientific procedure and I can provide it to you." Oddly enough, when I later wrote to them and asked if I could buy their software (I had received the grant with added funds so I could do so), one never did answer my query and the other, ahem, was "having some minor problems with his computer program and would contact me later." Needless to say, neither of these people responded, as a system of this type still does not exist except on an interactive basis (i.e., where the human operator selects the vowel from a spectral display). Yet the myth prevails, even among sophisticated scientists, that the automatic identification and processing of vowels is easily done from free-flowing, continuous speech.

On the other hand, some of the things that are possible can boggle the mind. For example, a laser system actually exists that can project a beam against a window pane, capture its varying vibrations (via the reflections), store them and then analyze them for the speech going on inside the room (2). Of course, this is a very complex (and expensive) system to use and lots of analysis has to be carried out if even an approximation of intelligible speech is to be had. To be successful here, it also is necessary to be lucky with respect to the type of window, the size and shape of the room, room noise, the placement of the talkers, how they talk and dozens of other variables—all of which can affect the end product of understandable speech. Nevertheless, this "space age" technique actually is a reality. Another example: not very long ago, crude, light-writing galvanometers provided the only method for studying brief acoustic events such as electronic clicks, gunshots and impact noise. Today it is possible to analyze these events by reducing the acoustic signal into its component parts a great number of times each second and assessing the resulting patterns or values (see again, Figure 4-14). In any case, we skirt the borders of science fiction on what it is possible to do—and technology is advancing rapidly. On the other hand, our expectations sometimes run away with our logic.

So what will be incorporated into this chapter? Primarily the basics of electronic surveillance; that is, surveillance by electromechanical systems, not by visual or physical means (which are techniques of another type). Moreover, I divide this area in twain and describe only those portions relevant to this book. That is, I like to think of electronic surveillance as separated into two parts: tracking and monitoring. Tracking involves the use of either electronic devices which permit a target to be observed visually (infrared detectors, light amplifying and photographic systems) or beacons that can be placed on vehicles (or humans) so that their movements can be followed. Another example involves electronic devices that indicate if a person is attempting to leave an area (say, if he or she is under house arrest).

The monitoring types of electronic surveillance devices, systems and/or approaches to be described here are primarily those which Van Dewerker (16) refers to as "audio eavesdropping" methods. They will include telephone taps, room and body bugs and related techniques; countermeasures will be considered also. I recognize that there are some systems that are not yet perfected, others that are secure and even some where the proprietary aspects prevent much of a description (see also 3, 4, 5, 8, 12, 16). Nonetheless, the great majority of all systems fall into the three categories I cited: (1) the telephone tap, (2) the "bugging" of some space—a room or a car and (3) the "wiring" of an informant.

These three approaches will be discussed in reverse order; subsequently, a few paragraphs about other potential systems will be added.

THE BODY BUG

The Nature of the Body Bug

One of the most common forms of electronic surveillance is to place electronic gear on an informant and send him out to meet the target (as suspects sometimes are called). The system involved may terminate on the person of the informant (i.e., in the form of a tape recorder) or at some remote place (i.e., over a radio to a colleague who will record the events at a monitoring station). What is common to both systems is that the informant must wear a microphone and some sort of power pack. The microphone should be (and usually is) relatively unidirectional as well as sensitive in the speech range. Most often, it is taped to the person's chest or is placed somewhere (a button, a belt buckle) on his or her upper torso. A microphone and power pack may be seen as items A and C in Figure 5-1 (they are worn under the informants clothes). Once the signal is captured and transduced over a wire (item B), it then can be stored in a miniature tape recorder on the informant's person (see item D on Figure 5-1). Alternately, the informant can be provided with a small FM transmitter and the signals being picked up by the microphone can be transmitted through the air in

Figure 5-1. Drawing of an individual fitted with a body bug. Of course, all of the observed components must be concealed. They consist of a microphone, a powerpack, and either a tape recorder or an FM radio transmitter. A, mike; B, line; C, power; D, tape or radio.

the form of radio waves. In this case, they are received and decoded by an FM receiver situated somewhere within a few hundred meters of the informant—and then stored on a tape recorder coupled to this receiver. There are, of course, other systems but these two constitute the bulk of this kind of surveillance equipment.

Problems with Body Bugs

The three main problems with this type of eavesdropping equipment are (1) its physical presence on the informant (i.e., its detectability), (2) equipment limitations and (3) noise on the recordings.

Problem 1: Detectability

The first of the problems is self-evident. Any time equipment is physically placed on the body of an informant, it is vulnerable to detection—electronically or by tactile/visual observation. Sometimes, a body bug is not actually placed on the person's body but, rather, is situated in packages, briefcases or the like. In "The Case of the Excessively Ambitious Politician," two men met a number of times, ostensibly conspiring to trade illegal favors for substantial campaign support of a financial nature. The informant was met by the politician and taken to a motel he owned or controlled (the informant did not know ahead of time where the "meet" was to take place). When they were finally ensconced in the motel room, the target insisted that they strip to their shorts and leave their clothes in another room. These two virtually naked men talked for nearly two hours and everything they said was recorded—clearly and precisely. But … where was the tape recorder? Did the informant swallow an entire system? Not at all. Both men held scanning, debugging units in their hands; the informant's had been modified to contain an additional system consisting of a microphone, power pack and tape recorder. All he had to do was keep his "debugger" near the politician!

Of course, the target will not hear the operation of any of the types of equipment used in body bugging (unless the unlikely event occurs where the tape transport squeaks). On the other hand, if the target or his or her associates are using debugging equipment, they can detect tape recorder erase/bias operation if their unit is fairly close to the tape recorder and can detect frequencies in the 30-150 kHz range. The operation of a radio transmitter can be detected (if the informant is using one) if the system used (1) can lock onto the transmitter's frequency, (2) can scan all frequencies and/or (3) is sophisticated enough to detect transmission, even if the unit's frequency has been set very close to that of a powerful or nearby broadcasting station.

Problem 2: Limits

The second problem with body bugs is as serious as the first—and often contributes to it. The issue here is the trade-off between equipment size and fidelity. The smaller the microphone (of any type), the more difficult it is to maintain good frequency response and directionality. Moreover, a wire ordinarily connects the microphone to the rest of the equipment and potentially it can be broken (or seen). Tape recorders tend to be a little bulky—due to their need for tape transport motors/reels and the tape itself. And you will remember (from Chapter 4) that there is a serious trade-off between the quality of a tape-recording on the one hand and recorder speed and/or tape thickness on the other. Yet you would want the tape recorder to run as slowly as feasible and the tape to be as thin as possible so operation would be uninterrupted for long periods of time. Yet "smaller-slower-thinner" can add to the existing problems—ones that tend to degrade the utterances you want to capture.

Power is always a problem. Naturally you will want to use only tiny batteries—but, ordinarily anyway, the smaller the battery the less "electricity" it can store. In some applications this limitation is not a problem. In surveillance, however, you are attempting to run either a tape recorder (both the transport and electromagnetic circuitry) or a radio station. Thus, there is a series of size/power/life trade-offs that can operate in this case. Worse yet, when batteries are tested without a load, they can show full voltage even though they are near the end of their effective life. Even when relatively large battery packs are utilized (larger are more easily detected visually than are smaller, of course), they still limit the length of time one can use the surveillance systems described.

Yet other types of problems arise if the decision is made to use a radio transmitter as part of the body bug system. The equipment array utilized ordinarily is the same as that used with a tape recording system (i.e., microphone, wire and power pack), except that a radio transmitter is substituted for the tape recorder. There are some supercompact units that are composed of an array consisting of a microphone, power pack and transmitter. While these systems have the virtue of being extremely small, they are limited in range, operational life and fidelity.

Due to size, range, efficiency, power requirements and cost, most transmitters are of the frequency modulation (FM) variety. Usually they are built to broadcast at a single (crystal controlled) frequency level, but multiple frequencies may be possible. The monitoring/recording station is outfitted with an FM receiver that can demodulate the assigned frequency and transfer it (hard-line) to a tape recorder where the messages are stored. Transmitters of the type specified tend to emit signals of between 30 and 500 MHz at output levels of 20 milliwatts to 1 watt. Although there now are multistage (and somewhat bulky) packs that are powered to 5 watts, the values listed by Van Dewerker (16) have not changed much in the last 10 years. Most of these devices are power dependent with half-watt units effective up to a half mile—that is, if there are no obstructions. A great deal is known about these small transmitters (power requirements, effective range, fidelity, and so on). If you wish specific expertise in these areas, substantial additional training would be required. In the interim, the reading of some of the reference materials associated with this chapter would be a good place to start.

One final issue in this area. The manufacturers of these and related devices tend to be pretty secretive and/or proprietary about them; others will sell their equipment only to law enforcement agencies. Some of their secretiveness actually is hype (maybe most of it). Indeed, nearly all of the systems I have analyzed fall into two groups: (1) they do not accomplish the tasks their manufacturers indicate they will or (2) they are just a collection of simple units packaged as a system. A good example of the first group (i.e., one that does not perform as touted) may be found in Chapter 13; the following example should serve to illustrate the second group.

The SK-9 surveillance system—"constructed" by Honeywell but also sold by "Special Operations Group" Waltham, Massachusetts—is an example of a system that is said to be complex and of a nature that should not be described. Yet neither of these statements is accurate. All this system consists of is a "T-2A" body bug: a microphone with a rather bulky power pack and transmitter/antenna array, and, on the reception end, an ordinary briefcase fitted with a standard FM radio receiver (with antenna), amplifier, and a SONY (small size) TC-110A tape recorder. Of course, a few extra switches and minor features have been added to the system but there appears (to me anyway) to be little to no justification for the secrecy that seems to surround this pedestrian device. What is so mysterious about a simple crystal-operated transmitter fitted with a microphone and a briefcase containing an FM receiver, power pack and small tape recorder? Nothing! The reasons for keeping the SK-9 secret appear to be that law enforcement groups do not wish to let the criminals know what they are doing, the manufacturers wish to keep the competition to a minimum and the people using such a system do not wish the "other" side to be able to evaluate their efficiency. As with so many of the devices utilized in the world of electronic surveillance, there is as much myth as fact surrounding their nature and use. On the other hand, excepting for its size, the SK-9 is a good system. I have tested it, as well as a number of related devices, and found that, if they are operated properly, they will receive and transmit speech adequately at distances up to a quarter mile, even if the signal has to travel through a number of walls. As a matter of fact, a unit of this type worked reasonably well when I transmitted through a large number of obstructions (five ordinary walls plus four concrete and steel load-bearing walls and two all-steel walls). The signal was not seriously degraded except to be weakened substantially. However, when the amplitude of the recorded speech was raised for "easy" listening, the ambient noise level was also increased and a little masking took place. Thus, it can be said that most body bug systems work fairly well. They do have specific limits and these should be observed.

Problem 3: Noise

The third problem with body bugs perhaps constitutes the worst one of all; it is that of noise. This problem would become quite evident if you attempted to decode a tape made in the field on virtually any one of the devices or systems discussed. Indeed, while the potential sources of noise appear endless, only a few of the primary ones will be considered. First, there is system or "shot" noise. Many of the smaller devices generate noise fields that can interfere with speech intelligibility by masking it—especially if the speech is of poor quality anyway. Second are environmental noises of many types: wind and car noise, background music, overlapping speech, clothing noise, intentional masking countermeasures and so on. In "The Case of the Gleeful Killer," the noisemaker was a rocking chair on a wooden porch. In this instance, a man got into a fistfight in a bar and lost. Later that night he and a companion crept up to the house of his adversary, saw him in bed with his girlfriend (through a window), and shot and killed both of them. Since the killer was known to the police, they sent an informant to his house in an attempt to record an admission of guilt. The informant (a cousin of the assailant) was able to do so, but the noise made by several rocking chairs on the porch where they discussed the murders made decoding of this dialogue very difficult.

Actually, it is the noise created by clothing rubbing on the concealed microphone of a body bug that perhaps is one of the most common of all interferences to intelligible speech. Since any microphone placed on an informant must be concealed, most are placed somewhere under the informant's clothing and, as he or she moves, the microphone rubs against the cloth (or vice versa) and an intermittent noise field results. Worse yet, it appears as though this broadband noise is most often at its loudest when crucial parts of the recorded discussion take place (Murphy's law?). Care in microphone placement helps somewhat. Nevertheless, since it is best to have the microphone on the upper part of the body, it naturally will come into contact with clothing. Body bugs sometimes can be placed more securely on women due, at least in part, to their physiology and the nature of their underclothes; also they are somewhat less likely to be suspected or searched.

A third type of noise is that which is introduced by the target as a speech-masking or countermeasure device. This noise can take many forms but usually is loud and involves speech, music, running water or the like. Finally, transmission noise can result from the use of a radio receiver configuration. Here interference to the intelligible recording of speech can occur if there are a great number of structures blocking the transmission, if the system is not operated appropriately or if environmental noise adds to the noise resulting from system use. In "The Case of the Battling Businessmen," only unintelligible speech was recorded from such a system, because the two men sat in a very noisy restaurant and the policemen did not operate the equipment efficiently (even though they were in a car just outside the building).

In the chapters that follow, I will consider how speech can be enhanced if it is recorded as a weak signal and/or in various of the cited noise fields. In yet other chapters, I will address the decoding issue associated with degraded speech. Thus, discussion of these issues will be deferred to those sections.

Detection of Body Bugs and Countermeasures

Descriptions of countermeasures will be included here, because you will better understand the problems they can create if you also comprehend their nature. As has been stated, monitoring equipment is placed on an informant so he or she can participate in face-to-face conversations with a target or targets and record incriminating statements. Since these systems must be placed on the informant's person, their detection ordinarily can be accomplished by a thorough body search. An alternative method is to detect the signals relating to the transmission and either mask, or block, them in some manner.

The most serious problem here is that the criminal or target does not know which of the many people he or she talks to may be "wired" and, hence, is an informant. Just imagine the problems that would be created if you were a criminal and required that everyone you saw subject themselves to a strip search and/or scan—or if you would only talk to them by whispering in their ear while an audio system blared music. Of course, there are some people that criminals suspect and search, but often it is a person that they trust who carries the electronic surveillance equipment. Nonetheless, if a tape recording has been made, your greatest problem (if there is one) will probably result from the masking effects of noise—either environmental or due to countermeasures.

TELEPHONE TAPS AND ROOM MONITORING

It is rather difficult to discuss the monitoring of telephone calls separately from room monitoring as the two areas overlap substantially. I will include them in the same general section and subdivide it into two parts. The first of the two involves monitoring procedures that are carried out in an attempt to capture the utterances/messages that take place over a telephone system or systems (11); the second involves those that take place in any space (such as a room or an automobile) and by any means—included is the use of telephones as monitors. Incidentally, I have no intention of reviewing case law relative to who can legally tap telephones or monitor meetings. Suffice it to say that we are concerned here with how such activities can be carried out rather than if they are legal or not (17). A pamphlet on that subject (case law) is available from Forensic Communication Associates, Gainesville, Florida.

Pen Registers

Before continuing with a general discussion of the ways and means of monitoring telephone conversations, it would appear useful to define and describe pen registers and related equipment. These systems are used to determine the numbers being dialed from a particular telephone (14). Specifically, a pen register is a mechanical device attached to a given telephone (or telephone system) which records all numbers dialed from that line. It often is installed at a central telephone facility (it can be placed elsewhere, of course) and provides a permanent record of outgoing calls. Devices of this type cannot be used to identify incoming calls, nor do they reveal if any of the calls were completed. Pen registers are not involved in the monitoring of any of the conversations that take place; they simply record the outgoing numbers dialed and whether they are local or long distance. Some dial decoders print out the date, time and number called on a paper tape; others record this information on magnetic tape which can be accessed at a later time (on a monitor screen or by hard copy).

Incidentally, pen registers can be used to decode numbers "dialed" either on a conventional system or from touch-tone telephones (the registers that do the latter are called pulse decoders). In the past, great mystery surrounded dial decoders and pen registers. It is another mystery that should not exist, as they simply are devices which detect, decode and record the outgoing numbers dialed from specific telephones.

There is no way you can defeat a pen register except by using a telephone to which it is not coupled—a situation that is difficult to handle if you do not know that such a unit is in use on your line. Moreover, it is quite difficult even to detect application of a pen register, especially if it is installed centrally at a telephone facility. On the other hand, devices such as dial/tone decoders and pen registers soon may join the technological scrapheap, as they will be outmoded by ESS (electronic switching systems). AT&T (and its subsidiaries/associates) are now installing ESS in their new switching stations as they replace the old mechanical ones. These systems will be used to maintain records of those numbers dialed— plus the date, time and duration—for *all* calls (both local and long distance) made from a particular phone. It always has been possible to obtain information of this type on long distance completed calls; now data on all calls—completed or not—will be easily available to those groups who "have a legal need to know."

Telephone Taps

Functionally there are two reasons to tap into a telephone line. The first is to hear—or record—the conversations that are going on over that telephone or the telephones on that line. The second is to utilize the telephone as a monitoring device for whatever goes on near it or, if possible, all conversations carried on in the room. This section will focus on the first of these two operations; comments on room monitoring will be found in the discussion which follows it.

Self-Monitoring

The most obvious and simplest form of telephone monitoring is for the person involved to tap his or her own telephone. There are at least three ways to do so. The first—and by far the poorest—is to purchase a small microphone/suction cup device, stick it to your telephone and plug it into a tape recorder. As you would expect, inexpensive units such as these (they cost but a few dollars) do not work very well. If placed right at the earpiece, the two-way speech can usually be decoded, but it will have a restricted frequency response and be particularly susceptible to distortion by noise.

If you are handy with a screwdriver and pliers, you can utilize the second approach. Here your telephone is disassembled and you connect your tape recorder directly to the appropriate terminals on the inside. Three problems arise here. First, of course, you have to understand how both telephones and tape recorders work so that they can be coupled together in proper fashion. Second, this approach often results in at least minor distortion to the signal; I have noticed that hookups of this type tend to exhibit echoes or "hollow" sounding transmissions. Finally, you are limited in the amount of time you can operate the recorder unless you (1) physically are there to keep changing the tapes or (2) use a voice-activated unit.

The third system of this type is one that can be purchased at electronic stores for around $20.00. It is a simple little device that can serve to activate (i.e., turn on) your tape recorder whenever the telephone is lifted from its cradle. To use this equipment, all you have to do is insert it into the telephone line—i.e., connect the telephone to it and, in turn, plug it into the appropriate junction. All that remains then is to couple a tape recorder to the unit and you are set to record any call—in or out—that takes place over any telephone on that line. I have checked out numerous of these devices and they work very well. Of course, the legality of tapping your own telephone can come up. However, issues such as this one will not be considered here, even though they are important. You should note also that the use of these units sometimes can backfire in other ways. For example, take "The Case of the Turncoat Politician." As the title suggests, a particular politician in a large metropolitan area was caught red-handed conducting a little political mischief. To save himself, he agreed to turn against his partners-in-fraud and, among other things, record all conversations that were made on any telephone in his house. While he was able to collect some of the evidence desired by the police, tremendously long listening periods were required to check out the hundreds of nonrelevant telephone conversations that were dutifully recorded by his little array of snooper equipment. And imagine his embarrassment when one of these conversations turned out to be between his young daughter and her boyfriend as they planned the where and how of a sexual interlude.

Surreptitious Telephone Monitoring

Quite different problems arise when an individual attempts to overhear other people's conversations, as opposed to his or her own. Here the coupling of the listening device or tape recorder to the telephone line will be carried out in a manner that, if at all possible, will prevent its detection. As you might expect, even this seemingly simple act can prove to be quite complex. Please note, however, that I am not going to spend time on the claims and counterclaims you can read in the more sensational literature. I really do not care if a telephone eavesdropping system self-destructs when approached by a person (they presumably are triggered by body heat) or that it can be buried deep underground. Such fanciful dialogue only serves to increase confusions, and I am more concerned that you understand the basics of surveillance rather than the "what ifs" about it—especially since they may not be totally accurate.

Basically, there are two types of wiretaps that permit telephone calls to be intercepted. The first involves connecting the equipment directly to the telephone wires (hence the term *wiretap*); the second uses an induction coil. The first of the two involves physically coupling a set of wires to the telephone line at some accessible location. Hard-line connect systems can be designed in such a manner that they do not result in any detectible disturbance/change in the telephone operating voltages (see below). However, if inappropriate equipment is used, or improper installation procedures carried out, detectible line voltage shifts can result. More important, the wiretap can be visually observed at the location of its insertion. However, the farther away it is from the target telephone, the more difficult it is to find. The output of the hard-line intercept devices can be directed to earphones, if the physical presence of an agent is required, and/or to a tape recorder or radio transmitter so permanent copies can be made at the site or at some remote station. Incidentally, optical transfer systems sometimes can be used over short distances and under the proper conditions. These devices usually involve the use of a laser beam modulated by the audio signal. When detected, the light signal is decoded and the information stored (usually as an audio analog on recording tape).

The induction coil works somewhat differently than a direct tap. In this case, no physical connection to the telephone line is required. It is only necessary that the induction coil lie close to the telephone line of interest. This type of system responds to the variations that occur to the magnetic field which is associated with current flow through the telephone line. At once, this approach is difficult to detect and difficult to implement. The primary problem is that the magnetic field is of very low energy; hence, a correspondingly low signal will be transduced by the sensing coil and an appropriate amplifier must be included somewhere in the system. This approach does nothing to disturb either the voltage or current in the telephone line. Hence, it can be detected only visually. Again, once amplified, the signal can be directed to earphones, a tape recorder or a radio transmitter. While the inductive coil approach is less easily detected than the direct connections of the hard-line approach, the latter (i.e., the physical tap) often is preferred because (if properly installed) it is highly reliable and provides much better fidelity.

Countermeasures

As has been suggested, there are numerous firms that tout systems which will detect intercepts of the type just discussed. Most rely on voltage or current variation. For example, when a telephone is removed from its cradle, there is a rather substantial drop in its line voltage; the shift usually is from around 48 volts to under 12 volts. The exact voltage that will show across the terminals, however, will depend on system characteristics, temperature, humidity, the number of phones (on that line) off the hook, and so on. What will not show up—despite manufacturers' claims—is a voltage change due to the presence of a properly installed hard wire or induction coil intercept. Thus, the only infallible (or nearly so) methods by which these approaches may be foiled is by (1) finding them, (2) not using the telephone to transmit information you do not want intercepted and/or (3) the use of some sort of scrambler. Scrambler systems can be digital or analog; both serve to code the speech signal in some manner before it passes over the telephone lines (6, 7, 9, 15). Of course, systems such as these are not totally secure, as the speech has to be decoded (or unmixed) at the other end of the line, and an eavesdropper could obtain and use a similar device and its codes. Finally, if a radio transmitter is used to transfer the information to be picked up at another location, a radio frequency detector might be employed to determine its presence and permit jamming. Ordinarily, however, surveillance by these procedures is limited only by system inadequacies.

Room Monitors

This section overlaps significantly with the previous one. However, here we are dealing not with the interception of a telephone conversation as transmitted over an appropriate line but rather with detecting everything (audio, that is) that goes on in the room under surveillance (see Figure 5-2 for a summary of some of the available approaches). A telephone can be used for this purpose—but so can other systems. However, I will start with how a telephone is utilized as a room monitoring device.

Telephone Eavesdropping

Basically there are three ways that a telephone can be used as an audio detection device within a room. They include the implantation of a microphone somewhere within the telephone, modifying the telephone to act as a microphone and infinity transmitters. The first two are related; they involve access to the telephone and the technical ability to modify it. The microphone embedded within the telephone itself can be linked to the listening post either by a radio transmitter or the telephone lines themselves. That is, the microphone and transmitter may be "dropped in" or a microphone installed within the telephone with its output sent out over a pair of the unused lines. Alternately, the telephone microphone itself can be employed as the pickup transducer (by an additional modification of the cradle disconnect). These devices are sometimes called "on-line" microphones and require some amplification or preamplification at an early stage. Naturally, the range of these devices is sharply limited, as the transmission can take place only up to the first major (telephone) switching facility. The use of the telephone microphone itself as a listening device involves its modification and is fairly complex. In any case, both of these approaches provide audio information with respect to (both ends) of telephone calls and the dialogue (and other sounds) existing within the room. However, they do so within the frequency response and sensitivity limitations of the drop-in or telephone microphones.

The third approach, the infinity transmitter, is a rather misunderstood system. While there is no magic associated with it, it is a rather clever device. Sometimes called a harmonica bug, infinity transmitters also are related to "call backs" and "keep alives." Basically, it is not a transmitter at all—nor can it intercept conversations from infinite distances (as the original manufacturer claimed). Rather, it is simply a tone-controlled switch coupled to the telephone line of interest. Input usually is a microphone/amp combination; output is either the eavesdropper's telephone or some system connected to the telephone line. Once in place (installation may be a problem, of course), the switching mecha-

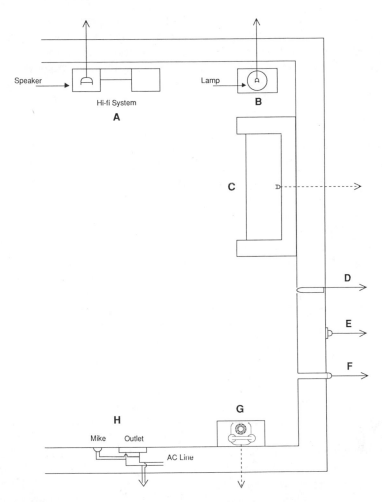

Figure 5-2. A schematic of a number of ways room surveillance can be accomplished. An existing transducer may be modified to operate as a microphone (A). Microphones may be "hard-lined" to furniture such as a lamp (B), or "dropped in" as in (C); a transmitter is needed in the latter case. A spike microphone (D) may be used to penetrate a wall; a transducer may be placed against the wall if it is solid (E) or placed on the far side of a hole drilled in the wall (F). Also included in the figure is the suggestion (G) that a telephone may be employed for room surveillance in several ways (see text) and that the electrical circuitry to the room may be utilized (H) to carry a signal to a listening post (once it has been received).

nism is easily activated. The eavesdropper simply dials the number of the target telephone and then immediately transmits an activation tone. He must do so after the circuit is complete but (preferably anyway) before the phone rings. In turn, the tone activates the switch which "answers" the phone electronically rather than by having someone in the room do so physically. It is by this means that the microphone in the target telephone is activated and the eavesdropper can listen to any sounds that are made in its vicinity. Thus, a clever operator can call the desired number, quickly transmit the tone and then listen in on the various sounds and discussions occurring in that room. Moreover, all is not lost if the telephone does ring before the infinity transmitter activates the target phone (thus, cutting off any chance that it will ring). In this case, the eavesdropper responds to the person answering by pretending to have called a wrong number and then activates the infinity transmitter after the target telephone is back in the cradle. Please note also that if the target subject attempts to use his or her telephone, the eavesdropper simply hangs up, thereby disconnecting the unit. Early models were activated by a single tone, usually A above middle C (i.e., 440 Hz) or middle C (263 Hz), and the tone was transmitted by sounding that note on a harmonica (hence the term harmonica bug). Currently, other frequencies or even a series of tones are used—a procedure that makes counter-measures somewhat more difficult. Finally, a related device is the "keep-alive" or "listen back." These systems are much simpler then the infinity transmitter and, while they require an installation in the target telephone (specifically in the cradle mechanism), they do not require a tone to activate them. Rather, the installed microphone is turned on simply by calling the number of the target phone. They operate as a microphone "keep-alive" once the call has been completed and the telephone has been replaced on the cradle. Deactivation of the system occurs as a result of the line voltage change when the eavesdropper hangs up.

Room "Bugs"

No matter what simple or complex configuration room-monitoring systems take, they can be reduced to two components: (1) a microphone (with its accompanying amplification devices) and (2) a listening post (see again Figure 5-2). The microphone may be hidden almost anywhere; transmission may be hard line or by radio, and the "listener" may be a person with earphones or simply a tape recorder. In all cases, however, ingress to the room (or, at least, the area to be monitored) must precede eavesdropping. Let me review some of the major configurations that can be used.

Use of Available Lines/Transducers. The snoop who is to acoustically monitor a room may choose to utilize either existing transmission lines or devices that may be turned into microphones. Telephones could be used, but these approaches already have been discussed (see G, Figure 5-2). So, what other "in-room" systems are available? Although severely limited, one such approach involves coupling a microphone to the electrical circuits within a room or a house (H). In this case, the system is designed to pick up the audio signal and superimpose it upon the 60-Hz electrical current in a manner similar to the way much higher radio frequencies are modulated for transmission of messages. The record system here must be directly coupled to the same circuit as the microphone, as the modulation can be blocked (unless a by-pass is constructed) by transformers and intrabuilding circuit splitters. These very low frequency (VLF) or current carrier devices are not very efficient but can be made to work under some circumstances.

A second class of systems (A) is that which utilizes available equipment, such as an existing speaker system, which can be modified so as to convert its magnetic transducer (loudspeaker) into a microphone. A simple survey of your own home will reveal that most residences, businesses, and the like, contain a variety of such units. Among them are the loudspeakers in radios, television sets, home music systems and intercoms. As stated, here the transducer is modified (ingress to the area is required, of course) so as to permit it to function also as a microphone; lines are then run to the listening post or transmitter. The reason that such modification can take place will be remembered when the preceding chapter is considered. That is, a magnetic loudspeaker is constructed in a fashion quite similar to that of a dynamic-type microphone—i.e., a diaphragm is mechanically coupled to a coil/magnet array. When the system acts as a loudspeaker, the electrical current activates the cone. This process is reversed when the transducer is not in use as an output speaker but, rather, acts as a microphone. The small electrical signal thus generated is amplified and sent on to the listening post by radio or hard-line systems.

Implanted Microphones. Naturally, the most common room-monitoring system involves the use of a microphone or microphones placed in the room or in/against the wall of the target room. A hard line then is run to an amplifier (ordinarily outside the room and some distance away from it) and then on to the radio, earphones, or tape recorder used in the monitoring process. Several types of miniature microphones can be employed, depending upon where they are planted or hidden within the room (C). These microphones can be hidden in lamps, bedposts, sofas, chairs, radiators, and so on. The size and sensitivity of the transducers utilized is the main consideration in its selection.

Unlike the microphones that can be hidden within a room, size is not a consideration if the listing transducer is placed in the wall; nonetheless, a smaller one still is more easily affixed than a larger one. There are several techniques that can be used here. First a dynamic, ribbon, electret or condenser microphone can be placed in the wall or even on the other side of the wall (F). In such case, however, it is necessary to link the microphone directly with the air in the room by means of an open hole or hole with a tube. In turn, this approach can present some problems—the two most important are that the hole might be observed and/or the tube leading to the microphone might create some speech degrading resonance peaks and damping.

Finally, microphones can be embedded within the wall or placed against it (E) whenever the surface is contiguous with that of the other side (i.e., if the wall is solid or at a stud)—or if the microphone is designed to be part of a spike that can be driven into the wall (D). In these cases, ceramic, crystals or similar microphones appear to work best; however, the way in which they are used is bound to create some distortion in the captured signal. Good descriptions of these two approaches may be found in Van Dewerker (16).

Countermeasures

You will remember that I have been providing an occasional review of the additional problems that can result from the application of surveillance countermeasures. I have been doing so in order to alert you to some of the problems that may result from these actions. Of course, if the countermeasures are successful, there will be no surveillance materials to process or analyze; if they are partly successful, they will create some of the problems which have been outlined previously. In short, the rationale for these discussions has been to review their effect on the activities of the forensic phonetician.

Yet, while it is rare that individuals in our specialty area would be required to find bugs or sweep a room, the chapter would seem incomplete if I did not provide a somewhat more specific review of the issue of interest, i.e., surveillance countermeasures. Hence, I have decided to do so—even if such a discussion is a little tangential to the main thrust of this book. However, when reading the section, please do not forget that the purpose of this chapter is only to provide you with a generalized appreciation of specified electronic surveillance techniques. That is, no attempt was made to turn you into an accomplished snoop or eavesdropper. Rather, a general discussion of many (or most?) of the sources of the problems you will face was provided so you would be able to understand the strength and weaknesses of the devices employed as well as their capabilities and limitations, and their diversity and nature. This knowledge, in turn, should permit an understanding of what may have to be done to make the recovered speech more understandable, to authenticate what was recorded, establish who was talking, and so on. That particular thrust was why I did not go into greater detail relative to the methods described, and why I have not listed the manufacturers, dealers, costs or model numbers of the equipment used. This same general approach will be taken with countermeasures, as it is not the function of this treatise to turn you into a countersnoop.

The approach ordinarily employed to counter the eavesdropping techniques we have been reviewing is often referred to as "discover and/or defeat." That is, if telephone and room taps can be discovered, they can be defeated (i.e., eliminated). However, sometimes they can be defeated even if their presence is only suspected—in this case primarily by masking or taking the conversation elsewhere.

Telephone Tap Detection. It has long been known that it is difficult if not impossible to detect properly installed telephone monitoring systems except by observing them visually. Indeed, irrespective of manufacturers' claims, only somewhat minimal efficiency can be expected of countermeasure systems purported to be effective in this area. Methodologically, these devices attempt to exploit a telephone's normal switching functions by either drawing current from the line when the telephone is not in use or measuring telephone line voltages. The first of these draws current from the line in such a manner that it triggers the telephone company's switching exchange and causes the line to be (continuously) busy—that is, if additional current is being drawn off by a tapping device. On the other hand, line voltage measurement equipment is used in an attempt to detect voltage changes caused by the attachment of a tap. Neither approach is very effective. A somewhat more sophisticated method of detection is based on hardware which sends pulses of energy down the telephone line; in turn, these pulses are reflected from the various electrical junctions along that line. At least some taps show up as new electrical junctions. This approach works only if you have an accurate blueprint of the relevant installations and are aware of the existence of all the legitimate junctions.

The primary problem with telephone tap detection results from the nature of the telephone system itself. A tap can be placed anywhere on the line between the telephone switching exchange and the target instrument. The length and complexity of those lines make a tap very difficult to detect from the instrument's end of the line. Moreover, as I have indicated, the electrical characteristics of the telephone lines can change with length, weather, temperature, humidity and equipment additions within the system. These changes often will override the effects of a telephone tap device, making it almost impossible to detect. Finally, the only wire systems which are easily detectable are those which draw excessive current from the line (causing an unusual change in system voltage); they can be detected by either a voltmeter or those devices specifically manufactured for this purpose. No countermeasure devices can detect wire attachments or voltage-actuated switches which use: (1) matching networks, (2) systems inductively coupled to the telephone or (3) a single telephone wire and earth ground. All of these techniques are currently available for use in electronic surveillance. Finally, one of the basic approaches to this problem is to check the telephone lines wire by wire; usually this technique is accomplished with the aid of a commercial unit. Here the operator selects any two wires found in the telephone line and checks them for modifications. Certain kinds of intercepts can be detected by this process; the problem is that sometimes thousands of pairs have to be tested before a particular modification can be detected.

Radio Transmitter Detection. While it is rare that the operation of a tape recorder (situated at the listening post) can be determined by the detection of the erase frequency, such is not the case when the telephone tap involves a radio transmitter. That is, electronic detection of a monitor transmitter installed on or very near the target premises is quite similar to the detection of any radio frequency unit. Indeed, the presence of a surveillance transmitter may be discovered by radio frequency (field strength) detectors of several types, by spectrum analyzers and by all-wave surveillance receivers—but, of course, only when the unit is being used (or only by visual means when it is not).

Field strength meters measure the relative radio frequency energy present at some given point in space. The device contains an antenna, a diode detector, and a sensitive amplifier which drives a meter or other indicator device (e.g., a light or audio signal). Most field strength measurement devices can provide several optional approaches to ordinary energy measurement. One option is to normalize the meter to the local environment. Another involves a limited tuning ability whereby a single large band of energy can be broken down into its smaller component parts. An associated technique is to activate an audio-frequency generator through an amplifier and loudspeaker in the room to be examined. The usable radio frequency spectrum is then swept with the receiver, and if a transmitter is operating, the generated audio modulation will be received by the surveillance receiver as feedback or a squeal. The sweeping must be done in an extremely careful manner, of course, since it is quite possible (in the tuning process) to quickly dial past the transmitter frequency without noticing its output. Moreover, sensitivity is somewhat low with respect to the broad tuning range of the cited receivers, but these radio frequency detectors also may be obtained in a highly tuned mode. The argument for the tuned models is that they are more sensitive than are those that are untuned. On the other hand, the tunable models must be switched through their frequency spectrum all the while the testing is being conducted, while the untuned models need merely to be moved about the area.

Still other problems are associated with telephone-related radio taps. As a general rule, the telephone must be in use before a radio spectrum analysis can be performed, and radio frequency searches are not effective unless the transmitter is within range of the detecting device. For example, a field strength measurement device is not very efficient unless the tap is inside the telephone instrument itself. Thus, you can see that systems of this type are decidedly limited. They exhibit broad spectrum width, large variation in sensitivity, poor selectivity, inability to detect carrier current devices and susceptiblity to standing wave reflections which can occur in some rooms. Nor do they permit detection of low-level eavesdropping devices when high radio frequency energy backgrounds are present. To sum, while field strength measurement devices probably should not be used as the principal means of radio transmitter detection, they can be a useful supplemental tools nonetheless.

Spectrum analyzers also constitute a valuable instrument in the electronic countermeasures field—primarily due to their flexibility. This type of equipment provides capability for a visual display of sophisticated modulation processes as well as displays of both large portions of the radio spectrum and the corresponding side bands (which may contain audio signal information). Indeed, these devices can be used to analyze audio and carrier signals in a manner not possible with audio amplifiers and countermeasure receivers. However, they do exhibit some limitations, primarily in the form of low sensitivity—a factor which requires that the analyzer be in the proximity of the surveillance device in order to detect it.

An entire chapter could be written on radio countermeasures, but the brief review above should demonstrate that there are gadgets available that permit the seeker to locate radio transmitters of all kinds—from telephone taps to drop-ins to those transmitting the output of hidden room microphones.

Room Monitoring Countermeasures. Several major approaches have been developed for use in this third of the various types of countermeasures. Here, the presence of (1) radio transmitters, (2) microphones and (3) infinity transmitters is sought. The radio countermeasures have been covered above (at least briefly); the other two approaches will be described below.

As with all sweeps, it is first important to attempt to visually locate a microphone or microphones. All lines/wires in the room (and leaving it) should be identified and a physical search instigated. As with radio detectors, a number of manufacturers provide systems (at a cost, of course) which they say will find hidden microphones; most of these do not work very well. Apparently, many of these detection devices are designed to permit you to determine the placement of a microphone by identifying either its low-level voltage signature or, more often, the magnetic field associated with it construction (i.e., especially the magnets in dynamic microphones). Still other units permit introduction of sound into the room and the tapping into unidentified lines with a loudspeaker. If the line is coupled to a microphone, a squeal or howl will result. As with most devices, however, eavesdropping microphones are best found by physical search—and a very thorough one at that.

Detection of infinity transmitters (when they are in use anyway) appears to be quite simple. Just call the number of interest from an adjacent phone and see if a busy signal occurs. There are, however, other ways to detect the open line associated with these devices. Commercial systems designed for this purpose can be used, as can an ordinary voltmeter. If an infinity transmitter is in use, the voltage on the line (the phone must be left in the cradle of course) will read between 6 and 12 volts rather than the 48 or so volts expected. In other words, an open line will exist where none should be. While the detection of an active infinity transmitter is quite easy, the triggering of an inactive one is much more difficult—especially if the unit is one of the new multitone or time-series-activated devices. Nevertheless, either basic tones or a tone sweep (which emits various frequencies within the audio spectrum) can be played over the line in an attempt to activate the infinity transmitter. Once activated, the measurement of line voltage will detect it's presence. In short, infinity transmitters—and similar devices—can be detected once their use is suspected.

To summarize, eavesdropping devices often can be discovered by a careful search; electronic countermeasures also can be effective. Indeed, for every electronic surveillance device, system or technique, there is a countermeasure that often can be effectively employed. However, it should be pointed out once again that the "game" of eavesdropping and countermeasures creates problems for the forensic phonetician—and many of them result in poor quality tapes. Let me provide you with a few examples. A person who wishes to pass intelligence may do so over a public telephone. However, if he or she does so and law enforcement agents become aware of it, they can obtain permission to tap that phone. If they do, however, the street and related noise in this environment can degrade the speech/messages obtained (it is also expensive to monitor all that goes on at a public telephone). A second example: if you were to become interested in the issue, you would find that there is an entire literature on telephone line scramblers—both analog and digital (see again 6, 7, 9, 15). Some are rather good; all require both encoders and decoders at both telephone stations in a link. However, it is possible to decode the transmissions with detecting equipment, at least if you know such equipment is in use and its codes. Simple analog systems are fairly easy for an eavesdropper to decode; technologically more complex digital and shifting speech "window" approaches are of greater challenge, but decoding can be accomplished if the eavesdropper has the time, money, equipment and skill at his or her disposal. Unfortunately, the resulting product may be one that suffers degradation. Finally, still other problems can occur. For example, it even has been suggested that the space between the walls can be saturated with noise (13)—or that utterances can be masked if people talk while taking a shower. We certainly do know that tiny radio-type systems can be fitted even under the skimpiest of bathing suits—and that tape recorders can be hidden inside "debugging" equipment (see again "The Case of the Overly Ambitious Politician"). In short, it appears that anything one side can devise can be thwarted by the other in this give-and-take game of electronic surveillance. It is the quality of the speech or the speaker's identity that suffers; either may be degraded or impaired. Sometimes the forensic phonetician can negate these problems—sometimes not.

FROM THE SIMPLE TO THE SUBLIME

Surveillance techniques can vary from the super simple to the exotic. Of course, many of the clever little devices that are advertised in the popular press either work poorly, have extremely limited function or do not work at all. In any case, I have attempted to organize this area into a reasonable set of "component parts" and describe the basics of each. In doing so, let me conclude by describing yet two more devices that you may have heard about. Neither works particularly well, but both can be used in certain circumstances. The first technique involves devices that are only quasi-electronic; in this case, the sensor is not electronic but rather a mechanical unit. These systems are often referred to as passive reflectors and they function in a manner similar to when you place a drinking glass against a wall and use it to listen to what is going on in the next room. Actually, a hollow tube of this type can be used in two ways: (1) it can be placed against a "vibrating" surface such as a wall or (2) made as a closed (but hollow) metal tube with a diaphragm covering one end. The passive reflector can be set up either with a microphone and hard-lined to a tape recorder, or it can be subjected to a beam of radio energy. In this second case, the radio beam is modulated by the audio signal and sent out via an antenna physically attached to the unit. A pretty exotic "simple" system is it not? Actually, it works fairly well, but the speech energy transmitted often is so faint that it is obscured by room/equipment noise and distortion. Finally, microwave systems can be used to detect the radio beam associated with these pneumatic systems.

The last approach to be discussed was referred to early in this chapter; it involves the now famous use of a laser beam to intercept conversations from outside a building. In theory, what is done is to aim a laser beam at an appropriate window and pick up reflection (as it is varied due to window vibrations) by a specially constructed decoding device. The speech in the room is then extracted—presumably from the pattern that occurred when it modulated the laser beam. As I indicated, there are very real problems with this procedure. First, window panes do not make very good acoustic "diaphragms," so the pickup frequencies are rather distorted. Also, a great deal of speech is needed so that algorithms can be established for each of the talkers. Worse yet, the system is incredibly expensive to fabricate and use. It probably can be defeated by placing a sound source near or on each window of the room in which sensitive information is being uttered—or, perhaps, by having conferences only when it is raining.

CONCLUSIONS

As can be seen, a rather substantial variety of electronic surveillance techniques exist: from agent recorders/transmitters to passive reflectors, from infinity transmitters to room microphones, from telephone taps to laser beam receptors. Some are rather simple, others elegant in their conception and/or immensely complex. Most work pretty well but can be detected if the target only has the sense to look for them. Finally, these descriptions have been included because they are among the keys to most of the discussions to follow. That is, the cited problems tend to be created when the messages are intercepted and stored. The questions include: (1) what was said (speech enhancement and decoding), (2) who said it (speaker identification), (3) how was it said (stress in voice) and (4) is the stored account an accurate one (transcripts and/or tape authentication)?

CHAPTER 6

The Problem of Noisy
Tape Recordings

INTRODUCTION

Without a doubt the effectiveness of most law enforcement agencies would be reduced by a magnitude if suddenly they could no longer utilize tape recordings in support of their investigations. In fact, it is quite possible that analysis of information on tape recordings constitutes one of the single most powerful tools investigators currently have at their disposal. Yet their use in the storing, processing and analysis of messages, events and information has become so common that many investigators, crime laboratory personnel and related professionals tend to overlook or underrate their potential. Sometimes they simply neglect to utilize this effective technique (even when needed), or they use it poorly. In any event, tape recording techniques could be exploited to a far greater extent than they are at present. Moreover, with somewhat improved knowledge and upgraded procedures, the amount of information captured—and ultimately utilized—could be expanded by a substantial factor. That is, present technology, if properly employed, would permit a considerably more effective use of tape recordings than currently is the case.

One of the more common uses of tape recordings is in crime management. There are many other uses, of course, but this example will be used as the principal one in this chapter primarily because most of the problems that arise are related to that type of operation. Specifically, one of the most common types of information law enforcement groups wish to record (i.e., store), and then utilize in relevant investigations, are conversations among criminals or suspects. The data contained in these communicative interchanges very often reveal details of a crime that is about to be, has been, or is in the process of being committed. Often included is specific information about the participants, the place of the crime, its nature, and so on. Intelligence such as this can be utilized to prevent crime and to assist investigators in identifying and capturing the criminals; it often can be used in courts of law to verify that a crime has been committed or to establish the participation of those accused, and so on. However, as has been seen in previous chapters, the recordings used for these purposes rarely are of "studio quality;" indeed, they often are quite poor, as distortions of all types can and do occur. The most common of these problems is that noise is introduced onto the tape recording. Thus, the messages/information they contain are obscured by unwanted sounds. Other types of distortion can occur also. These difficulties will be discussed in this chapter.

THE PROBLEM AND ITS SOURCES

Reasonably good insight about the source of tape recording problems should result from a combination of the information about equipment contained in Chapter 4 with that found in the immediately preceding chapter on surveillance. To be specific, the equipment available or used, the techniques employed, and/or the field situation itself can lead to conditions where the sought messages are obscured by masking signals or are distorted in such a manner that the speech is unintelligible—or, at least, difficult to decode. However, all is not lost if these problems occur, as there are techniques that will permit the speech signal to be enhanced—often to the extent that the relevant information can be reclaimed. Accordingly, the focus of this chapter will be on approaches to speech enhancement, with specific techniques relevant to decoding and transcript development discussed in the next chapter. However, before speech enhancement techniques can be established, it is necessary to understand how and why these problems occur in the first place.

Basically, there are two main sources of noise/distortion of tape recordings. The first set of circumstances (which may serve to degrade or mask the speech contained on these recordings) results from the nature of the equipment used, the recording techniques employed and operator error. The second domain is that of the acoustic environment in which the tape recordings were made (5, 9). Why and how do these two problems occur? Let us consider them in turn.

Recording Procedures

A number of causes of speech degradation are inherent within the equipment utilized or in the recording process itself. They result from such conditions as: (1) the reduction of signal bandwidth, (2) harmonic distortion, (3) the addition of noise (of all types) to the speech signal, (4) the intermittent reduction in (or elimination of) the speech signal, (5) frequency distortion, and so on. The most common origins of these problems are the inadequate selection, or improper utilization, of pickup transducers (microphones, bugs, telephones) or recording equipment and/or inadequate transmission links. Several specific examples of these problems and their impact on the resultant tape recordings will be found below. However, two relationships should be kept in mind: (1) these illustrations are not all-inclusive and (2) the recording conditions are not always under the control of the investigator/agent.

Transducers and Transmission Lines

The pickup transducers utilized in criminal investigations, business meetings and the like take many forms. They range from good-quality laboratory-type microphones, miniature microphones, and body microphones, to telephones, direct line taps and suction cup transducers (see again Chapters 4 and 5). To give you an idea of what all this may mean,, the frequency response of several such transducers are portrayed in Figure 6-1. Traces A and B were made by analysis of good-quality laboratory-type microphones; they can be seen to have a relatively flat frequency response between 20/40 Hz and 16/20 kHz. In their normal operating modes, they are more than adequate for the transfer of speech, for, as many authors point out (11, 17), the frequency region 200-5000 Hz is particularly important for good speech intelligibility. Thus, these units (A and B) should properly transduce all five of the vowel formants and their transitions, as well as energy associated with even the most extreme of the consonants. Note

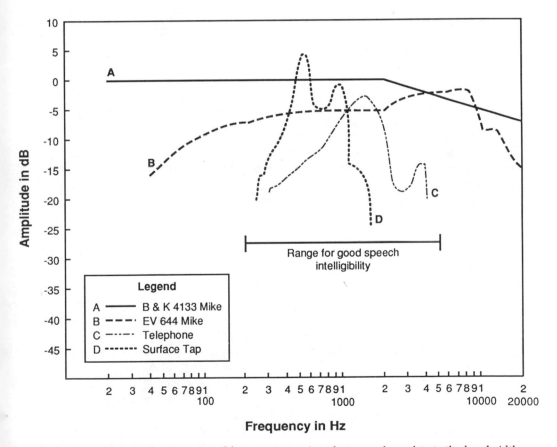

Figure 6-1. The frequency response of four common microphones as they relate to the bandwidth for good speech transmission. These curves are based on actual laboratory measurements.

also Curve C—a passband fairly consistent with that of a telephone link. We obtained this configuration by actual measurement of several telephone transmissions and, as you will note, the passband here proved to be approximately 280-3600 Hz. However, in many instances, an even more limited frequency response can be expected for recordings made over telephone circuits. However, it should be stressed that a passband such as this one still permits reasonable speech intelligibility to be transferred and recorded, that is, if there are no other competing or confounding factors present. The frequency response (see Curve D) of a microphone of the type that is still occasionally used in police surveillance demonstrates the problem that can be encountered with field-type transducers. In this case, the frequency response is seen to be quite variable; worse yet, it only extends from about 240 Hz to, at best, 1400 Hz. A limited-passband device of this type will sharply reduce the speech intelligibility of the recorded message, and it is difficult to enhance the intelligibility of speech which has been degraded in this fashion. Moreover, as had been stated, problems of this nature also can result from inadequacies in transmission lines, (channel distortion); in any case, they occur whenever limited passband or variable frequency response exists anywhere in the entire system. That is, the problem can lie in the transducers, the transmission lines, and/or even the recording equipment used—especially if it is old, of poor quality or if malfunctions occur.

Inadequate Equipment/Operation

A second set of recording problems relates to inadequacies in equipment selection and/or operation. Inexpensive or very small recorders, while useful in surveillance and undercover work, often do not have sufficient fidelity to permit the recording of speech intelligible enough to be easily decoded—or, perhaps, decoded at all. Use of such equipment often will result in conditions of limited frequency response, harmonic distortion or system noise; poorly maintained equipment also fosters similar problems (as well as variation in tape speed and intermittent short circuits).

There are other problems associated with the selection and use of poor quality or inappropriate equipment and/or recording procedures. A few of the more important include:

1. *Excessively slow tape recorder speed.* Obviously, long recording times are desirable in surveillance work (even if the tape recorder is a tiny one) and very slow recording speeds permit a great deal of information to be captured before the tape has to be changed. However, these slow speeds result in reduction in frequency response, loss of signal level and sharply reduced intelligibility, as too much material has to be crowded onto very small amounts of recording tape.
2. *Very thin recording tape.* This type of tape is used for the same reasons as are the very slow recorder speeds. However, it is fragile and often has an emulsion coating that is uneven or too thin. The result can be speech

3.   dropouts, reduction in signal strength, print-through, tape stretching—and reduction in speech intelligibility.
3.   *Batteries with an inadequate charge.* This condition can lead to signal reduction, recorder stoppage or variation in tape speed.

Finally, the misuse of the equipment by the operator, or his or her lack of understanding of its proper operation, can result in significant problems. For example, in "The Case of the Squabbling Businessmen," one of the tape recordings was virtually useless because the operator (1) let the principals arrange to meet in a crowded restaurant and (2) did not bother to thoroughly check the equipment beforehand. Hence, the tape was marred by excessive noise due to the din in the restaurant and from the fact that the antenna of the FM receiver used was not properly attached; consequently, little intelligible speech was recorded.

In sum, the sources of speech degradation from system inadequacies and misuse are many; sometimes it is extremely difficult, if not impossible, to compensate for them.

Problems Resulting from a Noisy Environment

The most common form of speech signal degradation is caused by masking signals being recorded onto the tape along with the speech. These unwanted sounds include noise from all sources plus "forensic noise," i.e., competing speech (other persons talking simultaneously with the target), music, and so on (9). Noise of many origins can be recorded: it can be broadband or narrow band; have a natural frequency (or frequencies); be steady-state, intermittent or impact.

Steady-State Noise

A typical noise of this type is 60-cycle hum (and its multiples of 120, 180 Hz, etc.), a signal which can be induced into a system, and ultimately recorded onto the tape, from any 60-cycle AC electrical source. While noise of this type has a masking effect on speech, its effect often can be reduced or eliminated—that is if notch filters are used (see below).

Another type of noise you will encounter is broadband in nature and can result from such friction sources as the wind, fans/blowers, vehicle operation, clothing movement, and so on. Some of the effects of this type of noise may be mitigated by the elimination of that part of the total noise spectrum that exists outside of the speech range—i.e., by the use of filters that pass the frequency band between 350 and 3500 Hz, for instance. Analog filtering techniques are particularly useful in this regard.

Finally, certain types of noises are produced by mechanisms that have what may be considered "natural frequencies" (due to cavitation or their speed of operation); motors, fans and blowers are illustrative of such devices. In such cases, analysis of the noise spectrum sometimes will reveal peak frequencies and a relatively narrow noise band. A great deal of this type of energy can be filtered from the recording, even if it is located within the speech range, because its band is narrow and steady-state. While digital filters are particularly useful in combatting this type of noise, notch filters also can be utilized.

Competing Speech/Music

Perhaps the most difficult "noise" to eliminate from a tape recording—that is, without simultaneously removing the speech that is to be enhanced and decoded—is that which results from the speech of other talkers and from music. In this case, the unwanted sounds have virtually the same frequency spectrum as does the targeted speech. Indeed, in some cases, little processing is possible that will enhance the speech intelligibility of interest—especially if the level of the competing signals is relatively high. However, in other cases, judicious filtering is useful, as human auditors sometimes can focus on a specific signal among several, especially when specialized binaural techniques are used (see below and 10, 11, 17, 18). Better yet, spectral analysis can be carried out on the noise and the filter settings based on the observed patterns. Finally, it should be stated that several schemes for the electronic separation of the speech by two talkers have been proposed. In my opinion, while they have not yet achieved operational significance, they do exhibit good potential for use in the future.

Intermittent/Impact Noise

Noise of this type can take many forms: street noise, gunshots, pinball machines, bells, horns, explosions, doors closing, and so on. Impact noise is of short duration and tends to obscure speech only intermittently; that is, it will mask a particular utterance by a particular speaker. Unfortunately, in some instances it is the content of the obscured message which is the very one most desired. Since these impact noises (as well as their sources) are extremely variable, it is well nigh impossible to list all of the events/relationships that reasonably could be expected to occur. Nor will it be possible to describe all of the potential remedies that could reduce these negative effects upon speech intelligibility. Rather, about the only advice I can offer is to point out that, when it is necessary to combat the effects of impact noise, you should do so by utilizing and applying the general principles enumerated below.

In short, there are many ways that the speech you want to hear and/or analyze can be degraded—and there are many sources of these distortions. You have only to consider the equipment you have used (or that utilized by some other agency or group), the realities of surveillance, and some of the remarks above to understand why so many tape recordings need to be processed/enhanced before the speech they contain can be decoded. The wonder is that even a higher proportion of these recordings are not severely degraded. In any event, the procedures that follow should be helpful when you need to understand (or carry out) tasks of this type.

BASIC TECHNIQUES OF SPEECH ENHANCEMENT

As stated, the focus of this chapter is upon those basic techniques that can be utilized to enhance the intelligibility of speech on tape recordings, or of any speech which has been obscured or degraded in some manner. First, it should be acknowledged that a number of scientists are developing powerful and sophisticated machine techniques for the analysis and reconstruction of degraded messages. They employ approaches such as bandwidth compression, cross channel correlation, mean least squares analysis, all-pole models, group delay functions, linear adaptive filtering, linear predictive coefficients, cepstrum techniques, deconvolution, and so on. Most of them are utilizing advanced technologies (3); some are attempting to approach the problem on a systematic basis (12, 13, 14, 15). As I indicated, however, none of these techniques currently appear to be fully operational (i.e., valid and inexpensive); most are extremely complex, time consuming and costly—at least, they are too costly to apply to the routine material produced for law enforcement, business, security or military purposes. On the other hand, a number of these approaches have demonstrated excellent potential both for future development and for use with those extremely important distorted speech samples which do not respond to analog and first-order digital filtering—and where cost is not a factor. As these techniques develop, they should prove invaluable for the enhancement of speech where distortions are severe. While it seems premature to discuss approaches of this type, you can obtain a list of relevant articles from Forensic Communications Associates or you can carry out a relevant search of engineering and IEEE publications. In short, the procedures to be described in this chapter are those practical approaches that we developed and have been using for some years now (see, for example, 2, 3, 5, 9, 16). However, I should like to reiterate that they are not all-inclusive; indeed, they are constantly being refined and improved.

Operator Background/Training

Enhancement of the intelligibility of speech on tape recordings is best carried out by an individual with specific training obtained from a university-level program in forensic communication and/or the phonetic sciences. At the present time, some law enforcement agencies are successfully providing in-house training of this type for agents with academic/technical backgrounds in electronics, audio-engineering, and the like. In most cases, this training appears appropriate and, what is more important, adequate. Accordingly, even though the specialist in forensic phonetics is the most desirable "operator" in this area, many individuals in the second group cited probably can develop skills suitable for the tasks described below; some already have done so. However, to be effective, these individuals should be proficient relative to the processes they are to employ, the specific equipment they are to use and, especially, the speaking processes (i.e., phonetics). University-level training, of course, is most desirable, but a good understanding of the information contained in this book, and from such elementary publications as Denes and Pinson's *The Speech Chain* (6), is helpful—at least for a general understanding of the processes involved. So is practical knowledge about forensics and related tasks in the forensic communication area. In any case, the most effective processing will result from a combination of appropriate equipment and good technical training/experience on the part of the operator. But, what are some of the relevant processes that can be applied?

Tape "Dubbing"

The first step in the speech enhancement procedure, and a prelude to all of the operations described below, is to make a good-quality copy of the tape to be processed. It is not at all desirable to utilize the original tape recording as a working copy as its repeated use will ultimately result in signal deterioration due to breakage, stretching, twisting or friction wear to the oxide (or recording) side of the tape. It is especially important not to accidentally erase any part of an original recording (just imagine the problems encountered if you destroyed or compromised important evidence) nor damage the tape in any way. Incidentally, it is well to remember that if the original tape recording is in cassette form, you should punch out the two little tabs (if someone has not already done so) so that accidental rerecording can be avoided (9).

The Log

The need for a detailed and accurate written account of all processing activities would appear obvious; yet it constitutes a step that is sometimes neglected. It is important to record all of the procedures and equipment you use (as well as the equipment settings) in order to provide for technical efficiency and the identification of the techniques you found most useful from among those attempted. It is especially important to be able to recall the exact procedures you used so they can be replicated, or described/demonstrated, if you are called upon to testify in court. Moreover, a log will permit quick identification of troublesome sections.

The log serves a second purpose also. Prior to the examination and processing of a tape recording, it is good policy to learn as much as possible about its nature and contents. Any information about how the recording was made—as well as where and by whom—will be useful. As is obvious, a written log can serve as the repository of information of this type; the account then can be reexamined during the analysis procedure for useful information relative to the conditions which must be mitigated or processed. Such material also can be helpful, later on, to the decoders (see Chapter 7).

Listening to the Tape

It is important to listen to the entire tape recording one or more times (before you attempt to process it) in order to develop a good working knowledge of its contents and the types of interference and degradation that exist. As several authors (10, 11, 17) point out, decoders follow this procedure also, as it assists them in identifying the number of individuals on the recording (as well as their identity and sex), the different dialects exhibited by the speakers and at least some of the specific problems to be met. When speech enhancement is attempted, you will want to assess the tape for those reasons and in order to identify the different types of masking noise, signal-to-noise ratios and competing speech signals that occur.

Spectral Analysis

Special techniques are available if noise is the primary (or even one of the several) detrimental factor(s) interfering with acceptable speech intelligibility. If it is, you will want to learn all you can about its location, intensity, natural frequency or frequencies, bandwidth, and so on. In such a case, spectral analysis can provide a helpful approach. We have found t-f-a spectrograms to be of somewhat limited effectiveness in this regard, but they are better than no analysis at all. My group prefers to employ a somewhat more sophisticated technique; we digitize the signal and apply a program that provides a series of individual ("instantaneous") spectra over time. An illustration of this type of grouped spectra can be found in Figure 6-2. As can be seen, the noise "bars" peak around 800 and 2000 Hz. This technique can be used to obtain a great deal of useful information about the nature of the noise—especially if sections of it can be

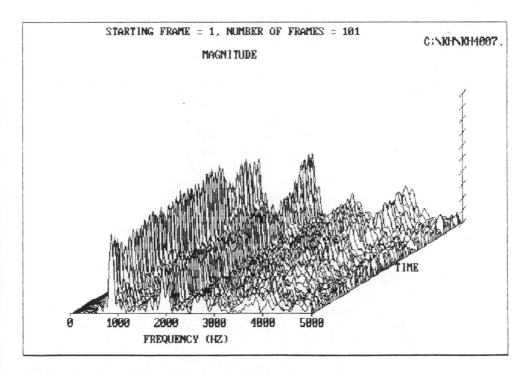

Figure 6-2. Three-dimensional printout of a digital analysis of a noise signal. Note that the lowest frequencies already have been filtered out and that there are energy concentrations around the frequencies of 0.8 and 2.0 kHz.

found and analyzed where no speech is present. To summarize, it is desirable that you learn all you can about the problems you face from any sensory, hardware, hybrid or software processing techniques you may have available.

Filtering Techniques (Analog)

The several types of frequency biasing and filtering techniques to be described possibly constitute the most useful approach available for "scrubbing" a tape recording. The methods to be used may be best understood by observation of Figure 6-3. It will be noted from the figure that our approach often is to conduct the filtering in two phases or stages. While we sometimes find it possible to carry out all of the filtering in a single phase, the two-stage approach incorporates a number of advantages. Specifically it permits attention to be focused on selected elements during the first phase and on still other specific problems during the second. Alternately, the process can be analog filtering followed by digital. Moreover, if a multistage approach is utilized, it is not desirable to cascade a large number of filters in a single equipment array. This is an important point, as when filters are cascaded, they must be isolated from each other (no matter what their manufacturers tell you) so as to avoid equipment interaction (see the section on isolating filters below).

An additional relationship must be understood before we proceed. That is, energy at a lower frequency will tend to mask those around it and above it, whereas energy at a higher F0 will not mask lower frequencies to as great an extent. Figure 6-4 provides simplified and stylized information about these relationships; it is based on presentations by several authors (1, 7, 8, 19, 20). In any event, it presents information about the frequencies masked by a sine wave of, and a narrow band noise centered at, 450 Hz. First, the sinusoid. Here you will notice that the frequencies around 450 Hz (and very close to it) will be masked maximally, with the higher frequencies slightly more affected. Note also that sinusoids above 450 Hz will be masked, especially if they are multiples of that frequency. The effect is systematically reduced for frequencies which occur at greater and greater distances from 450 Hz. Finally, it also can be noted that (1) the masking effect is somewhat reduced right at the frequency (or its multiples), (2) beats occur when the two frequencies are very close to each other and (3) except for those in its immediate vicinity, the masking frequency tends not to interfere with those below it. The second curve shows the masking effects of narrow-band noise—a case more relevant to the forensic model. Here you will note that there is some masking at frequencies below this noise band, the most severe effect is within the band, and serious masking is continued for frequencies above it.

What are the implications of these effects? One example would be to apply them to the passband for speech (roughly 350-3500 Hz). Of course, frequencies that are within this band will mask the speech signal to the greatest extent and will be the most difficult to remove. However, we now can see that noise below 350 Hz also will mask the speech to a substantial extent (and be distracting also). Fortunately, much of it can be removed by good filtering techniques. Hum (60 Hz) is an example here. If such energy is confined to its fundamental frequency

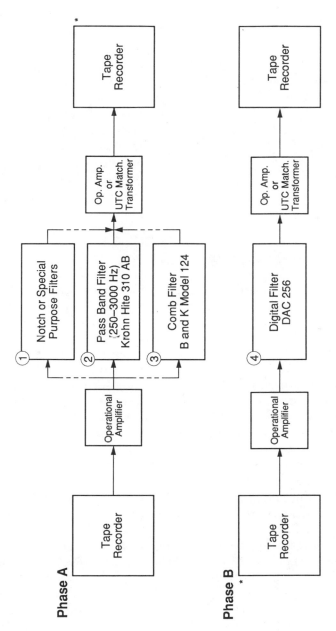

Figure 6-3. A block diagram demonstrating how analog and/or digital filtering can be accomplished. The three analog filters (1–3) can be used singly or cascaded. Note the dashed lines; this indicates that multiple analog filters cannot be employed simultaneously in parallel. A typical configuration would be to place a comb filter and a digital filter (both isolated) in series.

*For single-phase use, remove these tape recorders and the operational amplifier and couple directly to 4.

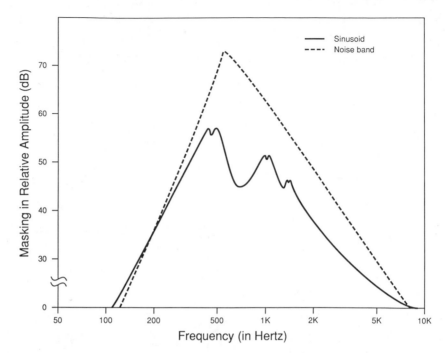

Figure 6-4. A somewhat theoretical graph of how certain sounds mask other sounds. It will be noted that there is a strong tendency for low-frequency sounds (either sinusoids or noise) to mask higher frequencies but not so much the reverse. Masking frequency is at about 450 Hz.

(i.e., 60 Hz), its effects are fairly easy to counter; a notch filter is used for this purpose. If hum multiples (120, 180, 240 Hz, etc.) are present also, its debilitating effect is fairly high both because these other frequencies will mask higher ones and because some of them will be within the speech range. Finally, even though its presence can be quite annoying, noise above 3000 Hz will not mask speech to any great extent. Moreover, it can be reduced in level/effect by either analog or digital filtering. You should keep these relationships in mind as you (1) approach the problem of enhancing speech on noisy tape recordings, (2) read reports about such processing or (3) listen to tape recordings in either processed or unprocessed states.

Now back to analog filtering techniques and systems. There are a number of methods and concepts here; Figure 6-5 should assist you in understanding these relationships. In this figure, the frequency response of a series of stylized and simplified low-pass, high-pass, bandpass and notch filters—with varying slopes—are depicted. Each curve relates to one or more of the filters discussed below and will be considered in relation to the appropriate descriptions when presented.

Frequency Biasing

Anyone who has a home music system is familiar with the bass and treble controls on their amplifier. In the simple sense, the systems to which these terms

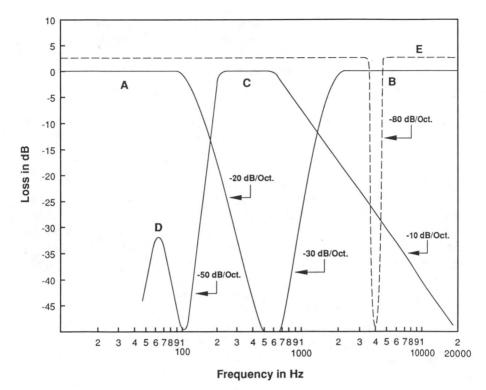

Figure 6-5. This figure shows the filtering capabilities of low-pass (A), high-pass (B), bandpass (C) and notch filters (E), as well as filtering slopes that are shallow (upper C), moderate (A, B), steep (left side of C, E) and which exhibit rebound (D).

refer are low-pass (bass) and high-pass (treble) filters with very shallow slopes (12-15 dB/octave) coupled to an amplifier circuit so that automatic compensation occurs for signal energy loss due to the filtering. Biasing controls (and, hence, systems) often can be found on tape recorders and amplifiers. More complex systems, such as Dolby, simply operate as a series of high-pass, low-pass and bandpass filters with preselected characteristics. In short, the manipulation of circuits such as these often can serve to mildly enhance speech intelligibility on a tape recording; they do so by moderately reducing the level of the unwanted (noise) signals that lie above or below the speech band. In short, the manipulation of circuits such as these often can serve to mildly enhance speech intelligibility on a tape recording; it primarily does so by moderately reducing the level of the unwanted (noise) signals that lie above or below the speech band.

Notch Filters

If a spectrum analysis shows that a noise source is producing a relatively narrow band of high energy at or around a specific frequency, a notch filter centering on that frequency may be employed to reduce its debilitating effect on speech. The effects of a notch filter are depicted by curve E in Figure 6-5. In this case, the filter is designed to reduce energy at or around 4 kHz; it will be noted that its slopes are very steep; to obtain this configuration, active or dynamic filters probably would be required. Theoretically, you could build a simple (and passive) notch filter with the characteristics depicted if you had a little technical knowledge in electronics. However, it would be difficult to do so without also producing some undesirable side effects (see below). Nevertheless, reasonably good notch filters can be fabricated/purchased for most frequencies under about 2 kHz; units with a center frequency around 60 Hz are particularly good for reducing the speech-masking effects of AC "hum."

Bandpass Filters

As has been stated, highly intelligible speech needs only a frequency passband of 200-5000 Hz; good-quality speech (especially for decoding purposes) can be obtained if the passband is 350-3500 Hz; and reasonably intelligible speech can be had with passbands that are even more sharply limited. Hence, even if there is a substantial amount of noise in the lows and/or the highs, speech may be enhanced by subjecting the tape recording to a bandpass filter with characteristics of approximately 350-3500 Hz. Curve C in Figure 6-5 illustrates this type of passband filter; however, in this case, its frequency limits are not 350-3500 Hz but rather 200-800 Hz. If you will ignore the particular cutoff frequencies shown, curve C can be utilized to describe some of the problems encountered in bandpass filtering. First, you will note that the slope associated with the high-frequency limit of the filter (800 Hz) is about 10 dB per octave (-10 dB/oct.). A slope such as this one tends to be "clean," and little or no "rebound" can be expected. On the other hand, it also can be noted that attenuation of those signals above 800 Hz is gradual (as in frequency biasing procedures) and, hence, not very much reduction in noise would occur even at those frequencies which are some distance from the filter roll-off. Occasionally, a shallow filter slope (such as this one) is desirable, as some of the competing noise can be reduced (when it occurs within the speech range) without excessively reducing the energy level of the speech itself. On the other hand, this type of filtering is not very desirable for the elimination of noise outside speech range, as it does not attenuate such signals sharply enough. The low-frequency slope (i.e., the one at the 200-Hz "cutoff") of filter curve C is shown to be around 50 dB per octave. The effects of such a steep slope are quite different than those for the one described above. First, even frequencies which are very close to the filter roll-off are sharply attenuated; however, undesirable side effects sometimes occur when energy is decreased this rapidly. That is, the filtering may exhibit a characteristic referred to as "rebound" (see section D of this curve). When rebound occurs, it simply means that some of the frequencies below (or above, as the case may be) the "cutoff" frequency are not attenuated. Further, it can be noted from the illustration that, in the case of curve C-D, the rebound occurs around 60 Hz. In an actual situation, a rebound at this frequency would be an undesirable occurrence, for "hum," which could be present on the tape being filtered, would not be attenuated. In sum, filters that can pass speech frequencies but materially reduce higher and lower frequencies are especially useful in the enhancement of speech intelligibility because they tend to eliminate masking signals without seriously degrading the speech itself.

"Comb Filters"

A comb filter is a device that consists of a series of separately controllable bandpass filters—each with a relatively narrow frequency response. In a sense, a comb filter operates in a manner similar to a large group of variable notch filters arrayed in a systematic sequence from low frequency to high. Its characteristics (i.e., slopes) tend to be superior to the "equalizers" found in audio stores even though it looks like them (externally anyway). In any event, a comb filter can be used to continuously modify the spectrum of a signal by selectively attenuating the undesirable frequency bands throughout the operating range of the device. For example, it can be utilized to operate simultaneously as a bandpass filter and one or more notch filters, or it can be cascaded with other units in order to increase the filtering effects of the total system. Comb filters are particularly useful due to their great versatility. Indeed, troublesome sections of a tape recording can sometimes be enhanced by playing them repeatedly through a comb filter with the operator adjusting the various settings by very small increments for each run.

An illustration of how you can use analog filtering to solve the problems of a noisy tape recording occurred during one of my earliest investigations/trials. I call it "The Case of the Crooked Judge." It seems that the presiding judge of a particular circuit court enhanced his income by "selling" cases. As any attorney can tell you, it is quite difficult to obtain a conviction (or an acquittal, if you are on the defense) if the presiding judge does not desire that specific outcome. What happened in this particular case was that the police, who long had been aware of the judge's illegal activities (but who had not been able to obtain enough evidence to arrest him), finally got a break. An informant turned up. Basically, a young prostitute caught "breaking and entering" agreed to cooperate with the police and record her deal with the judge who had sent word that he could be "bought." The young woman was "wired" and met with him at a restaurant. They discussed what it would cost her to either be acquitted or, at least, receive probation. Unfortunately, the informant did not realize at first that she and the judge were sitting in the restaurant beside an air conditioner blower. By the time she noticed it and got their table changed on some pretext, the meeting was half over. Hence, much of the speech on the first half of the tape was obscured by both restaurant noise and the noise from a blower. This problem was intensified by the nature of the case. First, if a sitting judge is accused of criminal activity by a previously convicted criminal, the evidence against him had better be very strong. In this case, the jury must be able to hear the bribe clearly and succinctly. Worse yet, if you try someone as important as a judge, the "court" must be a person who is both a distinguished jurist and one beyond reproach. The jurist selected for this purpose met these criteria, but he was in his 70s and had a mild hearing loss. What to do? Since this was a case early in my career, it served as an excellent test of my ideas about analog processing. In short, my assistants and I found the dominant frequency of the blower plus those for some of the other sounds (by wave analysis), and by cascading a series of analog filters, we removed enough noise so that the speech could be heard. We also learned that sometimes you have to carry out your procedures in the courtroom during the trial (as we did in this case) rather than simply processing the tape in the laboratory and playing it later in court (as we have in other cases). We also learned that the use of personal headsets for all jurors, and other relevant personnel in the courtroom, was a good technique to use—especially if all of the individuals involved could control the gain to each of their ears independently. The case went well for the prosecution and although the presiding jurist had to take the tape recordings home (to listen to them until he could understand what was said), he permitted them to be entered into evidence.

A Reminder

It is very important to isolate filters from each other and from any other electronic device (such as tape recorders) coupled to the system. The reason for such isolation is that filters have a marked tendency to interact with each other (and other units) and, as a result, produce a variety of unwanted side effects (attenuation rebound, signal distortion, etc.). Quite obviously, any process that increases the distortion to the speech signal—rather than reduces it—is an undesirable one and is to be avoided. These interactions essentially can be eliminated by coupling both the input and the output of a filter to other equipment through either operational amplifiers or isolation transformers (see again Figure 6-3). Usually operational amplifiers are preferred since they can be utilized to maintain signal level. That is, since filtering attenuates some of the frequencies within the spectrum of a signal, it also tends to reduce overall signal strength. Thus, if tape-recorded speech is passed through a series of filters without any amplification at all, the overall level can be reduced (in the worse case, anyway) to where the speech would not be heard well enough to be decoded. As indicated, the use of operational amplifiers as buffers mitigates this problem.

Digital Filters

Digital filters take two forms: hardware and software. The hardware types (such as the DAC 256 or 1024) are quite expensive and are relatively complex in their use. The digital filtering that can be accomplished by software programs such as Signal Technology's ILS or the Livermore Laboratory's SIG programs require a minicomputer, or pretty large microcomputer, as storage becomes a problem if the speech segment (on the noisy tape) is more than a few minutes long.

Basically, filters of this type digitize the signal a set number of times each second (say 20k); they then determine the energy (especially steady-state) in the frequencies above, below and between the specified limits, remove this energy and convert what remains back into an analog signal. As you might expect, the process actually is somewhat more complicated than that described; however, this definition should serve to provide you with an operating concept of this type of equipment. A functional review of the DAC 256 can provide an example of how these systems operate (it is one of the simplest models, yet it works well). It has two modes of operation; both involve automatic processing. Basically, it is a 256th-order filter which rapidly designs its own filtering so as to remove unwanted noise by adaptive predictive deconvolution. It works best for linear noise (most noise signals are predictive) but can process nonlinear noise by "short-time correlation." The second mode is yet more powerful, as the noise (linear) is fed to one channel as a reference, and that noise plus speech to the other. The process, then, is one of adaptive noise cancellation.

As stated, digital filtering can be carried out by computer if appropriate software and extensive memory are available. Actually, the process is quite similar to that described above, as "hardware"-type digital filters simply perform the process in a hybrid manner (i.e., some of the components are hard-wired together). In short, when software approaches are utilized, a computer is programmed to seek a systematic energy band within the signal (i.e., the noise band) and then to "remove" it by only reconstructing the time-varying speech signal.

In practice, the digital approaches can be very helpful—especially in certain circumstances where analog filters cannot remove the unwanted energy. They have their weaknesses, however. Often they remove some of the speech along with the noise; in other cases, the resulting signal is distracting, distorted or includes what sounds like an echo. We have found that it is best to employ analog filters wherever possible. They are easy to understand and use and, if the speech can be sufficiently enhanced for decoding, there is no need for digital filtering. Hence, we save the more powerful techniques for the more difficult, specialized or complex tasks. Further, we have found that analog filtering followed by digital filtering and, then again, analog filtering provides both the most intelligible speech and that which sounds the most natural. Of course, these statements should not be construed as constituting a technical "how to" or cookbook approach; hence, you must accept the fact that it requires further training plus experience to be able to match the particular hardware/software procedures to the noise problems found on a particular noisy tape. Appropriate training in engineering is quite helpful and a strong background in the phonetic sciences is a must.

Binaural Listening

As I have pointed out, problems related to the actual decoding of the speech itself are not the focus of this chapter (but rather the next). However, all of the techniques discussed here are aimed at mitigation of that problem. Further, the technique I now wish to discuss relates both to decoding (Chapter 7) and the enhancement of speech intelligibility by the reduction of the masking and distracting effects of noise. This process is one which is related to established auditory theory and, especially, to the integration of incomplete stimulus patterns by the process of binaural hearing (see reference 4 for an excellent discussion of these effects). Basically, we have carried out research in which it was possible to demonstrate that the intelligibility of the speech signal (to the listener) can be markedly improved by a technique we developed. What we do is split and filter the signal. The filtered product is fed to the decoder's dominant ear at a relatively high intensity level and the unprocessed signal simultaneously to the contralateral ear at a level just above the threshold of hearing for speech (see Figure 6-6). I should stress that it is important for the filtered signal to be directed to the person's dominant ear if this procedure is to work well. The easiest way to determine which of your ears is dominant is to see which eye is dominant. Simply take a tube and look through it. The eye you use is the dominant one; it is associated with the dominant ear. When this technique is used, we have found that the speech seems to "pop" out of the noise to an extent that it often can be decoded—even if it also is distorted in other ways. Not only is intelligibility enhanced, but the perception of the filtered speech as being rather "artificial" in nature is markedly reduced. The equipment configuration for this technique is a simple one. A good-quality, dual-track tape recorder is used and the noisy tape recorded on both channels. The recorder now is coupled to a second recorder (or phones), with the channel-"one" output fed through an attenuator to the appropriate channel of the second unit. Simultaneously, the signal from channel 2 is fed through all filtering equipment to the parallel channel on the new tape recorder. As can be seen, this technique utilizes the equipment already employed in the filtering process. All that is now necessary is for the decoder to know which of his or her ears is the dominant one. As many decoders who have utilized our process can attest, the HBF (Hollien Binaural Filtered) approach to decoding constitutes a very powerful tool.

Variable-Speed Tape Recorders

Variable-speed tape recorders also can be useful in enhancing the intelligibility of speech on tape recordings. Devices of this type come in two classes; each is used to produce a different effect. With the first, only a simple, manual increase or decrease in recorder speed is possible. These units are especially useful in situations where the speed of the original recording was varied for some reason—a problem which can result from mechanical malfunction, fluc-

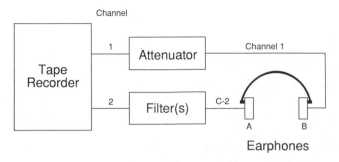

Figure 6-6. Schematic of the Hollien Binaural Filtered approach to speech decoding. As can be seen, the speech is fed simultaneously and stereophonically to both ears. The dominant ear (A) receives the highly filtered product, the contralateral ear (B), the full signal but at an energy level just above threshold.

tuation in the recorder's operating power, or some such event. Sometimes the speed of the tape recorder slowly decreases; in other cases, it will vary in either a systematic or random pattern. When any of these events occur, they usually are accompanied by degradation of speech intelligibility. As would be expected, the specific prescription for speed variations of this type is to play the recording on a variable-speed tape recorder coupled to yet another recorder. While the problem recording is played, the operator can manually control the speed of the first (variable-speed) unit in a pattern that compensates for the speed variations which were first induced by the defective operation of the original system (hum tracking is especially useful here—that is, if a 60-Hz signal is on the tape). Some talent and practice is necessary if this operation is to be successfully carried out. However, as the operator becomes skillful, the speed of the resulting tape recording often can be returned to near normal, with a corresponding enhancement of speech intelligibility. Please note, however, that it is much easier to compensate for problems of this type if the incorrect speed is steady-state rather than variable. Finally, speech intelligibility can sometimes be enhanced by varying tape recorder speed so that it is faster or slower than normal. In this case, either the effects of noise are reduced by changing its spectrum or a talker's speech becomes clearer simply on the basis of change in tape speed. However, these techniques are based on subjective impressions. Thus, their success (or lack of it) pretty much results from trial and error, with proficiency subjectively based on operator skill and experience.

The second class of variable-speed tape recorders is typified by the Lexicon, Varispeech II. In this case, expansion and compression circuits have been added to the device so that the speed of the recording can be altered, yet the perceived speech not appear to be distorted—i.e., in those ways typical to the speeding up or slowing down of a system. That is, when the tape speed is increased, or is slowed, an appropriate circuit is activated which compensates for the resulting upward (or downward) shift in the frequency spectrum (especially for the vowels). Accordingly, neither the perceived pitch of the talker nor any of his or her articulatory characteristics appear to be essentially altered. Manipulations of this type often serve to enhance speech intelligibility—especially when they are utilized in concert with filtering. At present, the reasons for these effects are not completely understood. Apparently, certain relationships among phonemes are altered by this technique; certainly the perceptual relationships among the noise signals on the tape and the speech to be decoded are changed. Nevertheless, no systematic explanations currently are available either about the underlying causes of this effect or relative to the extent of speech improvement that can be expected by application of the process. However, since the technique has been shown in the laboratory to enhance the intelligibility of speech in noise (at least, in some cases), its use on an experimental basis can be recommended.

TO CONCLUDE

It must be conceded that the techniques for enhancing the intelligibility of speech on noisy tapes presently are a little primitive. The state-of-the-science in this area of forensic phonetics probably is not more advanced because the need for such capability has only recently been recognized. However, a number of other conditions also have served to retard appropriate R&D (research and development) efforts in this area. First, law enforcement agencies have not yet begun to articulate their needs in this area. Until they do, it is not likely that either relevant "support" groups or the phonetics/engineering scientific community will direct any realistic proportion of their energies and/or resources to programs designed to solve the issues. Quite to the contrary, it is a reflection of present priorities that only a few individuals, who have both appropriate scientific background (in phonetics and engineering) and an interest in these problems, are conducting research programs relevant to *any* of the forensic phonetic needs of law enforcement agencies. Moreover, the research currently being carried out tends to be somewhat uncoordinated, or even piecemeal, in nature. It often results simply from relationships that develop between a specific law enforcement agency (with a particular problem) and a specific individual (or small group) willing to attempt a practical solution. Somewhat more advanced activity can be found in the military, overseas and in certain industrial/management firms. In these cases, there often are in-house personnel (usually engineers) with qualifications appropriate for the solution of at least some of the transmission/storage problems associated with this area. Quite obviously, a series of relevant, and funded, projects are needed here.

The final point to be made relates to an issue implied earlier; specifically the training of specialists in forensic phonetics. To our knowledge, no highly developed training program of an appropriate kind has as yet been established. Indeed, the few courses and skeletal "certificate" program now available at the University of Florida probably constitutes the only focused educational thrust of this type in the United States. However, it may be possible that, in this case also, awareness of the problem will lead to the development of more extensive programs. In any event, an adaptation of modern technology and modification of existing programs should result in accelerated solutions.

Speech Decoding and Transcripts

INTRODUCTION

As you will see, this chapter is a natural continuation of the preceding one. That is, the processing techniques described in Chapter 6 were presented in order that you could better understand (1) how speech on a noisy or distorted tape recording is processed for improved message intelligibility and (2) how speech enhancement techniques can be used in support of speech decoding. Thus, the materials contained in this chapter will overlap with those found in Chapter 6. They will focus on methods that can be used to decode heard speech and convert it to a reasonably accurate and complete written copy or transcript. Please remember that, in this chapter, we are considering the decoding of materials that have been degraded in some manner (sometimes quite seriously) and not simply the secretarial process of transferring ordinary spoken dialogue into text. That process is itself difficult, but it is not nearly as challenging as those to be described here.

Before the main topic is addressed, however, it should be helpful to again list some of the places and situations where these problems will be encountered. They include: (1) court transcripts which were made from recordings under less than optimal conditions, (2) the recorded product of electronic surveillance of any and all types, (3) any dialogue or utterances that were recorded under less than ideal conditions and (4) spoken material that is inadvertently added to a tape recording being made for another purpose.

Problems and Their Sources

At the risk of being redundant, let me again stress that the primary reason for making a forensic-related tape recording is to provide a permanent and accurate record of a spoken message or related event. Moreover, if a tape recording is to be useful, the speech it contains must be comprehensible, and you will remember that its intelligibility level can be affected both by system (or channel) and speaker distortions. If neither exists, there will be no problem, as the speech will be intelligible and it can be converted to written form by any competent secretary. On the other hand, if problems (distortions) do occur, parallel procedures which permit the successful decoding of the message must be applied. The first procedure is to identify, understand and eliminate the distortions insofar as practicable (see Chapter 6). The second part of this thrust is to develop specialized techniques that permit decoders to deal with distorted speech and understand as much of it as is possible (13, 16, 24).

A word of caution: before attempts are made to decode any speech material, you should try to determine the cause of the distortions. Doing so will aid you immeasurably in anticipating the form the decoding challenge will take. Reference to the following list should be of assistance as you go about this task.

1.   *Causes of Channel Distortions*
    a.   Inadequate recording systems: poor-quality transducers, tape recorders and radio equipment, telephones, body bugs, etc. The result will be speech distortion caused by inadequate frequency response, harmonic distortion, speed variations, and so on.
    b.   Inadequate recording tape: poor-quality tape, tape too thin, inadequate emulsion coating. The result can include print-through, speech dropouts, crosstalk and broken/twisted tape.
    c.   Noise: broadband, narrow band, continuous, impact, forensic, etc. The result is masking of the speech, distraction to the decoder, and so on.
    d.   Improper equipment use or breakdowns: inadequacy of operators, operator carelessness, poorly maintained equipment, etc. All types of problems can occur as the result of these events—among them are the loss of the recording, noise, fade-outs or dropouts, crosstalk and broken tapes.
2.   *Speaker Distortions*   Difficulty in speech decoding can result from a number of intended and inadvertent behaviors by the talker or talkers.
    a.   Disguise (almost always intentional)
    b.   Dialects/foreign languages
    c.   Variation in speech rate (often unintended)
    d.   Effects of stress/fear
    e.   Effects of alcohol/drugs/health states
    f.   Multiple speakers; interruptions by other speakers

Any of these conditions can degrade speech intelligibility and make decoding difficult. As with system distortions, they should be identified, whenever possible, and dealt with individually. For example, the use of specialized decoders for foreign language dialects might be warranted.

PERSPECTIVES ABOUT DECODING

There are a number of relationships as well as some specialized information that can materially aid you in understanding the decoding process. They should be helpful whether you are a decision maker, a supervisor, a decoder—or if you have to select decoders and/or evaluate their work. If you wish to become a specialist of this type, however, you will need to develop skills that extend far beyond the principles outlined in this book. Please note also that the "perspectives" are not presented in any particular order. Nevertheless, they all bear on the decoding process.

Noise and Masking

A large part of the previous chapter was devoted to the masking effects of noise on speech. It is a topic that requires a great deal of attention. Yet, it is important to keep the noise-speech relationship in perspective. For example, you may be a little surprised to discover that noise is not always as debilitating as you might suspect, as the presence of speech often can be detected, even when accompanied by rather intense nonspeech signals. In some cases, speech itself barely can be detected yet much of the message can be understood. This situation is due in part to the internal redundancy of language and the structure of an utterance. For example, if a competing broadband or thermal noise is only twice as intense as the speech, the spoken message ordinarily will remain almost completely intelligible. Even more surprising, the intensity of the interference signal sometimes can reach a level as much as four times as great as that of the speech (depending on the type of noise, of course) before it completely destroys intelligibility. Thus, the spoken message is not always hidden by an accompanying interference signal. In fact, if you will remember the several discussions on the effects of noise on speech in the preceding chapters, you also will remember that the problem often is more one of distraction or irritation than it is of signal degradation. Thus, the experienced decoder often is not overly concerned about the simple presence of high signal-to-noise ratios; they may not prevent efficient decoding.

Auditory Effects

This issue is one that is closely related to noise and masking; it involves several auditory illusions and effects that were implied but not fully discussed in the hearing section of Chapter 3. There are three issues of importance to the decoder: (1) foreground-background processing, (2) binaural listening and (3) auditory illusions—especially those related to speech.

You already should be familiar with the concept of foreground-background processing. Almost everyone has seen the picture in which a white vase can be observed if you look at the middle part of the figure (foreground), but the silhouettes of two (identical) people facing each other will be seen if you look to the sides. In our case, however, the concept is an auditory one and refers to a person's ability to attend selectively to a particular portion of a heard stimulus. In the case of speech in noise, the human auditor can listen to the noise, if he or she wishes, and relegate the speech to the background. It also is possible to bring the speech to the foreground and attend more closely to it than to the noise. Much of this processing occurs at the cortical level; it is aided by the process of binaural listening. It also is one of the reasons why, in my judgment anyway, humans make better speech decoders than do machines—at the present state of technology anyway (see reference 22, but also 17, 18).

Binaural listening simply means to hear a signal simultaneously with both ears. As you will remember, what is heard can be monochannel (one microphone) or stereophonic (two microphones with two channels one to each ear). It is well established that binaural hearing aids both in foreground-background relationships and in deciphering speech (4, 5, 11). While the process involved is complex, it is commonly experienced. All you have to do is alternately listen to speech through a single earphone and then through two. Individuals in law enforcement often are amazed at how much better they can hear a recorded conversation when we use good equipment and play it to them through binaural earphones.

The speech decoder is aided by auditory "illusions" also. Indeed, no special training is necessary, at least for limited use of these phenomena, as most people have learned to process distorted or partly heard speech on a natural basis. Additionally, direct experience and trial and error aid in enhancing your ability here. Most of the relevant processing of this type takes place at the cortical level, but the nonlinearity of the ear may contribute also. What appears to happen is that we "intuitively" learn to fill in the parts of speech that are distorted or missing and properly decode the degraded elements by attending to coarticulation and the environment within which phonemes are heard. For example, a vowel and its transition alone often can provide enough information to permit you to correctly "hear" the missing consonant; certain speech sounds within a word can be obliterated (or replaced by noise) and yet be understood when "heard;" a talker's fundamental frequency is perceived even though it has not been passed to the listener because of limited system frequency response (over a telephone, for instance). Actually, there is no mystery about these auditory illusions (27), as their nature is lawful; they depend partly upon the experience of the listener, partly upon training and partly on his or her neurophysiological structure. In any case, they serve to aid the person involved in a difficult speech-decoding task.

Channel Distortion

Various distortions can be present without affecting the peculiar retention of intelligibility within speech. For example, the speed of recorded speech samples can be doubled—or halved—with only a minor reduction in intelligibility level. Moreover, it can be interrupted with silence or with noise, the peaks of speech waves can be clipped or various frequency ranges can be filtered from speech without a critical degradation of intelligibility. Indeed, speech can retain reasonable decodability despite being simultaneously distorted by a number of factors. However, I should hasten to add that, while speech intelligibility is resistant to a single fairly severe distortion, it decays much more rapidly if two or more are present. The review of these relationships should enhance your understanding of some of the positives and negatives of the decoding task.

Phoneme Characteristics and Word Boundaries

A portion of Chapter 3 was dedicated to a description of vowels, consonants and other phonemes. Basic knowledge about these speech elements and their nature is a fundamental part of the decoders repertoire. Indeed, comprehension of phoneme place and manner (as these factors interface with basic acoustics and physiology) will provide the decoder with useful insights especially when the task is troublesome. As you will remember from descriptions of those rather nasty murders I described in earlier chapters ("The Case of the Nervous Killer"; "The Case of The Overheard Murder"), it was knowledge of the basic phonemic relationships that led to the correct decoding of particularly difficult material.

Another rather important set of relationships with which the decoder must be familiar is word structure, and especially the characteristics of word boundaries (21, 23). There are linguistic rules for word structure (just as there are for sentence structure), and these rules provide important information about what a word might be (or should be) when it cannot be clearly heard. Knowledge about the characteristics of word boundaries is just as important; it bears especially on spectrography, when it is utilized to provide a visual "picture" of the utterance as an aid to the auditory perception process. The decoder not only will be aided in a general way by a solid understanding of word and phoneme boundaries/characteristics but also whenever he or she is faced with a particularly difficult decoding task.

Lexical Stress and Accent

Decoders will find analysis of linguistic stress (exhibited by a speaker) to be quite helpful in the preparation of accurate transcripts. The many nonlinguistic gestures a person uses to enhance the meaning of a message are well known (1, 2, 6, 7, 9, 10, 19, 20); they often are referred to as supersegmentals (the segments of speech being the vowels and consonants). The paralinguistic elements used to create emphasis include variation in F0, phoneme/syllable/word duration, vocal intensity, and so on. Familiarity with these features and how they affect speech can provide important clues to the individual who must transfer heard discourse into written form. Knowledge of the nature and characteristics of dialects (3, 8, 25, 26), either foreign or regional, also can be of aid to the decoder. For one thing, recognition of a dialect by a particular talker within a group can provide an assist when it is necessary to correctly link each speaker with the messages produced. For example, we found differences in dialect to be of critical importance when we attempted to develop transcripts from recordings associated with "The Case of the Well-Endowed Hooker." This person agreed to be wired and attend a party which included a number of drug dealers. As it turned out, it was just as important to know who made a particular statement as it was to learn what was said. Fortunately, several of the talkers exhibited dialects or lexical stress patterns that were fairly unique to them. Had they not, a reasonably accurate transcript would have been an impossibility.

Coarticulation

The concept of coarticulation has been discussed at length; hence, very little additional explanation should be necessary at this juncture. As you will remember from Chapter 3, coarticulation refers to the fact that each speech sound uttered affects all others near it. Little wonder that an appreciation of the effects this feature will have on perceived speech can aid the decoder with his or her processing. Indeed, several of the concepts/methods previously discussed relate directly to coarticulation. Any individual who wishes to understand how decoders operate (or develop a career in this area) would be well advised to enroll in courses that familiarize them with the specifics of this speaking phenomenon.

THE DECODER

A number of references have been made to decoders. Thus, it would appear timely to review their characteristics and training (at least those that are desirable), as well as other elements that may serve to contribute to their skill. As you might expect, effectiveness in this area varies from person to person, with some individuals appearing to have more natural talent than do others for decoding distorted speech. Moreover, a given professional's efficiency will vary somewhat from situation to situation. But, what skills are necessary if an individual is to be effective in this area?

Personnel who are utilized to decode tape recordings should have good hearing, be familiar with police, security or intelligence operations, be trained for the task and enjoy this type of activity. First, and as you might expect, at least normal hearing is a must. Moreover, some people appear to be able to detect the subtleties in quasi-intelligible speech better than others—especially as they gain experience. Naturally, individuals with these talents tend to make the best decoders. Second, basic familiarity with the types of speech associated with law enforcement activities and the courts is critical. Yet this type of background is a little difficult to obtain. Most of the people currently working in this area have developed their understanding primarily from experience. Perhaps internships would be helpful in this case. We have a program of this type in place; it appears to be working well.

Unfortunately, I presently know of no academic programs which are specifically designed to create decoders. Yet there appear to be other types of professionals who can be trained to become competent in this particular area. For example, individuals trained as phoneticians, linguists and speech specialists (especially speech pathologists) appear to be good candidates for this type of work—especially since they will be quite familiar with the information reviewed in the preceding sections. However, I realize that it is not always possible to obtain newcomers who are as highly skilled as are these people. As an alternative, I would suggest that individuals who have had training with degraded speech or difficult transcriptions also could be developed into decoding specialists. In this regard, a military background (especially in aircraft control towers) might be appropriate, as could secretarial experience with law enforcement agencies and/or the courts; indeed, court reporters would be expected to exhibit good potential for this type of work. On the other hand, very few of the several types of people listed are fully qualified; hence, they also would need some kind of specialized training. To illustrate, while the phoneticians/linguists would need training in forensics and/or some background with law enforcement, the secretaries/reporters would need at least some formal training in phonetics and linguistics. It is perhaps this second group that needs the most attention. As I have pointed out, there is little question but information about the manner or place of phoneme or word production, as well as about the acoustics/physiology of speech, is required if reasonable transcripts are to be developed from highly distorted speech material. Phonetics courses are the source of such training/information. Moreover, training on a more technical level would be necessary if the decoder found it necessary to carry out electroacoustic analysis of particularly obscure segments.

Finally, it has been proposed that individuals who are blind or partially sighted might make good decoders (15). As is well known, the blind often exhibit other sensory skills (such as hearing) that are highly developed. What would be necessary in this case is to provide the blind decoder candidates with basic training in phonetics, supervised experience and a method of recording the transcripts (either a braille typewriter or a second tape recorder). In short, there are several classes of individuals who exhibit a potential for successful careers as forensic decoders—assuming, of course that supplemental training and experience is provided to compensate for their deficiencies.

THE MECHANICS OF DECODING

This section is included in order to provide an understanding about the mechanics of the decoding process. It is not designed to train you as a decoder but rather to permit you to understand the process and/or interpret the product provided you by this type of specialist.

First of all, you should be aware that any attempt to obtain a "quick and dirty" transcript of distorted speech probably is doomed to failure. That is, if the method utilized by the decoders does not involve a thorough and structured approach, the result probably will be inadequate and yet additional problems will be created. For example, major textual errors can be expected, and additional hours will have to be spent by someone in an attempt to find and correct these problems/errors. In short, it is important to employ a thorough and systematic approach to decoding. If you do so, the transcript will be as accurate and unchallengable as is possible within the limitations of the material to be decoded. Please note, also, that the person receiving the transcript often can evaluate its accuracy simply by checking the rigor and thoroughness utilized in its development.

Preliminaries

The Log

The first thing a decoder should do is develop a log. It is the starting place for just about every procedure or process encountered in this book. Indeed, it is very important that an accurate log be kept of all decoding operations, as it usually will prove to be invaluable as the project advances. It will aid you in locating sections of interest, especially if disputes/confusions occur, and will be indispensable if you are required to testify in court.

Dubbing

Unless speech enhancement personnel deliver two or more decoding-ready tape recordings, a high-quality copy (or copies) of the original should be made by means of a hard-line link between two matched, laboratory quality, tape recorders. High-speed copiers can be utilized too, especially if there are alot of tapes to duplicate. It is important that the original tape is never used in the processing (except for the dubbing, of course), as accidents can occur even when experienced professionals are involved. The original recording should be stored away in a protected environment and only the copy used in decoding.

Equipment

Good-quality tape recorders should be utilized in the processing, as should a set of high-quality earphones with adjustable volume controls for each ear/channel. Their use permits binaural tapes of all types to be played. They also deliver the best signal possible to the decoder, block out unwarranted environmental noise and, since they are comfortable, reduce listener fatigue.

Process and Technique

Let us now assume that you wish a transcript made of a problem tape recording. How would you proceed if you had to carry out the task yourself and/or how would you evaluate the specialists who did the work and their product? The methods, approaches and techniques that follow should shed some light on the actual mechanics of the decoding process.

Listening

Once the enhanced/filtered copy of the tape is available, the necessary equipment has been assembled and the decoders are identified, it is possible to begin the task. The first procedure (after the preliminaries) is for the decoders to listen to the entire tape recording. This technique constitutes more than a simple familiarization process. It also permits the log to be initiated, particularly diffi- cult material to be identified, proper names to be learned (when possible) and any idiosyncratic characteristics of the recording to be noted. The listening process then is repeated (usually one or more times) as the decoders begin transcript development. This process is a straightforward one. The decoder simply starts at the beginning and records the heard utterances in sequence. Codes are used to indicate where there are minor questions, where decoding may be possible but is questionable and when the words are found to be inaudible or unintelligible. Please note that it is necessary for the decoders and/or their supervisors to continue this process until no further improvement in the written transcript can be made.

Panels and Specialists

The most common approach to the decoding process is simply to have a trained, experienced individual carry out the task. However, a somewhat more efficient approach is to have one decoder process the tape recording and then have a second specialist review and refine it. Probably the most efficient approach at all (especially if the speech on the tape recording is severely degraded) is to assemble a panel of listeners or decoders—at least for the final draft. Of course, you should recognize that to empanel a group of specialists can be quite expensive. I have found that this procedure is particularly effective with recordings associated with aircraft disasters; when the speech involves "street talk," foreign languages or dialects; if the material is highly technical; or if it contains language not familiar to ordinary decoders. Finally, if a decoder is not already knowledgeable about "street language," he or she should attempt to learn as much about it as possible, as it is being encountered with increasing frequency; either that or specialists should be used.

Codes

Once the listening procedure is complete and a reasonable transcript has been developed, it is necessary to apply the codes that have been devised to identify the talkers, problem portions of the transcript and other events. For example, you will want to identify each talker by number (sometimes by name) and by sex. Moreover, in order to insure good communication between the decoder and decision maker, it is necessary to systemically identify questionable words/phrases, inaudible words, pauses, competing speech and similar events. A system such as this has been developed by Dr. P. A. Hollien (16); it is a reasonably good one and will be used as an illustrative approach here. P. A. Hollien employs this system in order to insure that her personnel organize the transcript to clearly describe all of the events contained on the tape recordings. Two examples should suffice to illustrate this system. If sections are found where speech is audible but not intelligible—or where the speech of multiple talkers' interferes with decoding, brackets are used and the approximate number of missing words listed (e.g., [* 2-3 words] or [* 10-14 words]). This approach provides far more information than does the word "inaudible." A second way in which the flow of events is documented is by including a description of the occurrence using a star and slash lines, as follows: "*/footsteps, door closing, two gun shots, loud thump/." Of course, any systematic set of codes is acceptable, providing they are utilized in a consistent manner and an appropriate legend is provided. Other useful information should be included also. The cover page of the transcript should be organized to include: (1) the name of the case, (2) the case number, (3) the name of the relevant attorney, (4) identification of the tape recording or recordings and (5) a case summary or abstract. A legend of the code system used also should be placed on the cover page or prior to the beginning of the text. A typical legend may be found in Table 7-1(16).

Finally, it should be noted that a document which can be called a "first-order transcript" becomes available at the end of the initial stage of processing. It is important that the decoder develop a working copy of this type as soon as possible; it should be one where plenty of room is left for corrections, additions and deletions. Once the first-order transcript is completed, attempts can be initiated to upgrade it to a final version. That is, the work can be reviewed, or a second decoder (or panel) can complete the effort using the available transcript.

Settlement of Disputes

Disputes are bound to occur whenever more than one person is involved in decoding speech from a difficult tape recording. Here again, several options are available. Either the decoding supervisor or (ideally) a panel of listeners should make a final judgment, but only after fully debriefing both of the decoders involved in the dispute. Ordinarily, this approach will provide a remedy. However, if (as it sometimes happens) the segment simply is unclear, you may have to qualify certain portions. That is, it may be necessary to place them in paren-

TABLE 7-1. The Type of Legend that Typically Would be Associated with a Decoding System

Male 1:	First male voice heard on tape (sometimes it is possible to use the person's name).
Male 2:	Second male voice heard on tape (The same procedure is used for females).
[* 2-3 words]	Approximate number of words that are unintelligible, or explanation of events.
(word):	Words found in parentheses are questionable; that is, it is not possible to verify their correctness.
000 to N:	The approximate number (found on the tape recorder meter) where a particular event took place. Also listed (somewhere) must be both the initial number plus the counter speed.
—	Pause or break in the flow of speech.
Misc. Info.:	As needed. Miscellaneous information usually comes at end of the recording or may be described within parentheses.
Time (if needed):	In minutes and seconds.
+ (Proper names or places):	Proper and place names may be identified ahead of time. If they are not, and any confusion exists, they should be spelled as they sound and identified as problemsome by placing them in parentheses.

theses so as to indicate uncertainty; occasionally it is helpful to provide both versions of the disputed section. A very difficult sentence, then, might appear as follows (see Figure 7-1):

145   Male 3:   (If we) are to meet [* 2 words] (Bor'-chen-ko), [* door closes], (he/we) can't—can't be — in ah—(Lake-land) in (September)...

Proper Names

It should be reiterated that proper names often are quite difficult to decode. While speech and language are internally redundant—and markedly affected by text and coarticulation—there is little to no external information inherently associated with a proper name, i.e., that which can aid the decoder in determining its structure. Of course, the problem is mitigated a little if the name is repeated throughout the recording. However, it often is necessary to obtain a machine processing "assist" here if the decoder is to accurately identify severely distorted proper names (and related types of material). As a matter of fact, it is considered legitimate to consult with those individuals familiar with the recording in order to obtain a list of the names which will be encountered. Such information will provide assistance in decoding difficult names, or in differentiating between two names that are similar. Accurate identification of proper names can be especially important if the issue is to determine which of several people produced a specific utterance.

Binaural Listening

Several references to binaural listening have been made; in any of its several forms, this approach greatly increases decoder efficiency. Moreover, a specialized binaural technique was described in the preceding chapter. As you will remember, this procedure was reviewed in some detail; however, a brief reiteration of its characteristics appear to be in order.

As far as we can tell, speech processing carried out at the cortical level permits highly distorted discourse to be reconstructed by a number of means; selective attention, foreground/background processing and binaural hearing are among them. As you will remember, we have developed a technique that utilizes these operations in order to enhance the intelligibility of distorted speech. Specifically, we utilize a highly modified (usually filtered) speech signal which is channeled to the auditor's dominant hemisphere and a low-energy (but complete and unprocessed) signal which is sent simultaneously to the contralateral ear (hemisphere). The mixing of the two signals at the cortical level results in the impression of reduced distortion and enhanced speech. The sensation that often occurs is one where the decoder or listener hears reasonably intelligible speech and the noise fades into an ambient background. As stated, it is extremely important that the paired signals reach the listener's ears simultaneously; that is why we recommend that both parts of a dual-channel recording (from a single recording) be processed simultaneously. This method has proved to be quite effective and can be used whenever simpler techniques do not work. Incidentally, it is "portable" in the sense that, if necessary, the processing can be carried out right in the courtroom.

The Final Transcript

Once the decoding process has been completed and the confusions resolved (whenever possible), the entire transcript should be retyped in final form and carefully evaluated for errors. The potency of the written word is not to be underestimated and, as with other people, juries can be powerfully influenced by a transcript. Indeed, it can prove to be the deciding factor in a trial. Thus, the portrayal of the messages found on a tape recording (and the identity of the individual speakers) must be determined as accurately and fairly as possible. On the other hand, if careless errors (even simple typing errors) are detected, the transcript tends to be impeached. It certainly loses its credibility, and perhaps unfairly so. Thus, it is the obligation of a decoding team to provide as precise a transcript as is possible.

"The Case of the Dirty Sewer Inspector" can be used to illustrate the importance of proper decoding. It seems that the inspector in question was not really interested in his job. Rather, he would approve a building contractor's sewer hookups or septic tank simply by being paid to do so. One contractor resented this practice, went to the police and agreed to be "wired" in order to record the inspector's duplicity. When approached, the inspector took the contractor to his cottage on a lake, where they sat on the porch and made the deal. As it turned out, the tape recording contained about two hours of a general uproar (cricket and frog noises, walking sounds, the creak of rocking chairs on a wooden porch, and so on) with speech heard but faintly in the background. However, after the police sent the tape to our group for enhancement, enough speech could be heard (especially with respect to the bribe) to support an indictment and trial. The jury was composed of six rather elderly women and the presiding judge was a stickler for proper procedure. Hence, he made me (1) play the entire tape and (2) carry out the speech enhancement right in the courtroom. No transcript was permitted.

The tape was played. After about 45 minutes of listening to swamp noise (the bribe occurred near the end of the two hours), the judge turned to me (to be truthful, at this juncture, I was nearly asleep on the witness stand) and said, "I can't understand any of this; hence, I'm throwing out the tapes." Since the entire case depended on this evidence, the prosecutor was apoplectic. Almost as an afterthought, the judge said to me, "I can't understand what is being said and I'll bet you can't either." "Oh, yes I can," I retorted, "That's my specialty." He then said, "It's lunch time. Go write out a transcript of the tape where the bribe was made and bring it to me with just that part of the recording." I did so, and after lunch, the judge listened only to the 10-minute portion of the tape that included the bribe while reading the transcript. He then said, "Fine," and ruled that the jury should read my transcript while listening to the bribe portion of tape. What a remarkable turn of events! The jury now was permitted to hear evidence of the bribe—and see it all written down—rather than not being provided any evidence at all. An aside: the participants on the tape recording indulged in a great deal of swearing. After hearing some of it, the jury forewoman became so indignant that she left the courtroom in a huff. The judge had some difficulty in persuading her to return. It was the only time I have ever seen a juror attempt to walk out on a trial.

SUMMARY

As many prosecutors and defense attorneys have discovered (sometimes to their distress), it is only those transcripts of tape recordings which are accurate and reliably developed that ordinarily can be utilized effectively in the courtroom. Yet the decoding of distorted or masked speech is not a simple task; rather, it can involve a long and rigorous process. As has been pointed out, efficient decoding demands a good understanding of the law enforcement milieu, the sources of distortion, the acoustics of speech and language, phonetics and the actual decoding process. Further, the decoder must be able to identify problems, possibly enhance the speech on the recording and be familiar with the procedures used in dubbing, filtering, development of binaural recordings and, of course, practical decoding techniques. Nonetheless, the end product of these efforts can be quite valuable in investigations and/or trials, as a good transcript can stand as a solid piece of evidence—even if it has been developed from a poor tape recording.

CHAPTER 8

Authentication of Tape Recordings

INTRODUCTION

As you are aware, tape recordings are now part of almost everyone's life, especially here in these United States. They are so common that the magnitude of their use actually is difficult to comprehend. Indeed, this already extensive utilization of both audio and videotape recordings is spreading at an accelerating rate. Witness the recent DeLorean case where federal agents attempted to demonstrate that the defendant had violated the laws involving controlled substances by the use of surreptitious video recordings. That DeLorean was not convicted is beside the point; what is relevant is that this technique is becoming an important one for gathering evidence. It is also useful in crime countermeasures, intelligence work and the courts.

The question now arises: are abuses possible? Can a person successfully modify a tape recording to alter a situation or for personal gain? For example, is it possible for (1) an enthusiastic agent to edit a tape recording in order to enhance the case against a suspect, (2) a businessman to alter a tape recording in order to improve his bargaining position, or (3) a suspect to modify one in order to absolve himself from a crime? The answer is a qualified "yes." Hence, procedures must be developed that will permit neutral parties to discover if an audiotape or videotape recording has been modified in some manner or if it is authentic in all possible respects. The focus of this chapter will be upon these issues. Please note, however, that I will feature the techniques used to validate audio recordings, as they are basic to the problem and, in any case, many of the methods used for authenticating videotapes parallel these (audio) approaches anyway.

But, who uses tape recordings in the first place? By now it should be clear. They are employed by numerous groups; included are law enforcement agencies, hospitals, businesses, the military, intelligence agencies, security firms, educational institutions, and so on. Indeed, the nearly monumental increase in the use of this inexpensive and attractive method of storing voiced messages has led to a substantial number of problems related to the technique itself. Some of these problems have been discussed in previous chapters; it now would appear timely to examine the ways by which the integrity of a tape recording may be upheld or discredited.

THE PROBLEM

The problem of tape recording authenticity is a rather serious one, as any challenge relative to validity suggests that someone has tampered with evidence or falsified information. Worse yet, a challenge can arise at any time: when the recording is being made or monitored, when its contents are being processed for some purpose, in a court of law and so on. It usually is made by one of the relevant parties, who will claim that the tape has been tampered with or in some manner does not represent the actual events that took place (either quantitatively or temporally) at the time it was made. This issue of tape recording validity is being encountered with increasing frequency and is one that must be met in a systematic and thorough manner.

General Definitions

One of the current problems in this area is the number and types of people who are attempting to validate or challenge tape recordings. Obviously, the people who should be responsible for these tasks are relevant and experienced scientists or, possibly, those audio engineers who have had secondary training in phonetics and/or speech. One appropriate class of scientist is, of course, the phonetician—an individual who is trained in the acoustics and physiology of speech, language and linguistics, the hardware of engineering, the software of computer sciences and perception/psychoacoustics. A second group of appropriate scientists includes electrical/computer engineers who also have some background in the phonetic sciences; scientists of either type must also be experienced in forensics. Nevertheless, many other individuals—no matter how unsuited they are—attempt to validate or impeach tape recordings; included are agents, private detectives, electronic technicians and even laypeople (6). Few use a systematic approach; very few do a complete analysis; and some use rather odd techniques that apparently they think are of relevance.

A number of other problems exist also. Some relate to the definitions employed (or lack of them); others relate to philosophical considerations. For example, some practitioner's suggest that, as long as a tape recording was not "tampered" with after it was made, it is "authentic" (2, 11, 13). They ignore the fact that all kinds of manipulations could have been carried out during an interrogation or telephone call in order to modify what actually happened. To illustrate, an individual could tap his or her own telephone, call someone, and ask: "Did you steal my wallet?" and then shut off the tape recorder. In the ensuing minutes, this same individual could so harass the person being called that when he or she then asks: "Do you think I am being unfair?" and turns on the tape recorder, the poor recipient would be heard to scream an affirmative answer. Examples of this type are virtually endless.

In my judgment, it also is poor procedure if the practitioner does not carry out an authentication of the entire tape recording. From sworn courtroom testimony (11, 13), I have discovered that the FBI agents who are assigned this responsibility only examine those portions of the tape recording that are challenged. It appears from this testimony that they are primarily concerned with refuting challenges directed at tapes which have been made by law enforcement agencies rather than determining their actual integrity. Of course, I must concede that they probably receive many more requests for service than they possibly can meet anyway. Moreover, the problem is complicated by the fact that some tapes are continually interrupted due to federal laws that prevent complete recordings from being made in some surveillance situations (more about this "minimization problem" later). On the other hand, whether or not special agents should be authenticating tape recordings in the first place is open to some question, especially since they insist that they have not established any procedures or rules to govern their work (11, 13).

For my part, I would judge it manditory to establish guidelines as to what is and what is not an authentic tape recording—and what procedures and techniques permit this question to be satisfactorily answered. The approaches and materials that follow are based on my own experience and research in this area (5, 6), as well as on the work of others (1, 8, 9, 16).

A Definition of Authenticity

My definition of an authentic tape recording is predicated upon the following five assumptions or relationships. First, it must have captured all of the audio events that occurred during the entire target period. Second, this "period of interest" must include the entire series of happenings relevant to the intelligence contained by the recording; that is, a tape recording cannot be initiated at some juncture after the conversations have been going on or before the entire interview or relevant dialogue has been completed. Third, it must be shown that the tape recording has not been interrupted in any manner (i.e., the entire recording was made at one time and with no omissions) and fourth, that none of its sections have been removed. Finally, it also is mandatory that nothing has been added to the tape recording; that is, it must contain only that material which was originally recorded. Thus, I believe you can see that to be "authentic," a tape recording must include a complete set of events, and nothing can have been added, deleted or changed at any time during the recording or subsequently. As stated, I am aware that federal laws have been passed that require law enforcement personnel to minimize tape recordings in some situations. Apparently, these statutes were designed to prevent agents from invading the privacy of innocent citizens and/or tampering with surveilance tape recordings. The processes involved here are quite awkward both for the agent and the (tape) examiner. What eavesdroppers must do is listen to a conversation for a short while and continue the recording only if incriminating dialogue is heard. Otherwise they must stop listening and turn off the tape recorder. Recordings of this type are quite difficult to defend as valid; sometimes it proves possible, but other times the hurdles presented are virtually insurmountable. Finally, as you can see, the definitions provided above focus on audio recordings. However, it is but a short journey from audio to video. Admittedly, there will be some additional tests/procedures to be carried out with videotapes but the two processes are quite similar.

Assumptions

Certain assumptions must be made by the scientist or practitioner prior to making any attempt to authenticate a tape recording. First, it is important to remember that no tape authentication examiner actually can tell anything about a recording other than whether it has or has not been modified in some manner. That is, even if a tape recording appears to have been altered, there is nothing in the processes involved that can provide any real information about the intent of the person who (somehow) modified it. Thus, it is impossible to tell if a recording has been "tampered with, doctored, and/or fraudulently created" from the analysis process alone. These terms imply intent—and a reprehensible, devious one at that! However, since all an examiner can do is demonstrate that a tape recording does not meet all five of the cited criteria for validity, the descriptive words "tampering," "doctored," and "fraud" should be strictly avoided. There simply is no way to determine if the person who made the alteration did so innocently or for nefarious purposes. The fact, that these (somewhat negative) words occasionally are used in the text to follow should not dilute this admonition in any way. We all know that fraudulent events occur; hence, I feel free to discuss them. Yet no one can assign intent to a tape edit, because there is nothing in any processes we can utilize that will tell us why the alteration occurred.

The second assumption involves the two-stage processing that must be carried out. If the examiner is to meet his or her responsibilities properly, the tape recording first must be treated as if it *had* been modified, tampered with or edited in some manner. The reputation or presumed integrity of the individual/agency making the tape recording should have no effect on the thoroughness of this examination. Indeed, only a painstakingly rigorous and objective examination will insure that evidence of tampering will be uncovered if it exists, or that any section of the tape that exhibits a "suspicious" event will be appropriately analyzed. The second stage of the process is one which requires that every effort be made to explain each questionable area, or event of concern, which is encountered. Indeed, events ordinarily can be found that appear suspicious, yet are not caused by alterations at all. Thus, the actual cause for each of these occurrences must be determined. It is just as important to avoid the identification of an innocuous event as a modification as it is to miss an alteration.

I must admit that during my testimony, the "other side" always gleefully responds to the first part of this two-stage model. They seem to find it helpful in their attempts to turn me from an unbiased expert into an advocate (incidentally, so far they have not been able to do so). They often take the first part of the paired assumptions out of context and present it in the form of an accusatory question. Apparently, they use that strange set of perceptions that permit some people to blithely use partial data for their own personal bent. But, of course, they should not be allowed to do so. The expert simply cannot become an advocate (see Chapter 16). What must be done is to patiently point out that if an unbiased and objective decision is to be made about a tape recording, it should be evaluated rigorously and appropriate procedures must be followed. Therein lies a problem. Some examiners appear to have difficulty in resisting a client's wishes (a client can be a person or an agency) to read more into data than actually exists. Appeals of this type must be ignored, and both parts of the two-stage method I have suggested carried out. To follow any other course would be either unethical or dangerous. Personally, I find that I have to disappoint my clients over half the time when they wish a tape recording challenged and nearly a third of the time when they wish one authenticated.

Finally, it is only fair to indicate that there are limitations to the authentication techniques to be described. For example, it is probably true that an appropriately trained team of phoneticians and audioengineers could fabricate a recording which would be difficult, if not impossible, to detect as having been edited. At least, they could do so if they were provided enough time, appropriate equipment and large quantities of the speech of those individuals to be heard on the recordings. As a matter of fact, my wife (Dr. P. A. Hollien) and I have been able to create a training tape of this type. We made some of the modifications so obvious that they are easy to identify, others difficult to find and a few just about impossible to detect. However, it is my opinion that the creation of a totally undetectable fake recording constitutes so formidable a challenge that the probability of it actually happening is relatively slight. Hence, the techniques reviewed below should be quite adequate for any but the most extraordinary authentication task.

GENERAL PROCEDURES

As has been implied, the procedures to be described were developed in response to the needs of law enforcement agencies, public defenders, state and federal courts, defense attorneys, the military and business organizations. Over the years, our general approach has proven to be stable and effective. However, we have been able to upgrade some of the procedures as new technologies have become available. When considering our techniques, please remember the criteria for authenticity, i.e., to be validated, a tape recording must contain all of the acoustic events that occurred as they occurred; no portions can have been added or removed. Finally, a number of the listed procedures are employed and re-employed at various stages of the examination, whereas others are used in parallel with each other. Attempts will be made to point out these situations wherever they exist.

The discussions to follow will be divided into four parts: two major and two minor. The first major section involves the preliminary steps to be taken—an area that includes both analysis and housekeeping. The analyses described can be carried out only on the original tape recordings and equipment. The focus of the second major section is on the analyses that must be carried out once the preliminary steps are complete. The two final sections are short. The first will cover the special problems encountered when a tape recording is "minimized," and the second, the authentication of video recordings.

PRELIMINARY STEPS

Listening to the Tape

Quite obviously it is important to first listen to the tape recording in question—in its entirety—in order to (1) fully understand its general nature, (2) develop tentative impressions concerning the potential areas of difficulty and (3) locate sections that must be intensively analyzed at a later time. It is desirable (but not absolutely necessary) to listen to the original tape when you first encounter it—even before the physical examination takes place—as doing so will aid you in insuring that the copies you make are accurate ones and that you will not miss anything relevant when you make the physical examination.

The Log

It would seem almost too obvious to suggest that a detailed written log be kept of all activities carried out. Nevertheless, the need to record each and every procedure employed is mandatory if you are going to remain organized and be able to focus attention on those sections which require intensive and/or complex analysis; it will be of even greater importance if you are required to testify in court. Moreover, certain problem areas will emerge repeatedly as the several analysis techniques are applied; you may detect others only by one of the procedures. Since all such questionable events must be intensively examined, a log permits their accurate and quick location as the evaluation process proceeds. Most important, it prevents accidental omissions of analyses that should be conducted.

The Physical Examination

As stated, the physical examination of a tape recording constitutes an important phase of the authentication process. There are several events/items to consider here: (1) the amount of tape on the reel, (2) physical damage to (or condition of) the reel/cassette, (3) splices, (4) the accuracy of the working copies and (5) the equipment. It is at this stage that attempts are initiated to determine if the recording in question actually is an original.

Amount of Tape

It is important to determine, insofar as is possible, if the "correct" amount of tape (i.e., the amount intended by the manufacturer) is on the reel or in a cassette. Of course, it is possible to make this determination only within certain limits. However, I have found that many manufacturers bring the wound tape to within 5-7 mm of the reel edge; others simply indicate how many feet of tape are on the reel. Small variations (plus or minus 5%, say) provide very little informa-tion, but large ones suggest that something has happened to that particular tape. Cassettes require a slightly different approach as they usually are calibrated by time (a 30-minute tape, etc.). It is fairly easy to time the amount of tape on a cassette and determine if it is of reasonably appropriate length. In both cases, it is useful to examine the amount of tape on other reels/cassettes (of that same type, of course) sold by that particular manufacturer.

Physical Condition

Examinations in this area tend to be confined primarily to cassettes. It is important to examine the cassettes for pry marks or damage to the screws that hold them together. Negative evidence here is cause for concern. It is well also to evaluate the history of the tape itself. Has the evidence pouch been opened? Are there inappropriate identification marks on the reel or cassette? Is there evidence that the tape was used previously?

Splices

One of the more critical (potential) modifications an examiner must attempt to detect is the presence of splices on the recording tape. If they are found, it must be assumed that the tape has been edited. While the reason for such an alteration may have been an innocent one, there is no way for the examiner to know how much of the recording has been removed (or added) or for what reason. Hence, if spliced, the tape is compromised.

There are two major types of splices: adhesive and heat. In the first case, the two ends of the interrupted tape are cropped—usually at an angle—so that they butt together smoothly—and a piece of splicing tape applied to the back (the nonoxide side). Ordinarily the splicing tape is of a different color than the recording tape and is easily seen. In a heat splice, the two ends of the tape are overlapped and melted together. Heat splices are more difficult to see, but they create an abnormal thickness in the tape at the point of the splice.

Portrayal of a reasonably good technique used to monitor a tape for splices may be seen in Figure 8-1. It should be noted that the examiner is listening to the tape as he visually monitors it. Sometimes the presence of a splice is revealed by an audible click as the tape passes over the playback head—at least if it is poorly made or magnetized blades/scissors were used. Note also that the examiner is allowing the tape to pass over his finger after it leaves the playback head. The human fingertip is very sensitive and splices often can be felt as well as seen and/or heard. The mounted magnifying glass is to assist the examiner in locating splices. This procedure also permits tape distortions of an innocuous nature (viz., stretching, crumpling, twists) to be detected and logged. It is important that such events be identified, as they often create distortions in the recorded signal or add extraneous signals to the recording. Obviously, proper identifica-tion of these events is important as the click caused by a twist in the tape may sound like a splice.

It also should be pointed out that, occasionally, a tape is accidentally broken

Figure 8-1. Photograph of an examiner checking a tape for splices. Note that he is listening to the recording, observing the tape through a magnifying glass and letting it run over his finger. While somewhat more awkward, the process is the same for a cassette tape.

due to mishandling. In such a case, the person repairing the tape should have had the good sense to carefully place the torn ends in approximation with each other and splice them together. If a splice is found, the oxide side of the tape should be magnified at the point of the splice and the ends examined. If they are ragged and found to match each other, it can be concluded that the splice was made only to repair an accidental break and that no portion of the recording has been removed. However, if the two ends do not fit together, or if they have been cut to permit a smooth splice, it must be assumed that an unknown quantity of tape has been removed, or perhaps added.

Making the Duplicate

At this juncture, one or more good working copies of the tape recording should be made so that further tests can be carried out under laboratory conditions—and so that there is no chance of damaging or destroying evidence. It is very important that the copy be an accurate one, because an alteration could be missed, or one found that did not exist, if the copies were not exact duplicates of the original. Hence, they should be made on high-quality, calibrated tape recorders or on a high-speed professional dubbing system. Moreover, the recorders should be directly coupled together (hard-line, not speaker to microphone). Very little that is of relevance to the authentication process will be forfeited if care is taken with the duplication process. Finally, all copies should be evaluated against the original in order to insure that the dubbing process is error free.

Is the Tape Recording an Original?

One of the problems any expert in this area will have to face involves whether or not the tape recording being examined for authenticity actually is the original. This issue is not a trivial one, because it is not possible to make a judgment as to whether a tape is authentic unless the original is examined. Moreover, if it was cleverly altered and then a copy made, the modifications can be quite difficult to detect. But how does one determine if a tape recording is an original or a copy of some other tape? I have supplemented my own efforts here by observing the work of several other individuals (2, 16). They indicate that determination of originality is an easy task but I am not persuaded that it is. On the other hand, a reasonable conclusion often can be drawn. Of course, the courts accept the "originality" of a tape recording based on an unbroken chain of custody. If the evidence package is sealed and signed properly, a jurist will assume that no one had access to the tape except those individuals who have placed their names on it. Perhaps so, but this logic seems a little tenuous to me as it may be the very people who have had custody of the tape who have altered it. In any case, some of the procedures to follow can assist an examiner in determining if a tape recording is an original.

First off, the electronic signatures associated with the operation of tape recorders can be used to evaluate the tape's originality. For example, if it can be established that only one such unit was used in making the tape, it also can be inferred that positive evidence of originality has been uncovered. These data become yet more meaningful if it is found that the recorder purported to have been used for the recording actually was the one employed (see below and Chapter 14). Third, if hum can be detected, it can be utilized also. Of course, hum results from AC to DC leakage due to a faulty or poor power supply; hence, battery-powered units do not tend to create this type of signal on a tape. If the unit is known to utilize line voltage and but a single hum is observed, this event can be assumed to support the notion that the tape is an original.

Most of the time, originality is presumed due to the absence of evidence to the contrary. If hum is present on a tape made on battery-powered equipment, if incorrect or multiple tape recorder signatures are found, rather strong (but circumstantial) evidence exists that it is not an original. In any case, the examiner must be sensitive to this problem and no amount of authoritative assurances should dissuade him or her from carrying out extensive tests in order to determine whether or not a specific tape recording is the "original."

Incidentally, it should be noted at this juncture that sometimes these preliminary examinations can be deferred if a good-quality copy of the tape is available. That is, the laboratory analyses (see below) can be initiated first and the physical examination of the original carried out at a later time. Moreover, there have been several instances where I found no need to examine the original or the equipment—and for good reason. In each instance, analysis of the copy led to the inescapable conclusion that further tests would be a waste of time, as there was no evidence at all that the tape in question had been modified. Obviously, these findings were disappointing to the client, but it is not possible to go any further than your data will permit.

Sometimes it is difficult to obtain access to the purported original. Nevertheless, it is very important that the examiner persevere in doing so. Let me illustrate this contention by citing "The Case of the Overeager U.S. Marshall" (he was the defendant). In this instance, I was asked to authenticate a tape which was purported to be an exact copy of the original. As you might expect, I had asked to examine the originals (and make my own copy) but was denied access due to "security" reasons. When I pointed out that I had security clearance (both military and civilian), the statement was reiterated but with the word "our" before "security." In any event, I found evidence that the tape had been altered but also that the copy might not be genuine. At this juncture, I asked for and received a second "first copy of the original." This second copy was found to be different from the the the one I had received initially. It also appeared to have been modified but in different places than the first. My third request to examine the "original" finally was granted. I did so (it was physically unremarkable), made a copy and analyzed it. This tape was quite different from the other two and, ironically, had only one or two questionable events on it. The important point to remember here is that authenticity decisions can only be predicated by examinations of original tape recordings (ultimately anyway) and to base your conclusions on an untested copy could lead to disaster. Anyway, anyone who settles for anything short of a full analysis is not behaving ethically.

Unfortunately, if an original tape does not exist, there is no way you can authenticate it. I was drawn into this type of dispute in "The Case of the Careful Killer." In this instance, several college students were living together but having some difficulty getting along. One apparently felt that he was in mortal danger so, on a particular night, either lured, invited or permitted one of the other students access to his room. He then proceeded to shoot and kill his visitor, all the while recording the event. His contention was that the tape recording proved that he acted in self-defense. Nonetheless, he was convicted and sentenced to a jail term. After spending several years in prison, his attorneys reopened the case. By then, however, all of the evidence (including the tape recording) had been destroyed. At this juncture, an investigator came forward saying that he had made a copy of the cited tape recording for his "collection." Unfortunately, the tape recorders he used were poor ones and he made his copy by a speaker-to-microphone process in an open room. The tape in question was inferior at best; it exhibited several clicks and dropouts. My position was simple. This tape recording could not be authenticated because it was not the original and that relationship alone destroyed its integrity. The fact that there was evidence suggesting it may have been manipulated, at least at some juncture, was immaterial. In this instance, my judgment was countered by some federal agents who claimed that this tape was as good as an original. They were wrong, of course.

Equipment Evaluation

There are a number of reasons to examine the equipment actually used in making the tape recording you are examining. For one thing, you often can tell something is wrong (or not wrong) just by looking at it; a pretty obvious example would be if the tape is reel-to-reel but the recorder is a cassette unit. Moreover, you will want to obtain the recorder switching "signatures" and any information you can on its idiosyncrasies. Hence, tests on the *original* equipment must be carried out in order to determine if it actually was used and if the recording specified as the original was made on the system cited. The procedures to be utilized involve making a series of test recordings under conditions of quiet, noise and speech—and repeating them while serially operating all switches on all devices within the system. Evaluations then must be made in order to determine if the signatures found on the recorded tape are the same as those produced by the equipment which supposedly was used for this purpose. Moreover, any idiosyncratic features exhibited by the apparatus often can be used to demonstrate that events they add to the tape recording actually are innocuous. In any case, I cannot stress strongly enough that it is important to learn all you can about how the tape recording was made and about the nature and operation of the equipment used.

Evidence of Stop-Start Activity and of Rerecording

The final step of the physical examination of a tape recording is not routinely carried out by most examiners. Nevertheless, it is one that can be quite important in certain instances and, hence, should be among those approaches considered. It involves examination of all or, at least, certain sections of the oxide side of the tape recording. That is, one or both of two methods may be employed to determine if: (1) the tape recorder has been stopped and restarted, (2) portions of the recording have been erased or, even, (3) a portion has been erased and a second, or overrecording, has been made. Obviously, if the tape recorder has been stopped and restarted, there is no foolproof way to tell if the recording was interrupted for a moment, for an hour or for a day. However, if such evidence is found, it demonstrates that the recorded materials or messages are not complete and the recording, therefore, is compromised. You will remember that, if a section of the tape has been erased, it is possible to measure the length of the period during which the recorded materials were obliterated. However, due to the powerful action of the tape recorder erase head, it will not be possible to determine what was removed (see again Chapter 4).

As stated, the physical processes by which evidence of rerecording or stop-start activity can be obtained is of two types. The first of these involves the locating of the marks or tracks a tape recorder mechanism sometimes leaves on the oxide side of a tape when it is started, while running and when it is stopped. These marks reveal little but that the tape has been played or recorded. However, occasionally, they are unique enough to be utilized in identifying the specific tape recorder used and in some instances they can provide evidence of how the recorder was operated. These markings often can be detected by observation with a large magnifying glass or a low-power microscope.

Some of the events cited above can be better detected by a second process—that of observation of the recording patterns themselves (see Figure 8-2). That is, certain solutions, powders, or manufactured devices will permit the magnetic recording pattern to be visualized and any disturbances in it perceived. For example, the Minnesota Mining and Manufacturing Company (3M) markets a "magnetic tape viewer" (Scotch brand) of this type; several types of fluid also are available for this purpose. However, it should be remembered that unless the tape recording is extremely short, this procedure is so tedious and time consuming as to be potentially counterproductive. Rather, it is a method that should be utilized on a selective basis and, especially, when evidence of a potential interruption has been found. In such instances, the technique is important because these discontinuities may permit observation of the interrupt, off-on, or splice patterns (if, indeed, there are any).

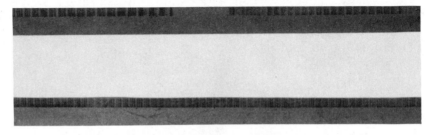

Figure 8-2. Photographs of the magnetic patterns seen on quarter-track tape recordings. Above, the pair of tapes were treated with Kyread DIP-C magnetic tape developer. The tape pattern below was processed with a 3M viewer; note the interrupted configuration. This break shows that the tape has been spliced and then rerecorded.

LABORATORY EXAMINATION

Once the physical examination is complete and good working copies have been made, an intensive laboratory analysis may be carried out. It should be noted at this juncture that, even though much of the description of tape recording authentication appears in the early part of the chapter, most of the analyses are carried out on working copies. Thus, the lengthy review of the bases employed in testing the integrity of a tape recording and the details of the physical examination should not lead you to believe that most of the work now has been completed. Quite to the contrary, long hours of analysis and interpretation follow if a thorough, objective evaluation is to be accomplished.

Auditory Analysis of the Recorded Signal

Constant reference has been made to the need for multiple auditory monitorings of the material recorded on the tape or tapes being examined. So far, however, no description has been provided of the potential cues that are sought and their importance. Moreover, up until this point, the tape recording probably has been heard only once or, at the most, twice and but few entries have been made in the log relative to what we call "areas of concern." It now is necessary to listen to the entire tape recording a number of times, all the while making detailed notes relevant to problem events. As has been stated, if the examiner is thoroughly familiar with the material that was recorded (and how it was recorded), he or she now can concentrate on locating the events that need to be identified as either modifications or innocuous happenings—that is, if they know what to look for critically. What are some of these occurrences?

Pulses/Clicks

As it turns out, most of the auditory events to be located, studied and hopefully identified are overt in nature. For example, many take the form of heard clicks, pulses, thumps, clangs, rings, crackles or other such transients. Any such occurrence is potentially indicative of an alteration and must be evaluated. It is necessary to stress that an appropriate examination of each of these events should be conducted, even though it is recognized that signals of this type can result from a large number of causes, only a very few of which might be due to modification of the recording. Clicks and related signals can result from (1) innocent events occurring anywhere in the entire system (e.g., short circuits, operation of motors, internal activation of switches), (2) operational changes to other units in the system (e.g., an automatic turn on, if an operator utilizes a switch to phase in another device, a telephone hang-up), (3) events external to the recording system (the closing of a door; environmental thumps near the microphone, the click of a pencil) and/or (4) the operation of relays if the recording is made over a telephone network. In short, the presence of clicks, pulses and similar phenomena need not reflect alterations, but, since they usually occur if the recording has been modified (by turning the tape recorder "off" and then "on" or by splicing out a section and then rerecording the entire tape), each and every event of this type must be thoroughly examined. Incidentally, the use of a tape recorder with a counter or timer is useful, as you can keep track of the amount of tape that has been played and return to a particular place at will. In any case, if the cited identification procedures are followed, the relevant sections will begin to emerge as potentially "troublesome" areas and can be noted and logged.

A second category of suspicious events involves changes (especially abrupt ones) in recording level. This type of phenomenon can signal the existence of manipulation, as it could result from a section of the tape being removed in such a way that two different gain levels are butted together. However, these events also can result from (1) artifacts in the recording procedure, (2) operation of some nonrecorder related equipment or (3) a shift in the distance between the signal being recorded and the pickup microphone. Again, however, any changes of this type, especially if abrupt, must be individually examined in an attempt to determine their cause. Just as important is a sudden change in background and/or if the ambient noise level abruptly changes (see below). Additionally, an altered tape recording sometimes can be identified by other aberrations in the heard signal—such as perceived echoes, impressions of multiple recordings, fade-outs or dropouts and so on. Indeed, very abrupt fade-outs and fade-ins (of 500 ms or less, say) are particularly suspicious, as they may signal a place where some type of editing has occurred. As stated, each of these occurrences must be evaluated for its cause.

Finally, it is important to greatly amplify any section of the recording where the signal either disappears or appears markedly reduced. It is sometimes possible, by this method, to reconstitute that portion of the message that has been accidentally damped in its intensity or even "lost" by (1) inadvertent reduction in input gain, (2) certain types of short circuits or (3) changes in the impedance among the component circuits. Perhaps more important, amplification of such sections sometimes can lead to a determination of whether the reduced signal occurred accidentally or might have been intended. As an example, if loss of signal is accompanied by other evidence of stop-start activity (at the points where the signal is lost and where it reoccurs) and it cannot be amplified enough to decode the message, it might be concluded that an attempt was made to remove the messages and/or sections that originally had been recorded between those two points. On the other hand, if the signal can be amplified enough to be heard, and/or there is no evidence of stop-start activity, signal loss probably is due to some accidental occurance. The word "probably" is especially relevant here as this problem occurred in "The Case of the Serial Killer"—one which involved a young man who took pleasure in raping and killing young women. He had been captured and problems arose during his interrogation. We were asked both to decode what was said during these sessions and to be ready to testify that the tapes were authentic. We very soon discovered that the defendant was a very clever person and the way he behaved created the difficulties. When questioned, he would make teasing statements—ones that would excite the interrogators. Their loud speech coupled with his very soft speech and a series of clicks he made with a soft drink can created severe decoding difficultes (of his speech) and the tape recording appeared to have been altered. We were able to demonstrate the source of the clicks plus recover his very soft responses to questions. In short, the cited evaluations provided the prosecution with a transcript plus a demonstration that the tape was a valid one.

Visual Observation of the Recorded Signal

Two methods can be utilized to permit visual examination of the signals on a tape recording; both may be seen pictured in Figure 8-3. Note again that the examiner is listening to the recording as these procedures are carried out. The first technique involves observation of an analog of the recorded signal; it appears as a trace on the cathode ray oscilloscope screen (it is seen on the examiner's left). By listening to the tape and observing the patterns that can be visualized from the CRO, questionable events can be identified and, often, related to causal factors. Basically, the technique is utilized as follows. Any episode (a click, for instance) that the examiner wishes to analyze may be both heard and simultaneously visualized on the CRO; it may be evaluated repeatedly simply by replaying the tape recording. Admittedly, no permanent record is provided by this process, but a comparison of the relative amplitude, pattern duration, etc., of the click with other events and signal features often permits conclusions to be drawn relative to the cause of the intruding event. For occurrences of longer

Figure 8-3. An examiner is shown listening to the tape and visually observing the signal on a CRO. Also shown (upper right) is a computer-processed digital display. A hard copy of either of the plots can be made at the discretion of the examiner.

duration, a quick estimate of the frequency of the signal being studied can be obtained by a careful operation of the frequency-synchronization control circuit of the CRO. In short, visual analysis of this type can provide both primary and supplemental information about questionable sections of the tape recording.

The examiner photographed in Figure 8-3 also may be seen making a permanent record of the tape-recorded signal on the computer to his right and on a high-speed level recorder—a device that produces a (relative) amplitude-by-time trace. Devices of this type include the Bruel and Kjaer Model 2305 level recorder, the Kay Elemetrics spectrometer (operated in its time-by-amplitude mode) and the Honeywell 1508A Visicorder (unfortunately, they all have inertial problems to overcome). In short, this technique provides analog patterns of the damped wave of a signal as a function of time. Although utilized extensively by some groups (11, 13), this approach is a rather crude one. It does provide an approximation of the analog trace but with only fair time resolution. Nevertheless, information of this type can be utilized to supplement observations resulting from other more sophisticated evaluation methods. For example, the extent of intensity changes (in relative dB) that occur can be determined, and some patterns associated with stop-start activity can be quickly visualized; observations of these types would lead to the development of computer-generated serial spectrograms and digital signal analysis, respectively. That is, if it is suspected that the tape recorder has been stopped and restarted, appropriate signal activity can be compared to that created for known "off-ons." If the disturbances are similar, more sophisticated techniques can be applied; if they are nonexistent, it must be assumed that the click in question resulted from some other happening. In short, high-speed level recordings can provide a useful dimension to the overall authentication approach and their use is recommended especially during the preliminary analyses.

Noise Analysis

Any unwanted signal on a tape recording reduces the probability that the message(s) it contains can be decoded easily. Indeed, as I pointed out in Chapter 7, such signals can be classified as "forensic noise" by individuals who are involved in decoding tasks, as they interfere with attempts to accurately transcribe the taped utterances. On the other hand, noise can be helpful in speaker identification cases, as its analysis can provide information about the speaker and/or his or her location irrespective of the voice-to-voice matching process. These signals include music and competing talkers, as well as those resulting from wind, clothing, street and motor noises. More to the point, analysis of noise of these types often can serve a useful purpose when you are examining a tape recording for authenticity. For example, if a song from a jukebox or television, heard in the background, changes abruptly (to another song), evidence is provided that the tape recording was interrupted or edited. Related indications of manipulation would include relatively abrupt changes in the level of an ambient noise, or in its spectral characteristics. On the other hand, if a click was observed, but it was unaccompanied by direct physical evidence of a splice or change in recorder operation, and analysis of the background noise revealed no change in ambient level or spectral components (or the click occurred within a word), the examiner could be reasonably confident that there had been no alteration of the tape recording. In short, the examiner often can utilize noise analysis to determine the source of a particular event found on the tape recording being studied.

Electronic Analyses

The techniques and procedures cited above will provide evidence—pro or con—about most of the events of concern; indeed, many already will have been identified as innocuous or, perhaps, as possible evidence of alterations. On the other hand, there may be some events which are difficult to explain or that require more sophisticated analysis than that already discussed. For example, time-frequency-amplitude spectrography can be useful in providing graphic impressions of what the acoustic events look like over time. A more sophisticated approach, as seen in Figure 8-4, can provide an indication of spectrum change either at a particular point in time or over time. These data are computer generated and digital; they can be analyzed quantitatively as well as graphically evaluated on a pattern-matching basis. There are many relatively sophisticated electronic or computer techniques that can be applied selectively to the tape

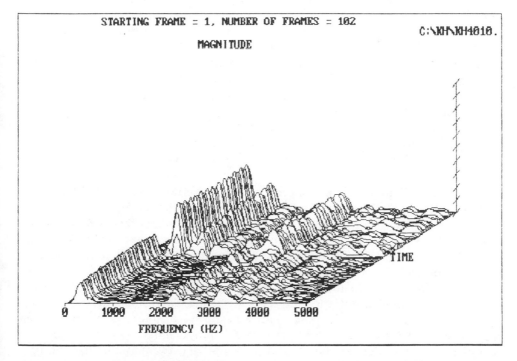

Figure 8-4. A splice has been found. When a click was heard, the examiner digitized the relevant section and displayed it spectrographically. The very abrupt change from one speech pattern to another signals the presence of a splice—one that was made on an earlier version of the recording.

authentication process. However, so many of these analysis combinations exist that it would be virtually impossible to list them all. With this limitation in mind, let me provide a specific example of the way clicks can be evaluated by digital processing.

As you will remember, I indicated that while high-speed level recorders and Visicorders could be useful in studying clicks, many far more sophisticated approaches were available. These more advanced techniques may involve the use of (1) specialized electronic hardware, (2) hybrid systems or (3) computer (software) analysis. To illustrate this type of approach, let me use as an example the clicks made by the on-off operation of a tape recorder and the correlative signals these events will place on a tape.

The click engendered by the recorder being turned "off" and then "on" usually can be heard easily; however, it is not so easy to identify it as being different from other types of clicks and/or as an electronic "signature" associated only with a specific machine. The question arises as to how you go about identifying an individual click as being created by operation of a particular tape recorder—specifically by manipulation of one or another of its switches. There are a number of procedures that can be applied; one of ours involves computer digitization (at 20k) of the click and its environment. To accomplish this procedure you will need a minicomputer (or a large micro) with an A/D board and substantial memory. Also needed will be one of the several commercial digitization programs now available. Once the signal is in digital form, the output can be analyzed for wave characteristics. We use our specially written DOER program for this purpose. The DOER output can be analyzed digitally or presented graphically. "The Case of the Oversexed Surgeon" can be used to illustrate this approach, that is, in its graphic mode. The individual in question made it his practice to have sex with as many of his female patients as possible and videotaped these trysts. However, the tape that was challenged was one made after his arrest and during an interrogation. Sections of this tape were analyzed by application of the cited procedure and, by this means, it was demonstrated that the tape was not complete. Specifically, the anatomy of two of the clicks found on the tape can be seen in parts B and C of Figure 8-5. When these configurations were compared to that of A—which is a specified "off-on" — it was discovered that they were "unannounced" interruptions to the flow of the tape recording. Note that the "off" pattern of B is almost identical to that of A (and, hence, can be shown to be switching activity), but there are slight differences between the configurations of A and C. Even though these differences were minor and probably can be explained by operator variation, they do tend to reduce (at least slightly) the probability that pattern C also is unidentfied switching. Note also, that these patterns (and the quantitative data they represent) can be used to investigate whether or not one tape recorder or more were used in the creation of this tape. In any event, the defendant was shown to be telling the truth when he indicated that he had been interrogated "more extensively" than had been revealed by the evidence tape recording. Worse yet, by manipulating the process, the agents involved impugned the tape's integrity.

A caution must be associated with this approach. While useful under relatively controlled conditions, it cannot be employed indiscriminately. That is, in

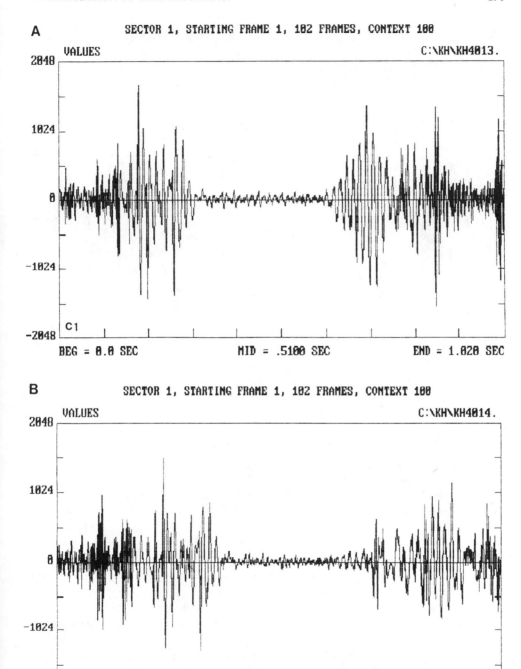

Figure 8-5. Three frames drawn from an actual case. The first (A) demonstrates the patttern of an announced interruption of a tape recording. The other two (B and C) are instances where the recording also was interrupted but the modification initially denied.

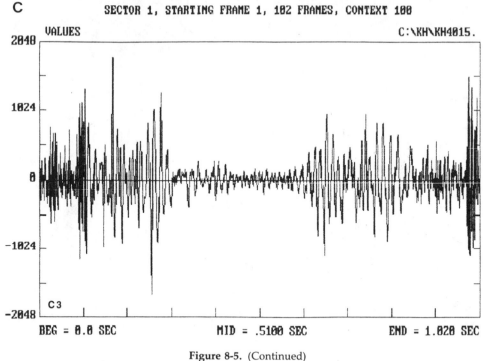

C

SECTOR 1, STARTING FRAME 1, 102 FRAMES, CONTEXT 100

VALUES   C:\KH\KH4015.

Figure 8-5. (Continued)

the case cited above, we had a pre-identified "off-on" event available to us and, hence, could contrast it to other potentially like occurrences on the tape. On the other hand, if this technique is to be utilized in a general way, the assumption which must be made is that each and every tape recorder has its own electronic signature and this signature is unlike those produced by any other tape recorder under any operating conditions. Many phoneticians and engineers support this assumption and have found themselves testifying to that effect on the witness stand. I have done so myself, even though I always temper the concept somewhat. As a matter of fact, some examiners even go so far as to indicate that they can study the gap between the record and erase head signals, first to identify them, second to identify activity in subcircuits ("that's the erase head turning off"), and then to identify the particular tape recorder used. Perhaps so, but I would like to see more hard data on this subject before I become an advocate of the procedure.

In an attempt to clarify the matter, I had a literature search carried out and, to my horror, found that no definitive studies at all were available. There may be some, but my team of able young scientists could not find any. Hence, we set out to determine if tape recorders have an operating signature unique to themselves and if these signatures are unlike those of any other tape recorder. Figure 8-6 shows the patterns for several units. They all are quite different are they not? But what happens to traces like these if: (1) the operator varies the force and/or

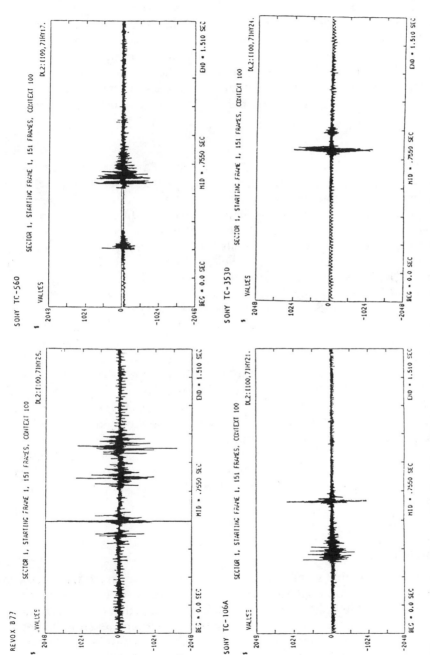

Figure 8-6. Patterns from "off-on" activity of four tape recorders. As can be seen, these configurations are unique enough to be of some value in determining if a particular tape recorder was used to make a specific tape recording and, perhaps, even to identify an unknown tape recorder from the electronic traces it leaves on the tape.

speed of his or her controlling movements,(2) there are different types of noise present, (3) the tape recorders are of exactly the same make and model and made serially within a batch or (4) the recorders are used, reused and used again over a long period of time? The number of potential events and relationships that could be listed here (and could affect these signatures) is lengthy. Hence, I now temper my statements about tape recorder operation rather dramatically—at least until the two very large studies (7) my colleagues and I are carrying out are complete (see Chapter 14 for more about these studies). In short, you should avoid overstating relationships in this regard. The cited technique can be a useful one but, as with so many others in this young field, it must be applied with caution.

Coarticulation

Usually the application of the several techniques described above will permit the examiner to identify most, if not all, of the questionable sections on a particular tape recording and—subsequently determine the nature and cause of those events. However, from time to time, situations will arise where a particular occurrence cannot be explained easily. For example, a segment could be spliced out of a tape recording and then the remaining material rerecorded in the presence of a noise field. In such cases, the examiner often would be aware that something had happened (often on the basis of coarticulatory discontinuities; see again, Chapters 3 and 7) but not be able to specify the exact cause of this problem. Thus, coarticulation analysis, and evaluation of associated spectral correlates, sometimes can be useful. That is, application of an advanced spectral analysis technique will permit the examiner to study the acoustic makeup of the consonants, vowels and vowel transitions that exist prior to and following a suspected edit. An evaluation of this type ultimately will permit application of acoustic theory of speech production so that a decision can be made as to whether or not the observed patterns exhibit appropriate phonemic and coarticulatory relationships. Moreover, various filtering techniques could be employed concurrently (in order to remove system noise) so that coarticulatory effects could be studied aural-preceptually. Thus, by this use of a battery of advanced procedures, it might be possible to determine if the tape recording had been modified in the manner suggested.

Flutter Analysis

It has been noted that small variations, or flutter, in tape recorder speed can be caused by wear or other mechanical imperfections (see reference 10 as an example). It now is the opinion of a number of scientists that such information may be unique to a particular recorder model and, perhaps, even to a specific unit. The problem with making flutter measurements is that there must be some sort of steady-state signal on the tape (such as hum) and specialized equipment is needed. However, given these two requisites, the flutter analysis technique appears to be a useful addition to the examiner's repetoire.

The Report

Up until now, there has been very little need to consider the development of formal reports. For example, where the problem is one of the enhancement of speech on a tape recording or the decoding of distorted speech, the resulting product is either the improved tape recording or a written transcript. Now, and for the first time, it is necessary for us to consider the need for, and nature of, a written report. While I do not consider it my function to teach report writing, it might be useful to outline the elements that should be included in all such reports. I do so primarily because I have been literally stunned at the casualness exhibited by some examiners when they approach the authentication process. Some do not submit any report at all; others do not provide a detailed report. Yet others do not even bring their results to court or even keep systematic logs. In one case, an examiner said he did not even know when he had carried out the analysis (11). Incidentally, the material that follows also should be useful as a guide for reports you might want to write relative to some of the other areas within forensic phonetics. In any event, I submit that you should consider including the following elements.

1. A cover page including an identification of the case and principals— plus your address and the date submitted.
2. A detailed description of the materials sent, and when they were received.
3. A general overview of the authentication processes employed.
4. Details of how the copies of the tape recordings were made.
5. Description of the entire physical examination—and your specific findings.
6. Description of all additional tests and findings as well as the dates on which they were performed.
7. A table listing all events of concern; this schedule should include all innocuous events found and their presumed causes. Other tables and figures may be useful also.
8. A detailed description of any events that appear to be the result of alterations—if any are found. It is possible also that you may wish to include information about their probable causes if you have it.
9. A list of other circumstances of interest you have observed (relative to the tape recording), even if they are a little tangential to the primary task.
10. A list of your conclusions—and your opinion as to the authenticity of the tape recording. You must defend its integrity if it is authentic or, if it cannot be shown to be valid, provide specific evidence for your negative opinion. However, it is imperative that you do *not* overstate your opinion in either direction. "Let the data do the talking" is a useful scientific adage. It can be most helpful here, as it is important that you avoid becoming an advocate. Finally, sometimes a statement as to the estimated probability of the accuracy of your conclusions provides a useful perspective.

THE MINIMIZATION PROCESS

As was stated, some types of surveillance (and, hence, the tape recordings associated with them) are carried out under a federal law which does not permit the surveillance tape recorder to be turned on and left on. Apparently, this legislation was enacted so that the privacy of the innocent could be maintained and to prevent law enforcement groups from falsifying tape recordings (how tape "minimization" would serve to achieve this second goal is a bit of a mystery, however). In any case, agents operating a tape can listen in on the dialogue going on for a minute or two. If some law is being violated, they can activate a tape recorder. If not (or if someone not involved is talking), they cannot record the conversation or even continue to listen to it. A tape recording of this type is quite difficult to validate; it is almost as difficult to challenge (that is, if it has been modified). However, several of the techniques described above can be used to carry out at least a partial analysis. For example, (1) the same tape recorder signature should occur at each and every interruption, (2) if hum is present, its form should not change, (3) the activation of the tape recorder should follow the beginning of the suspects' discussion (that is, if illegal activity is observed, the tape recorder can be turned on but, since it cannot be activated before this determination is made, onset should be some time after the initiation of the conversation), (4) the general environmental (acoustic) conditions should not vary—and so on. The challenge to the authentication process is substantial if minimization has been mandated. You should only attempt evaluations of this type if you have had considerable experience in the area.

AUTHENTICATION OF VIDEOTAPES

Not a great deal of space will be allotted to the authentication of videotape recordings. First, nearly all of these tapes will contain an audio channel (a tape recording) and it can be processed in much the same way that ordinary audio tapes are evaluated. The "preliminary" procedures you would have to structure and carry out would be predicated on the fact that the audio channel constitutes but a single track on a fairly wide and complex magnetic tape. On the other hand, once the physical examination is completed and the working copies made, the other analyses to be carried out are virtually the same as for any audiotape recording.

As you might expect, a successful evaluation of the video portion of the recording to be evaluated requires specific equipment and specialized techniques. Again, it is important to examine and test the equipment on which the original recording was made, as there is at least some evidence that electronic signatures unique to a particular unit can be determined. Unfortunately, this area of inquiry is so new that not much hard data are available; hence, you must approach this task cautiously.

Having written this admonition, let me point out that there are some events that can suggest a videotape recording has been altered—or at least is not the result of a single pass over a previously pristine tape (i.e., a new one). For one thing, the "noise" that can be seen on a previously unrecorded tape is different from the "noise" generated by erase heads. Thus, a spectrum analysis employed in the proper manner here should effectively supplement the visual impressions of the examiner. Additionally, it is almost universally true that when a second video sequence is rerecorded over the first, a series of angular flashes occur. Finally, abrupt "turn ons" and "turn offs" (of the video picture) also suggest that editing has taken place.

A final comment: a device you can use in evaluating video recordings is easily procured; it has an action that somewhat parallels the frame-to-frame fviewers utilized in motion picture film processing. Of course, video is not created in the frame-to-frame mode. Nevertheless, the observation of "stills"— coupled to tiny advances of the tape—often can reveal interruptions and/or disparities in the video portion of a recording.

Once again, the reader should be cautioned that the techniques for video authentication are not as well developed as are those for audio (indeed, they are quite primitive). A good deal more science plus some practical experience are needed if the efficient and accurate authentication of this type of recording is to become an everyday occurrence.

TO CONCLUDE

There are three reasons for you to be asked to authenticate a tape recording: (1) to challenge its integrity (the client believes that "tampering" has occurred), (2) to defend its integrity (the client wants to be able to demonstrate its validity), or (3) simply to determine what has happened to it. However, I must stress and restress that the reason for carrying out an authentication procedure is totally immaterial to the process, and you must approach the problem in a systematic, thorough, complete and ethical manner. You must do so no matter who made the tape and/or under what conditions it was generated. To do less is inexcusable. As I indicated earlier in this chapter, I have had to disappoint clients many times by indicating that a tape they hoped was valid actually was not—or the converse. Your findings are what the data dictate and you only can go as far as they will permit.

Finally, you can expect two things to occur in the future. First, new and better technology will become available, and second, schemes designed to insure that tape recordings are authentic, and have not been edited in any manner, will be developed. Indeed, some firms are touting "tamper proof" tape recording equipment even today. However, their approaches tend to be rather simplistic in nature (a timing signal recorded on a second channel, for instance) and, without doubt, could be defeated. Thus, please remember that the materials found in this chapter are not all-inclusive. Rather, they are ones I have found to be both stable and effective. As such, they constitute initial guidelines for the understanding—and advancement—of the authentication process.

PART III

Speaker Identification

CHAPTER 9

Historical Issues and Perceptual Identification

INTRODUCTION

Almost anyone who has normal hearing, and who has lived long enough to read these words, has had the experience of recognizing some unseen speaker (usually someone familiar) solely from listening to his or her voice. It was from this common everyday experience that the concept (or is it a myth?) of speaker identification was born. References to the process in novels, comic strips, the movies and television have resulted in a perpetuation and refinement of this "myth" to a point that presently many people believe such things as: (1) the identification of a talker by listening to him or her is infallible—or nearly so, (2) technologically we can carry out voice identifications with exactitude, (3) "voiceprints" are the direct equivalent of fingerprints, and so on. Therein lies the structure of a so-called myth.

On the other hand, this particular legend, like practically all others, is based in part upon solid evidence. We are finding out that there is a certain validity to the process of voice/speech identification and we even are beginning to understand some of the relationships which permit it to happen. For example, while we do not as yet know if every one of the five billion people who now exist produce voice and speech that is so idiosyncratic in nature that it is unique to each of them and differentiates them from all others, we do know that we often can discriminate auditorily between and among different speakers. Indeed, it is not difficult at all to remember the times you have identified family members, friends and/or celebrities just from hearing them talk.

DEFINITIONS

But what do we know about speaker identification? We know that it is one of two forms of speaker recognition—the other is speaker verification. Specifically, speaker identification is defined as the process of identifying an unknown speaker from samples of his or her voice. To do so you would need to know a great deal about that person's speech characteristics (a rare occurrence) or be able to match the voice of the "unknown" talker to one from a group of suspects or subjects. As you might expect, this process is a rather difficult one. It is particularly difficult because the task must be accomplished in the face of channel/system distortions (telephone, bandpass, noise, etc.) or speaker distortions (stress, disguise, emotion, etc.). The speech here is never contemporary and the subject is usually uncooperative, especially if there is a crime involved. Often a match is not possible; either the unknown is not represented among the suspects or the tape recordings of the unknown voice simply are too poor to be of use.

Conversely, when speaker verification is at issue, the subject wants to be recognized. Here, high-quality equipment is used, and many reference samples of the talker's speech are available and can be continually updated. Speaker verification is one of several methods utilized to authenticate the person talking when he or she is unseen; it also is (or can be) used in banking by telephone, communication with people in space capsules or with personnel in remote locations. This is the process which you use when you attempt to identify friends, acquaintances or family members. More detailed descriptions of these issues will be found in Chapter 11.

PERSPECTIVES

What else is known about speaker identification? We do know that anyone who attempts to carry out tasks of this kind will enjoy some logic and research in support of their efforts. But, we also know that there are severe—sometimes very severe—problems associated with the practical application of any method, technique or process in the area. Chief among them, of course, is the fact that we simply do not know, as yet, if intraspeaker variability is always less than interspeaker variability—in all situations and under all conditions. Simply put, we are not at all sure that you will always produce speech that is more like your own than it is like *anyone* else's, no matter how you talk, no matter how you feel, no matter what the speaking conditions. I recognize that this dilemma constitutes a functional nightmare for anyone attempting speaker recognition. However, even if the speech of a particular person is not totally unique under all conditions, there may be ways of identifying differences among talkers anyway. But first, what are some of the practical problems to be faced in speaker identification?

Problems in Identifying Speakers by Voice

The first problem is one that often is very little appreciated. It is that the speech of a talker being analyzed will never be contemporary, and it is well-known that noncontemporary speech creates difficulties in any recognition task (9, 10, 12, 37). Of course, once in a while, near-contemporary speech is found in speaker verification, but in the world of speaker identification, noncontemporary speech is the rule. After all, if a bomb threat caller is apprehended as he makes the call (contemporary speech), there would be no need to apply speaker identification procedures.

Two other classes of problems are associated with speaker identification and even can occur (under special circumstances) in the speaker verification milieu. You should be quite familiar with them by now; they are system (or channel) distortions and problems with speakers. As you are well aware, system distortion occurs as a result of such things as reduced frequency response (telephone conversations, for example), noise, interruptions, and so on. In such cases, some of the information about the talker is lost or masked and, just as in speech decoding, such losses increase the difficulties in successfully completing the task. Additionally, speaker distortions also are debilitating to the identification process. As you would expect, most criminals experience fear, anxiety or some sort of stress-like emotions when they commit a crime. The usual effect of these emotions is a change in one or more factors within their voice or speech. These shifts can make it more difficult to match the recorded voice sample to exemplars made at a later time. So too can the effects of ingested drugs, alcohol or even temporary health states (such as a bad cold) interfere with the identification process. Worse yet, the criminal rarely will be cooperative and may even attempt voice disguise either when committing the crime or when providing voice exemplars. In any case, there are a number of speaker "distortions" that can occur (sometimes they are not known to the examiner), with the result that the speech being analyzed is seriously degraded for identification purposes.

Given all of the above theoretical and practical problems, what speech elements are there which would suggest that the serious scientist or practitioner could attempt identification/differentiation among voices? For one thing, it has been postulated (10, 12, 34, 37) that a given individual's speech signal contains features which are sufficiently unique and consistent to permit at least some successful identifications to be carried out. Indeed, both available data and logic permit the assumption that certain elements within a talker's speech tend to be relatively idiosyncratic and are so as a result of the habituated speech patterns employed. Social, economic, geographic and educational factors as well as maturation level, psychological/physical states, sex and intelligence tend to affect speech in relevant ways. Obviously, these factors can be combined with those idiosyncrasies of a given talker's anatomy and physiology to create a unique cluster of speech and voice features. Yet a further point can be made. If one were to measure *several* dimensions within the speech signal, it might be possible to successfully discriminate among talkers on the basis of a composite analysis or profile. We subscribe to this postulate. Specifically, we contend that while there may be no attribute within a person's speech of sufficient strength and uniqueness to permit that particular individual to be differentiated from all other talkers, the use of a group of features may permit successful recognition. An elaboration of this position will be found in Chapter 11.

AN HISTORICAL OVERVIEW

Some people erroneously believe that speaker identification originated with the infamous Joseph Stalin. Now, there was an adroit man—sick and brutal, of course—but clever nonetheless. Moreover, since his contributions to speaker recognition are rather intriguing, it might be of interest to briefly describe them before proceeding with a more accurate historical review.

At the beginning of World War II, literally millions of the people under Soviet dominance defected to the invading Germans; indeed, in one case an entire army from the Ukraine did so. Later on, the Germans captured huge numbers of loyal Soviet soldiers and civilians in their drive toward the cities of Moscow, Leningrad and Stalingrad. After the war was over, large groups of both these deserters and legitimate captives returned, or were returned, to the USSR. At this juncture, Stalin was faced with a serious dilemma. Who among this mass of people had been loyal and who had not. His solution was a simple one: he treated them all as deserters (whether they were or not) and imprisoned them. However, not all of them were sent to die cutting down trees in the Gulags. Those individuals who were highly trained, and/or practically educated, were sorted out and sent to jails where they could be used to carry out more sophisticated tasks. Included among these groups were several who were put to work on developing systems for identifying speakers by voice. Indeed, the famous author Solzhenitsyn wrote about one such team of scientist/engineer prisoners in his novel "The First Circle." The individuals in this particular jail had been put to work on a number of projects, with one outfit focusing on speaker identification. You surely can understand how important it would be for the masters of a police state to be able to identify their "enemies" simply by voice analysis. In any case, Solzhenitsyn is quite amusing as he relates the imaginative strategies utilized by the scientists and engineers to delude their inspectors into thinking they were making progress. As you might expect, substantive efforts in the speaker identification area still go on in the Soviet Union. Work in this area did not originate in that country, however.

Early History

In reality, at least primitive efforts in voice recognition probably antedate recorded history—and were continued down through the subsequent centuries. We know also that some relevant discussion about the issue occurred in English courts several hundred years ago. Indeed, the admissibility of aural-perceptual testimony in that country may be traced back to at least the year 1660, when voice identification was offered in the case of one William Hulet. More recently, such evidence has been accepted by courts both in the United States and Great Britain. For example, in the state of Florida (20), acceptance of aural-perceptual identification testimony is noted as early as 1907. In this particular trial, a hitherto unknown, unseen, cross-racial defendant was identified as a rapist by his having spoken two sentences: "I have got you now," and "I don't want your money." At least the victim said it was him. The court agreed and explained the decision by means of the following logic:

> The manner, time and place of his assault upon her threw her instantly into the highest state of terror and alarm, when all of her senses and faculties were at the extreme of alert receptiveness, when there was nothing within her reach by which to identify her assailant but his voice. Who can deny that under these circumstances that

voice so indelibly and vividly photographed itself upon the sensitive plate of her
memory as that she could forever afterwards promptly and unerringly recognize it on
hearing its tones again. (20)

This early decision is accepted today as an appropriate legal precedent for
the admissibility of aural-perceptual (identification) testimony in many courts
both within Florida and throughout the United States. As it turns out, however,
other judges take a differing point of view. Their position is that a woman being
raped is so stressed that she could not be expected to later remember even the
most prominent of her assailant's features—much less those subtleties in his
voice that would permit identification solely from an auditory impression.
Which of these two extreme positions is the more accurate? Some research on
this issue will be described in a later section of this chapter.

As you probably are beginning to understand by now, there is a rather long
history of admissibility and nonadmissibility of aural-perceptual voice identifications in the courts and, although a review of case law is not part of this book, a
few comments in this regard would appear justified. While some confusion
exists, it appears that most courts will permit a person to testify about the
identity of a speaker (from voice judgments), providing that witness can satisfy
the presiding judge that he or she "really knows" the talker. This approach is a
reasonable one (as we shall see from the experiments described later in the
chapter). If the witness has been in close contact with the individual to be
identified for a long period of time, he or she probably can accurately recognize
the speaker solely from hearing his or her voice. Two problems arise, however.
First, there are judges who take a rather conservative position on this issue. In
these instances, it is difficult to convince them that the witness knows the
defendant well enough to permit voice/speech recognition, and individuals who
should be allowed to testify might not be permitted to do so. On the other hand,
there are other jurists that are quite permissive with respect to such testimony.
For them, any contact at all is sufficient and, often, people who barely know the
person in question are permitted to testify. And, of course, there is the famous
case of the judge who permitted a witness to testify that he could recognize a
particular dog from his bark (38).

Use by Police

The general uncertainty in this area has led both scientists and practitioners
off in various directions in their attempts to find relevant solutions. One consequence is that both basic and applied research has been carried out in this area.
Moreover, police have attempted to remedy the situation by conducting "earwitness" lineups. They take an exemplar provided by the suspect and place it in
with a group of three to six speech samples spoken by other people. Presumably
the witness is required to listen to all of these voices and pick out the "correct"
one. The police may even attempt to carry out this process live. However, this
approach has come under fire (2, 25) as it exhibits several weaknesses. First off,
the procedure should be carried out in a manner that is fair to the suspect. That
is, his or her exemplar should not be compared to speech uttered by individuals
who speak in quite a different manner. An example of an unfair lineup would be

one where the voice of an uneducated black suspect is contrasted to exemplars made by several white assistant district attorneys. In that instance, listeners probably would pick the black (if asked to identify the "criminal") even though they had never heard any of the talkers before nor knew anything about the case. It takes little imagination to see the many ways even the most well-meaning police could err when conducting an auditory lineup.

Consider "The Case of the Lazy Extortionist." A divorced woman with several children had one of her teenage daughters kidnapped. Just about the time the police found the daughter's body, the woman received a telephone call from a man who said he was the person who had kidnapped the girl, that she was safe and well, and that she would be returned to the mother for $6,000 (a rather small sum, you surely will agree). Because of this call (which was recorded, of course), the police did not release information about finding the girl, but rather set a trap for the extortionist. An agreement was made and the money was to be placed in an particular alley next to a dumpster. The entire area was staked out and, after several hours had elapsed, a man entered one of the apartments near the dumpster. Later he was seen to carry a container of trash into the alley. After depositing the trash in the dumpster, he noticed the sack containing the money, picked it up, and looked in it; he then looked both ways and returned to his apartment. He was arrested and held. During this period, he was asked to make a voice exemplar and did so. Four other exemplars were provided by two policemen, a parole officer and a social worker. Excerpts from the five tape recordings were played to the mother over a telephone during a session when neither the suspect nor his attorney was present. She identified the suspect as the extortionist; whereupon he was indicted and brought to trial—but only for extortion as it was clear he was not involved in either the kidnapping or murder. When I analyzed the "voice lineup," I discovered that the defendant's voice actually was quite different from any of the foils and, because of this, probably provided the witness with cues that may have had little to do with the actual identification. Therefore, I proposed that the witness repeat the evaluation but with the suspect's sample imbedded in a set of exemplars where the speech of any given foil was not so similar to that of the other foils yet inherently different from his. This request was denied, but I was permitted to have the woman repeat the original test while on the witness stand. Since only the judge had the key, he was able to track the accuracy of her performance. I had reasoned that, if she could systematically identify the defendant, he undoubtedly was guilty (albeit, pretty darn lazy); however, if she could not, the evidence would be to the contrary. As it turned out, the courtroom test was not conclusive. The witness identified the actual extortionist 75% of the time and the defendant somewhat less, but still at a level better than chance. The defendant was convicted and perhaps justifiably so; I do not know. I do know that I still wish I could have administered a valid test.

A number of statements and assumptions have been presented about the aural-perceptual identification process. Accordingly, it should be obvious that most of these relationships are grounded in data/concepts that are the product of scientific inquiry. It now would appear useful to examine the results of some of these investigations. The basic research will be considered first; it will be followed by a short review of some of the more applied studies which have been carried out in the area.

BASIC AURAL-PERCEPTUAL RESEARCH

Among the earliest experiments of the modern aural-perceptual speaker identification type was one triggered by the Lindberg kidnapping case. Charles Lindberg was elevated to national hero status after he became the first man to fly solo across the Atlantic Ocean. Hence, when his son was kidnapped, and later found murdered, most of the people in this country joined him and his wife in mourning. Indeed, the emotional level ran so high that when, later, Bruno Hauptmann was arrested and indicted, there was great concern that the authorities would not be able to protect him. I can still remember one of my granduncles telling me about the pressure placed on him during the time he was one of Hauptmann's prison guards.

Lindberg apparently had heard the kidnapper's voice twice: once on the telephone (an old-style one with very poor fidelity) and once (briefly) in person but at night. Two years later (during the trial), Lindberg testified that he recognized the voice of Bruno Hauptmann as that of the kidnapper. What a sensation this created; no one doubted for a moment that he could and did make a valid identification—that is except for a psychologist by the name of Frances McGehee.

Whether Hauptmann was guilty or innocent apparently was not at issue with McGehee (substantial physical evidence supports the notion that he was, however). What interested her was the identification Lindberg made two years after having heard the voice of the kidnapper. In response she carried out two studies (21, 22). Her procedure was to have auditors listen to an individual and then identify him within a group of other talkers at various times (one day to five months) subsequent to exposure. All the speech samples in the first of the two studies were "live;" hence, she had the speakers produce all of their utterances from behind an opaque curtain; she used recorded samples in her second study. To be brief, McGehee found that the voice identifications were quite high and that falloff in accuracy was gradual but steady—from 83% correct identifications the day following exposure to a voice, to only 13% after five months had elapsed. Moreover, correct identification patterns of the recorded voices (also of people who were unfamiliar to the listener) were similar to those for the live subjects, and they were extinguished just about as rapidly. It has been suggested (4) that a decay process of this type is quite complex. It can be inferred that it is one which is governed by an individual's ability to store information relative to both short-term and long-term memory.

Contemporary research tends to substantiate McGehee's conclusions only in part and to indicate that reliance on aural-perceptual identifications, particularly those of a previously unknown talker, may not be as robust as is desirable. However, few of these experiments replicated McGehee's (even in part) and, therefore, the status of our knowledge about aural-perceptual speaker identification must be pieced together. There are a number of key studies. For example,

Bricker and Pruzansky (3) reported 98% correct identification of familiar speakers by listeners when sentences were provided as stimuli; however, identification accuracy fell to only 56% when the samples were short—and others have reported similar results (15, 17). As early as 1954, data (27) became available which suggested that identification accuracy improved with increasing speech sample duration up to about 1200 ms; for longer periods, accuracy did not appear to be related to duration, but rather to phonemic repertoire (see also 6, 7, 17). Moreover, a number of investigators have observed that, when the speech signal is degraded in various ways—for example, by (1) increasing the number of speakers, (2) substituting whispered for normal speech, (3) the use of different speakers, (4) the use of different speech materials, and so on—listener's performance was poor, or they needed much longer speech samples in order to permit a reasonable level of identification for even known speakers (5, 6, 7, 17, 35, 36, 39).

Other confusions exist. For example, several authors report that speaker disguise, dialects, noncontemporary samples and a large number of speakers reduce identification accuracy (9, 10, 14, 23, 28, 34, 39). Moreover, it has been demonstrated (30) that listeners will exhibit error rates as high as 58% when noncontemporary samples of the same speakers are presented, and that accuracy is yet further reduced when a speaker's voice is paired with one that sounds similar to it (sound-alikes). Worse yet, little research has been carried out on the effects on speaker identification of emotion, speaker disguise and distortion (1, 9, 14, 23). It is known that psychological stress affects the voice (11, 13, 31, 33, 40), but the extent of its exact effects on correct identification have not as yet been ascertained.

On the other hand, some of the research reported in this area suggests that there are certain features within the speech signal that can be identified and which appear to be natural components of these organized (acoustic) productions. That there are speech-related characteristics within our utterances that we can "extract" for identification purposes is very important to the overall process—primarily because it also may be possible to identify/analyze them by machine and develop automatic or semiautomatic identification methods that will be both valid and efficient.

One of the first of these features is mean speaking fundamental frequency, or SFF (6, 15, 19); perceptually this attribute is heard as pitch level and variability. A second includes vowel formant frequencies, ratios and transitions (15, 24, 36). There is little question but that these features provide important cues in the perceptual identification of speakers. As a matter of fact, attempts have been made (6, 24) to compare the relative importance of source (voice) and vocal tract (articulatory system) transfer characteristics for speaker identification purposes; it was found that these features contribute additively. In addition, phonemic effects on the identification task have been investigated. It has been reported that the level of correct perceptual identifications varies as a function of (1) the vowel produced, (2) consonant-vowel transitions, (3) vocal tract turbulence and (4) inflections. Finally, voice quality, speech prosody/timing, and many other vocal characteristics all appear to affect the identification process. In short, there are quite a number of features that relate to aural-perceptual speaker identification.

The lists I have presented probably are a little confusing and/or difficult for you to organize. Accordingly, let me arrange them first into an inventory of the positives and negatives related to aural-perceptual speaker identification, and second, into a catalogue of those elements which can be employed to structure practical evaluations in this area.

The Pro-Con Framework

Most of the following are considered to be among those positive relationships associated with the perceptual identification task.

1. Speakers who are known to the listener are the easiest to identify by voice, and accuracy here can be quite high (10, 14, 27).
2. If the listeners' perception of a talker's speech characteristics are reinforced from time to time, correct identification will decay more slowly than if appropriate stimulation is not provided (13, 21, 22). This relationship holds both for listeners who know the talker and those who do not.
3. The larger the speech sample—and the better its quality—the more accurate will be the aural-perceptual identifications.
4. Listeners can be quite variable in their ability to make speaker recognition judgments (14, 29), but some of them are naturally quite good at it.
5. Listeners appear to be successful in using a number of the "natural" characteristics found within speech/voice in the identification task.
6. Phonetic training and task organization appear to aid in successful identifications.

Some of the events that operate to reduce the accuracy of the aural-perceptual speaker identification process can be listed also. The following are among the more important.

1. Talkers who are not well known to the listener are more difficult to identify than are those whose speech is familiar.
2. The greater the number of talkers there are in a group, the more difficult will be the speaker identification task.
3. Degradation of the signal (produced by the talker) will tend to impair the identification process.
4. Noncontemporary speech makes the identification task more difficult.
5. Talkers who sound alike can be confused with each other even by listeners who know them.

Features Useful in Identification

Evaluation of the scientific literature generally available in this area—and specifically those presentations reviewed in this chapter—inevitably leads to the postulate that people attend to certain features within the speech signal and use them in the recognition process. A number of these features have been identified; they include the following.

Speaking fundamental frequency (SFF, F0) or heard pitch. The focus here is on general pitch level (high, medium, low) as well as on the variability and patterning of pitch usage. Many individuals exhibit habituated pitch patterns that can aid the listener in identifying them by voice.

Articulation. The focus in this case is especially on idiosyncratic vowel or consonant production as well as on vowel formant levels and ratios. The controlling word here is idiosyncratic, for to be useful in identification, an individual's phoneme production must be in some way a little different from that of others, or perhaps somewhat unique to him or her. Coarticulatory effects are important here also.

General voice quality. There is little doubt but that the general quality of a sound-producing mechanism aids us in identifying which instrument is providing the auditory percept. For example, if the same person plays the same note (at the same intensity) first on a clarinet and then on a violin, you would have no difficulty in determining (from the heard signal alone) which was which—or, at least, that they were two different instruments. The same strategy can be utilized in voice recognition.

Prosody. Although not much research has been done on how a person's speech timing, or the temporal patterning of speech, affects our ability to identify him or her, we do know that we listen to how slow, or fast, a person talks; how smooth or choppy is his or her presentation. Thus, the timing and melody of a person's speech can be used to provide cues relative to identity.

Vocal intensity. So far, vocal intensity, while identified as a recognition feature, has not been investigated at a level necessary for good understanding. Moreover, in practice it is very difficult to determine absolute intensity because even small changes in the distance between the talker's head and the microphone (or receptor) can result in variations in energy level. Nevertheless, it is obvious that we listen to how loud a person speaks and how they vary their vocal intensity when they talk. Accordingly, it is theorized that evaluation of this parameter is often useful for speaker identification purposes.

Speech characteristics. This category should *not* be considered a wastebasket term equivalent to "other." Rather, I am referring to specific speech elements such as (1) dialect, (2) unusual use of linguistic stress or affect, (3) idiosyncratic language patterns, (4) speech impediments and (5) idiosyncratic pronunciations. These features extend beyond the simple articulation or prosody considerations discussed above, and can provide very powerful cues in speech recognition. The problem, of course, is that they are difficult to quantify.

By now it should be clear that people who identify each other by do so only after carrying out a great deal of auditory processing of the heard signal. This processing may be completed very quickly, but it is accomplished nonetheless. In any case, the listener may take into account all, or only some, of the six sets of attributes listed above (along with a number of subfactors) when they make a judgment. Conversely, they may be forced to base their decisions on but one or two of the sets or subsets when the others are degraded by some kind of distortion. In short, when they are taken as a group, these six data sets provide a reasonably robust basis for aural-perceptual speaker identification—I certainly use them for that purpose. They also can be used as the conceptual substructure for machine approaches to the problem (see Chapter 11).

A PRACTICAL APPLICATION

The immediately preceding section included review of the more relevant of the (basic) studies in the area of aural-perceptual speaker identification. These relationships also were utilized to develop (1) listings of the positive and negative features of the process and (2) analysis procedures that could be useful in systematically determining whether heard speech samples were produced by one, two or a number of talkers. The question now may be asked: can anyone actually apply this approach? In my estimation, trained phoneticians often can do so—especially if their training includes experience directly relevant to the forensic milieu.

Of course, some people would challenge this statement. I would respond to their criticism in two ways. First, there is some research that supports my position and, second, the phonetician has the advantage of being able to structure his or her analysis. The first of two studies I would like to review was carried out by Shirt (32). She developed a test based on 74 recorded voices provided her by the British Home Office; she then asked 20 phoneticians and an equal number of untrained controls to carry out three fairly difficult listening tasks based on rather short samples. Essentially, she found that, while the best control did as well as the best phonetician, the phoneticians overall did a rather better job than did the untrained subjects. However, neither group appeared to utilize a structured analysis of the type described above. On the other hand, Köster (16) reports that his phoneticians did very much better than his controls in several experiments where they attempted to identify people they knew—again unstructured procedures were used, as were short speech samples. In this case, not one of the phoneticians made even a single error. These studies, plus additional evidence, suggest that phoneticians can carry out the identification process better than can an untrained person, even under conditions where unfamiliar talkers are employed, the task is unstructured and/or the samples are short. Specialized training in identification, plus the systematic structuring of a good aural-perceptual analysis procedure (one of the type described above), should permit this class of professionals to do a reasonably good job with forensic-based identification tasks. Please note here that I said "reasonably good," as we have little data available which are focused directly on this issue.

A SECOND APPROACH

As we have seen: (1) speaker "lineups" may not be either effective or valid enough to use at all, (2) the courts seem not able to provide us with boundaries as to what is and what is not permissible with respect to speaker identification by witnesses and (3) the one-on-one auditory-matching procedure is not foolproof even when the process is highly structured and utilized by trained phoneticians. Are there any alternatives? Are there any methods that will permit reasonably good aural-perceptual speaker identification to be carried out? First, let us consider data from studies which were organized with law enforcement needs in mind. They should aid you in better understanding some of these relationships as well as what may be possible in this area.

Applied Research

In 1982, two colleagues of mine and I reported data on the accuracy of listeners in recognizing talkers under a variety of conditions (14). The study addressed the known-unknown talker controversy. That is, some authors contend that listeners have to know the speakers in order to make highly accurate judgments of their identity, whereas others suggest that listeners can identify talkers even if they do not know them. There also are individuals who would challenge either of these fairly extreme positions. In response to the controversy, we carried out several experiments in which we attempted to: (1) estimate listeners' capabilities to resist the effects of disguise and stress, (2) determine how fast recognition is extinguished and (3) assess the importance of the auditors being acquainted with the talkers. Our speakers for these experiments were 10 adult males who had recorded speech samples under three types of speaking conditions: (1) normal, (2) stress (electric shock) and (3) disguise. Three classes of listeners were utilized in a highly controlled environment (see Figure 9-1): (1) a group of individuals who knew the talkers very well, (2) a group that did not know the talkers but were trained to identify them and (3) a group that neither knew the talkers nor understood the language that was spoken. As may be seen from Figure 9-2, the analyses indicate that the performances among the groups were significantly different. Listeners who knew the talkers performed best, while the non-English-speaking listeners produced the lowest level of correct identification. The "middle" group, i.e., the English-speaking listeners who did not know the talkers (but were "trained" for over an hour to recognize them), also were subdivided into groups on the basis of their ability in learning to identify them. However, even in this case, the best of the subgroups still was significantly less competent in the identification task than were the listeners who knew the talkers. The least competent subgroup performed at about the same level as the auditors that did not speak English. Finally, analysis of the three types of speech revealed that, in most instances, the normal and stress conditions were not very different relative to identification level, whereas the disguised productions resulted in significantly fewer correct identifications, even when the listeners knew the talkers very well. In short, these experiments provided a few of the answers we need. First, it appears true that you can accurately identify a talker if you know him or her very well, and you can do so under rather difficult conditions. Second, we found that it sometimes is possible to fool a person who really knows you (but not too often). Third, you can expect that at least some people can be trained to recognize a talker with reasonable efficiency even if they do not know him or her. Of course, the correct identifications will be higher if the conditions are optimum and the listener is trained in speech analysis. However, anything that degrades the situation will tend to reduce performance. Fourth, people who do not know a language are no better off than those that do. Fifth, at least certain kinds of stress do not appear to reduce the recognition level very much—but disguise does. Finally, listeners

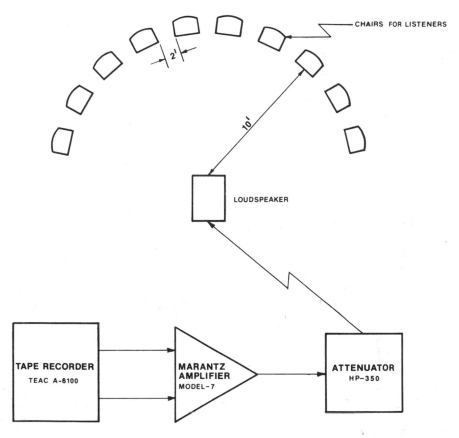

Figure 9-1. Equipment array and subject placement for aural-perceptual experiments using groups. If placed in a sound-treated room or area, this configuration will permit the generation of data which are as valid as those obtained from highly controlled single-subject experiments.

vary markedly in their ability to carry out speaker identification tasks. Individuals who wish to work in this area should be prepared to demonstrate their ability to perform effectively.

Another and related experiment was carried out in order to study the effects of stress or arousal on speaker identification (1). The question asked here was: can the victims of a crime perform better aural-perceptual speaker identifications than can people who are not aroused in this manner? In order to discover if stress or arousal enhanced or degraded accuracy levels, a group of young females was prescreened for potential sensitivity to stressors. The 20 most susceptible to stress, and the 20 least likely to be threatened (controls) were selected as experimental subjects. The "stress" group was presented 10 minutes of violent video stimuli (attacks on women, rape scenes, death of children) while a male voice read a threatening commentary; the controls saw a pastoral video sequence (primarily of a horse being exercised) while hearing a male voice read neutral material. We monitored subjects' responses to the stimuli by means of a standard polygraph technique. A procedure involving speaker recognition (of

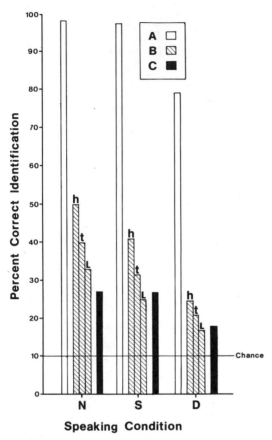

Figure 9-2. Correct identifications of a group of 10 talkers speaking under three conditions: normal (N), stress (S) and disguise (D). Group A knew the talkers very well: group C, while trained to task, knew neither the talkers nor English. The group B listeners—also trained to task—were evaluated on the basis of three groupings: high (h) or low (L) correct response level on a pretrial test and by total group (t).

the male voice) was carried out and we found that the aroused women made significantly better identifications than did the women who were not stressed. Further, the aroused subjects sustained these (better) identification scores over time. In sum, it appears that, other things being equal, fear/stress/arousal can improve a person's ability to make the relatively complex judgments required for auditory speaker recognition.

The third of our investigations contrasted earwitness and eyewitness identification (13). Specifically, we undertook to investigate and contrast visual and aural-perceptual identifications of a simulated crime from a set of photographic and tape-recorded exemplars. Auditors were law school students who were divided into four groups. Group A made three identifications (serially) one day, one week and two weeks after the "crime" took place. Group B saw the photographs and heard the tapes only once, a week after the incident and Group C only after two weeks had elapsed. Witnesses in a fourth group (D) followed the same schedule as did Group A; however, they were presented with an imposter who was similar in appearance and speech to the actual "criminal." Both the imposter and actual "criminal" were presented (in the photographic lineups only) at the final judging session. Eyewitness "lineups" have been challenged

(8); however, the results from our investigation demonstrated that visual identifications can be quite accurate. By contrast, (auditory) speaker recognition levels were relatively poor (see Figure 9-3). Surprisingly, no strong trends were observed as a function of elapsed time, either for repeated trials or for procedures involving different initiation latencies; nor did confidence levels appear to be related to accuracy of judgment. These results support the position that testimony of the earwitness type should be viewed by judges and juries with greater caution than may have been the case in the past. Indeed, the weighting for such testimony probably should be on the negative side, as high levels of misidentifications can occur—especially if the witness is not the victim. Of course, the visual identifications were predicated upon optimum conditions, i.e., the eyewitnesses (1) enjoyed good lighting, (2) were reasonably intelligent, (3) had adequate eyesight, (4) were reasonably close to the simulated crime (and could see it) and (5) were asked to remember the criminal. The situation for the earwitness identifications was optimum too but, as seen, the results were not.

A New Analysis Procedure

A number of relationships now should be apparent. First off, we have seen that phoneticians may be able to assist law enforcement personnel with speaker identifications based on heard stimuli. At least, they should be able to do so if they have available reasonably good speech samples, have had experience with this type of activity and employ structured analysis techniques. Moreover, the

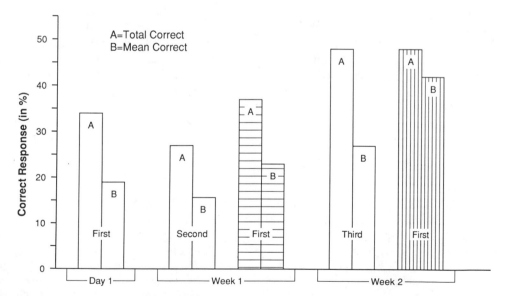

Figure 9-3. Ability of listeners to identify a talker heard speaking during a simulated crime. Three groups of subjects are represented. One group (no shading) completed trials after one day, one week and two weeks, a second group (horizontal lines) after one week and the third (vertical lines) only after two weeks. Correct responses were low but seemed to improve—up to two weeks anyway.

three experiments just reviewed provide yet additional information about human capabilities in the speaker recognition domain. That is, when combined, these results can be used to demonstrate that individuals who are not phoneticians can carry out auditory identifications at least at some success level. Of course, the task has to be highly structured and the auditors must be motivated, trained (at least to some extent), have native ability for the task, and so on. On the other hand, it must be conceded that numerous events/relationships exist which can serve to degrade success rates; they include low listener arousal, speaker disguise, unstructured presentations, speaker stress, and so on. Thus, aural-perceptual speaker identification appears hazardous in most instances and even the extensive training enjoyed by phoneticians provides no guarantee that they will be highly effective in their efforts.

But how can the aural-perceptual speaker identification process be upgraded? Some practitioners utilize techniques that involve either the contrasting of two or more voice samples by alternately comparing them on two tape recorders or by making up many pairs of samples so that a series of rigorous and systematic comparisons can be carried out. I prefer the latter technique. However, these procedures still do not require that identifications to be made from, or within, a field of talkers or that the phoneticians (or practitioners) provide data on their ability to make correct identifications.

A far better approach is one that utilizes the paired comparison, or ABX, technique plus what are referred to as "blind" panels. In this case, solid information is provided for use in the decision-making process. Please note that tens of thousands of experiments of this type have been carried out with human beings as subjects. The obtained product does not constitute an opinion but, rather, consists of structured/measured responses. That is, subjects are utilized here as machines or meters and the obtained data processed for trends. Much of what we know of human and animal sensations has resulted from such investigation.

Now, having pointed out the suitability of the approach for use in forensics, let us return to its description. First, when applying the technique, it is best to use two classes of listeners. One group should be highly trained professionals such as phoneticians and the other, untrained controls. As would be expected, the data obtained from the trained examiners will be quite powerful. However, it is important to use a control group also. The reason for doing so is not just to verify the data provided by the professionals, but also to insure that the observed relationships are robust enough to be obvious to just about anybody. Second, the operational procedure I favor is a rigorous one; it is utilized with both types of listeners. Basically, it requires that the subjects operationally demonstrate that the data they provide are valid. That is, they are tested on three levels: (1) can they hear the samples presented to them, (2) can they tell when a pair of samples is produced by the same speaker and (3) can they determine when each of the pair actually is uttered by a different person? To be specific, each volunteer first receives a hearing test and then (after a few familiarization exemplars) is presented with 75 to 90 pairs of samples on a quasi-random basis. It is important to include a large enough number of samples so that the test is valid, yet not have it so long that the auditors become fatigued, bored or even angry. In any event, the test is made up as follows: 20-30% of the samples are spoken by the same person, 35-45% are uttered by two different talkers and 25-35% are experimental in nature. The "experimental" samples contrast the known and unknown talkers. To qualify as subjects, all auditors must pass the hearing test (minimum acceptable level: 92% correct), demonstrate that they can recognize two samples when they are produced by the same person (at a level of 80% or better) and show that they can tell when two samples were not produced by the same person (at an 85% criterion level). Any individual who does not meet all three criteria simply has his or her "experimental" data discarded. In my judgment, this approach is a powerful one. The subject is required to demonstrate that he or she can properly carry out the task, or they are not used. I have completed a number of experiments of this type wherein all samples were fully controlled (i.e., all talkers were known to me). The experiments sometimes involved a positive match, and other times the two talkers actually were different people. The resulting data showed a mild correlation between the evaluation scores and the ability of the subjects to perform the task properly. It is not until the criterion scores were reduced to around 60-65% correct identification on both internal tests that the experimental scores begin to suffer. That is, as long as the subject could make a match, or identify different talkers within a pair, at least two-thirds of the time, they could be expected to perform satisfactorily with the "experimental" pairs. Finally, this approach has been used in the field—and compared to our machine method (see Chapter 11). In both instances, an effective performance was noted. When subjects are required to demonstrate their ability to make accurate judgments, they also prove effective as a group in correctly contrasting "known" and "unknown" talkers—even within a large field of speakers.

To summarize, we now know a great deal about people's ability to make aural-perceptual speaker identifications. For example, it is clear that most auditors use strategies involving *natural* speech features for this purpose, that specialized training greatly aids in task success (as does motivation) and that some people are better at making identifications than are others. We also are aware that noise, distortion, noncontemporary speech and very short speech samples, plus large groups of talkers, degrade the effectiveness of the process. Finally, it is clear that while aural-perceptual speaker identification has marked limitations, fairly good results can be expected if the task is highly structured—and/or the listeners are required to demonstrate their competency.

CHAPTER 10

The "Voiceprint" Problem

INTRODUCTION

"Voiceprints" are a problem that simply will not go away. For example, as late as 1981, the proponents of this method of speaker identification claimed that their approach had been accepted by courts of law in 25 of the states within the United States, by two military courts, plus by two courts in Canada (29). Perhaps more alarming, yet other courts (including several appellate and supreme courts) have admitted "voiceprints," and these techniques have even been accepted in some European countries. Of course, whether the method can be successfully introduced into other courts, and continued in those that have accepted it previously, is open to question. Nevertheless, this approach to speaker identification appears to be holding on (at least marginally) even in the face of numerous setbacks, negative research and general disapproval by the relevant scientific community. How could this situation occur in countries as technologically advanced as are those cited? An answer is not easily provided.

Ordinarily, I first would include a section describing the nature of the issue/method being considered. However, in this case, I have chosen to initiate the discussion with some of the history surrounding the controversy. This approach should provide you with perspectives useful in evaluating the method when it is reviewed. Suffice it to say at this juncture that the speaker identification technique of "voiceprints" is based on t-f-a (time-frequency-amplitude) spectrograms and the attempts of "examiners" to use them in a rather crude pattern matching paradigm.

PERSPECTIVES ABOUT "VOICEPRINTS/GRAMS"

Establishing relevant perspectives about "voiceprints" is not all that easy—primarily because of the confusion, and the many contradictions, which appear associated with the technique. Several of the problems appear to result from: (1) a lack of interest (or concern) about these issues by the relevant scientific community, (2) proper perspectives relative to the extreme seriousness of the problem and (3) the unwillingness of the "voiceprint/gram" proponents to have their methods evaluated. The first two points are related; the consequence is a lack of sufficient research on the subject. But, what is so unusual here is that members of the scientific community do not seem willing to focus a major research effort on the issue. To appreciate their reluctance, it is necessary to understand scientific response to problems such as this one.

Speaker identification simply is one of the many applied areas that bridge the phonetic sciences and engineering. In the ordinary course of events, any dispute about an applied technique (such as "voiceprints/grams") simply would result in a flurry of laboratory inquiry. Indeed, differences in scientific opinion of this type are quite common. One needs only to attend any phonetic sciences congress or a convention of the Acoustical Society of America to discover that, on any given day, numerous scientific controversies are presented, discussed and/or debated. Occasionally, one is even resolved. That is, it is well known that differences of opinion are very common in the ebb and flow of scientific life. They relate to theory, interpretation of data and relationships among events; indeed, they reflect nearly every facet of the process of science. And what is the usual response of the scientific community to an issue such as this one? Debate, of course, but most important, the competing ideas are tested, retested and yet further tested. Eventually, the fundamental relationships are discovered or some sort of resolution is worked out. Moreover, it is common for many scientists to work on a single dispute. Only rarely does a very small group of scholars investigate (or be privy to) a given issue—at least, any but the most trivial. Thus, in the give and take of everyday science, many investigators may contribute to the development of a theory, to the testing of a controversy, to the solution of a problem. And that is how it should be. Under ordinary circumstances, the "voiceprint/gram" issue would have been handled in just this manner.

Unfortunately, the cited controversy is not a simple instance of scientific difference of opinion. In this case, the proponents of the technique are producing a "product," hence, they have a proprietary interest in it. Small wonder that they have continually argued that the "relevant" scientific community agrees that their procedures are valid. By excluding from the "relevant scientific community" all individuals except those who agree with them, they are functioning pretty much in the manner of any businessman who is enthusiastic about a product and advertises it in a way that reflects his ardor. However, some professionals have argued that the "voiceprint/gram" proponents go beyond the boundaries of good business procedure and operate more as cultists—wherein only the true believer can evaluate or criticize the art or activities of the group. Thus, if their recently defunct professional association, the International Association of Voice Identification (or IAVI), actually was some type of a fraternity, there would be little need to evaluate their activities on a scientific basis, as it would be faith (not reason) which would govern their behavior. On the other hand, if (as they say) their methods are bonafide, someone should test them to see if they meet the criteria for validity. But, since "voiceprints/grams" appear to be a product, the typical scientist is somewhat reluctant to carry out the basic validation research, indicating that this process should have been handled by those individuals that developed the method in the first place. In any event, it appears that these relationships (plus a number to follow) are among those which tend to discourage appropriate investigators from entering this particular arena.

Second, there is a clear societal or sociological component to the "voice-print/gram" issue—and situations of this type are decidedly foreign to many scientists. Moreover, these same individuals do not recognize that the resulting confusions can be downright dangerous; a situation that, perhaps, is illustrated by "The Case of the Sullen Indian" (10). In one of the rural areas of Canada there is a consolidated school which is attended by a mixture of various types of Canadian pupils; included among them are Indians. One of these Indians was a teenage schoolboy who was rather bright—quite bright as it turns out. Since high intelligence among Indians apparently is not viewed favorably, at least by some Canadians, this young man experienced many frustrations. His response was to ingest large quantities of "firewater" — a behavior that served only to compound his problems, as he then became both an Indian and a "drunk." As you might expect, the Royal Canadian Mounted Police gives short shrift to teenage drinkers. Anyway, a series of bomb threats were directed to the consoli-dated school in question—so many that a tape recorder was coupled to the school's telephone line. At that point, yet another threat was received and recorded. The voice on the tape was one of those growly-whisper types that often occur when a person speaks softly but under tension. One of the distinct features of the voice was the caller's use of vocal fry (the lowest voice register; the one with a rough popping quality). When the Mounties heard the recording, one of them said, "Aha, that's our young Indian friend." At this juncture, the schoolboy was arrested, brought to police headquarters and convinced that the only way he could prove his professed innocence was to provide the police with a "voice exemplar." He did so. The exemplar and the tape-recorded call were sent to a Canadian "voiceprint examiner" who indicated either that they were not the same voice or that he could not arrive at a decision. They then were sent to another examiner (one in the U.S.) who indicated that the two voices had been produced by the same person. In the ensuing trial, it appeared that the "voiceprint/gram" technique had again been defeated (as usually is the case when the opposition presents anti-voiceprint experts). However, the decision swung the other way after six local Mounties testified that they believed the bomb threat caller to be the defendant. The youth was convicted and sent to jail for two years. When released, he demanded and received a review—even though the Canadian legal aid society refused to support him with counsel. The conviction was upheld by two of the three appellate judges, but it was the third and dissenting judge that made an observation which has created more night-mares than I wish to count (10). In discussing the "errors" related to the trial, he pointed out that he did not think the boy was guilty because (1) he had been out of the sight of school officials for only a few minutes at the time the call was made, (2) a teacher who knew him well said it was not his voice on the tape, (3) there was no cafeteria noise on the tape recording, even though it was lunch time and the only phone in the school (other than the one in the principal's office) was in a hallway outside the lunchroom and (4) the phone used in the call obviously was of a different make from that in the school—and there was no phone like it within many miles. It is the fourth of these points that is the most important. The phone used in the bomb threat call was of European manufacture, i.e., one where the number is dialed, a tone is heard when the party is reached and then the coins must be deposited. It was not an American unit, as was the one in the cafeteria hallway (i.e., where the coins are deposited first and then, after the person dials, a connection is made). Since both the tone and the dropping of the coins were heard on the recording, the phone used for the bomb threat call could not have been of the Western Electric type situated at the school. Hence, it follows that the young Indian simply could not have made the call. Had I been more observant, he would not have had to spend two years in jail for a crime that he could not have committed.

Since "voiceprints/grams" still are employed by a few law enforcement agencies—and, sometimes, even by the FBI (25)—the previously cited social problems continue to exist. As stated, the average scientist finds them peculiar, confusing and (occasionally) abhorrent. Since scientific investigators deal with basic or applied research (or with the current scientific fad of modeling), the societal implications of the use of speaker identification techniques such as "voiceprints/grams" tend to be beyond the scope of their interest or even attention. Finally, the urgency associated with this problem is perhaps the element most often misunderstood by researchers. We need to know if the "voiceprint/gram" approach to speaker identification is a valid one, and we need to know it now, as this approach already is in use in the courts. However, even though these relationships are not apparent to most relevant scientists, their lack of concern about the problem may not be as reprehensible as it appears on the surface. It is the unusual nature of this issue that sometimes has led to what may appear to be inappropriate perspectives on their part.

Emotions Flare

Without question, the controversy about "voiceprints" has produced a great deal of emotional dialogue. Perhaps the reason for these intense feelings is that the issue is proprietary to some; unproven to others. However, it does not seem acceptable to send an individual to jail solely on the basis of a procedure that many scientists believe does not work. Small wonder then that I have testified (32, 35, 37) that: "I believe voiceprinting to be a fraud being perpetuated upon the American public and the Courts of the United States." Not to be outdone, the proponents of "voiceprints" have indulged in emotional outbursts also. For example, Truby (46) has indicated that the tactics of those opposing "voiceprints" are "inappropriate and ethnologically anachronistic," "hysterical," "indefensible;" that their behaviors constitute "outlandish demonstration;" that they are "misinformed" and have acted "impetuously, naively, aggressively and … dissently;" that they are guilty of "latter day book burning or worse;" exhibit "professional ineptness" and "engage in dissension for dissension's sake." Apparently, he also feels that anyone who opposes his beliefs on "voiceprinting" is engaged in "some ill-designed, witch-burning adventure and should be severely censured as a troublemaker." Indeed, even today, the scientist who ventures into the courtroom to counter the claims of the "voiceprint" enthusiasts is made to feel that he is somehow equivalent to a person who believes the world is flat (this analogy actually has been used). However, it never is mentioned that for every "new idea" that a given group of scientists incorrectly oppose, there are thousands that they properly discredit.

Nevertheless, no matter how inappropriate are these passionate outbursts, the fact remains that this technique has been accepted by a considerable number of courts, even in the face of more rational reviews (4, 5, 6, 18, 19), and a few are still accepting it. Hence, the problem has yet to be resolved. Some of the more relevant reasons for this situation follow.

Lack of Opposition to "Voiceprints"

One of the more obvious reasons why the "voiceprints" proponents have been successful when taking their technique to court (especially in the past) is that they have been unopposed. That is, in the majority of early cases, and even recently, the opposing attorneys were not conversant enough with the procedure to avail themselves of consultation or expert testimony by scientists and others knowledgeable about its inadequacies. In many instances, the attorneys did not have the funds to enlist appropriate aid but, in others, they simply were not aware that the vast majority of the scientific community did not accept "voiceprints" as a valid speaker identification technique. Indeed, because they were not conversant with the problems associated with the method, otherwise capable trial attorneys found it a difficult process to impeach, even though they intuitively found it lacking. After all, it carried a kind of surface validity. Perhaps even more disquieting is the fact that, when opposition appears imminent, indictments or suits frequently are withdrawn; indeed, they have been in nearly half of the cases for which my testimony has been sought. I believe you can see how the "voiceprint" proponents use this approach to protect their product; they simply withdraw from the scene if scientific opposition appears likely. In short, the "voiceprint" method was accepted early on by a number of courts, and precedents were set that could be utilized by its supporters in yet other cases. Small wonder, then, that the unsuspecting jurist often could see no reason to deny acceptance of this technique in his court. Moreover, there also are general legal precedents that have a bearing on the courtroom acceptance of "voiceprints." The major one among them is called the Frye test.

The Frye Test

The legal criterion which most scientific testimony is required to meet is one based on the 1923 case of Frye *vs* the United States (12). Basically, this test states that a scientific method must be generally accepted by members of the appropriate scientific community before it can be accepted in a court of law as being reliable (or, more properly, valid). The proponents of "voiceprints," however, have managed to give the impression that their method meets this test. They do so by stating that the "scientific community" supports and accepts their approach. On the surface, a statement such as this one—especially when uttered under oath—would appear to be inaccurate or even irresponsible. However, the key is in their definition of the term "scientific community." This group is one which the "voiceprint" proponents define as including only those individuals whom *they* recognize as qualified. Thus, they blandly testify that only (1) voiceprint examiners can evaluate "voiceprints" and that other scientists (even those who actually are the most appropriate) are not qualified to judge their technique (9, 10, 31, 32, 35, 36, 37, 42, 44, 46). The "voiceprint" enthusiasts reject anyone (as being incompetent) unless they: (1) have made "thousands upon thousands of spectrograms," (2) have spent years attempting to use their procedures in speaker identification tasks, (3) agree that the "voiceprint" technique is a valid method for speaker identification and (4) are certified as qualified by other "voiceprint examiners." It is by this guise that they generate a scientific community of their own—one that consists of about a dozen and a half examiners plus an undisclosed number of trainees and "friends." Whether or not this small, self-appointed group is the only one in the world capable of making reasonable judgments about the "voiceprint" technique of speaker identification is open to serious question. However, they have convinced many courts that they are, indeed, the only experts in this area.

THE "VOICEPRINT" METHOD

At this juncture, I will attempt to describe "voiceprints." Unfortunately, this process has not been particularly well defined by its proponents. It also appears to be one that tends to change over time and from practitioner to practitioner. For example, a review of their testimony in the courts, the techniques they use and their opinions, all tend to reveal a rather substantial drift in technique. To be specific, Kersta (23) has indicated that he attempts to match the patterns of 10 common words, whereas Nash (37) sometimes testifies that he uses these words, but at other times indicates that he employs such things as the "bars, blades, blips and bands" seen on a spectrogram (35). On the other hand, Smrkovski (10) has indicated that he requires the suspects to provide exemplars of the exact phrases spoken by the unknown and then makes his matches based on an unspecified number of similarities (32). And finally, Truby (46) has unequivocally stated that he believes it to be unthinkable that anyone would even try to describe the pattern-matching process related to this technique and implies that it is one of such great mystery that there is no way to operationally define or quantify it.

Yet, no matter what definition is offered, the core of this process has been, and still is, some sort of pattern-matching procedure based on the configurations seen on t-f-a spectrograms similar to that found in Figure 10-1. As you probably are aware, while the development of this form of sound spectrography was an exciting event some half century ago, it is a relatively crude technique—at least in the light of modern-day technology. Unfortunately, the "voiceprint" enthusiasts apparently are not aware of (or choose to ignore for the sake of their consumers) the limitations of this process and the ways in which patterns produced

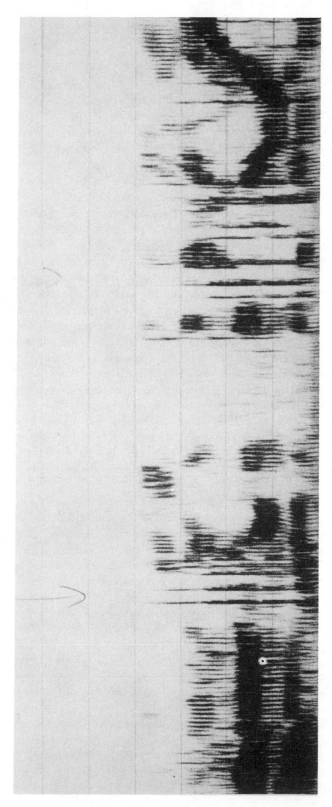

Figure 10-1. A time-frequency-amplitude spectrogram of the type utilized by the "voiceprint" proponents. This type of spectrogram also has been discussed in Chapters 2 and 4.

by this device can be distorted. Quite to the contrary—from time to time, they even have argued its infallibility (10, 24, 37, 46).

Generating t-f-a Spectrograms

As you know by now, time-frequency-amplitude spectrograms are produced by a device which employs relatively narrow (45 Hz) or wide (300 Hz) bandpass filters to sweep the frequency range of a segment of speech approximately 2.4 sec in duration. By this means a rather rough analog approximating the speech events processed is produced. Time is on the horizontal axis, frequency on the vertical and the relative darkness of the markings constitute an estimate of intensity (see again Figure 10-1). Of the three dimensions, time is the most accurate. Frequency, however, tends to be somewhat distorted with respect to its actual characteristics and for two reasons. First, most sound spectrograms used in "voiceprinting" utilize broadband filtering, a process which tends to remove representation of the actual partials within the speech signal. Instead, what is seen are rough outlines of where there are concentrations of energy. Taking vowels as an example, the areas of resonance—or the vowel formants— appear as black bars. It is by this means that the cited concentrations are outlined and the specific details of the acoustic wave (i.e., the actual partials) are lost. Of course, it is conceded that some useful features of the speech act can be observed and measured by this process but, in a very real sense, these configurations are artificial, because energy is seen where, in reality, it does not exist and removed from areas where it does. The observable patterns are yet further distorted because the frequency dimension is structured on an arithmetic basis (with the 1-kHz divisions equidistant) when actually this function is a geometric one based on a 2:1 ratio (i.e., the octave system); see again the frequency section in Chapter 2.

Probably the greatest weakness of this particular type of sound spectrography relates to its third feature—that of signal "intensity." Spectrographs of the t-f-a type provide rather minimal information about the energy patterns of speech sounds. These devices simply do not permit accurate quantification of energy as a function of frequency, even when the "sectioners" are used. Thus, as you might have guessed from the discussion above, it is relatively easy to accidentally or volitionally modify the patterns seen on a particular spectrogram. As anyone who has made a number of these records will concede, problems such as changes in calibration, variation in gain (at any stage within the process), filtering of any type, noise, internal distortion and/or any background signal can markedly bias the patterns seen on a particular spectrogram. Indeed, individuals using spectrographs for other purposes often change or enhance the pattern characteristics they wish to observe simply by manipulation of one or more of these very features.

An example of this problem occurred in "The Case of the Matching Clicks." Consider a rural town in the southern part of the United States—a town with but a single industry to support the bulk of its inhabitants. During the fall of a year not too long ago, a series of bomb threat telephone calls were received at the main office of this company. Since the firm in question had been exhibiting displeasure with its location, continued bomb threats—or an actual explosion—might trigger relocation. Thus, great pressure was placed on the local police to solve the case. One of the calls was traced to a particular residence and tight surveillance was placed around the house of interest. When yet another bomb threat call was received, the police closed in and found the house occupied by a single male. Since this male already was one of several suspects, the case appeared solved. However, when exemplars of all suspects were sent (with copies of the recorded bomb threat calls) to a "voiceprint examiner," he exonerated the man arrested at the house under surveillance and identified yet another of the suspects as the caller. During the trial, it became evident that the "match" had been based (to a great extent anyway) on a spike that appeared on the spectrogram of one of the bomb threat calls. There was no such "click" on the spectrograms made from the exemplars provided by any of the suspects except the one on trial. Of course, a spike such as the one observed could not be related in any way to the speech of either the unknown caller or defendant. About the only explanation that made any sense at all was that it related to some sort of malfunction (possibly intermittent) in the recording system used. It also was of interest to note that the "voiceprint" examiner could not explain why there was no noise on the tape recording, even though the defendant was known to be at work at the time of the call and the only phone to which he had access was situated in a very noisy part of the shop.

In short, t-f-a sound spectrography (of the type described) does not constitute very sophisticated technology. Logically, it is a technique that leaves at least some doubt in the minds of many scientists as to whether the observed patterns constitute an accurate and stable enough analog of the speech signal to permit any identifications at all to be made (in this regard, consider Figures 10-2 and 10-3). Questions also arise about the robustness of the technique in the face of the many distortions and stresses associated with the forensic situation.

The Listening Procedure

When the "voiceprint" technique was first used, attempts at matching the patterns of one spectrograph to those seen on another constituted almost the entire process. A second procedure was added to the overall approach during the 1970s. This additional task required that the "voiceprint examiner" listen to the voice of the unknown talker and compare it to that of the suspect or suspects. Thus, a possibly useful dimension was added to the method—which now appears to include judgments by the examiner as to whether or not the two voices sound similar or different. Neither the exact process employed in this technique nor research related to the approach has been articulated by the "voiceprint" proponents. However, from their testimony in court, it appears they feel that this supplementary procedure adds a rather important dimension to the overall process. In response, I refer you back to the previous chapter and the discussions there as to the hidden dangers in the aural-perceptual approach to speaker identification (especially relative to the one-on-one procedure)—and how these judgments must be structured if they are to be valid.

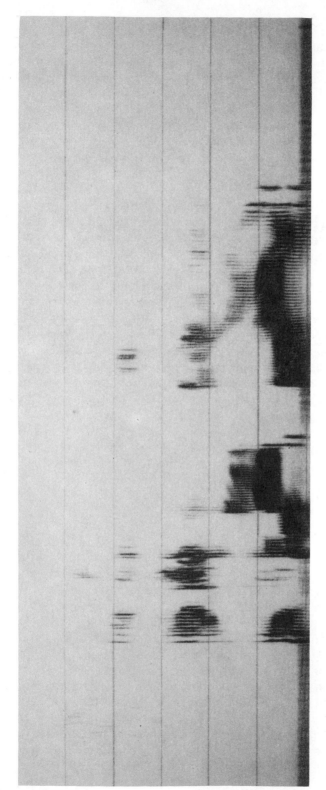

Figure 10-2. A pair of spectrograms produced by two different talkers speaking the same passage. Note how very much alike they are.

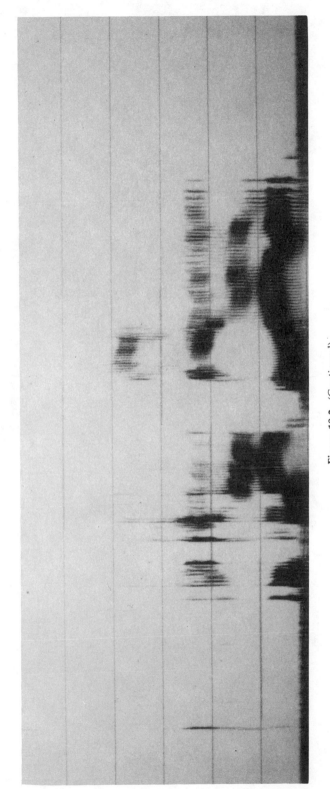

Figure 10-2. (Continued)

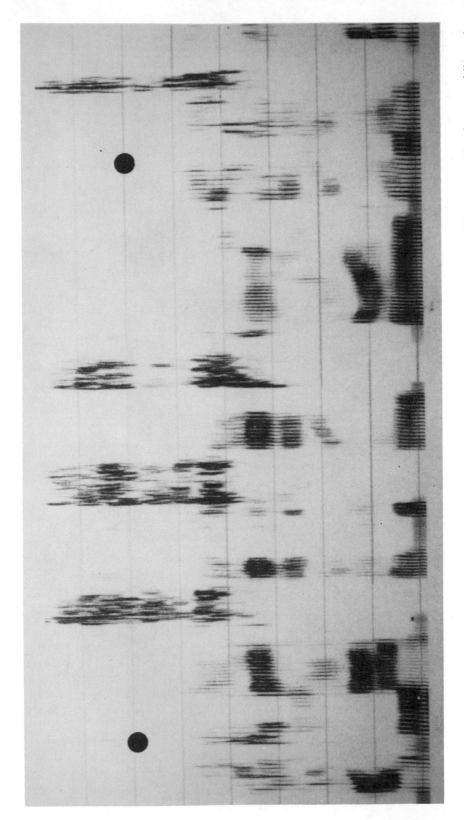

Figure 10-3. A pair of "voiceprint" type spectrograms of a *single* individual speaking the same passage but at different times. Note how very different they are with respect to timing and other relationships.

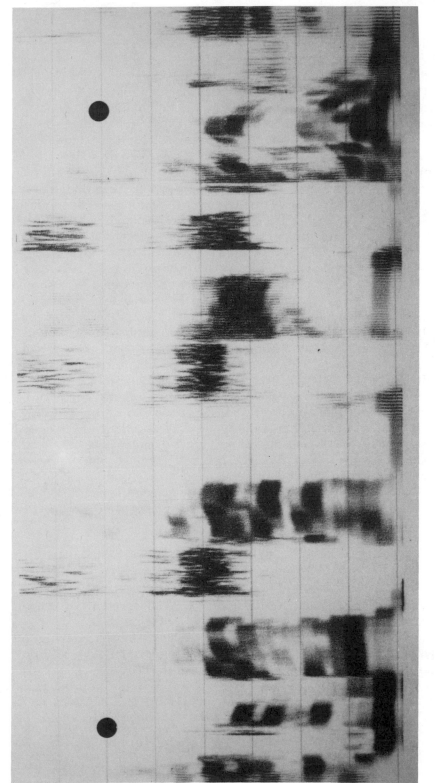

Figure 10-3. (Continued)

THE PROBLEM OF "VOICEPRINT" VALIDATION

If "voiceprints/grams" are a product, what is the proper stance to be taken by (1) their proponents and (2) members of the scientific community? As with any product, it is incumbent upon the organization producing it to demonstrate its nature, use and safe operation. That is, it would appear necessary for the "voiceprint" proponents to be the first to demonstrate the soundness of their product and the validity of their techniques. They could do so by carrying out appropriate (and substantial) research programs or by utilizing well-established logic and published research to support their position. They do not appear to have done so; they have not even attempted to demonstrate that intrasubject variability always is smaller than intersubject variability (see the Tosi study below). However, in this instance, they (perhaps) should not be taken too severely to task. There is always the possibility that the individual talker being studied may not exhibit enough idiosyncratic features to permit even the more sophisticated approaches to speaker verification/identification to be carried out successfully. Indeed, as I stated previously, the problem of the inter-/intra-speaker variation haunts all individuals working in the speaker recognition area. Nevertheless, no matter what your perspectives about these basic relationships, the fact remains that it is those who create a product who must first substantiate its validity and efficiency. In this instance, it also is their responsibility to experimentally demonstrate the ability of their technique to work properly in the forensic milieu with all its speaker and system "distortions." Yet, the "voiceprint/gram" proponents appear unwilling or unable to do so, and they have been reminded continuously of this responsibility over the past 20 years. Their response, usually, has been to invite others to carry out the necessary research—a stance that does not seem to me to be an appropriate one. Since they claim the technique is valid, and since they are the individuals who are exploiting it, they should carry the basic burden of, at least, primary test standardization. What have they done in his regard? They report only one large and a couple of small studies.

The Basic Study by Tosi

The research by Tosi and his coauthors (45) is advanced by the proponents of "voiceprinting" as primary research support for their technique. Indeed, they stress that one of the reasons courts and juries should attach credence to their claims is because this research has proven that "voiceprinting" is a valid process. They further describe the centrality of this project in such a manner as to exclude any information generated by other relevant research. In truth, this particular investigation is only one of many that have utilized this type of pattern-matching process in speaker identification, and there are a number of other studies that are just as relevant to the issues under discussion as is this one. Further, since the Tosi et al. study was a laboratory investigation—rather than one directly related to the forensic model—there also exist investigations that are far more relevant to the forensic process than is theirs.

The Research Design

The research by Tosi and his associates is a little difficult to follow, as it consists of a number of substudies combined into a relatively large project. Moreover, some of the experimental conditions varied over the investigational period (for example, there appeared to be a midproject reduction in both the number of examiners and the number of words used in the matches). Indeed, one of the consultants (Black) appeared somewhat surprised that the research came out as well as it did, considering "the apparent weakness" in the research design (37). Basically, the authors studied talker populations of between 10 and 40 individuals (drawn from a group of 250). Their examiners consisted of between one and three individuals (drawn from a group of 29). They claim that their 250 talkers represent a total population of 25,000 males and, thus, give the impression that a substantial population was evaluated, when in reality, the groups studied were of a size conventional for research of this type. Briefly, the subissues examined were if: (1) it is best to use six or nine cue words in the identification process; (2) the use of one, two or three utterances of the same word by a speaker has an effect on this process; (3) the effects of different types of recording conditions result in differences in identification; (4) correct identification levels vary as a result of the cue words being spoken in different contexts; (5) different size populations of speakers affect the data; (6) there are differences in the identification process resulting from the use of contemporary and noncontemporary speech; and (7) open and closed trials alter identification rates.

Tosi's Results

Tosi and his associates present their results with respect to two cycles or stages of the research. The percentage of correct responses is reported to have varied between a little over 86% to nearly 96%. The data also are presented with respect to the types of errors obtained (basically, false identifications and false eliminations) and with respect to the number of firm conclusions made by the examiners. In the discussion and conclusions, they stress that when they replicated Kersta's original research, "which involved essentially closed trials and contemporary spectrograms of cue words spoken in isolation," they were able to confirm his claim of an error rate of 1% false identifications. This particular statement is used extensively in the courts to suggest that even with respect to the forensic model, a level of 99% accuracy can be expected from the technique. Yet, a more significant set of data can be observed by examination of the findings for contemporary and noncontemporary samples. These data can be considered to be far more appropriate to law enforcement primarily because contemporary speech will never be found in the forensic milieu, that is, with respect to criminal/suspect comparisons. To repeat an earlier illustration, the only way contemporary speech would be obtained under forensic conditions is when an arresting officer is at the scene of the crime and immediately obtains a voice exemplar under exactly the same conditions which existed during its commission. Quite obviously, if these conditions prevailed, there would be no reason to attempt an identification by "voiceprints." In any case, for open trials (which most closely parallel the forensic model) and noncontemporary speech, the error rates were in excess of 18%—with somewhat over 6% being errors of false identification and nearly 12%, those of false elimination. It should be remembered also that these data were obtained from highly controlled laboratory procedures and not from the field! In any event, if the cited values are applied to a pool of 100,000 individuals—a number that could very well represent the population of "suspects" existing in a major city—12,000 criminals would be exonerated and 6,000 innocent people accused of a crime. These figures are somewhat bizarre of course; nevertheless, such relationships must be taken into account when the forensic model is considered.

Other Studies by "Voiceprint" Proponents

The "voiceprinters" also refer to other "studies" they have conducted. Some of these investigations appear to be ad hoc in nature (see, for example, the old report by Kersta, 24); others do not seem to constitute actual research. For example, Smrkovski has testified (10) that he examined "voiceprints" of the speech of twins and found that the spectrograms did not match. Studies such as this are not experiments at all (in the scientific sense anyway) but rather the kind of process that could be carried out by any curious and intelligent layman given access to certain types of machines. On the other hand, there have been a few studies which would seem to qualify as descriptive research. Most notable is Hennessy's M.A. thesis (17), which was carried out under "business" conditions; he used two "examiners." First, a pilot study was conducted; it involved 12 males and 8 females, most of whom were Asians. A 30% error rate was obtained. In the major experiment, carried out with 84 American subjects equally divided between males and females, the error level was even greater—41% In response to these rather unmanageable error rates, Hennessy concluded "it is the opinion of this writer that 'voiceprint' identification is a reasonable identification method ... the relatively low accuracy percentage rate is not discouraging."

Another thesis was carried out by Hall (14), who investigated the ability of Rich Little to mimic six celebrities. Unfortunately, none of the celebrities would cooperate. Indeed, the only individual who even responded was actor John Wayne, who suggested that Hall send him a phrase to read, "rather than have me attempt to mimic Rich Little mimicking me." Hence, the speech samples used in the comparisons were drawn from "prerecorded interviews, television appearances, and through the assistance of the Michigan State University Voice Library." Spectrogram matches were discussed (but not employed), fundamental frequency was obtained from the narrow-band filter of the spectrograph (Hall claimed that Little was not able to match the F0 of the subjects), and an auditory discrimination test by 20 generally untrained students was carried out in both quiet and noise. The listeners were able to identify the subjects as themselves 79% of the time and the mimic as himself 68% of the time, and when the mimic was attempting to sound like the subject, 74% of the time. These values were somewhat lower when noise was present. Hall suggests that it is possible to "discriminate spectrographically between the subjects' natural voices and their voices when mimicked by another person—even a professional." However, the results of this research are not very compelling, nor do they relate very well to the forensic model. Rather, Hall appears to have conducted some sort of speaker verification task and, even in this sense, the results were negative. They do little to support the claims of the "voiceprint/gram" proponents that their technique is 99% accurate.

Finally, a study of sorts has been published as a letter to the editor in the *Journal of the Acoustical Society of America* (25). In this letter, it was reaffirmed that the FBI would not use "voiceprints" in court but would do so in investigations. The author went on to indicate that over a period of 15 years, FBI examiners had exhibited an error rate of only 1% for those speakers where they made a positive decision (about 35% of 2,000 cases total). It certainly appeared that he was attempting to show that, while the procedure could not be used in very many cases, it was virtually error-free when it was employed. In reading this letter, however, I found that the author had not provided very much tangible support for his position. For example, the following observations (among others) could be made. First, references to other studies were quite sparse and tended to be those that reflected his particular bias; he did not include the dozens upon dozens of reports of experiments that do not support his position. Second, he did not seem aware that the type of spectrometer he referenced is only one of many types of sound (and other) spectrometers. Third, he in no way recognized, or made reference to, the extensive work carried out on machine approaches to speaker verification and/or identification (there are literally hundreds of references here; see Chapter 11 for a few). Fourth, and most important, he did not describe in any relevant detail just what he meant by "voiceprints" or how this process was accomplished. For example, it could be asked if the procedures actually utilized were consistent among the examiners and over the 15 years of work he cites. Further, it appeared obvious that, in some instances at least, he confused procedures for the handling of tape recordings for other purposes with speaker identification. Fifth, he did not establish the qualifications of his examiners. While he listed six requisites as necessary, only two appear particularly relevant (i.e., the completion of a 2-week course with a "voiceprint" examiner and "formal approval" by that person or another examiner). Sixth, he did not indicate if his examiners had completed the "two years of full-time experience" in (1) voice identification, (2) tape processing or (3) the filtering of tapes (the second two types of experience appear to be rather tangential) before, during or after their work was included in his survey. Seventh, it is not clear if the 1,000 "actual case examinations" his subjects would have had to carry out for "certification" were included also in the 2,000 cited in the letter to the editor, or were in addition to them. Also, I must confess to being rather uncomfortable with the author's assumption that scientific certainty was demonstrated when a decision made by an examiner was "consistent with case disposition" in question. Apparently, he expected the cooperating agency to inform him if any changes occurred in the outcome of the case; in my estimation, good scholarship would have required him to carry out a follow-up in all instances. Other questions can be asked, of course. Some are found in Shipp *et al.* (40); a counterresponse also is available (26). In short, it is a little surprising that the FBI would permit publication of an endorsement of a procedure in which it has so little faith that it will not permit its use in support of courtroom testimony.

Independent "Voiceprint" Studies

The "voiceprint" proponents have succeeded (at least in court) in giving the impression that they have conducted virtually all of the research in this area. To demonstrate this impact, the following statement was made in an article on "voiceprints" in the *Maryland Law Review* (2): "The only challenge to Tosi available to a defendant is the testimony of theoretically skeptical scientists whose testimony is in the opinion of some courts far less persuasive than Tosi's ... not because Tosi is right... but because he is the sole possessor of empirical data." Yet, a great deal of work in this area has been carried out, the experiments in question having been conducted by individuals within the actual scientific community—by researchers who have dispassionately studied variables that were as relevant (and often even more so) to the forensic model as were those of the "voiceprint" group. To be specific, in an important study, Stevens *et al.* (43) compared the ability of subjects to make speaker identifications spectrographically and by the aural-perceptual method. They report that the error rates associated with spectrographic examinations ranged from 21% to 47% but that their subjects were somewhat better when identifying speakers on the basis of the aural-perceptual method. Further, Young and Campbell (48) antedated Tosi in testing Kersta's claims and they reported far greater error rates than did either Kersta or Tosi. Even more to the point, Hazen (15) studied the cited process, utilizing both closed and open sets as well as identifications from same and different contexts. His error rates also were substantially higher (12-57%) than were Kersta's or Tosi's. As a matter of fact, Hazen concluded that "spectral similarities due to intraspeaker consistency are not apparent enough to outweigh the similarities due to ... phonetic context." In sum, none of the several investigators cited could achieve "hit rates" even close to those claimed by the "voiceprint" proponents.

Yet other investigators have addressed this problem. For example, Obrecht (33) became curious about statements by Nash (19) concerning the similarity of fingerprints and "voiceprints" where he (Nash) said: "As each one of the ridges of your fingers or on the palm of your hand differ from each other, so do all of the other parts of your body. They are unique to you ... including your voice mechanisms." A study was then carried out in which Obrecht found that examiners with experience in fingerprint analysis were no better at speaker identification than were those who lacked such a background. Even more to the point, it has been reported by Endress *et al.* (11) that spectrographic patterns and fundamental frequency vary substantially over time and with attempts at voice disguise; my associates and I have observed similar relationships (20, 30). As a matter of fact, we discovered that when subjects disguised their voices, very substantial changes occurred in F0 and in both the spectrographic and temporal patterning of the speech. Yet another recent study serves to underscore the problems relative to disguise faced by the "voiceprint" proponents. In a report on experiments relative to the effect of selected vocal disguises on spectrographic speaker identification (38), it was stated that these conditions led to identification errors varying from approximately 50% to nearly 78%—even when relatively high confidence ratings were reported by the examiners. These cited investigators also observed error rates of 40% and greater, even when the talkers did not disguise their voices. Finally, Rothman (39), who employed highly skilled examiners, reported an overall correct identification mean of but 20% when he used talkers that sounded similar to each other. He obtained his best identification scores (39%) when his examiners compared the same phrase and his poorest scores (6%) for the "sound-alikes" when the samples were noncontemporary.

It is interesting to note that none of the independent investigators were able to achieve the very high levels of correct identification reported by Kersta, Tosi and their associates. Certainly, no investigator mustered a level even close to the 99% correct identification rates they claim possible. Admittedly, in some instances the individuals used as examiners were not as highly trained for these tasks as the "voiceprint" proponents suggest is necessary. However, in practically all instances, the examiners were at least as skillful and well trained as those utilized in the Tosi *et al.* study; indeed, in other instances, they were highly experienced/educated in both the phonetic sciences and in identification tasks. How, then, does one account for the extremely high levels of identification reported by Tosi (and Kersta) and the uniformly lower scores obtained by all other investigators? Unfortunately, this question must remain unanswered, at least for the present.

THE "VOICEPRINT EXAMINER"

Another contention, made by the proponents of "voiceprints," is that the technique is a good one because their small band of examiners has developed exceptional skills in the identification process. However, they do not provide any hard evidence to support this claim. They do list the recommended requisites for their examiners and the general processes by which they should operate (3, 44, 45, 46). Perhaps these conditions are best iterated by Black *et al.* (3) who indicate that "voiceprint examiners" should meet the following criteria:

1. A voice identification trainee must complete at least two years of supervised apprenticeship dealing with field cases and possess academic training in audiology and speech sciences before applying for a test of proficiency to become a professional examinee.
2. A professional examiner in voice identification must be entitled to five alternate decisions after each examination, namely: positive identification, positive elimination, probability of identification, probability of elimination and no opinion one way or the other.
3. A professional examiner in voice identification must be entitled to use

as much time and as many voice samples as he deems necessary to complete an examination.

4.   A professional examiner in voice identification must be held responsible for the positive decisions he may reach after his examination.

Truby (46) further argues that being a "speech scientist" does not qualify an individual in the area of "voiceprinting." He would reject any speech scientist or phonetician who had not *"accumulated personal mileage poring over sound spectrograms"* and who had not scrutinized thousands of "voiceprints." For example, he writes "I contend that *constant immersion in voice identification exercises* is the only criterion for acquiring the indicated expertise. *NO AMOUNT* of substitute intelligence or professional intellect can approximate the experience of *DOING* " (emphasis Truby's). Unfortunately, he does not suggest how one is to determine if he is correctly carrying out the process and is making accurate judgments. Truby further argues against the idea that the "voiceprint" technique necessarily belongs

> in or to Speech Science exclusively. Expertise, to begin with, is a matter of specific training, talent, acuity, perseverance, interest and so forth. Speech Scientists are not by definition experienced acoustic phoneticians, nor applied linguists of a variety of expertness; and *no one* has a corner on pattern recognition, to be sure.

Indeed, he contends that "anyone capable of leveling *truly valid* criticism at voiceprinting should seek . . . certification and if capable of attaining same; either withdraw his/her criticism or thus *appropriately qualify* his/her objections" (again, emphasis Truby's). He does not say if all of the "qualified voiceprint/gram examiners" have "scrutinized thousands of voiceprints" or who the supervisors are that evaluated their work. As a matter of fact, he gives no details at all as to how you would learn the process or find out if you could successfully carry it out.

Thus, the proponents of "voiceprinting" stress that one of the major strengths of their technique (Truby calls it an infallible one) is that they use only "highly trained" professionals who presumably adhere to some set of regulations. To me, this argument appears as erroneous and self-serving as does the postulate that the scientific community accepts the validity of "voiceprints." What is sadly missing is the scientific evidence demonstrating that the "voiceprint" procedure actually is valid and that its "certified examiners" can (successfully) carry out the required tasks. Nevertheless, their positions about these issues have been reiterated so often that they are believed—at least, by some individuals and by some courts.

The Objectivity of the Examiners

There is no question but that the "voiceprint examiners" are serious about their craft. As to whether they are objective in their judgments is quite another matter. First of all, it must be remembered that these examiners are primarily law enforcement agents (not scientists) and are emotionally tied to the technique. While I would not venture to suggest that any of them have ever perjured themselves in a court of law, or have indulged in any unethical conduct, I must confess that I sometimes wonder about their biases. A bent of the type they have exhibited tends not to lead to objectivity but rather to a highly protective stance—occasionally one that is almost mystical.

The "voiceprint examiners" prejudices tend to crop up in other ways too. For example, Smrkovski (10) testified in 1976 that he had been using the "voice-print" method of speaker identification for about five years. He stated that, during this period, he had examined nearly 30,000 spectrograms. As you will agree I am sure, 30K spectrograms is alot of them. Indeed, to carry out the tasks he said he had completed, he would have had to (1) become familiar with the specific case or task in question, (2) listen to the relevant tape recording, (3) establish his records, (4) find the section to be analyzed, (5) record that sample on the spectrograph, (6) make the spectrogram, (7) log/identify it, (8) make his judgment (presumably concerning the matches), (9) record this judgment, (10) write his report and (11) communicate his findings. Could he have done all this at an average rate of 20 minutes per spectrogram? Probably not, but if he did and worked a 40-hour week for 50 weeks per year, it would appear that the process-ing of this many spectrograms would have required the entire five years. No trips, no coffee breaks, no testimony, no telephone calls, no conferences, no training could have been included! Just spectrograph analysis. Perhaps the worst case was when Nash testified (and on more than one occasion) that he had analysed over 100,000 spectrograms (30, 37). Even on the incredibly unrealistic basis that each spectrogram took only 10 minutes to process in its entirety, it appears that he was able to crowd about 15 years of full time analysis into the nine years he had been active in the field.

Educational Issues

The basic educational background of most "voiceprint examiners" and, hence, their comprehension of the complex communicative processes with which they are dealing also can be questioned. While it is quite probable that the relevant education of most of the examiners exceeds the basic 2-week course in "voiceprinting," their level of specialty education appears minimal for the tasks they are required to carry out—that is, excluding the two or three Ph.D.'s who do a little work in this area. Apparently, some members of this small group of individuals have earned at least some college-level credits; a few have won bachelors or even masters degrees. However, most who have completed degrees appear to have majored in the area of speech pathology or criminal justice rather than in the phonetic sciences—a situation which may or may not be a disadvan-tage to them. However, since details of their educational background and its relevancy to the speaker identification process are not easily discernible, only suppositions can be made about their basic knowledge in relevant areas. In any event, it is suggested that (with very few exceptions) their educational experi-ences are *not* of the type which would lead to an understanding of the challenges they must face. Since speaker identification clearly is not simple pattern match-ing, individuals working in his area should exhibit competency and knowledge in the appropriate sectors of acoustics, physiology, perception, engineering, psychology and phonetics. The fixation of "voiceprint examiners" on this rather archaic process (i.e., pattern matching rather than modern technology) is perhaps the best indicator of their level of sophistication. It is by this means that they sometimes reveal the extent of their understanding (or lack of it) about speaker identification.

"The Case of the Smart-Aleck Rich Boy" should serve to illustrate my argument in this regard. A well-to-do young man had completed college about six months before he could start law school. He spent this period working in one of the many "theme parks" that exist in this country. Before he left this position (for law school), he told his friends and supervisors just what he thought about all "that sweetness and light which we shoveled at the gullible public." Some months later two bomb threats were made to (and recorded at) the park's main office; the threats also involved extortion. As the young man was among those that had been tabbed as "trouble makers," the park's Chief of Security called him (and others) for "a routine employment follow-up evaluation" and recorded his voice. Of the several exemplars sent to a "voiceprint examiner," his was the one chosen as being the same as that of the bomb threat caller. I was retained by the defense and, after evaluating the examiner's work, found that he had erred in numerous ways. In one instance he had made a match where the patterns of the two sounds were similar in configuration, but were at markedly different frequency levels. The magnitude of this difference actually was so great that there was very little possibility it could have resulted from variation in the vowel "targeting" behavior of a single individual. Rather, it undoubtedly was associated with the production of speech sounds (perhaps even of dissimiliar vowels) by two different individuals. Apparently, this "voiceprint examiner" was not well-enough versed in the laws of acoustics to permit him to avoid a simple "error" of the type cited. Worse yet, he made numerous other errors. In any event, as the case developed, it also became evident that the two calls probably were made by two different people and neither of these "unknowns" appeared to exhibit a dialect remotely related to that of the defendant. When the part of the case based on physical evidence also collapsed, the indictment was withdrawn and the young man continued his law studies. Many other examples of this type could be cited. In short, I must confess that after considerable experience with "voiceprint examiners," I reluctantly have come to the conclusion that many of them are not familiar enough with the relevant concepts and knowledge to be able to carry out speaker idenification tasks of any type.

Finally, while the "voiceprint" proponents tend to be generally vague about the levels and types of experiences necessary for success in speaker identification, they do stress the need for background in forensics. To my mind, familiarization with law enforcement (and related) needs is quite desirable, but actual experience (i.e., as an agent) within the law enforcement community probably is not necessary. More important is the type of advanced training one receives in appropriate graduate study programs. Speaker identification is a very complex problem. Anyone attempting work in this field should be highly qualified in the phonetic sciences, engineering, psychology and related specialties. Moreover, specialized training and experience within these areas also is a must. Two-week courses simply are not an adequate substitute for proper training.

The Examiner's Apprenticeship

Perhaps one of the most disquieting claims made by the "voiceprint" proponents relates to the benefits of the 2-year apprenticeship each of the examiners must complete. Presumably, every trainee works under an experienced supervisor for this period of time. But who are these supervisors? Where did they come from? Who supervised them? Admittedly, a technique such as this one has to originate somewhere. However, I am unwilling to take on faith the supposition that the original supervisors actually possessed the ability to make identifications themselves—much less that they exhibit skills which will permit them to train other people in the area. As stated previously, the very fact that they accept the "voiceprint" technique as valid—and with no more scientific verification than it enjoys—brings their judgmental processes into question. And . . . where are the experimental (and independent) data relative to their success rates?

It is possible to trace the supervisory genealogy of some of the examiners— at least roughly. Apparently, the first was Lawrence Kersta, the individual who popularized the method. A number of people took his 2-week course; he then provided the supervision for their apprenticeships. Yet, Kersta's abilities have been seriously questioned; he certainly has made errors (7). One of Kersta's apprentices was Ernest Nash. In turn, Nash apparently was supervisor to L. Smrkovski and possibly F. Lundgren, and these two gentlemen appear to be among the current leaders of the "voiceprint" practitioners. Is Nash's record without blemish, or did he extend the legacy accorded him by Kersta? Perhaps the opinion of one jurist (35) will provide insight into Nash's abilities. This judge wrote:

> Regardless of the issue of admissibility, the opinion of Lt. Nash that the defendant was the speaker of the bomb threat to the Telephone Company on February 2, 1972, was not reliable in this particular case due to: a) Mistakes and errors in the preparation of the spectrograms used in making the identification, b) Failure to ascertain the existence of such errors, c) Demonstrated listening errors in the court while under cross-examination, d) Tentative misidentification of the court-ordered exemplar (Exhibit 2) prior to outside knowledge of identification and e) Failure to maintain accurate records/logs during conducting of tests on Exhibits 1 and 2.

Moreover, in a later case (31), Tosi was forced by the court to analyze some of Nash's spectrograms. He disagreed with Nash relative to the suspects' identity.

It can be argued that the issue as to whether one or more of the "voiceprint" supervisors made errors in judgment (or was not as effective as he might have been) is not as important as the issue relative to the validity of the technique itself. Nevertheless, I would submit that the skill/behavior of the leaders in an area is of substantial consequence—and that their conduct can be questioned in this instance. Even more important is the fact that these supervisors have not been objectively tested relative to their ability to perform the tasks themselves and/or train others in ways that appear relevant.

Finally, a number of fundamental questions can be directed at the apprenticeship itself. For example, what is the nature of this program; what are its prerequisites? How is talent/progress assessed by the supervisors; what skills are necessary for graduation and how are they tested? Personally, I would like to know just how the apprentice is supervised by the sponsor and if the relevant tasks are consistent and standardized. To my mind, the "voiceprint/gram examiner" apprenticeship does not appear to be similar to the close relationships established between graduate students and their professors—nor do they appear to involve the daily contact the typical apprentice enjoys with a journeyman or artisan. Rather, the interface seems to be sporadic in nature and carried out at long distance, either by mail and/or over the telephone. Perhaps this assessment is unfair. If so, the "voiceprint/gram" proponents have only to establish the nature of these apprenticeships by publication of appropriate detail. However, at present, it appears that the abilities and behaviors of their "examiners" constitute a liability rather than a strength.

TO CONCLUDE

There is little question but that confusion exists relative to the nature and merit of the "voiceprint/gram" technique of speaker identification. Among the major criticisms that can be leveled are that (1) it is an archaic procedure, (2) its validity is in question (due to insufficient and/or negative research), (3) it appears to permit decisions to be made only about a third of the time and (4) the training and competencies of its operators are largely a mystery. Moreover, its effectiveness in the field is uneven enough to suggest that the approach tends to lack merit. After all, in this case, practice does not make perfect; it simply makes "more of the same." Granted, these confusions may lead to unfair evaluations. However, it would be much easier to make intelligent decisions about "voiceprint/grams" if the proponents would only publish reasonable field data about the method as well as systematic reviews of the training procedures and evaluations used to develop examiners.

A final point should be made. Several individuals are making an effort to computerize "voiceprints." The project, which is being carried out in Los Angeles, has been underway for some years now. It has enjoyed a great deal of publicity but, to date anyway, I have not been able to discover if the relevant investigators have produced any useful results. Apparently, there have been no research reports in the scientific literature and the one general publication I have been able to find was not very informative (1). My guess is that, just as application of the best of modern technology would not permit you to fly nonstop from New York to London in a World War I aeroplane, the inherent weaknesses of a primitive method such as "voiceprinting" cannot be overcome simply by adding a computer to the pattern-matching process.

In the interim, the major hope for success in the field of speaker recognition—and especially for speaker identification—appears to be that of machine/computer processing by fairly sophisticated techniques. Since aural-perceptual (human) approaches appear impractical for forensic use, the only reasonable solution to the problem appears to be the development of some sort of computer-aided, machine procedure. Chapter 11 will provide information about the structuring and testing of such a technique. The actual development of a particular method of this type will be used as an example.

CHAPTER 11

Machine/Computer Approaches

INTRODUCTION

The speaker recognition scene changes radically when attempts are made to apply modern technology to the problem. Indeed, with the seeming limitless power of electronic hardware and computers, it appears that solutions are but a step away. Yet such may not be the case. For example, many years have passed since the earliest efforts were made to develop machines that would (1) type letters dictated by voice, (2) automatically translate the speech of one language into another, (3) understand spoken speech and (4) identify a person from voice analysis alone. Authors such as Hecker (40) insist that there are no machines which are both as sensitive and as powerful (for these purposes) as the human ear. What Hecker means by "ear" is, of course, the entire auditory sensory system coupled to the brain, with all its sophisticated memory and cognitive functions. He may be correct in his assumptions, but I do not think so. Hence, the issue I will address in this chapter is: can machines/computers be made to operate at least as efficiently as the auditory system for speaker identification purposes? That is, can they be made to mimic these processes or, if not mimic them, at least parallel the recognition task by some other method? Probably so, but the task is not an easy one.

Please be aware that it is not my intent to use this chapter to list or review all of the efforts that have been made to develop speaker identification by machine. Indeed, while some approaches have shown promise, most have not. Moreover, we also will see that very few groups have persevered in their efforts to solve this problem and develop a system that operates reasonably well under most field conditions. Thus, rather than a simple review of the work of others, I have chosen to outline the levels and types of research that must be undertaken if a speaker identification system is to be developed. This review will include description of the specific evaluation procedures I believe must be employed if a system—any system—is to be successful. Finally, I will describe in some detail one such method or approach. It is the one I know best, since a group of my colleagues and I have been working on it for the past 25 years. I include its description because it should nicely define the strictures and structures anyone will encounter when attempting a task of this type. Moreover, by describing it in this way, I can make the procedures involved freely available to anyone who wishes to use them. Indeed, several other scientists already are utilizing the system to be described—either in part or in its entirety.

PERSPECTIVES AND DEFINITIONS

First, it would appear useful to provide some definitions. Even though you may find them a little redundant (see again Chapter 9), they should improve your perspective about this area. At the very least, they are important to the understanding of the concepts that follow.

To be specific, there are three independent yet interrelated problems (within the general area) that are of importance to law enforcement and security organizations, the military, and diplomatic, intelligence, aerospace and related agencies. They are speech recognition, speaker verification and speaker identification. Even though rather substantial progress has been made relative to the first of these problems—and modest progress on the second—the fact remains that there actually are no fully operational systems currently in existence that permit reasonably effective speech/speaker recognition tasks to be carried out. There are many promising, but experimental, approaches—one or two of which show excellent potential (101). Nevertheless, I stand by the statement that as of 1988, there are no fully functional systems on line. But why are these areas so important?

Speech Recognition

If it were possible for machines to decode spoken or tape recorded utterances, it also should be possible for them to automatically: translate languages, control prisons (with very small numbers of personnel), activate and control machinery, operate drones/satellites, type spoken messages, activate weaponry systems (from secure positions), permit banking by telephone, and so on. Indeed, if electronic and mechanical devices could be operated by voice commands, the potential for improved military, business, government, law enforcement and other operations would be extensive. Yet, as has been pointed out (21, 101), speech recognition by machine currently is not possible—or, at least, it is restricted to a degree which permits only casual use. There are a number of reasons for this situation; prominent among them is the fact that when a speech recognition system with even a limited lexicon is placed on-line, it very often fails due to the fact that it is not speaker independent. In order to operate effectively, the device must first recognize the talker and then attempt to analyze his or her particular speech patterns (i.e., selectively decode the utterance). Thus, no matter what you read in the newspapers, there presently are no systems that can successfully perform these functions for extended populations of talkers and for a lexicon large enough to handle unlimited discourse.

Speaker Verification

The problem of speaker verification is generally on a par with that of speech recognition. However, in this case, it is not necessary to interpret what the speaker says but rather to verify his or her identity and, in the basic speaker verification paradigm, the talker *wants* to be recognized. The potential uses for a working system of this type are virtually endless. Access of a person to secure areas by analysis of his or her voice is one example; verification of the identity of an officer giving instructions over a radio, walkie-talkie or any channel where he cannot be identified by sight, is another. It also can be important to verify the identity of individuals who are speaking from airplanes, space capsules, hyperbaric chambers/habitats, tanks, or some other remote station or location. Substantial research is being carried out in this area by a large number of laboratories. Taken as a whole, the scientific effort on speaker verification is outstanding and literally hundreds of excellent experiments have been published. If you are interested in this area, you would do well to read some of them; a few are listed for your convenience (see references 1-5, 7-9, 11, 15, 19, 20, 22, 27, 28, 30-32, 51, 52, 54, 56, 58, 65-70, 72, 73, 75, 77, 80-86, 88-94, 102-104). This set alone should provide you with a healthy introduction to the speaker verification area and to some of the more important approaches utilized by relevant investigators. The verfication task, while formidable, is relatively straightforward in nature. The individual talker ordinarily is cooperative (that is, unless he or she is an impostor), and, even though the speech sample cannot be contemporary, the equipment utilized ordinarily is of high quality and the nature of the sample controlled. Then too, extensive "reference" sets can be developed and redeveloped for each talker. Nevertheless, rather substantial problems remain to be solved here also, and there, as yet, do not appear to be any on-line operational systems that permit the universal verification of large numbers of individuals solely from analysis of their voices(5).

Speaker Identification

You will agree I am sure, that, of these three problems, the most difficult one to solve would be the identification of an unknown speaker by voice analysis—especially when he is talking in an environment which distorts or masks his utterances. For example, the speech exemplars analyzed never are contemporary, and the talker is usually uncooperative. He may attempt to disguise his voice or suffer from a number of intrusive conditions, i.e., the (varying) effects of health, ingested drugs, emotional states (especially stress or fear), and so on. System or channel distortions (limited bandpass, harmonic distortion) and noise (intermittent, continuous, narrow-band, broadband, etc.) also can interfere with attempts to establish the identity of a talker. Worse yet, the identification task always involves an "open set" — that is, one where the unknown talker may or may not be represented in the suspect/subject pool. This problem is quite serious because one member of any group always will sound more like the unknown talker than will any of the others, whether or not he actually is that person. Hence, the processes/criteria utilized in speaker identification are of critical importance.

Yet, the uses are many for a system which can be effectively applied to determine which talker, from among many possible talkers, is actually the "unknown" speaker. For example, it might be necessary for you to decide: (1) which of the several pilots or astronauts was the one who uttered the message, (2) if the individual on the telephone is the kidnapped child, (3) which of the suspects is the obscene caller, (4) if the individual who made the threats over the telephone actually committed the crime. While there currently may not be a system which can provide accurate identifications under every and all conditions, the need for one continues to grow. As such, an appropriate response must be formulated. Hopefully, the approach which will be described toward the end of this chapter is one that may lead to a successful solution of the problem.

APPROACHING THE PUZZLE OF SPEAKER IDENTIFICATION

The way to develop a machine-based speaker identification method is to (1) formulate an approach and (2) begin to test it. Since many ideas and approaches have been proposed, it would seem that the first of these two maxims would be, or should be, easy to achieve. Yet, that relationship does not necessarily hold. For example, the approach you decide to pursue should be in and of itself rooted in strong logic and/or prior research. Hence, you should have some idea about the potential of your approach even before you start testing it. Worse yet, the second part of the process (i.e., the research itself) is even more difficult to accomplish—primarily because it involves the completion of so very many experiments. Consider Figure 11-1. Portrayed here is a reasonable approach to the research-based development of a speaker identification system. In this instance, a number of elements, or vectors, are employed. In turn, a vector can consist of any analysis which you assume (from your prior modeling or literature study) will be useful as an identification cue. It could be made up of a group of parameters that "describe" speaking fundamental frequency, the number of axis crossings found in the signal during a predetermined period or just about any set of related measurements that you think are idiosyncratic enough to permit the identification of a particular speaker. Yet, there probably are no vectors which are robust, or all-encompassing, enough to permit efficient identifications under any and all possible conditions. Hence, if you are to be successful, you probably will have to develop a number of them—each one testing mutually exclusive elements within the speech signal.

Permit me to describe a reasonable scientific approach to this issue. Indeed, the experiments to be carried out should not be haphazard in nature. Rather, you should employ a systematic and organized program of research. The first series of investigations should be designed to test the ability of a selected vector to discriminate among talkers within a fairly large group of subjects. These early studies should be designed so as to permit gross changes to be made as needed in the parameters (or parts) that make up the vector. Once it begins to show promise, you then should evaluate it in situations where distortions are present.

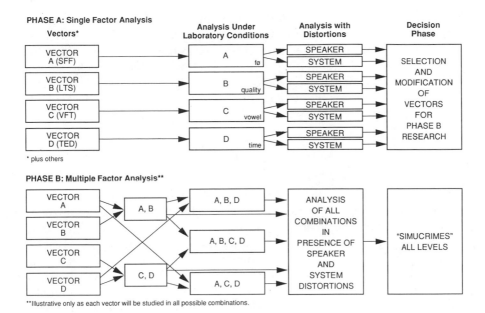

Figure 11-1. Model of a highly structured research approach for the systematic development of a "machine-based" speaker identification system.

Channel distortions, for example, could include telephone (frequency) bandpass and noise, whereas talker distortions could include speech samples produced under induced stress and/or disguise. The first phase of the process, then, is to continually test (and modify, if necessary) the vectors you have chosen until: (1) they appear robust enough to aid in the identification process and (2) you are aware of the conditions under which they are the most accurate or which reduce their efficiency. This initial process may take a fairly long time to complete.

The second phase of the research program would be to attempt to increase the power of the system by combining the vectors on some basis. As can be seen in the lower part of Figure 11-1, this process is a very complex one. To carry out all potential combinations of a set of only four vectors would require 11 separate research programs—each involving multiple experiments under normal conditions and with distortions present. Further, the work probably would have to be replicated after revisions were made to upgrade the system. In our case, this process has resulted in the total elimination of some vectors; it also permitted us to upgrade those that we found useful.

The final phase of a system development is to test the procedure in the field. In this instance, two approaches can be utilized; the first involves the solution of simulated "crimes" generated under field-like conditions, and the second, the application of the system to actual "real-life" cases. Either approach will provide good information relative to the validity and efficiency of the system, but both have their limitations. For example, even well-designed "simucrimes" are a little artificial and only roughly parallel real-life situations. On the other hand, the use of actual investigations permits only nonscientific verifications (i.e., confessions and convictions cannot be validly substituted for data). Nonetheless, the inclusion of these approaches is important, as these types of relationships can demonstrate if the procedure is one of merit or if its accuracy is lacking. In our work, this final step proved invaluable, since it led to the two-dimensional profile approach that we now believe to be of substantial value. In short, the development of a useful speaker identification system is not a trivial task. Indeed, we have discovered that it takes years of work and the completion of hundreds of experiments if the effort is to result in a successful approach.

A RESPONSE TO THE PROBLEM

When considering this area, it appeared to me that a detailed review of the ups and downs of the many studies carried out in the speaker identification area would be counterproductive. As with speaker verification, such discussion would be highly technical in nature and, more important, it would be off the point, as we want our focus to be on successful efforts. Anyway, except for projects being carried out in Eastern Europe, very few (if any) systematic research programs of the machine or computer-based type are being carried out. Of course, a few top flight experiments at laboratories associated with Bolt, Beranek and Newman and the German Bundeskriminalamt have been reported; however, unlike the thrust in speaker verification, these programs do not appear to be extensive and/or long term in nature.

Conversely, our program began in the 1960s and we have been conducting research now for well over 20 years. Since it is the program I know the best, it will be the one used as an illustration of the machine approaches to speaker identification. In all, eleven scientists, plus a large number of research assistants and technicians, have been involved with the project (most are named in references 45-50). Review of this work should provide a good illustration as to how you can go about developing a speaker identification system. Not only does our approach—which we call SAUSI, or Semiautomatic Speaker Identification (system)—provide a good example as to how one can apply the standards we suggest to research of this nature, but it is public domain. That is, if you wish, you can utilize any portion of the system or the research we have reported for your own purposes. Indeed, a number of scientists already are doing so. Now let me review how we approached the problem, the criteria we developed, and the system which resulted.

SAUSI

Our response to the speaker identification problem was to identify and evaluate a number of parameters within the human speech signal in order to (1) study some of the basic relationships involved (i.e., intra- and interspeaker variability) and (2) discover if any of these parameters could be used as identification cues. These investigations included both basic (laboratory) research and, later, investigations involving the potential (speaker/system) distortions that are known to occur in the field. We discovered early on that traditional approaches to (laboratory-type) signal processing, no matter how sophisticated, were rendered functionally inoperable when attempts were made to apply them to forensic problems. Indeed, these approaches also are sharply degraded for verification purposes when field-generated distortions occur. At this juncture, we shifted our focus and began to investigate a selected group of *natural* features (within the speech signal)—those which were thought to be potentially idiosyncratic of an individual speaker (44, 46, 106).

How did this perspective develop? As stated, we first noted that traditional signal-processing techniques were incompatible with the forensic model. Yet, we could not escape the fact that humans often carry out successful speaker identifications even under difficult conditions and that they do so simply by auditorily processing speech and voice signals. Stimulated by this observation, we reviewed the aural-perceptual literature (see especially Stevens, [96] and Chapter 9 for a review of those features people use in aural-perceptual speaker identification) in an attempt to discover which parameters might provide useful cues for our purposes. As you will see when our vectors are described, the features we were able to identify included speaking fundamental frequency, voice quality, vowel quality, the temporal patterning (or prosody) of speech, vocal intensity, and so on. Indeed, as our research with these speech/voice features progressed, we discovered that many of them tended to be resistant to forensic-type distortions. Better yet, this resistance could be enhanced in some instances, and different vectors were seen to resist different types of distortion. As a result of these investigations, we now are persuaded that the most robust approach to speaker identification is one based on the analysis of natural speech features and that the elegant but traditional types of signal processing, carried out by individuals working on speaker verification, are far less resistant to the distortions found in the typical forensic situation.

The Profile Concept

It also was very early in the development of what now appears to be a functional speaker identification procedure when we noted that no single vector seemed to provide high enough levels of correct identification for all of the many field distortions associated with law enforcement activities. Our first response to this problem (see again Figure 11-1) was to combine the vectors. However, in doing so we soon discovered that, sometimes anyway, such combinations resulted in a reduction of the correct identification scores. These results apparently were caused by the "diminishing returns rule" relative to the number of parameters we were applying. That is, the sensitivity of a system will continue to increase as parameters are added until it reaches an asymptote. At that point, further additions will result in the system moving onto the negative slope of the performance curve—and this situation is only exacerbated by the addition of yet more parameters. Our first solution was to reduce the number of parameters in a vector and mathematically combine vectors on a normalized basis rather than to simply add more and more parameters to the total.

The second relationship which resulted in degradation of system sensitivity by combining vectors turned out to be a methodological one; it related to the severe tests we employed in the research. That is, our experimental protocols reflected the forensic speaker identification model and called for but a single reference sample for each subject/condition. Thus, as the multidimensionality of the vector space increased, the reference points for each subject were forced farther and farther apart and the probability of correct identification was reduced. In short, we began to have too few points in too large a space, with little to no intrasubject variability and we were forced to try and find these points rather than to match one area to another. A partial solution here was to increase the number of references per individual and/or use longer speech samples. However, we soon discovered that this was a poor response because, as the number of reference samples increased, the imbalance between the number of parameters and population size also was reduced.

It took some time, but ultimately we were able to enhance the robustness of our vectors and compensate for the methodological constraints we had logically built into our research and, hence, into the identification approach. These efforts culminated just recently in our second modification, i.e., the development of a two-dimensional profile in which all of the vectors are represented—but on an equal and normalized basis. The normalization process also has helped prevent dominance by a particular vector simply because its calculated values are greater than those of the others. In any case, we found that the most sensitive procedure was to test a sample of a particular unknown speaker against a series of (speaker) reference sets made up of the unknown speaker's utterences, that of the known (or knowns) and those of a series of foils. It was by this method that effectiveness of the procedure was determined internally—primarily because the test sample for the unknown talker always should match best with his or her own reference set. Further, the known-unknown relationship never would be attempted on a one-to-one basis. In any event, estimates could be made as to whether or not the speech sample produced by the unknown talker matched that of any of the knowns. Practical demonstrations of how well this profile approach works will be found in the following sections.

A Summary

A number of postulates and perspectives have been presented in this section; they can be summarized as follows. First, the development of a system designed to identify speakers from voice samples should be initiated only on the basis of available data and/or sound theoretical constructs. Second, it is important to carry out a large number of experiments on the chosen approach—at least enough of them to demonstrate the validity and reliability of the selected procedures or techniques. Third, we suggest that a research program should culminate in a extensive series of field tests. Fourth, natural speech features appear to be the most robust of all the identification cues. That is, in practice, we have found that, to be successful, a forensic-related approach to speaker identification must be grounded in a vector system that employs signal analysis of this type— as natural speech features are the only ones which will be resistant to the many types of distortion encountered in the field. Fifth, we would argue that no single vector can be expected to provide a powerful speaker identification cue under any and all circumstances. Rather, some type of profile must be developed. Finally, any procedure employed must be one which will provide direct comparisons within a field of talkers; that is, all evaluations must extend beyond a simple one-on-one match of speakers.

THE NATURE OF THE SYSTEM DEVELOPED

It is my hope that I have been able to accurately describe the criteria and processes that must be followed if an effective speaker identification system is to be developed. The rest of this chapter provides a specific example of the results that can accrue if these principles are observed.

The Experimental Vectors

We found that Stevens (96) had cataloged a number of speech features which, when applied, could lead to the successful identification of talkers; these features included fundamental frequency, glottal volume velocity, formant frequencies/bandwidths, turbulent phonemes and nasal consonants. We tended to agree with Stevens—at least, relative to most of the stated features—but added several others to the list. Thus, the structuring of our approach was based on the features selected plus several related operations, viz, ones that exhibit: (1) generally high probability for discrimination among speakers, (2) enhanced utility when combined with other parameters, (3) resistance to distortion, (4) availability and (5) compatibility with computer processing. These criteria were not developed all at once; rather they were organized as a function of our ongoing research program. In any event, the vectors which have emerged as useful speaker identification cues are described below.

The Long-Term Speech Spectra Vector (LTS)

Analysis of power spectra has had a relatively long history relative to research on speaker recognition. We postulate that LTS provides an effective index of general voice quality and that as such, it is a good cue to a speaker's identity. A number of authors (9, 16, 20, 32, 34, 37, 60, 78, 98) have reported utilization of average spectra as a basis for specific cue materials in the identification process. However, it has been our group (23, 24, 49, 71, 107) that has systematically and successfully explored its use. We discovered that LTS can predict the identity of speakers at very high accuracy levels, especially in the laboratory and when data are normalized. We also have been able to demonstrate that LTS is relatively resistant to the effects of speaker stress and to limited passband conditions. However, it does not function well as a predictor when talkers disguise their voices. At present we extract the LTS data from speech by means of an FFT Real-Time Spectrum Analyzer (Princeton, model 4512) coupled to one of our DEC PDP 11/23 computers. The vector utilizes up to 40 individual parameters (or elements within the speech signal) to generate a power spectrum curve covering a frequency range of 60-10,000 Hz. The evaluation process involves the normalization of Euclidean distance data; a comparison of two such curves can be seen in Figure 11-2.

The Speaking Fundamental Frequency Vector (SFF)

Perception of the fundamental frequency of voice (F0 or SFF) has been shown to be a reasonably good cue for speaker recognition (17, 53, 62, 68, 97). However, prior to our efforts in this regard, acoustic/machine analysis of this speech feature had not been exceptionally encouraging (1, 25, 53, 55, 89, 95, 103). Neither were we able to report that this vector was a very powerful one in our earlier research, but it was our belief that this early lack of success resulted from the utilization of a vector with too few parameters. The situation appears to have changed now that we are utilizing an approach involving measurements of up to 30 parameters; indeed, the results continue to show substantial improvement (23, 50, 53). To be specific, the parameters making up this vector include the geometric mean and standard deviation of all the fundamental frequencies produced by the talker plus intervals, or "bins," of semitone width containing energy and the number of waves in each of these semitone interval bins. Fundamental frequency data are obtained automatically by means of our FFI-8 (Fundamental Frequency Indicator; see Chapter 4): a system operated in such a manner that its output is fed directly to one of the PDP 11/23 computers. As stated previously, FFI-8 is a digital readout F0 tracking device which consists of a series of successive low-pass filters, with cutoffs at half-octave intervals, coupled to high-speed switching circuits which are controlled by a logic system (50). FFI measures each wave (it does *not* "sample") by producing a string of pulses, each of which marks the boundary of a fundamental period extracted from the complex speech wave. These data, in turn, are delivered to the computer in the form of a square wave. At this juncture, an electronic clock records the time from pulse to pulse, and these values are processed digitally to yield the desired statistical data (see Figure 11-3 for an example of the FFI output).

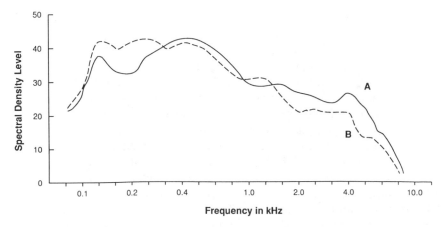

Figure 11-2. Graph portraying a pair of power spectra. The two subjects (A and B) will continue to produce multiple LTS curves similar to the first. Hence, the data contained in these curves can be utilized to mathematically establish intra- and intersubject relationships for identification purposes.

```
FFI  Reference  Freq. --- 16.35Hz    Clock Rate --- 1000    Cast Limit --- 6
     1012 FFI Cycles were validated in 6 Buffers for 0.91913E+05 Counts
========================================================================
                    LOW-RUN      HI-RUN       CAST        GOOD       TOTAL
# of Cycles          52.00       46.00      193.00      1012.00    1303.00
% of Cycles           3.99        3.53       14.81        77.67       1.00
# of Seconds          4.73        0.10        1.77        10.19      16.80
% of Time            28.15        0.62       10.54        60.65       1.00
========================================================================
```

A. Mean (St): 33.24 Mean (Hz):110.1 Standard Deviation: 2.79 (Semitones)

B. DISTRIBUTION TABLE:

ST	HZ	NO.	SECS	%
22	58.3	1.	0.0	0.2
23	61.7	1.	0.0	0.2
24	65.4	6.	0.1	1.0
25	69.3	6.	0.1	0.9
26	73.4	10.	0.1	1.4
27	77.8	16.	0.2	2.2
28	82.4	29.	0.3	3.7
29	87.3	45.	0.5	5.4
30	92.5	76.	0.8	8.6
31	98.0	114.	1.1	12.3
32	103.8	143.	1.3	14.5
33	110.0	173.	1.5	16.6
34	116.5	143.	1.2	12.9
35	123.5	116.	0.9	9.9
36	130.8	74.	0.6	6.0
37	138.6	23.	0.2	1.8
38	146.8	17.	0.1	1.2
39	155.6	7.	0.0	0.5
40	164.8	4.	0.0	0.3
41	174.6	2.	0.0	0.1
42	185.0	2.	0.0	0.1
43	196.0	3.	0.0	0.2
44	207.7	1.	0.0	0.1

C. HISTOGRAM:

```
17                    *
16                    *
15                   **
14                   **
13                  ***
12                 ****
11                 ****
10                *****
 9               ******
 8               ******
 7               ******
 6              *******
 5             ********
 4            *********
 3            *********
 2           ***********
 1         ****************
   +----+----+----+----+----+----+----+----+----+----+----+
ST 15   20   25   30   35   40   45   50   55   60   65   70
HZ 39   52   69   92  123  165  220  294  392  523  698  932
```

Figure 11-3. Printout of speaking fundamental frequency data for one subject. The actual values (seen at the left) can be used to generate an SFF identification vector.

The Vowel Formant Tracking Vector (VFT)

Much use has been made of vowel formant center frequencies, bandwidths and transitions by individuals using time-frequency-amplitude spectrographic techniques in speaker identification (14, 26, 36, 38, 39, 41, 48, 54, 59, 76, 87, 97, 99, 105). While their approach has not been a particularly sophisticated one (especially when used as "voiceprints"), the research conducted by these individuals suggests that vowel formants and their nature definitely are important to the speaker identification process. Moreover, research both in the aural-perceptual area (10, 17, 53, 62, 64, 164) and relative to study of the issue via machine approaches (13, 25, 29, 33, 35, 73, 74, 78, 79, 80) can be used to argue the importance of elements within the formant structure as speaker identity cues (61). We agree and have developed a VFT vector. On the other hand, some controversy exists about which of the VFT features and subfeatures are the most unique to an individual and the most consistent over time (13, 26, 53, 62, 74). Accordingly, we have focused our VFT parameter selection process on two features: (1) the center frequencies of the first three vowel formants (F1, F2, F3) and (2) the ratios among these three formants (F1/F2 and F2/F3). It now appears that F1, F2 and, to some extent, F3 center frequencies are good indicators of speaker identity, especially when several vowels (such as /i,a,u/ plus the syllable /na/) are used in the sample. Moreover, there is some logic for selecting formant ratios as identification cues; it is as follows. Formant frequencies are generally dependent on the size and shape of the vocal tract, therefore, they are established and shifted by articulatory movements. However, since the range of formant frequency shifts and the F1/F2 and F2/F3 ratios probably cannot be significantly altered at will, they should convey idiosyncratic information about a specific talker (99). Finally, data of this type appear to be resistant to many kinds of system distortions. In short, selection of this vector was predicated on (1) the stability of an individual's vocal tract—its size and shape, (2) vowel position and (3) the presumed resistance of these features to distortion and/or interference. The approach we utilize provides for a VFT vector of up to 28 parameters. The vowel formant frequency windows are preprogrammed, and our high-speed Fourier analysis hybrid system currently provides the spectral data. This vector is proving to be a robust one.

The Temporal Vector (TED)

Very little research on speaker identification has focused on any of the temporal parameters that can be extracted from the speech wave (23, 24, 57). Nevertheless, there appears to be strong logic that there are speaker-related prosodic speech elements that can be extracted and used for speaker recognition purposes. For example, given the hypothesis that talkers differ with respect to speech durational factors (i.e., syllable, word, phrase, sentence), it is possible that the time a person utilizes to produce a specific amount of connected discourse may be useful in the identification task. Moreover, certain individuals may employ a greater number and/or longer silent intervals in producing a linguistic message than do others. In any case, a rather substantial number of temporal speech features are amendable to study and certain experiments support their use (42, 43, 57). The measures we have developed for this purpose include: (1) Total Speech Time (TST), defined as the period (in ms) it takes to produce an utterance of a set number of syllables, (2) Speaking Time Ratio (S/T), defined as a measure of the total time for which acoustic energy is present during a specific utterance, (3) Silent Interval (SI), a reciprocal of speaking time (S/T), (4) Speech Rate (SR), a measure of the speech material completed during a fixed time period (based on syllable rate, not word rate) and (5) Consonant/Vowel Duration Ratios (C/V), or the time ratio between a particular consonant and a vowel in a specific CV utterance. Each of the three main TED features (TST is a base measurement) are, in turn, built from several parameter sets (see Figure 11-4), and data for each set are obtained at 10 interval levels (above a predetermined base) for the entire sample. Hence, there will be an S/T-10, S/T-20, S/T-30 and so on. Data for this vector are obtained by use of a rectifier-integrator coupled to one of the PDP 11/23 computers by means of an A/D converter. Special processing software has been developed for this vector.

Other Vectors

Finally, several other vectors either have been used unsuccessfully in the past or have been identified as possible identification cues. These speaker characteristics are at a revision stage, under study or being developed for use in the SAUSI profile. They will not be reviewed here, however, because I do not know at this time if any of them will prove useful enough to be employed on a routine basis.

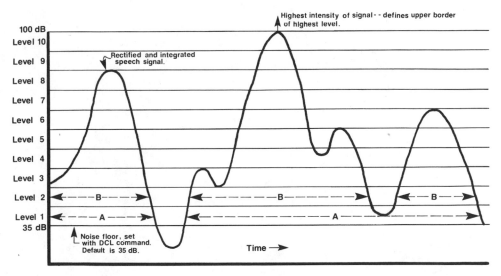

Figure 11-4. Trace illustrating how the TED vector functions. A number of measures are generated. Among them are 10 sets of the number and duration of speech bursts (A and B are examples) for each of the 10 equidistant levels. Data of this type can be used to identify a subject and discriminate him or her from others.

Developmental Procedures—General

The vectors generated by this research have been tested singly and in combination many times: (1) in the laboratory (included were simulated field conditions) and (2) in the field, where attempts were made to "solve" simulated, but structured, crimes; see again Figure 11-1. Many experiments—both successful and unsuccessful—were carried out under the laboratory phase of this project and most of our basic information has been generated by these studies. However, it was the second set of procedures which permitted us to refine the system for operational use, at least on a preliminary basis. As may be seen in Figure 11-5, the actual process we utilized is servomechanistic in nature. It provides for the continued evaluation of the vectors developed and the reanalysis of their robustness as they are upgraded. As I have stressed previously, I believe that this approach—or a similar one—is very important for the proper development of a speaker identification system. Given that it has not yet been shown conclusively that intraspeaker variability is always less than is interspeaker variability, the strength and efficiency of any approach must be demonstrated by

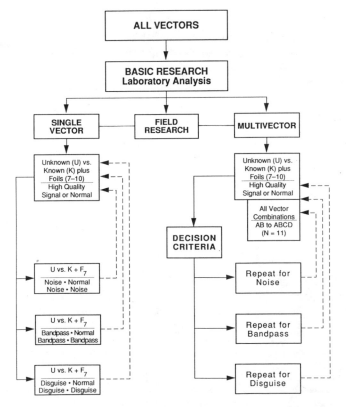

Figure 11-5. Block diagram of one of the several plans that can be utilized to field-test speaker identification vectors or systems. Here the forensic model is used, but the experiments are laboratory controlled or simulated. Once the data are satisfactory, the procedures can be taken into the field for real-life analysis.

those who develop it. This process is the only one which will insure that appropriate experiments—and enough of them—will be completed prior to operational use of the system; i.e., that the approach will be validated before it is activated.

In response to our stated criteria, we have carried out a large number of basic and applied experiments appropriate to our goals; in each instance, we attempted to determine the uniqueness of the feature or features tested and the strength of the vector as structured. We did so by variously degrading the speech signal utilized in the investigations and by using a large number of talkers—included were subjects whose speech tended to be difficult to analyze and others that "sounded" like each other. When a vector (or cluster of vectors) began to show potential as a speaker identification cue, the research effort was shifted to the field. At that time, the forensic model was investigated and the profile approach applied (see below). Thus, as might be inferred, our work here has progressed through many phases and through many stages; it was supported by a number of research grants and contracts.

The Data-Base Utilized

It would appear useful to describe (at least briefly) the large and varied data-base that was developed for this research. It consists of nearly 2000 recordings of well over 400 speakers (both males and females) variously producing over two dozen types of utterances. For example, experimental samples include normal reading/speaking, spoken digits, free/controlled disguise, multiple dialects and induced stress (several types). Moreover, various classes of noises have been mixed with these recordings and they have been transmitted over telephone lines. These samples constitute the experimental materials ordinarily utilized in the basic testing of our vectors. However, a second data-base was developed for the field studies. In this case, recordings of the actual voices of agents, suspects, criminals and the like were collected until well over 150 samples were added to the data-base; most of these utterances tended to relate to criminal activity. Some of them were made over the telephone, others in police stations, and so on. As stated, these samples were used in many of our field investigations. We prefered to use them in that milieu, as they were drawn from real-life situations yet had been recorded under known or controlled conditions.

Procedures Utilized

No attempt will be made to detail the long and tortuous history of all of the experiments that have been carried out on this procedure over the past 25 years. Rather, I will simply highlight a few of the findings so that you can understand what we have done and something about the product of these efforts. As I pointed out before, I will concentrate only on the system I know the best (45, 106). Other approaches have also been tried (6, 10, 12, 19, 20, 28, 56, 67, 68, 84), and some have shown substantial promise. If you are interested in them, you should refer to the cited literature.

The actual procedures used in our experiments can be best understood by reconsideration of Figures 11-1 and 11-5. As can be seen, the vectors are evaluated singly and in combination first in the laboratory and, later, in the field. In the past, the only levels of identification which actually approached 100% (under most conditions, that is) were for the LTS vector and certain multiple-vector analyses. However, the other vectors are beginning to provide very high identification levels also—even when used alone. Further, they now are being used successfully in a multiple-vector profile—and the specific conditions under which each vector is individually most robust are emerging. To this end, several of the earlier experiments have been replicated on the basis of the profile concept and the results have been encouraging. Additionally, the sensitivity of a variety of mathematical distances (Euclidean and Steinhaus among them) have been, and are being, evaluated. We now feel that we have identified a reasonably valid operating system and, as with the other of our techniques (most are found described in this book), are willing to have any qualitied person or agency use it (some already are doing so).

But back to the research. Please remember that the approach used here addresses the very severe limitations imposed upon the identification task by the forensic model (i.e., one referent, one test sample). Coupled to this rather harsh research design, we initially chose to force matches (or nonmatches) from the large field of voices—i.e., the known plus 25 foils (or controls)—and to utilize the nearest-neighbor statistical approach. In any case, many investigations of this type were carried out both under good conditions and with the signal degraded (often severely) in numerous ways.

A very early experiment demonstrating the effect of combining the vectors (used at that time) into pairs is shown in Table 11-1. We were most interested here in what would happen to the identification levels of LTS and SFF when they were combined with each other and with other vectors. Since we had found that correct identifications by single vectors employed under these conditions (especially those relative to distortions) ranged from 12-85%, it was here that we first discovered that levels of correct identification sometimes were reduced by multiple-vector processing. The reasons for this relationship already have been discussed, and, as can be seen in Table 11-2, once steps were taken to minimize them, the situation improved.

Table 11-3 demonstrates another approach; it illustrates the results of application of the forensic model to data from the LTS vector alone; nine small experiments are reported here. Basically, a closed-set test was utilized, with the speech of the different talkers contrasted against another sample of their own voices plus seven randomly selected foils. An identification test was carried out with Euclidean distance values calculated and a three-nearest-neighbor approach utilized. As can be seen, this process permitted the speaker to be correctly identified in all nine cases. These results are particularly impressive due to the marked homogeneity of the subject population utilized. Moreover, research designs of this type are particularly useful, as they permit identification of those other talkers who are (or could be) confused with the target speaker. This particular study has been repeated many times with each of the vectors. We now know when very high levels of correct identification can be expected and when it is necessary to be cautious (for example, the effects of disguise when LTS is used alone or noise degradation of TED).

TABLE 11-1. Percent Correct Classification When Individual Vectors Are Combined into Multiple Vectors

	Talkers					
	Run A			Run B		
Vector and condition	1	2	3	1	2	3
Normal/Normal						
SFF/LTS	58	64	75	62	73	81
INT/LTS	46	54	58	42	50	54
TED/LTS	42	64	73	58	58	65
SFF/INT	30	35	59	42	50	62
SFF/TED	46	62	62	54	58	73
INT/TED	27	31	39	27	27	42
Noise/Normal						
SFF/LTS	31	35	50	42	50	62
INT/LTS	27	42	46	35	46	59
TED/LTS	30	36	62	35	50	65
SFF/INT	27	27	50	27	35	42
SFF/TED	35	50	62	31	42	54
INT/TED	19	27	31	27	31	36
Bandpass/Normal						
SFF/LTS	46	50	65	39	62	62
INT/LTS	27	42	46	23	27	35
TED/LTS	42	42	50	35	42	46
SFF/INT	27	31	46	27	35	35
SFF/TED	31	46	58	31	42	54
INT/TED	15	23	31	12	15	19
Noise/Noise						
SFF/LTS	54	69	81	46	73	73
INT/LTS	46	46	62	42	54	59
TED/LTS	27	46	62	31	39	46
SFF/INT	36	39	46	35	42	54
SFF/TED	27	31	54	31	50	58
INT/TED	27	31	36	27	27	36
Bandpass/Bandpass						
SFF/LTS	50	65	73	73	73	85
INT/LTS	23	27	42	27	39	42
TED/LTS	46	59	65	46	50	62
SFF/INT	39	46	59	35	39	58
SFF/TED	42	50	59	35	46	54
INT/TED	19	27	31	23	31	35

Note. Data are from an early (1972) set of experiments. Subjects were 26 young men controlled for age, dialect and education; text was also controlled. The three-nearest-neighbor approach was employed.

Two additional evaluations are provided to illustrate some of the more practical tests (and somewhat more recent ones) that have been carried out. In the first of these experiments (see Table 11-4), the speech of a known talker (K) was contrasted to nine other individuals. Speaker U (unknown) was believed to be K but the recording was made in the field and was of relatively poor quality.

TABLE 11-2. Summary Table of Two Experiments where Vectors were Combined by an Additive Procedure

	Condition	
Vector	Distortions	Normal speech
SFF	54	68
LTS	76	88
TED	46	62
VFT	68	85
SFF/LTS	78	88
SFF/TED	56	66
SFF/VFT	70	84
LTS/TED	76	88
LTS/VFT	80	90
TED/VFT	67	86
SFF/LTS/TED	78	88
SFF/LTS/VFT	82	91
SFF/TED/VFT	70	86
LTS/TED/VFT	78	89
All vectors	82	90

Note. The nearest-neighbor (serial and normalized) approach was utilized. Subjects were 25 adults males.

TABLE 11-3. Summary Table of LTS

Test subject	Experimental subjects							
1	1 1*	F6	F9	F11	F14 3	F18 2	F21	F23
5	F2	5 1*	F9	F14 3	F18 2	F20	F21	F25
9	F4	F8	9 1*	F10 3	F16	F18	F22	F24 2
12	F1	F5	F9	12 1*	F15	F20 2	F24	F26 3
15	F3	F7	F12	15 1*	F17 3	F20	F23	F26 2
17	F2	F4 3	F8	F15	17 1*	F18	F21	F25 2
23	F1	F6	F13 2	F14 3	F19	F21	23 1*	F24
24	F2	F7	F12	F15 3	F18	F23	24 1*	F26 2
25	F3	F6	F11	F14 2	F17 3	F19	F22	25 1*

Note. Subjects were a homogeneous group (age, size, health, education) of young males; 1* = correct identification.

TABLE 11-4. A Field Test of Four SAUSI Vectors by the Three-Nearest-Neighbor Ranking Procedure

Vector	Speaker								
	K	F1	F2	F3	F4	F5	F6	F7	F8
SFF	1	—	2	—	—	3	—	—	—
LTS	1	—	2	—	—	—	—	3	—
VFT	1	—	—	2	—	—	—	—	3
TED	2	—	—	—	1	—	—	—	3
SFF/LTS	1	3	—	—	—	2	—	—	—
SFF/VFT	1	—	—	3	—	2	—	—	—
SFF/TED	1	—	—	—	—	3	—	—	2
LTS/VFT	1	—	—	—	3	2	—	—	—
LTS/TED	1	—	2	—	—	—	—	—	3
VFT/TED	1	—	—	2	3	—	—	—	—
SFF/LTS/VFT	1	—	—	—	3	2	—	—	—
SFF/LTS/TED	1	3	2	—	—	—	—	—	—
SFF/VFT/TED	1	—	—	2	—	3	—	—	—
LTS/VFT/TED	1	—	—	—	—	—	3	2	—
All vectors	1	—	—	—	3	2	—	—	—
Estimated % probability subject is U	88	C	C	C	C	19	C	C	C

Note. An unknown talker was contrasted to the known talker (K) plus eight foils (F). U = unknown; C = chance or near chance.

The eight foils (F) were drawn variously from field recordings and from our database (sound-alikes of K were sought). Four SAUSI vectors were applied singly and in all combinations. As can be seen in Table 11-4, K was selected as U in all cases except one—in that case, he was the second choice. When the probability was estimated, it appeared that there was about an 88% chance that K was U, a 19% chance that F5 was U, and a lesser probability (i.e., chance) that the other foils were U. It was concluded that SAUSI permitted the identification of the "suspect" (K) as the criminal (U). As it turns out, K admitted to being U—not scientific evidence, of course, but nonetheless a rough verification of the accuracy of the technique.

The second example of a field evaluation (see Table 11-5) involved an open set, as the actual criminal was not known to be among the suspects (however, K was the prime suspect). The basic sample of the unknown (U) was derived from a conversation he had over the telephone with a second person. Moreover, all speech was in a foreign language and the principals used low, often soft, conspiratorial voices. There were three exemplars of the prime suspect. The first (K1) was taken from the audio portion of a television tape of K giving a public address in a large hall. The second tape recording (K2N) was made under circumstances more like the original speech, with the third recording (K2F) made from K2N by processing it through a telephone bandpass. Because there were several exemplars, only five foils or controls were utilized (all were native speakers of the language spoken by U and K), with foil K4 specially selected as a

TABLE 11-5. Summary Table of Normalized Distances Based on the Closest Match when the Unknown Talker was Compared to Himself, the Knowns, and the Foils.

Test/Vector	U	K2F	K2N	K-1	F1	F2	F3	F4	F5
Unknown									
LTS	0.127	—	0.116	0.649	1.559	1.973	1.487	1.468	3.214
TED	—	0.005	0.032	0.008	0.014	0.011	0.012	0.010	0.014
VFT	0.216	1.173	0.216	0.628	2.174	0.216	—	2.628	0.381
Total	0.343	1.178	0.364	1.285	3.747	2.200	1.499	4.106	3.609
	1	3	2	4	8	6	5	9	7
Overall (four rotations)									
Distance	4.072	2.356	6.858	6.176	11.794	14.642	11.724	11.060	14.882
Rank	2	1	4	3	7	8	6	5	9

Note. Also presented are the combined means of several rotations. Three vectors were employed; all values are distances from the closest match.

person who (subjectively) sounded a great deal like the unknown. In this case, only three vectors were used: LTS, VFT and TED as the SFF hardware was being repaired at the time of this particular experiment. First U was compared to another of his own reference samples and to all of the other eight. Subsequently, the process was replicated for the three Ks. The resulting distances were normalized and coverted to functions of, or distances from, the target. As can be seen from the overall values appearing on Table 11-5, U, K2F, K2N, and K-1 all clustered around each other. None of the foils, including K4, were competitors. Soon after the report listing these data was submitted to the agency requesting it, it was learned that K had admitted to having made the phone call in question. Again corroborative evidence of a sort.

The Profile

As more and more research (both basic and field) was completed, it became increasingly apparent that we probably were on the right track. However, we continued to be concerned about the problem of the differential robustness of the vectors as a function of the type of degradation to the signal. We also were concerned that we were not always successful in increasing the power of the system when we combined the vectors. At about this time, we began to normalize our scores (so as to reduce unfair weighting by the "large number" vectors) and combine the data additively. A composite of this type was seen in Table 11-5. However, it should be remembered that this particular approach was just one of many we routinely employed in data analysis. At about this point in time, we began to graph these particular data for both simulated and real-life field experiments.

The relationships seen in Figures 11-6 and 11-7 will illustrate the robustness of the technique utilized. In the first case, the identification of the unknown (U) was sought in a closed set of knowns (K) and foils (F). The data from the four

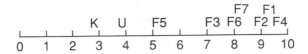

Figure 11-6. A two-dimensional continuum based on the summation of the normalized data from four vectors. This simulated field experiment involved closed-set trials with K ranking as high as U (they were the same person but different samples) and the position of the "sound-alike" (F-5) approaching those of the U and K speakers.

multidimensional vectors described above (LTS, SFF, VFT and TED) were normalized as described, combined into a table (such as 11-5) and then plotted on a two-dimensional continuum. As can be seen, K appeared to be more like U than did U himself (it was the same talker, of course). Moreover, the foil (F5), selected because he sounded like the unknown, approached identification, to a degree anyway. Note that the other foils cluster some distance from U. Figure 7 provides a similar display but from an entirely different experiment.

In other cases, where the known is not (or not thought to be) the unknown, the positions of the various individuals along the continuum appear somewhat random. Indeed, Figure 11-8 illustrates this situation; it is drawn from a real-life investigation which I call "The Case of the Embattled Entrepreneur." The evaluation was focused on two unknowns, two knowns and a number of foils (one of which was thought to sound like the U's and K's). As it can be seen, unknown X was first selected as himself, with the data for unknown Y placing him very close to unknown X. The knowns and foils appear in a different part of the continuum—an area which was fairly remote from that of unknown X and unknown Y. What can be concluded here is that the two unknowns probably are the same speaker but that none of the knowns or foils are either X or Y. This particular case cannot be discussed in detail, as it is still in progress as I write this; however, there is now other evidence to suggest that unknown X and

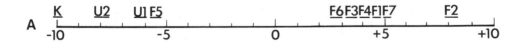

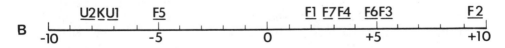

Figure 11-7. Two rotations (or separate trials) for several talkers drawn from a real-life situation. Here there are two (noncontemporary) samples of U, with K almost surely the same person as U. Again a foil who sounded like K was sought and placed in position F5. The rotations of the text-independent samples were carried out first with U1 contrasted to himself and all others and then with U2 evaluated similarly. Note how an increase in the number of rotations enhances the sensitivity of the procedure.

Figure 11-8. Another example of a real-life case but one where the unknowns (X and Y) may or may not be the same person and K and N are related; K5 again is a "sound-alike." In each rotation, the unknown talker was found to match best with himself. It also appears that X and Y may be the same person but that K is not either of them.

unknown Y are the same person and that none of the knowns or foils actually are the unknown. Moreover, the evaluation seen in the figure was replicated (independently) several times. All of the relations (i.e., the contrasting of the various U's and K's against the other talkers) resulted in profiles that were highly consistant with those reported in Figure 11-8. In short, the independently replicated data served to confirm the stated relationships.

In summary, it must be remembered that all of the illustrative subprojects described have been structured on the basis of the forensic model and, thus, we have tested SAUSI under relatively stringent conditions. To be specific, we ordinarily utilized: (1) a statistically small population, (2) only one reference sample per subject and (3) test samples that were short plus language independent. Moreover, noise and telephone bandpass distortions were virtually always present. A yet more rigorous forensic model was employed in the field cases cited— they involved samples that were noisy, bandpassed, noncontemporary and text independent. The overall results indicate that the strength of an *individual* vector varies somewhat from test-set to test-set. Indeed, while none of them provided consistently high levels of correct identification under any and all conditions, they appeared to compensate for one another and to do so especially when they were combined into a normalized two-dimensional profile. Thus, while the matches afforded by the vectors when used singly did not always result in an exact K-U match, they did so (that is, when K and U were the same talker) at very high levels when combined. Hence, the procedure of using multiple vectors, controls and normalized distances appears to be one that can be considered valid for voice identification. Indeed, the use of natural speech vectors in a structure of the type cited appears to lead to a speaker identification system that is both robust and reliable. Finally, since this approach as been developed primarily by public funds, it can be freely used/adapted by an competent scientist or practitioner (if appropriately referenced, of course).

PART IV

Stress in Voice

CHAPTER 12

Psychological Stress and Psychosis

INTRODUCTION

To understand how a person is feeling just from hearing his or her voice is not something that is very easy to do. Perhaps it is a nearly impossible task. Yet, there are times when an individual (a police officer, for example) has little else but the heard voice to tell him or her what action the talker is intending to take. While some of the relationships between vocal behaviors and emotions are known or suspected, they are tenuous enough that you cannot expect this chapter to be replete with illustrative cases or with descriptions of systems which would allow you to interpret a person's mental state from listening to his or her voice. Nonetheless, this area of study is an important one and probably will prove amenable to development over time—that is, as more and more relevant research is completed.

Please note also that I plan to concentrate discussion on the negative types of psychological states rather than on those parameters that reflect emotions in general. While it may be just as important to determine if people are happy or excited as it is to know if they are angry, anxious or psychotic, the "reading" of negative emotions probably is more appropriate to the forensic situation. I certainly do know that, of all the research which has been carried out in these areas, most of it has been on topics such as stress and psychosis.

Note also that this chapter will contain two sections. I would divide the material into two separate chapters, but the issues of stress and psychosis are so closely related that a dichotomy of that type probably would be artificial. Thus, we first will consider psychological stress as it appears to affect voice and then those speech/voice cues that can be (or may be) associated with psychosis. Entire books have been written on each of these subjects; hence, the thrust here is but an overview—one that is pretty much focused on the needs of law enforcement agencies, attorneys and the courts.

PSYCHOLOGICAL STRESS

Why is the determination of stress in voice so important? One element is its significance relative to interaction among people. We have been attempting to assess the presence, absence and/or magnitude of threatening and/or stressful behavior from the speech and voice production of other individuals since primitive man added a true cognitive overlay to his repertoire of oral signals. As a matter of fact, it is quite possible that crude assessments of this type were attempted even before organized communicative sounds existed among the members of our species. As implied, these analyses were (and are) attempted for a rather substantial number of reasons, some of which fall within the scope of forensic phonetics. They include assessment of the presence and magnitude of such emotional states as hostility, aggressive intent, fear, anxiety and so on—as well as deceptive or divisive behavior; even psychopathological states can be included under this rubric.

There is little question but that emotional and/or behavioral conditions of the types cited do exist and that their detection is of some consequence. For example, it can be important to monitor the levels and types of stress present in personnel who are physically separated from the control site (such as pilots, astronauts, aquanauts, police and others) irrespective of the message content of the spoken interchange. It is desirable also for a worker at a crisis control center to be able to tell if the caller actually is going to commit suicide, or merely wants to talk about it, and to make these judgments simply from the manner in which the caller speaks. Knowledge about the acoustic and temporal speech/voice clues which correlate with psychosis can be important to clinical personnel with respect to their interaction with, and assessment of, patients. In short, there are many instances where information about the behavioral intent or emotional states of an individual would be quite helpful to the auditor, and the needs of law enforcement personnel rank high in this regard.

To be specific, there is no question but that agents and police would find a system or procedure useful if its application permitted them to reliably identify (1) the emotions being felt by the talker, (2) the presence of deceptive behavior or (3) the presence/absence of psychosis. Moreover, if accurate procedures of this type could be carried out rapidly, effective on-scene decisions could be made— ones which currently are not possible. In any case, it appears that the activities of law enforcement, intelligence and security agencies all would benefit if the several stress states cited above could be better defined, coded and identified.

Linguistic Stress

Before any attempt is made to discuss the possible vocal correlates of emotions of any type, it will be necessary to clarify a number of terms. For example, the concept of stress is, in and of itself, quite difficult to define. For one thing, there are two kinds of stress: linguistic and psychological. In the first case, the focus (that is relative to phonetics) is on the emphasis patterns an individual uses when uttering a spoken message; the ways by which such linguistic emphasis is produced have been studied (see, for example, 9, 18, 20, 21, 36, 41). However, while these speaking characteristics are important to speech decoding and speaker identification, their significance is minimal when the issues outlined in this chapter are considered. It is the second of the two classes of stress that will be reviewed in the first part of this chapter; it can be referred to as psychological stress. Definitions of this type of behavior and data relative to its vocal manifestations will be found below.

Definitions of Psychological Stress

What is psychological stress? Is it fear; is it anger; is it anxiety? Scherer (56, 57) indicates that the question of definition is a serious one. The problem appears to result from "the lack of a precise specification and description of the emotional state underlying the vocal expression, independent of whether it is induced, posed or studied naturalistically." In laboratory experiments, stress often is identified in terms of the applied stressor. However, this type of definition is not very useful because, even though the stressor itself is described, the emotion(s) being experienced by the subjects actually are unknown. On the other hand, when emotions (including stressful ones) are specifically identified for research purposes, they often are simulated by actors. The reason for doing so is due to the fact that it is rarely possible to record the speech of an individual who is experiencing severe stress during the period it is occurring. Moreover, the situation is confounded by the fact that it also is difficult to obtain similar, contemporary (but unstressed) utterances by that same individual.

Two of the major dilemmas to be faced when we attempt to assess the vocal correlates of psychological stress have been considered in the preceding paragraph. The first is: given that we can detect the presence of stress, what exactly does this "feeling" represent? Is it fear, anger, anxiety or some combination of these three emotions? It can even be asked if a particular stress state is totally negative in nature. In any event, there is little question but that this problem is a major one when stress is studied. The second of the two difficulties relates to the differences between real and simulated stress. When actors and actresses are used, are they portraying stress accurately or are they parodying it in some way? For example, if professionals of this type consistently provided us with a particular caricaturization of a stress condition, we eventually would begin to recognize it as such, even if they distorted its actual characteristics in some manner. In any event, it is the rare author that reports any data at all on actual stress (5, 25, 26, 30, 32, 57, 66).

A third problem, and one that is perhaps more serious than the others, relates directly to the level of the stress state. That is, the issue here is, first, whether or not stress is present and, if it is, the extent of the emotion—i.e., the intensity of the effect. No matter how you approach research on stress, it is not adequate to provide your audience with only a general explanation of it plus a description of the stressor. Rather, both the presence and level of stress must be known before any behavioral response to it can be validly studied. Yet this approach is not the one ordinarily used and virtually all of the data on stress found in the research literature (except that for actors and actresses) have been obtained without the cited controls. It is little wonder, then, that many contradictions, and substantial variability, appear in the reported data. In short, you must accept the fact that many of the relationships and conclusions which appear in this chapter constitute but "best guesses" and most, if not all, of the operations described must be viewed with these cautions in mind.

Our Approach to Stress

No matter what problems are associated with stress, it will be necessary to base any research carried out on an acceptable definition. Obviously, this human condition reflects some sort of psychological state or states—especially one which is a response to a threat (3). Or, as Lazarus (35) points out, "to be stressed, an individual must anticipate confrontation with a harmful condition of some type." He suggests further that the strength of the stress response pretty much results from the magnitude of the threat. On the other hand, Scherer (55, 57) argues that stress can be either internal or external, with "adaptive or coping behavior required" — whereas others contend that it is not "imposed" at all but rather that it constitutes an individual's "response" to stressful conditions (8). The definition I prefer to employ is one first articulated at our laboratory (25, 26, 28); i.e., stress is a "psychological state which results as a response to a per-ceived threat and is accompanied by the specific emotions of fear, anxiety and/or anger."

When all of the warnings reviewed above are considered, it might seem that the materials to follow would be of limited use in the forensic milieu. In a sense, perhaps they are. After all, before you can tell if a person's voice is exhibiting stress, it probably will be necessary to learn something about how he or she sounds under ordinary circumstances. Moreover, the need to make a judgment may come and go so quickly that any analysis at all would be in the difficult-to-impossible category. Nevertheless, it often is important to learn all we can about the presence and level of stress in another person—even if the analysis is but an auditory one. Happily, there appears to be at least a few vocal correlates of stress. Accordingly, I will attempt to synthesize them and even to suggest a behavioral model you may find useful.

The Speech Correlates of Stress

This section probably should be entitled: "What we think we know about the vocal correlates of stress." Actually, this statement is not positive enough, especially since there are some stable relationships we can cite. For one thing, it now is accepted that listeners can identify some emotions from speech samples alone and do so at reasonably high accuracy levels (13, 25, 26, 28, 30, 37, 40, 51, 53, 54, 55, 57, 63, 67). For example, several authors (17, 37) have reported correct identifications of simulated emotions to be in the 80-90% range. As has been noted previously, most of the research cited above was carried out on "emo-tions" portrayed (vocally) by actors and it may be possible that they created some sort of artificial stereotypes. However, data reported by Williams and Stevens (66) can be used to argue that emotions which actually are being experi-enced can be validly identified also. If it is possible to accurately identify emo-tions simply by listening to the talker's voice, it also should be possible to identify the relevant acoustical and temporal parameters (within the voice sig-nal) that correlate with these states. What are some of these relationships?

Speaking Fundamental Frequency

Changes in heard pitch or speaking fundamental frequency (SFF or F0) appear to correlate with stress when it is experienced. For example, when Fairbanks and Pronovost (17) carried out their research with actors, they found that the SFF level was raised for the emotions of fear and anger but lowered or remained the same for the other emotions they studied (i.e., grief, contempt, indifference). This relationship is supported by others (52, 53, 54, 56, 67). As a further example, Williams and Stevens (66) analyzed the real-life emotions of pilots and control tower operators; they reported an increase in SFF as a function of increased levels of stress, and this finding essentially is confirmed by similar research (32). On the other hand, not all authors appear to agree that a strong pattern of this type exists. For example, Hicks (25) found only slight increases in SFF/F0 as a function of stress, and others (1, 23, 40) would argue against the positive correlation of pitch and stress on a universal basis, as some of their subjects exhibited such behaviors while others did not. In sum, it appears possible that, in most cases, moderate to substantial increases in F0 level are associated with psychological stress states. However, if this parameter really is to be useful, baseline data should be available for the subject. That is, it probably will be necessary to determine both the extent of the F0 shift and its direction—and to do so for each individual being evaluated.

At present, SFF and/or pitch variability appears to be a much poorer predictor of stress than does the level produced or perceived. Indeed, the data here are not very orderly. For example, SFF variability appears to increase for anger but not for fear. Moreover, if the variability findings are summarized under the general rubric of stress, the available data permit almost any position to be argued—i.e., that SFF variability related to stress (1) may increase, (2) may decrease, (3) may not change at all or (4) may vary from speaker to speaker (17, 25, 52, 55, 57, 67). Thus, a metric for pitch/SFF variability probably cannot be developed for use by law enforcement or other relevant groups. A speech component that could prove helpful, however, is the regularity (or rather the lack of it) that can be associated with speaking fundamental frequency. The authors of the above studies (and others) have noted that, when talking, stressed individuals exhibit behaviors such as voicing irregularities, discontinuities in F0 contours, irregular vocal fold vibration and even vocal tremor. However, while relationships of these types may be of potential use some time in the future, they currently provide us with little in the way of beneficial information.

Voice Intensity

Vocal intensity is another acoustic parameter that can be measured and correlated with the presence of psychological stress—at least to some extent. However, only Hicks (25) has reported measurements of absolute intensity; he found increases to correlate positively with stress. Other authors (19, 52, 56) pretty much agree with him, even though they used relative measures (11, 67).

On the other hand, investigations have been reported where increases in vocal intensity did not seem to be correlated with the presence of stress—or, at least, anger (31, 40). Nor did Hecker *et al.* (23) observe consistent intensity differences in the speech of their subjects when nonstressed and stressed speaking conditions were contrasted. Of their 10 subjects, 6 showed small and/or inconsistent differences (as a function of stress), 1 exhibited increased vocal intensity and the remaining 3 exhibited decreases. Nevertheless, based on a compilation of all the studies reviewed, the best evidence here is that vocal intensity is increased slightly for stress and anger, minimally raised for fear and perhaps contempt, and is reduced for grief. However, as with speaking frequency, these data exhibit some inconsistencies and, even where the shifts appear stable, it is necessary to compare the obtained values with those from subjects' neutral speech.

Temporal Characteristics

Identification of the prosodic characteristics in a voice reflecting stress is a relatively complex process. For example, when anger is taken by itself, it appears to be accompanied by rapid speaking rates as well as short phonatory durations and pauses (16, 40, 51, 52, 56, 67). Further, Fairbanks and Hoaglin (16) contend that fear can be similarly characterized, and a number of more recent investigators appear to agree with them (6, 54); on the other hand, others, notably Williams and Stevens (67) and Hicks (25), do not. One pattern reported by Hicks seems to be fairly universal; viz, it appears that fewer speech bursts occur if a person speaks while experiencing stress. Hence, angry/fearful individuals appear to speak in longer utterances than they would ordinarily. A final and rather important finding has been reported by Hicks (25). He has noted that nonfluencies appear to accompany stress. With only one exception (60), all of the other authors who have studied the speaking correlates of this emotion agree with him.

Summary

First off, you must remember that I have focused this discussion only on the stress-related emotions and have avoided any attempt to identify the speech/voice correlates of the more positive emotions of happiness, joy, satisfaction, love, confidence, and so on. Nor have I made but minor reference to other (negative) emotions, i.e., those of grief, sadness, contempt, indifference and boredom. Indeed, the discussions in this chapter have focused particularly on stress and its related emotions (or component parts) of fear, anxiety and anger. I have done so because stress is a key emotion to law enforcement agencies, the military, intelligence and related groups.

But can the relationships I have described actually be of some use in forensics? This question brings to mind a case I think of as "Highways Can be Dangerous." One rainy night, a young man made a left turn at the intersection of a dual highway. Somehow he did not see an on-coming automobile and rammed it, killing its driver, a young girl. There was some question as to whether or not he was drunk or had been been drinking moderately. In any case, he was tried for manslaughter. My involvement came from the fact that another motorist called

911 for aid and the resulting tape recording contained the defendant's voice also calling for assistance on an adjacent telephone. When they were compared to his normal utterances, the recorded speech exhibited all of the changes one would expect to encounter if a person was speaking under highly stressful conditions. In any event, I was able to testify (albeit very cautiously) that the defendant's speech was consistant with that of a person who was stressed rather than that of a person who was intoxicated. The main problem with this testimony was that I had to use the stereotypes of what the utterances of a person who is inebriated are like as there are no definitive data relative to "drunk speech." Worse yet, no agency in the United States appears interested in funding research on that problem. Hence, what little we know about the effect of intoxication on speech results primarily from reports by investigators residing in other countries. Thus, you can understand why my testimony was sharply limited, even though the defendant's speech met all of the criteria for an emotional state associated with psychological stress.

A Model

In an article I wrote some time ago (27), I made the statement that there are many commonly held notions about the way speech should sound when a person is experiencing stress or stress-related emotions. For example, some individuals would argue that anger "should" result in loud, harsh speech and fear in a high-pitched, staccato output. Indeed, almost any person you meet will venture at least a tentative identification of the voice and speech characteristics that they feel should accompany most of the more commonly felt emotions. I then reviewed the relevant research literature and was able to establish most of the relationships discussed in the immediately preceeding section. More importantly, however, I was able to structure these data in a manner that permitted the development of a predictive model. One that was somewhat tentative, of course, but also one that has proved useful in our attempts to understand how emotions are reflected in voice and speech.

An updated version of this model, one depicting the vocal correlates of stress, may be found in Figure 12-1. It is presented in an effort to portray what probably happens when a person speaks under conditions of psychological stress. When you examine the figure, you will note that stress appears to be accompanied (ordinarily anyway) by several changes in speech/voice production. These shifts include the following: (1) speaking fundamental frequency is raised, (2) nonfluencies increase, (3) vocal intensity rises moderately, (4) speech rate tends to increase slightly and (5) the number of speech bursts is reduced. Most of our own research tends to support this model but, just as has been noted by other investigators, deviation from these general trends occurs for some subjects. Moreover, since the observed characteristics result in shifts from the "neutral" speech state, they will be of greatest value in forensics when they can be contrasted with a reference profile based on that person's normal speech.

So here we are, almost back to the point at which we started. The problems to be faced are quite serious, but not enough consistant data are available. However, the cited model may be of some help here—as should those proposed

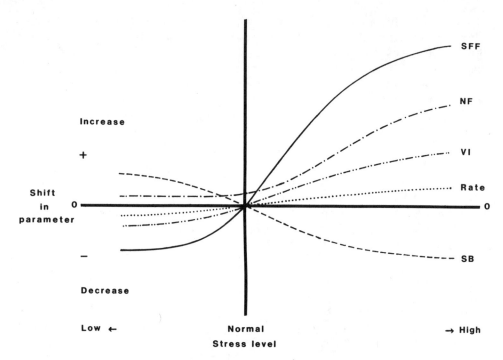

Figure 12-1. Model of the most common shifts in the voice and speech of a person who is responding to psychological stress. SFF is speaking fundamental frequency, NF is nonfluencies, VI is vocal intensity, and SB refers to the number of speech bursts per unit of time.

by Scherer (56, 57). He also has responded to the stress-voice enigma by developing a pair of models. One is based on a complex set of psychological constructs, the other upon the detailed organization of voice quality which has been proposed by Laver (33, 34). Without a doubt, the Scherer models help in providing a useful structuring of the complexities of stress as it is reflected in voice. It is quite possible that they will permit you to better understand some of the more subtle dimensions of stress and the resulting alterations to speech.

On the other hand, it should be clear that our model is substantially simpler than are any of Scherer's. In this instance, the focus is only on the major voice-related stress characteristics. While not originally organized in response to the needs of law enforcement (and related) agencies for applied assessment techniques in this area, it is, after all, consistant with their requirements. Moreover, the model provides a point of initiation for future research. The stress correlates in voice must be studied in much the same manner as Lykken (38) responds to the lie response. That is, we must first be able to determine when stress exists in the person and, especially, to what degree or level it is present. Indeed, it is only when we can quantify these states/levels that we will be able to precisely determine what happens to voice and speech when stress is present. The problems with any model in this area is that it is based on data where the presence of psychological stress is not fully contolled and its level (if present) is unknown. See Figure 12-2 for my interpretation of how anxiety levels can vary as a function

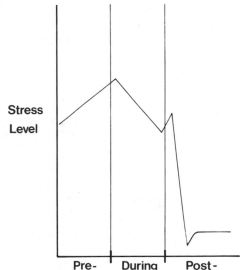

Stress
Level

Pre- During Post-

Figure 12-2. Predicted changes in stress level (for most people) as a function of response to a threatening or pressure-inducing situation.

of stressful situations. At what point in time do you measure the effects of the stress? Thus, precise information is not available in this area and it is badly needed. Perhaps the vocal correlates of psychosis will provide some useful cues about stress. They will be considered in the next section.

VOCAL INDICATORS OF PSYCHOSIS

Categorization System

There is no question but that psychotics experience some form of psychological stress, and there is very good reason to believe that such conditions manifest themselves in the speaking behaviors of these individuals. First off, it is important to identify the vocal correlates of these disorders (if they exist) for ordinary medical reasons. Moreover, it also is of some significance to do so for a reason that is not so easily recognized; i.e., that information about these relationships may provide useful data concerning the status of individuals experiencing short-term stress or psychotic-like episodes. Another purpose for studying the voice/speech of psychotics is one that relates directly to the forensic milieu. Can a psychotic be recognized as a person who is ill simply by the perception (or analysis) of his or her voice and speech? A review of the relevant research in this area would appear warranted as a precursor of any attempts at judgment.

In order to provide a reasonable basis for this discussion, a system of classifying psychotics must be adopted. It is recognized that there are a number of schemes available for doing so and that many of them are acceptable. However, the one upon which I base all present discussions is the American Psychiatric Association's DSM-III classification system (2). DSM-III provides a clearly defensible set of definitions and descriptions as well as a system which includes the following categories of psychosis: (1) Schizophrenia, with three subcategories based on age: (a) adult, (b) adolescent and (c) childhood; and (2) Affective Disorders, including: (a) Depression (general), (b) Involutional Depression and (c) Manic-Depressive states. The review to follow will utilize these classifications, in condensed form anyway, in order to permit a reasonably appropriate, yet consistent, analysis/interpretation of the research reported on the vocal correlates of psychosis. The only modification utilized (and a minor one) will be to reduce some of the subcategories into two major components: (1) Schizophrenia (adult/adolescent) and (2) Affective Disorders (Depression/Involutional Depression). The remaining categories will not be considered, primarily because so little useful research has been carried out on the speech/voice characteristics of these types of patients. In any event, it is unlikely that organization of the available data into these two relatively gross categories will do violence to the relationships being considered—especially since very few of the investigators we cite utilized more rigorous subject classifications.

Problems with Research in This Area

As with stress, we face a rather substantial set of difficulties when the vocal correlates of psychosis are being considered. The first of the problems is directly related to research on psychological stress. As with that emotion, investigators who study psychosis can only rarely assess the affect level of the disorder as the experiment takes place. This lack of information about severity level undoubtedly has led to inappropriate data interpretation. A second, and even more serious, problem is that most of the research in this area has been carried out on patients who either were sedated or were recipients of some sort of psychotropic drugs. For this reason, the observed relationships/data undoubtedly do not reflect the true vocal correlates of the particular psychological disorder under study. Rather, it is more accurate to suggest that the condition being tested is the effect of the prescribed drug upon the human subject. Indeed, this source of bias has been contolled in only a few of the many investigations which have been reported (10, 50, 64, 65). Yet, a third relationship should be recognized. To be specific, if a particular psychotic was found in an unmedicated, acute and (perhaps) violent state, there probably would be little need to carry out speech analysis in the first place.

To summarize, it is extremely important to keep the cited cautions in mind—especially those relevant to the lack of knowledge about stress level (or the immediate severity of the psychosis) and presence of mood-changing drugs. It is quite possible that they combine to bias the relationships discussed below.

The Voice/Speech Correlates of Schizophrenia

One of the earliest of the modern investigators in this area was Moses (42). He reported that the voices of his schizophrenic patients: (1) were similar to those of children, (2) exhibited very high-pitched phonation and (3) exhibited "inappropriate" accents or emphasis, as well as "rhythmic repetition of vocal patterns." On the other hand, Moskowitz (43) indicated that when they were roughly matched with controls, his patients exhibited "monotonous and weak speech with a flat colorless tone quality." Of course, these comments are subjective in nature and somewhat anecdotal. Nevertheless, they provide at least preliminary insight into the speech of schizophrenics.

Ostwald (45-48) also was a pioneer in this area but tended to study but one subject at a time. However, he reports that his schizophrenics exhibited: (1) patterns of rapid F0 shift, (2) intermittent sound production, (3) nasal voice quality, (4) impaired articulation and (5) poor breath control. These observations appear to be in rough agreement with those of Moses and Moskowitz (42, 43), especially with respect to the cited difficulties in articulation, the high SFF, excessive variability in speech rate/rhythm and the apparent lack of a finely tuned, integrated control of the vocal apparatus.

Ostwald (45, 46) also is responsible for one of those fairly rare instances where a psychotic patient was investigated both before and after treatment. His perceptual and acoustic analyses support the suggestion that several changes in speech had taken place as a function of treatment. He argues that these changes included: (1) a spectral power curve which displayed "a rise in intensity," (2) vowel formants which showed "appreciable change," (3) a voice that exhibited less "compactness" and (4) an oral reading rate which was increased (see also reference 7). While Ostwald's patients probably did improve as a result of therapy, it is a little difficult to interpret the significance of these presumably concommitant speech changes.

Spoerri (61) reports that he studied a very large population of schizophrenics $(N = 350)$. His listing of the voice/speech correlates of this type of disorder is somewhat reminiscent of the positions articulated by the earlier investigators. That is, he typified the speech of his patient/subjects as exhibiting: (1) strain, (2) harshness, (3) register changes (to falsetto), (4) dysarticulation, (5) volume changes (too loud), (6) speech changes with inappropriate alternations, (7) "gloomy, dull timbre" and (8) monotonous melody. Moreover, he related voicing irregularities to schizophrenia, and it will be remembered that this characteristic also was found in the speech of individuals experiencing high levels of stress.

A classic study was carried out in 1968 by Saxman and Burk (50). They contrasted a group of hospitalized schizophrenic females with controls relative to speaking fundamental frequency level (SFF), fundamental frequency deviation (FFD), and both mean (overall) and sentence reading rates. Perhaps, most important, they carried out their research 48 hours after psychotropic medication had been discontinued; hence, they are among the very few investigators to study psychotics when they were not medicated. These authors report that their schizophrenic patients exhibited a higher mean SFF than did the controls but that this finding was not of statistical significance. The schizophrenic group, however, did show significant differences (from the normal) relative to oral reading rates (slower) and frequency variability (larger). It should be noted that the findings of increased frequency variability are in contrast to most other studies of schizophrenia. However, since these investigators tested their patients after the discontinuation of medication, it is possible that they measured the schizophrenic process itself rather than behavior associated with the medication or its effects. Perhaps it is the medication variable which is controlling in (other) studies of this type. This investigation leads to the suggestion that a great deal more research of the type they conducted is needed before stable relationships about vocal correlates of schizophrenia can be established.

Finally, recent investigations provide a little additional insight into the speech-schizophrenic interface. First, Denber (14) found that speech power, vocal jitter and SFF differentiated his schizophrenic subjects from a group of controls. Moreover, at least some of his observations were confirmed by Hollien and Darby (29), who reported data relative to perceptual identification, SFF, frequency variability, reading time, phonation time and phonation-time (P/T) ratio. Interestingly enough, they report that the controls were (perceptually) identified as nonpsychotic 88% of the time but that their auditors were not as accurate in recognizing specific psychotic conditions from vocal samples. For example, even though the listeners were pretty adept at identifying psychotics, they were not very good in discriminating between schizophrenics and depressives (who also were studied in this experiment). Moreover, while their findings for SFF were not significant, the trend of lowered SFF for the schizophrenics was somewhat in variance with the findings of other investigators (see above, and reference 54) who have suggested that SFF is high for this class of patient.

In summary, it appears that robust voice/speech predictors of schizophrenia are not currently available. This lack of strong relationships undoubtedly is due to a combination of events/problems. Included are those cited above (stress level unknown, medication present) plus the position taken by several of us that the investigators involved employed methodologies so disparate that proper comparisons cannot be made. Of course, this lack of consistency among the observed relationships also could be due to the fact that there simply are no speech/voice features that typify schizophrenia. Yet, a thorough review of the evidence suggests that they probably exist and that, ultimately, they will be identified. In the interim, it is possible that certain tendencies are stable enough to be utilized as speech predictors of the presence of schizophrenia—especially, when the disease itself (and not the effects of medication) is considered. Admittedly, these factors are not very robust, but let me hazard the following list. It appears that schizophrenics exhibit: (1) a fundamental frequency level (SFF) which may be somewhat higher than that for normals, (2) a fundamental frequency variability which will tend to be reduced when they are medicated but increased when they are not and (3) deviant rate and rhythm behaviors which include prolongations of pause time, hesitations, elongation of certain words or phonemes and increased reading times. Of course, the final two of these prosodic features may be the result of medication. This list is tentative to be sure, but it may serve as a guide and/or a point of initiation for research which is more sophisticated than that carried out in the past. There also is the possibility that it might serve as a useful index for law enforcement personnel when they have to face a psychotic of this type.

Speech Attributes Relating to Affective Disorders

It should be remembered that there are several classes of depressed patients; the most common (other than mixed or general) are the involutional depressives and the manic-depressives. However, this review will collapse the *major* types of affective disorders into a single category—that of depression—primarily because, so far, no voice or speech analyses have emerged that permit differentiations between or among these subgroups. Indeed, it has not yet been conclusively demonstrated that depressives speak differently than do normals. It also should be remembered that, as with schizophrenics, virtually all of the research carried out on the communicative attributes of these patients has involved speech samples obtained when the subject/patients were medicated. Thus, the acute effects of this disease probably have been obscured by the effects of the drugs administered. However, a brief review of the relevant research may provide at least a little information about people who are depressed and how it may be possible (eventually) to identify these conditions from speech and voice analyses.

The modern research in this area appears to have been initiated in 1938 when Newman and Mather (44) reported data on the speech of a group of depressed patients whom they classified into several subgroups. Basically, they suggest that "classical" depressives exhibit voice qualities that can be termed "dead or listless." They further indicated that their subjects: (1) lacked adequate pitch ranges, (2) exhibited speech rates that were too slow, (3) produced too many pauses and hesitations, (4) lacked proper variability in (linguistic) emphasis and (5) exhibited too much pharyngeal and nasal resonance. Even though many related papers have appeared during the subsequent half century, it remains difficult to add to, or reject, most of the conclusions drawn by these authors. For example, Moses (42) also characterized the "depressed" voice as generally monotonous. He indicated that, when "tone" was lowered, intensity decreased proportionately and that it was this relationship which was responsible for the "monotonous" voice quality associated with the speech of his depressed patients. Several other authors agree (15, 49), indicating that they observed decreases in pitch, pitch range, rate and volume. However, it is possible that, since many of the subjects studied were quite old, some of the observed voice/speech characteristics could have been due to the physiological changes that accompany the aging process.

Mood changes also have been studied in the depressed (22) before, during and after treatment; here, spectral patterns have been observed to systematically shift with change in mood. Helfrich and Scherer (24) also carried out research of this type but reported that some of their subjects continued to exhibit a "depressed" voice even after mood change. They describe the voices of depressives as exhibiting reduced loudness, "dull, lifeless" voice qualities and diminished inflection. However, some investigators suggest that the vocal characteristics of the depressed may cluster into several different patterns and that each of these clusters could be associated with some subclass of the disorder.

After a period during which relatively little speech/voice research was carried out on the depressed, data (12) were reported on patients before and after electroconvulsive treatment. Prior to treatment, the voices of a number of depressed patients were perceptually characterized by a speech pathologist as "dull" and lacking in vitality. Following treatment, and with moderate clinical improvement apparent, the voices were judged by this same speech pathologist to have regained some of their normal "vitality." Additional perceptual analyses resulted in the observation that improvement occurred in articulation, increased pitch inflection and enhanced linguistic stress. Instrumental analysis also was carried out on these speech samples, but while commonly reported trends in speech power spectra, SFF, FFD and speaking rate were observed, they did not reach statistical significance. The lack of significant instrumental findings in this study is of interest, especially since a few of the observed trends were a little at variance with those from at least a couple of other studies (24, 46). Of course, these differences could relate to the different methods utilized in analysis. First, more stable data result from group analyses (as was the case here) rather than from the seperate evaluation of a number of individuals. Second, the focus here was on the effects of treatment rather than on the development of normative data (a thrust that is foiled in many studies by the lack of a sufficient number of subjects). Nevertheless, the major trends here were fairly consistant with those from most earlier investigations.

A number of studies (including two employing new approaches) have been reported recently. First, Hollien and Darby (29) utilized perceptual ratings, SFF, FFD, reading time, phonation time and P/T ratios in an attempt to differentiate among depressives, normal controls and other psychotics (i.e., schizophrenics). As will be remembered from a prior discussion, it was found that (1) the controls could be identified as "normal" 88% of the time, (2) the psychotics usually were identified as exhibiting psychopathology but (3) the judges could not differentiate appropriately between the two clinical groups. These authors also note that the depressive patients exhibited slightly lower SFF than did the controls (nonsignificant, however) as well as a slower reading time; the P/T ratios also proved useful in identifying the depressives. Another of the more recent studies was one carried out by Scherer (54), who investigated the voices of depressed patients before and after therapy. Of his several measures, only fundamental frequency differentiated the groups with a mean *decrease* in SFF following treatment. These data are at variance with those provided by most other authors. On the other hand, Scherer's reported findings on spectral bands appear to be consistent with the general literature in this area. Finally, he concludes that psychiatric treatment causes patients' voices to become more resonant and flexible—a change that, he suggests, is the result of increases in muscle tone.

In summary, it appears that depressives may exhibit speech that is slower and reduced in both energy and F0. I must concede, however, that these observations are rather tenuous and may not prove as robust, especially as new studies are completed. Nonetheless, they appear appropriate, at least, at this juncture.

New Approaches

In his most recent work (58), Scherer has attempted to develop a "Stimulus Evaluation Checklist" for use with psychotic patients (especially depressives). This test appears to be a combination of (1) Laver's (34) voice classification system, (2) a group of basic psychoacoustic techniques and (3) a set of semantic differential stimuli. He uses these materials to structure a model which he hopes will aid in the specification of the vocal correlates of depression. Scherer recognizes, as I do, that there are serious problems to be faced in conducting research of this type. Specifically, any scientist working in the area must respond to difficulties in classifying, choosing and sampling both the patients and speech/voice material to be studied—as well as in selecting the methodology and measurements to be employed. He also suggests that research should be carried out on the effects of psychopharmacological drugs on speech and voice as well as on patients who are free from medication. I agree. Indeed, there is no doubt but that Scherer is pursuing a logical and appropriate course of action. Indeed, the manner in which I currently structure my research is complementary to his. Moreover, I agree with most of his conclusions—possibly with the exception that I am a little more enthusiastic than he is that some of the vocal tendencies associated with depression can be identified.

On the other hand, I tend to deviate from most writers in this area in that I believe that there is a rather substantial reason for the speech of untreated depressive patients to be different than that of normals—that is, when they are not on a course of psychotropic medication. Specifically, both observation and research have demonstrated that depressives exhibit a strong tendency to withdraw socially. Hence, in my judgment they are severely stressed when they are forced to interact with their environment and/or make contact with other people. In turn, it can be expected that the powerful stress they experience will affect their speech, and it is my postulate that this relationship provides the basis for a better entry into the problem area than do the usual models.

As a matter of fact, we already have begun to evaluate this hypothesis. Specifically, a test originally developed by Talevera, but researched in assocation with members of my group (64, 65), has been applied as a stimulus to clinically diagnosed depressives who have been free from any psychoactive drug medication for at least three days. Even though we did not restrict subject selection to a bipolar disorder, all experimental subjects were diagnosed by our psychiatric associate as suffering from severe depression; he diagnoised them on the basis of the criteria established by DSM-III (2). Matched controls provided baseline data. All subjects were administered a series of tests (hearing, depression, anxiety scales, and so on) that served as selection criteria. Moreover, in view of our model, all were stress monitored during the experiment by means of heart rate and breathing patterns.

The experimental stimuli utilized here involved a 10-minute dichotic-listening procedure with subjects hearing the same (male) recorded voice speaking different passages to each of their ears; they were asked to repeat the utterances heard in the dominant ear. Errors (i.e., omissions, additions, repetitions, distortions and incoherent sounds) were scored and plotted for each of 10 one-minute segments and a binaural test was administered as a control during minute 11. As it turned out, the normals conformed to the expected error rate patterns by starting out with a mean of about 8%; this value subsequently fell to around 3% as they developed their response strategies. We hypotheszed that the test was short enough that fatigue would not inflate the scores toward the end and it did not. As a matter of fact, the normals exhibited an error rate of only 1% for in the binaural (control) procedure. As predicted (see Figure 12-3), the error levels of the depressives were 15-20% higher (a significant difference) than were

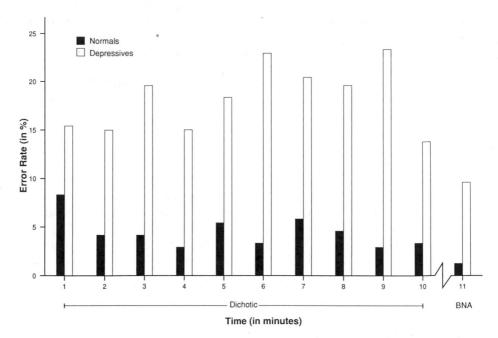

Figure 12-3. Error rates for a group of (nonmedicated) depressed patients—contrasted to those for normal controls—when they responded orally to a dichotic listening task. BNA refers to a binaural reading task which immediately followed the experimental trials.

those for the normals. In our opinion, the reason for this difference is that the administration of the test resulted in a violation of the defenses of the patients and forced them to respond to structured stimuli—a task that they could not, or would not, carry out effectively. A few preliminary measures were made on the speech produced by the two groups; they were found not to differ significantly (some trends were observed, however). Of course, the focus of this research was upon the dichotic listening procedure, not speech differences—i.e., can depressives be differentiated from normals in this manner or, even more important, can depression be predicted by a test of this type. Thus, a more complete evaluation of patients' speaking characteristics is needed, and one that should be carried out both before and after the test is administered. While we may have developed a new (speech) test for the diagnosis of depression, this particular experiment did little to add to our knowledge of the vocal correlates of that disorder. Apparently, the high stress/anxiety states we created counteracted the effects of the psychosis; i.e., the depressive state may have forced a speech feature to shift in one direction while the stress experienced counteracted that movement. We now are conducting follow-up research projects—several that we hope will be more directly relevent to the forensic model.

To summarize, the data and concepts about depression or affective disorders tend not to be as orderly as we would wish; indeed, they are rather difficult to organize. While the data suggest that depressive patients may utilize different speaking patterns than do normals, it also is possible that these patterns may not be universal or "classical" in nature. However, when all the data (especially those generated by patients who were not medicated) are taken into account, several voice-depression associations can be hazarded. Tentatively, it appears that depressives exhibit: (1) limited speaking intensity, (2) restricted frequency variability or pitch range, (3) slower speech, (4) reduced prosody and (5) a lack of linguistic stress. It now should be clear that, with the exception of speaking fundamental frequency and its perceptual correlate, pitch, this description somewhat parallels those for the emotions grief and sorrow. Please note also that, with certain exceptions, the speaking attributes for anger and fear appear to correlate, at least mildly, with those behaviors exhibited by schizophrenics. Thus, the vocal correlates of both of these psychoses suggest related emotional states. While it probably is rather dangerous to extend these analogies too far, the possibility remains that the relationships may be of some merit and that they could provide useful guidelines for law enforcement and clinical personnel. It must be stressed, however, that the cited relationships are rather tenuous and conflicting data exist in some instances. Hence, it is necessary to be a little cautious when attempting to generalize the speech/voice characteristics of psychotics for any purpose whatsoever.

A Conclusion

This chapter probably has been a little frustrating for you. If you expected to be provided with a set of clear-cut rules as to how you could identify a person who is either stressed or suffering from psychosis simply by analyzing his voice, you probably are pretty disappointed. Yet, the reality is simply that we do not have definitive information about the areas in question and anyone who tells you that they do is not being truthful. On the brighter side, however, you also have seen that some mild trends exist; hence, a few rules-of-thumb can be applied to these problems—especially to those related to psychological stress. That is, it appears that (1) speaking fundamental frequency, nonfluencies, vocal intensity and speaking rate are raised for stress; (2) depression somewhat parallels grief/sadness with a lowering of F0, vocal intensity and speaking rate reduction; and (3) the speech of schizophrenia may, to a modest extent, mimic anger/anxiety—i.e., with increases in SFF and speech bursts. Although rather tenuous, these relationships constitute a place to start both with respect to research and law enforcement. Better yet, they sometimes can be coupled with other suggestive behaviors in order to permit the decision-maker to arrive at reasonably intelligent conclusions about a given situation.

CHAPTER 13

Vocal Stress/Lie Detectors

INTRODUCTION

It is without question that law enforcement, security, intelligence and related agencies need an effective method for the detection of deception. Incidentally, "detection of deception" is the phrase used by many professionals when they mean lying. Whether a lie detector—were it to exist—would be used effectively, legally and ethically is not the focus of our concern here (however, these issues will be discussed briefly at the end of the chapter). Rather, I will stress the need for such a system and some approaches to the problem. But first, let us consider the basic issue: can lies be detected; is there such a thing as a lie response?

THE LIE RESPONSE

It is quite probable that Lykken (37) has articulated the key concept relative to deception. He argues that, if lies are to be detected, there must be some sort of a "lie response." That is, there has to be a measurable physiological or psychological event that *always* occurs when a person lies. He correctly suggests that, until a lie response has been identified—and its validity and reliability have been established—no one can claim to be able to measure, detect and/or identify falsehoods. The question remains, then, has such a lie response been isolated? Simple logic can be used to test this possibility, as the consequences of its existance would be extensive. As Lykken points out, the impact on society would be almost inconceivable. Consider the following. Since it would be possible to determine the beliefs, interests and intent of the leaders of any country, wars would become unlikely events—that is, unless the politicians simply refused to communicate at all. There would be no need for trials by jury; the guilt or innocence of anyone accused of a crime could be determined simply by asking them: "Did you do it?" Industry could shift the billions spent on advertising to product research and development. Consider also the impact an infallible lie detection system would have on family relationships!

Actually, there are a number of specialists who feel that they have developed approaches that can be used to detect lying with some degree of accuracy, even if there is not a universal lie response. Included among them are individuals who would accomplish the task by language or style analysis (see Chapter 15), others who claim to be able to do so by voice analysis (see below) and the polygraphers.

POLYGRAPHY

Polygraphers do not claim that they are able to tap into some sort of lie response. Rather, they contend that deception can be detected because it usually is associated with stress and that their approach permits them to determine if the person they are examining is experiencing this emotion. You probably are already aware that, by itself, polygraphy cannot totally fill the need for lie detection. While useful for these purposes, this technique is limited by the situation in which it is employed and, especially, by the skill of the operator. Of course, the basics about polygraphy and its uses have been pretty well established (36, 38, 43, 46, 52). However, a brief review of this technique and its accompanying procedures appears timely and, hence, will be included in this chapter. The primary reasons for doing so are to provide a perspective about the complexity of lie detection and a basis for our understanding of attempts to use voice analysis for the detection of both stress and deception.

The standard polygraph is an instrument which captures certain physiological data under relatively controlled conditions (see reference 43 for an excellent history). Its receptors, which are placed on the body, measure respiration, galvanic skin response, blood volume and pulse rate/amplitude (46). The activities monitored by these receptors are transmitted and amplified by the polygraph circuits in such a way as to allow the signal to be recorded by moving pens; in turn, these pens permit a trace of the signal to be placed onto paper moved by a kymograph, or hard-copy recording unit. As may be seen in Figure 13-1, the standard field polygraph unit contains a chart feed, from which paper is propelled at the constant speed of six inches per minute, as well as four pens used to provide a trace of each of the responses. Two of the pens record breathing patterns, while the other two record electrodermal (skin) response and cardiac output.

The polygraph's pneumographic subsystem measures respiration rate— i.e., breathing patterns. They are recorded as responses to pressure changes in two pneumatic tubes positioned around the subject's torso (at the thoracic and abdominal levels). Expansion in the area of the subject's chest and stomach during breathing causes stretching of the tubes, the movements of which are transmitted through bellows to the chart pens. The galvanic or electrodermal skin response (EDR) subsystem provides information on skin resistance as a function of the neural activity associated with stress, emotions and, possibly, deception. It is obtained by attaching electrodes to two of the subjects fingers and passing a small amount of electrical current through the resulting "circuit." Any variation in perspiration (a routine sympathetic response to stress) is detected and permanently recorded on the appropriate polygraph channel. Finally, the cardiosphygmograph subsystem is used to measure changes in the subject's

Figure 13-1. Photograph of an examiner conducting a polygraph test. The two pneumatic (respiration) tubes can be seen placed around the subject's chest and abdomen. The electrodermal response unit is placed on the fingers of his left hand and the blood pressure cuff on his right upper arm.

blood pressure and pulse. This measure is obtained by placing an inflated rubber cuff around the upper arm over the brachial artery; the forearm or wrist also can be used. As the heart contracts, it creates a blood volume increase that expands the arm, whereas when the heart is at rest, blood volume (and arm size) decreases; such changes result in parallel variation in the pressure in the cuff. An increase in pressure causes the appropriate polygraph pen to move upward, while a blood volume reduction results in a downward swing of the pen. Moreover, since the peaks represent individual heartbeats, and paper speed is both constant and known, heart rate (in beats per minute) can be calculated at least roughly. The physiological changes which may occur are revealed to some extent as variations in the frequency and amplitude of the heartbeats and as a function of the overall cardiovascular trends.

As might be expected, a theoretical framework underlies the use of polygraph measurements in the detection of deception. Specifically, alteration in the four physiological parameters described above are presumed to reflect arousal or stress states as a function of changes in the sympathetic division of the autonomic nervous system (ANS). It is well-known that the human body will respond physiologically to a stressful situation and responses of this type are induced by the ANS, which coordinates the activities of the endocrine system and smooth muscle tissue associated with the intestines, blood vessels and heart. More importantly, this system essentially operates involuntarily and, ordinarily anyway, cannot be brought under conscious control. Of the two branches comprising the ANS—the sympathetic nervous system (SNS) and the parasympathetic nervous system (PNS)—it is the SNS that is of interest here. That is, while the PNS is dominant when an individual is at rest, the SNS takes over when energy mobilization is required (2). Specifically, the SNS is activated by a perceived threat and, in response, prepares the body to cope with the emergency—i.e., to flee or to fight. When emotions such as fear, anger and anxiety (i.e., stress) occur, they stimulate physiological change. Among these responses are increases (discussed above) in blood volume and pulse rate, decreases in skin resistance and changes in respiratory rates. Thus, emotional states can be reflected by combinations of physiological responses and the polygraphers suggest that those cited can be monitored by their equipment. It is unfortunate, of course, but the strength of these responses can differ in an unknown or unmeasurable manner as a function of environment, basic physiology, subject, stressor and so on. Thus, universal baseline metrics for each of these elements or parameters have not been established and, excepting for heart rate, their specification on an experimental basis would be a little difficult. It must be remembered also that even if the mean changes (for people) were generally known, the data still might not predict how a particular individual would behave. A striking example here is the sociopath—an individual who may exhibit no physiological shifts when under stress or when lying.

As you might suspect, there have been some problems with the polygraph technique. The first involves a pair of underlying assumptions made by the polygraph practitioners; they specify that the procedure will detect stress and that stress is correlated with lying. In fact, both points, plus the relationship between them, have been challenged by a number of investigators. Chief among them is Lykken, who has written extensively on the subject (see especially, 36, 37). As you will remember, he suggests that there is no such thing as a lie response and, thus, the relationships specified above cannot hold. In any event, polygraph tests are carried out extensively, and while not often admissible in court (some states now permit them and they can be admitted by stipulation), they are widely used by law enforcement agencies in investigations. The method also is used extensively in industry for evaluating employee honesty. Much of the criticism leveled at the technique undoubtedly results from this second application, as most tests of this type are administered superficially and, hence, often are invalid.

Some of the negatives associated with polygraphy result from its inflexibility rather than its validity. First, the unit itself must be placed in close proximity to the subject, thereby making it difficult, if not impossible, to track the stress levels of (or deception by) individuals who are in remote locations. Such close placement of the equipment also limits gross movement or locomotion by the subject. Second, most polygraph examinations are regimented and, thereby, are time consuming—that is, they are if they are to be effective/valid. Third, subjects must remain relatively motionless during a polygraph examination in order to permit a baseline to be established/maintained and shifts in psycho-physiological functions observed. Even small movements—such as a startle response, for example—can prove detrimental to (stress/deception) assessment. Hence, the test is a rather awkward one relative to its administration.

Finally, I would be remiss if I did not point out a couple of relationships (relative to polygraphy) that keep me from being totally comfortable with it. For one thing, observations of polygraph traces are in and of themselves subjective. If an approach of this type is to be established as a valid detector of stress/deception, it must be refined to a level where quantification of a subject's responses is possible. In turn, if this level of sophistication is to be attained, a substantial (additional) amount of basic research on the physiological correlates of stress and lying must be carried out; the results must be quantified and then buttressed by applied studies. Second, it should be apparent that interrogator skills probably constitute the most important feature of the entire process. As is well known, certain examiners are able to obtain results that are far superior to those of others. These individuals appear to excel as interrogators—and one begins to wonder if it is not this skill which is important rather than the machine itself. Unfortunately, it is not easy to assess the attributes of polygraph examiners on a quantitative and unbiased basis. You almost have to judge them on circumstantial evidence. For example, certain relationships and/or behaviors suggest that a particular examiner is both effective and ethical; they include: membership in the American Polygraph Association, association with the military or law enforcement agencies, the refusal to carry out large numbers of examinations in relatively short periods of time and, of course, general reputation. Nevertheless, it must be said that, while physiological monitoring sometimes can provide information about the presence of stress (and, perhaps, deception), the standard polygraph and its examiners have yet to demonstrate that they can fully meet the challenge they face in these areas.

ANALYSIS BY VOICE

Whereas the polygraphers defend their approach in a rational manner, the proponents of voice stress evaluation operate much more haphazardly—and aggressively. They claim that their approach effectively meets the need for a system that detects deception and that it does so solely by analysis of the voice signal. A number of voice analyzers are now (or have been) commercially available (6, 9, 20, 23, 32, 33); all are purported to function as lie detectors. Indeed, a manual that accompanies one of them lists potential users as: "attorneys (negotiations, authenticity of information), employment agencies (employee evaluations), insurance adjusters (verification of insurance claims), reporters (determination of viable sources), psychologists (patient's stressful and important problems), security/service groups (stress analysis services), negotiators/investors (authenticity of information) and sales personnel/purchasing agents/

business personnel (verification of important verbal information)." But are the claims of the manufacturers of voice analyzers valid? Before addressing this question, I should like to briefly remind you of the vocal correlates of stress and lying (see again Chapter 12).

As you will remember, about half of the previous chapter was devoted to discussions of how stress is reflected in a person' phonatory output. And what did we learn? Primarily, that conventional research approaches to these relationships did not result in very powerful models. Of course, we were able to identify some tendencies (moderate increases in F0, nonfluencies, vocal intensity and speech rate; reduction in speech bursts), but, in all fairness, robust correlates simply were not to be found. Perhaps stress and deception occur simultaneously and it is the lie response that is vocalized (rather than stress). Indeed, while relatively little research has been carried out on any of these issues, it often is assumed that—vocalizations aside—lying and stress co-vary. However, you will remember that Lykken (37) disagrees even with this rather mild postulate. He maintains that stress can be induced when lying is not present and further, and perhaps more serious, that there are individuals (sociopaths, for example) who do not exhibit stress when lying. Moreover, it is well known that various types of lies can differentially affect stress behaviors—and do so especially as a function of the jeopardy involved. The problem is yet further confounded by the fact that neither the nature nor the extent of these relationships is known. Thus, while logic suggests that stress and lying may be related in some functional way, very little evidence of predictive value is available.

Some research has been carried out directly on the vocal correlates of deception (irrespective of the presence and level of stress). For example, several authors indicate that speaking fundamental frequency (F0) rises as a function of lying (28, 31, 47), but none of them found these shifts to be statistically significant; indeed, some were "mixed" in nature. Additionally, changes in other speech features, such as hesitations and staccato speech bursts (25, 47), may accompany spoken deception. Since not much other data are available on the stress/lie relationships, generalizations of any type would appear hazardous. In short, it must be concluded that the known vocal correlates of stress and lying, and the general stress/lie relationships, all are so tenuous that they cannot be used to provide a theoretical basis for the detection of deception through the measurement of some vocal parameter. Yet the proponents of voice analysis indicate that they can tell when a person is stressed or is lying simply by applying their technique to a voice sample. On what do they base their approach and what exactly do they do?

THE VOICE ANALYZERS

Presumed Theoretical Bases

When confronted with the stress/lie dilemma, the voice analysis supporters sometimes will attempt to list the constructs upon which their method is based and/or provide a theoretical foundation for it. Unfortunately, these models are not articulated in any one place or in any great detail. For example, relevant postulates can be found outlined (usually briefly) in the media, but in this case the thrust ordinarily is one of sensationalism rather than clarification. To illustrate, when psychological stress evaluator (or PSE) examiners have been interviewed about their procedure, they usually have cited "microtremors" (see below) as the theoretical basis for their approach but, then, have quickly shifted to discussions of their "results." For example, speech samples associated with the assassinations of both John and Robert Kennedy have been "analyzed" and with rather startling results: "Oswald (is) Innocent," "Sirhan (was) Hypnotized," (3, 15, 44). Other examples include discussions of the Patty Hearst kidnapping: she is "Not Guilty," "She Was Forced to Lie" (16); the so-called Washington scandals: "Ted Told The Truth about Chappaquidick" (14), "Hayes Lied but Elizabeth Ray Told the Truth about the Washington Sex Scandals" (21); and the truthfulness of statements by entertainers: "Lauren Bacall is Lying (about) Fords" (22), "Sinatra Told the Truth When He Denied Mob Ties" (13). However, media reports such as these provide little insight into either the theoretical or scientific bases for the method. In fact, their very nature tends to arouse suspicion about the techniques in question.

Yet another, but secondary, source about a possible (theoretical) basis for the method could result from analyses of the equipment sold by the manufacturers of the specified devices. That is, it would appear useful to determine the operating properties of such apparatus and use that information to infer the principles upon which the technique is based. Our analysis of the PSE circuits—excluding false elements but including those embedded in hard plastic—revealed that its typical operational mode probably parallels that of a low-pass filter. Indeed, VanderCar et al. (51) suggest that, excepting for the input and readout subsystems, the entire device consists only of a simple R/C circuit; one that could be built for a few dollars. Hence, while it is not possible to deduce underlying theory from circuit analysis, evaluations of this type permit at least some understanding of the approach employed.

When information such as that cited is coupled to descriptions found in the various operators' manuals and in articles such as Heisse's (23), it is possible to determine (roughly anyway) what the proponents of voice analysis probably consider to be the theoretical underpinning for their method. As stated, their approach is said to be based on microtremors—i.e., on the very slight tremblings that occur in some of the muscles of the human body. They contend that they are able to evaluate stress, and presumably lying, by demodulating the "subsonic frequencies" that are caused by these microtremors—specifically by the minute oscillations found in the muscles of the vocal mechanism. They argue that these microtremors are normal to any voluntary muscle activity, but that, in the person stressed, they are suppressed. Their devices, then, presumably measure frequency modulation within the (vocal) utterance—one which is presumed to be present for normal speech but is reduced (or disappears) for stress (23, 33).

There is no question that muscle microtremors exist. At least, they do in the long muscles of the human extremities—at rates varying from 8-14 Hz (12, 35). However, the proponents of the cited technique claim that such tremors also exist in the "voice," and presumably are created by some interaction between the laryngeal muscles and the airstream. They argue that these tremors (occurring when the laryngeal muscles are contracted and decreased when the talker experiences stress) can be processed by their instrument and identified in its output (usually graphically; see Figure 13-2). As expected, an explanation of this type triggers many questions.

The first that must be asked is: are microtremors present in the muscles associated with the larynx and vocal tract? Shipp and McGlone (48) tested this notion by embedding hook-wire electrodes in the lip and laryngeal muscles. They reported that none of these muscles showed tremor patterns similar to those found in the long muscles and thereby were forced to conclude that, if the voice analyzers work at all, their operation has to be based on some other set of principles. This research was replicated a few years later with the same results (49). In retrospect, McGlone agrees (39), arguing that tremors of the type in question usually are associated only with isometric contractions of the long muscles and seldom (if ever) occur in the small, fast-acting muscles of the vocal tract. Several other relationships also should be considered. For example, even if a microtremor occurred in a muscle activated to perform a single operation, the muscle groups of the larynx and vocal tract operate in a manner so complex that the effects of this (single) tremor would be wiped out. As voice and speech are produced, almost every group of laryngeal/vocal tract muscles will contract and relax many times within a relatively short period of time, and in concert with (or opposition to) each other and many other muscle groups. These rapidly shifting relationships clearly would mask activity of the type proposed; they would do so especially as workload varied. In any event, as the work of Eisenberg and Hill

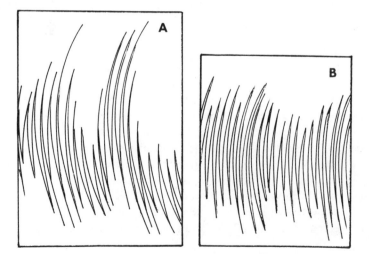

Figure 13-2. Configurations that are somewhat similar to the stress/nonstress readouts that appear in advertisements, descriptions and manuals associated with the PSE. The trace on the left (A) shows what is said to the "irregular" pattern associated with nonstressed speech; (B) the more orderly configuration said to accompany stress.

clearly demonstrates (17), the actual process of muscle contraction is substantially more complex than the voice analysis advocates suggest.

On the other hand, Inbar et al. (30) claim to have been able to observe a laryngeal tremor of the type specified. Unfortunately, they employed surface electrodes coupled to a low-pass filter system. As is well known, surface electrodes pick up activity created by any muscle in their vicinity and there is no way of knowing if the relationships reported by these authors were from a single muscle, a group of muscles, interaction among muscles or simply some sort of "laryngeal noise." Further, the results of other experiments do not support the claims made by Inbar et al. In the first of these studies (19), it was noted that firing rates of the vocalis muscle rose from 10 to 40 per second at the onset of phonation and remained there until after the cessation of sound. A second group of investigators (1) structured the vocal tract elements necessary for the so-called tremor to occur in voice and found them contraverting. In short, it would appear that the neurological evidence relevant to the claims of the psychological stress or voice analysis proponents tends to be rather negative. The available data simply do not support their position.

Studies also have been reported in which attempts have been made to locate evidence of tremors by analysis of the acoustic signal (spectrographically). In one case, the 5-100 Hz frequency band was studied for subjects who produced unstressed speech and others who were stressed by random electric shocks administered as they read a prose passage (40). No evidence was found that any energy bands existed at frequencies below subjects' SFF levels for either of the two conditions. Almcida et al. (1) report similar results, but the Inbar group (29) claims to have observed acoustic evidence of a "tremor" in the third formant of vowels. A statement of this kind both confounds the controversy and contradicts accepted acoustic theory relative to the operation of the vocal tract—i.e., very low frequency energy existing within the signal would be reflected throughout all formants and not just in one region. Perhaps a more telling argument involves the telephone, a link which is often used by voice analyzer personnel as part of the overall system. If the microtremor upon which they base their technique is in the 8-14 Hz frequency region, and the lowest frequency a telephone will pass is 250 Hz (at best), some other feature must be the one being measured. Thus, it appears that none of the required conditions appear to be met by the theories and/or methods proposed by the voice analyzer proponents. To be valid, voice analysis must demonstrate that the cited microtremors: (1) occur in the vocal muscles during speech, (2) are manifest in the acoustic speech signal and (3) are reduced or modified by psychological stress (45). Indeed, Bachrach (4) sums up this controversy rather nicely when he concludes: "There appears to be no conclusive evidence that ... a microtremor exists in the vocal apparatus ... the transfer from normal physiological tremor to the vocal cords appears unwarranted."

Research on Stress

In one sense anyway, if a system can perform the required tasks, it is more or less immaterial as to how they are accomplished. Unfortunately, the available research does not appear to support the voice analysis proponents' claims in this domain either. While there is indication that these devices can sometimes be used to detect stress if the level is extremely high (40), they appear ineffective if the stress level is moderate to low (5, 39, 41). If the technique is valid, it should operate effectively no matter what the emotional level of the subject.

The procedure appears to be a "tease" in other regards also. That is, data resulting from studies of its validity are rather inconsistent. For example, while Brenner (8) reports that his PSE analyses showed talker stress to increase somewhat as a function of audience size, these results could not be reconciled with other of his data, which were negative (9). The findings of Leith *et al.* (34) also add to the confusion. This group used PSE analysis to contrast severe stutterers with controls. They found an apparent lowering of stress (i.e., adaptation) as their subjects made a series of telephone calls. However, the results did not discriminate between their two groups: the stutterers, who experienced pathologically high stress levels at having to make the telephone calls, and the controls (nonstutterers) for whom the task induced little to no stress. Moreover, while the Nachshon and Feldman (42) data revealed no correlation between voice analysis and stress, positive correlations were reported by other investigators: i.e., for obstetrical patients (11) and for phobics when contrasted to controls (50). The results of the two studies by VanderCar *et al.* (51) are mixed also. In the first, they report that their PSE analyses correlated with stress measures of heart rate and scores on the STAI test for males speaking taboo words to females. However, when the experiment was replicated under nearly identical conditions, the PSE scores did not reflect stress or correlate with the other two measures.

In short, it appears that voice analysis of the type under discussion occasionally provides an indication of the presence of stress in speech—especially if the stress level is extremely high. On the other hand, it does not appear to work very well when moderate to lower levels of stress are investigated; nor can stress be detected consistently. Actually, however, research on stress is somewhat off the point as the primary objective of the voice analyzers appears to be the detection of deception by evaluation of an individual's utterances. Since such identifications also are the goal of the members of the American Polygraph Society, it might be a little surprising that they have not adopted or endorsed the use of these machines/techniques. Quite the contrary, in 1973, the APA Board of Directors voted against their use primarily because "the reliability and validity (of the technique) have not been demonstrated" (7).

Reseach on Deception

It should be noted that most of the studies to be reviewed below are based on analyses using but one of the available systems, i.e., the PSE. Indeed, not much research at all has been carried out on the effectiveness of any of the other devices. As with the experiments on stress, the PSE analyses related to lying tend to be conflicting at best. For example, Heisse (23) reports having tested the PSE by requiring a group of "trained" examiners to process 258 "evaluation replies;" he claims they were correct 96.1% of the time. Some concern can be expressed relative to the robustness of Heisse's study as he appears to have had close ties with the manufacturer of PSE equipment—at least at the time he published this paper. On the other hand, a number of investigators have challenged the ability of the voice stress analyzers to detect lying (5, 9, 10, 29, 32). The Kubis research (32) is pivotal in this regard; he used 174 subjects in a "simulated theft" experiment involving a thief, a lookout and an innocent suspect. In order to determine which of his subjects were lying and which were telling the truth, he utilized the polygraph and two "voice-analyzers" (the PSE and the VSA) operated by "trained" examiners. He also had the polygraph records reevaluated by independent examiners and obtained a subjective assessment of the recordings by the untrained assistants he used to monitor the interrogations. The primary accuracy level for the polygraph operators was found to be 76%; the independent polygraph personnel scored 50-60% and the subjective scores of the untrained monitors were equally as high. On the other hand, the results obtained from the voice stress evaluation procedures were roughly at chance levels. Even when the voice analyzer operators were provided with partial information, the obtained scores were well below those of the polygraphers. Kubis suggests that, because his untrained assistants were able to perceptually discriminate among his experimental subjects, he effectively demonstrated that the task he employed induced sufficient emotionality to be valid for its stated purpose.

The thrust of Barland's research (5) was somewhat different from that of Kubis. He studied both low-risk and high-risk deception. Barland reports that the PSE analysis was not sufficiently sensitive to detect lies if little jeopardy was involved; however, the results of his "high-risk" experiment were mixed. Specifically, all 14 polygraphers indicated that the subjects he studied were lying, whereas only eight of the 14 PSE examiners were in agreement (the other six PSE evaluations were inconclusive). While Barland's results are not clear-cut enough to resolve the issue, they do little to support the claims of the voice analysis proponents.

Brenner and his associates (9, 10) also have carried out research that bears directly on the ability of individuals to detect deception when using voice analysis devices. In the first study, these investigators report that when they offered their subjects a reward if they could "fool" the interrogators, most were able to do so. They state that, based on the obtained data, the PSE analysis "failed to identify correct responses beyond chance levels." In a second report, these same authors criticize the PSE (and similar devices) on the basis of five technical limitations: (1) scoring subjectivity, (2) variability due to the utterance chosen for analysis, (3) variation in recording quality, (4) interpretation differences induced by variations in transcription speed and (5) the potential that the person being examined can consciously control his or her responses. After a thorough review, they conclude that, "there is now enough technical evidence to seriously question the PSE as a practical lie detection device." Both an extensive review of the approach by Horvath (29) plus the studies he has completed support this position.

AN EXPERIMENTAL APPROACH TO THE PROBLEM

While most of the experimental data can be used to argue that psychological stress evaluation or, more properly, voice analysis is not a valid technique for the detection of either stress or deception, the fact remains that positive relationships occasionally have been reported. Of course, it is possible that (1) the data in certain of the studies were biased toward a particular relationship or (2) the research design utilized did not permit adequate testing, nonetheless, some of the reported results are a little difficult to explain. For example, why did the PSE data correlate with the other stress measures in one of the VanderCar studies but not in the other, and why did the Leith data show an adaptation effect even though the technique could not discriminate between subjects who were highly stressed and those who were not? Since, a number of these relationships appear to need clarification, we carried out two experiments which we believed would provide useful data about the controversy.

The Detection of Stress Experiment

Purpose. The goal of the first of the two experiments was to see if severe stress states could be detected by "voice stress analysis." It was our judgment that, to be fair, the stress level should be both very high and verifiable by other techniques, i.e., by procedures which are well documented as being both valid and reliable. Moreover, since it is not always possible to predict which stressor will affect a particular individual and by how much, we required that two different stress-inducing situations be employed and that the subjects' stress levels be externally monitored for both.

Subjects. Two groups of subjects of both sexes were utilized in this research ($N = 27$). All were healthy college students, 20-25 years of age, who exhibited normal speech and hearing. They were studied under two conditions: low (or no) stress and very high stress. The no-stress condition was determined by subject ratings, experimenter evaluations and a score of 7 or less on the MAACL (i.e., Multiple Affect Adjective Checklist) anxiety scale (53). To meet the high-stress criteria, subjects had to be appropriately ranked both on self and experimenter rating scales plus have received an anxiety score of 13 or more on the MAACL.

Induced Stress. As stated, different stressors were employed for each of the paired experiments—electric shock with the first group (laboratory stress) and a public speech for the second (situational stress). The first of the two subpopulations read a standard passage aloud under two conditions: while receiving random shocks from a Grason-Stadler "conditioning" system, and while not receiving shocks. Even though this procedure did not harm the subject, it caused enough discomfort to induce stress—and markedly so. The subjects for the second, or situational stress, procedure were drawn from a large number of volunteers who were recorded as they gave their first presentation in a public speaking course. Only those tape recordings obtained from individuals who met the cited stress criteria were selected for analysis. In this case, the two speech samples were different: (1) public address—high stress; (2) standard passage— low stress. While these two passages were text independent, they were judged to be of sufficient length (2-3 minutes) that no contextual effects would result.

Procedure. Subjects wore (and were permitted time to become familiar with) a specially constructed headset with a miniature (calibrated) microphone suspended from a boom. By this means, a constant microphone-to-lip distance could be maintained under any and all conditions; transmission was by an FM radio-link. All speech samples were produced in either a quiet classroom or a sound-treated room. Finally 20-second sections of all relevant speech samples were processed on a PSE-1 unit operated on the Mode III setting. Each segment was divided into four parts (one statement by each subject), coded, mounted and presented to the judges in a randomized sequence.

Judges. Three groups of judges were employed. The first group consisted of 12 college students who received a short training period (one hour) specifically based on the instructions found in the PSE training manual; they were not tested for competency. Members of the second group were recruited in a similar fashion. They were 10 college students who were provided substantially more training than the first group. In this case, the group received over two hours of training plus supervised practice with samples drawn from the PSE manual. The third group of auditors consisted of a group of advanced experimental phoneticians and psychoacousticians who had carried out substantial amounts of research involving analysis of analog traces. The third group also received the more extensive of the two training procedures.

Results. The results of this experiment may be found summarized in Table 13-1. The basic observation that can be made is that all scores hover around chance (i.e., 50%). Since these data are based on over 3,000 judgments, one might be tempted to discuss what appear to be trends in the data. However, it is dangerous to point out such "tendencies," since data such as these also could have been obtained by blindfolded subjects who simply guessed at the relationships. Accordingly, it only can be observed that (1) none of the scores deviated very far from chance, (2) the distributions were extremely variable and, in any case, (3) no value approached statistical significance.

When all of the data on the voice analysis technique for the identification of psychological stress are summarized, the following relationships may be observed. It appears that application of this approach occasionally results in the suggestion that stress is present in a speech sample (if the level is extremely high), but then so can virtually any stress measurement technique you can concepualize. Thus, it must be concluded that voice analysis of this type does not work very well. Worse yet, the procedure appears to lead to incorrect judgments when stress is not present (or is very low) and, if nonstress speech is often identified as reflecting stress, a serious danger exists—i.e., that unfortunate

TABLE 13-1. Evaluations of PSE Traces of Stressed and Unstressed Speech Produced by Two Groups of Talkers

Auditor group responses	Laboratory stress		Situational stress		Overall performance
	Stressed	Unstressed	Stressed	Unstressed	
Student Group I (Minimum training)					
Stressed	35	*	50	*	
Unstressed	*	45	*	64	48
Student Group II (Full training)					
Stressed	44	*	51	*	
Unstressed	*	45	*	39	45
Scientist Group (Full training)					
Stressed	45	*	48	*	
Unstressed	*	51	*	63	52
Group means	41	47	50	55	(48)

Note. *Reciprocal of the other value; data are provided for three groups of auditors. All values are percentages.

interpretations will be made about the talker's status. Indeed, the occurrence of a substantial number of errors of this type is simply unacceptable.

The Detection of Deception Experiment

We are sensitive to the claim by the voice analysis proponents that their techniques are not adequately tested in the laboratory because only low-risk lies can be studied under these conditions. For example, Heisse (23) argues that there are great differences between low-risk lies which (he says) cause the speaker little or no stress, and high-risk lies which cause a "great deal" of stress. Perhaps so, but the approach does not appear to correctly detect stress even if it is present; moreover, it would seem to me that a technique which cannot be used in most situations is of but very limited value. On the other hand, while it seemed logical to challenge the contention of the voice analysis supporters relative to their stress/deception argument, we did not have personal experimental data on which to evaluate the accuracy of their position. In order to counter this and related criticisms, we conducted the experiment described below. In doing so, we judged that a fair evaluation of the cited technique could be carried out if we required our experimental subjects to produce utterances (1) which they knew were untrue and (2) which would be particularly stressful to them. Accordingly, a procedure was developed in which all talkers would utter "high-risk" lies. That is, it was judged that, if subjects were convinced that an audience important to them was to hear them espousing a view which was strongly in conflict with their true feelings, their speech sample would reflect lying with substantial jeopardy.

Subjects. Volunteers were identified who were strongly opposed to animal experimentation and, in particular, to vivisection. Prior to the experiment, one of the investigators explained the seriousness and importance of the project to the potential subjects and requested that they volunteer. She also led them to believe that their colleagues and friends from the University and local community would hear their statements and, thus, identify them with a position they felt to be morally false. They further were led to believe that the purpose of the research was to see if auditors could discriminate when the subjects were lying and when they were telling the truth. Subjects were not told until after the entire experiment had been completed that the auditors would not actually hear their statements but rather "read" traces as coded by a PSE unit—and that neither they nor the speech sample they uttered would be identified in any manner whatsoever. In all, 44 individuals volunteered to participate in the research.

Procedure. Subjects first were required to view a series of visual materials which showed animals being severely abused during experiments. They were then asked to read, and tape-record, two 20-second statements: one strongly antivivisectionist in nature and the other strongly in support of animal experiments under any and all conditions. Three evaluations of the stress levels experienced by the subjects were employed: (1) self-reports, (2) experimenter observations and (3) scores on the MAACL test. High agreement among all three criteria was required if a volunteer was to be used as either an experimental or control subject. That is, to be included in the experiment, each volunteer had to feel/show high stress where required and low stress for their control reading. Specifically, they had to score between 1 and 8 on the MAACL after the low-stress (truthful) reading and between 10 and 21 in conjunction with the high-stress (lie) passage. Twelve individuals met all criteria. Conversely, to be a member of the control group, a volunteer had to show/feel no differences in stress and score between 7 and 12 on the MAACL for both reading conditions—with no more than a single point between tests. Seven individuals qualified for the control group. Most of the subjects who did not qualify for either group were rejected because their behavior and both test scores exhibited high stress. These relationships occurred, presumably, because the cited subjects found the task too difficult to carry out; indeed, several indicated that they felt strong anger during the entire procedure. In any case, all experimental subjects exhibited a sharp contrast between lying with jeopardy (high-stress patterns) and uttering a truthful statement with low stress. Finally, all experimental procedures paralleled those employed in the first of these studies—i.e., that investigating stress.

Judges. Again, three groups of judges were utilized: (1) college students who were "taught" to read PSE traces by means of the 2-hour training program; they were different subjects than those utilized in the first experiment, (2) the experienced scientists who had been employed in the prior experiment and (3) three trained/experienced PSE operators who volunteered to assist with the research.

Results. The results of this experiment can be found in Table 13-2. As may be seen, the "stress" group was judged to be lying less than 50% of the time by the students and PSE operators and only a little over 60% by the scientists when, in fact, they were lying 100% of the time. Statistical tests confirmed that the obtained results essentially were at chance levels, and even the 58% correct truthful

**TABLE 13-2. Summary Table of Percent Correct
Judgments by Three Groups of Auditors**

| | Speakers | | | |
| | Experimental | | Control | |
Auditors	Deceptive	True	Deceptive	True
Students				
Truth	*	40	*	39
Untruth	48	*	40	*
Phoneticians				
Truth	*	37	*	43
Untruth	62	*	54	*
PSE Operators				
Truth	*	58	*	48
Untruth	44	*	43	*
Mean				
Truth	*	45	*	43
Untruth	51	*	46	*

Note. *Reciprocal of paired value; experimental talkers were individuals
who recorded a true statement under low stress and a deceptive one under
high stress. Controls were individuals who showed low to moderate stress
for both conditions.

identifications by the PSE operators was not of significance. Further, I wish to
point out also that the PSE operators indicated that the subjects were lying,
when actually they are telling the truth, an incredible 42% of the time. As a
consequence, it appears to be very difficult, if not impossible, to defend the
validity of this approach. It is especially disturbing that various groups of examiners cannot discriminate among talkers who are (1) telling the truth under
conditions of low stress, (2) speaking a falsehood under high stress or (3) uttering (sometimes) either the truth or a lie under moderate-to-low stress. If this
method were valid, at least some of the conditions would have resulted in
statistically positive relationships. Accordingly, we concluded that the voice
analysis technique is of no value in the detection of deception.

SOCIAL ISSUES

In all good conscience, I could not end this discussion about voice stress
analyzers without commenting on their potential danger to society. For one
thing, even though the method's proponents argue that their technique can be
used in lie detection, we have seen that the available data support a very strong
case to the contrary. Negative arguments about this approach become much
more compelling when it is remembered that individuals who make claims about
a system must demonstrate the validity of their contentions. If they do not, their
entire approach is suspect—or worse.

Perhaps even more serious are the well-documented fears that the use of these units will lead to abuses; that civil liberties will be violated (especially when the method is employed over the telephone) and an individual's right to privacy will be invaded. Indeed, there are many instances where abuses appear to have been perpetrated by individuals who carried out these "tests." There is no question that activities of this type constitute a danger to anyone against whom they are directed. Finally, even though scientists working in this area are aware of the substantial need by law enforcement agencies for a valid tool of this type, the available research argues that currently none exists. Perhaps one of the more encouraging aspects of this problem is that, as far as I am aware, "detection of deception" by voice analysis has not been accepted by any court. Of course, a still better solution would be to entirely prohibit their use.

A POSTSCRIPT

So you think that the "voice analyzers" have folded their tents and silently stolen away? Don't you believe it! While writing this chapter, I received an advertisement from the National Institute for Truth Verification. It seems that they have revised the old Voice Stress Analyzer (VSA) and are now calling it the "computer voice stress analyzer" (CVSA). The device they picture appears to operate in virtually the same manner as the old VSA (or the PSE for that matter). Computer indeed! Additionally, and as stated in the advertisement, the system operates on the same "microtremor principle" as did the earlier models; in this case, however, operation is likened to that of a thermostat. Of course, the packaging shown is modern and attractive. Moreover, a set of "range" lights (low, normal, high) is included among the system's features; they presumably are used in conjunction with chart reading. All in all, this system does not appear to be any different from the old one (except for a newly designed box); certainly, no evidence is presented that it actually contains a computer. Unfortunately for us, it appears that "voice analyzers" neither die nor fade away.

PART V

Related Areas

CHAPTER 14

Signatures: Machine and Acoustic

INTRODUCTION

A number of subareas have emerged from the work being carried out in forensic phonetics. Several undoubtedly are as much the responsibility of engineers as they are phoneticians. On the other hand, and as you probably have deduced, most phoneticians have a rather extensive background in acoustics, electronics (at least with relevant equipment) and computers—just as they do with concepts about human behavior, physiology and speech itself. As has been seen, they are involved in such technical issues as the decoding of tape recordings, electronic surveillance, the authentication of tape recordings, speaker identification by machine, and so on. Careers that routinely encompass work such as this naturally involve related activities.

This chapter will focus on two areas: (1) the signature patterns created by machines as they are operated (and which permit them to be identified at a later time) plus (2) the signatures of impact noise signals (gunshots, in particular). The first area, that of machine signatures, is the natural outgrowth of tape recorder authentication; i.e., when attempts are made to validate a tape recording, it is necessary to know when the unit was started and stopped, which recorder was used, and so on. Indeed, the ability of the forensic phonetician to identify the electronic signatures created by tape recorders is becoming a very important skill. It is only logical then that he or she also should be able to identify signatures of telephones, the relays used in telephone transmissions, engines/motors (aircraft or otherwise) and a large variety of other types of machine noises as they happen and/or are recorded. Indeed, the general analysis of sound, and its electronic correlates, can be quite useful as an investigational tool.

Please consider again the concepts I have just presented. In a sense, they provide the basis of a postulate which may or may not be true. That is, many phoneticians and engineers believe that each and every device has its own—its very own—mechanical or electronic signature. Perhaps so, perhaps not. However, it is an idea that should be tested; after all, most myths are grounded in reality. Indeed, my colleagues and and I believe that we have found at least a tentative factual basis for a number of the relationships I will be reviewing in this chapter. To illustrate, I will first consider the operational characteristics of tape recorders and how they can be evaluated. This concept should not be new to you for, as you will remember from Chapter 8, this problem already has been discussed in some detail—particularly as it relates to the authentication process.

To be specific, tape recorders can be numbered among those devices that are thought to have signatures unique to a given machine; one that always can be identified and used to determine such important issues as: (1) if the recording in question was made on a particular unit, (2) if the recording is an original, (3) if more than one recorder was used to develop the tape, (4) if there are "off-ons" that suggest editing, and so on. But, is it true that each and every tape recorder has its own signature? Many writers think that they do. Indeed, some technicians even claim that they can identify when various internal circuits (i.e., erase heads, motors) are operated and/or shut down and that they can do so by examining the patterns created by the resulting electronic signal. Is this true also? You will remember from Chapter 8 that, after an extensive review of the relevant literature, I found this contention to be open to serious question. We really do not know if all of these suppositions are true and the reason we do not know is because research in this area is practically nonexistent. What a surprise! The legend about our ability to identify machines by their signatures would lead you to believe that these relationships are very well established. They are not. As yet, they have not even been thoroughly investigated.

In response to the problem, several of my colleagues and I are in the process of carrying out experiments in an attempt to uncover at least some of the basic relationships in this area. But is this the kind of project that will attract external funding? Of course not. It is necessary to carry out these experiments with available equipment and in our spare time. Nevertheless, we already have accumulated some data; they will be reviewed below. Also to be discussed is a related area: that of telephone signatures. By chance, we observed that some telephones showed rather complex and unique electronic patterns when the hand unit was returned to the cradle and the connection severed. A pilot study has been carried out and, so far, we have observed unit-dependent signatures; i.e., patterns that are unique at least to a class of telephones. These relationships will be discussed also, primarily as a second example illustrating the nature of machine signatures.

The second of the two areas to be covered is one that is mainstream to acoustics as a discipline, but not really fundamental to the field of phonetics. It involves identification of impact noises and, especially, gunshots. As it turns out, however, the phonetician can be included among the professionals competent to carry out analysis of this type. For one thing, he or she has background in quantitative measurement; for another, most are trained in acoustics and psychoacoustics. Thus, the phonetician is a "natural" for the study of impact noise—whether it is a stop-plosive, the click on a tape recording or a recording of a gunshot.

Perhaps you are wondering how often you might come across a case where analysis of gunfire is required. Such instances are more prevalent than you might think. Take the assassination of Senator Robert Kennedy for example. The gunshots involved there may have been recorded—when, where and how depends on your informants and/or analyses. A number of very important issues occur here, i.e., how many shots were there and where did they come from? In any event, there have been a number of instances where gunfire has been recorded—accidentally or on purpose—and controversy has occurred as to how the gun was fired, the sequence of firing or the position of the firearm when it was discharged. Even more common are earwitness reports of gunfire and, if there are more than one, these earwitnesses often contradict each other. Here again, tests on the signatures and nature of gunfire can aid the police and courts in determining what actually happened. Since I have carried out a number of projects in these areas, I will devote a later section in this chapter to the issue. It may be of interest to you.

MACHINE SIGNATURES

Nearly all electronic or electromagnetic systems produce a disturbance when they are operated. The acoustic click made by a switch when it is activated is but one example. However, the electronic signatures within a system that are of greatest interest here. Of course, sometimes the noise produced is not very useful. For example, it rarely is possible to discriminate objectively between one type of system hiss and another. However, many devices appear to create an identifiable (electronic) pulse or click when they are turned on and off or when a subcircuit is activated.

As I have suggested, electronic signatures of all types are very important to forensic phonetics. Hence, the bulk of this chapter will be devoted to their analysis. The signatures produced by tape recorder "on-off" switching activity will be examined in some detail, and telephone hang-up clicks to a lesser extent. But you must remember that these examples are only two among many. To illustrate, in "The Case of the Blue Box," it was requested that I identify the electronic (and/or mechanical) signatures of solenoids being operated in a telephone company switching room. The litigation was over the use of a device that permits a person to make long-distance telephone calls without paying for them. The operation of a number of these units had been tape recorded and I was asked to determine: (1) if the recorded noises were produced by solenoids typical to a telephone company switching station, (2) if specific classes of solenoids had been recorded and (3) if the operation of individual solenoids could be determined. Several of the techniques described below were utilized and I was able to demonstrate that solenoids similar to the ones used by that telephone company had been recorded. It was possible, even, to discriminate among different sets or types of solenoids. However, I was not able to discriminate amongst particular solenoids within a class. Thus, I had to conclude that, while operation of a solenoid results in a signature that probably is unique to this type of device (it relates perhaps to its size and power use), any member within a given class exhibits a signature that is virtually indistinguishable from those of its close relatives.

Another illustration: while 60-cycle "hum" often can be used to determine if certain circuits were operated (especially for devices that do not use batteries or employ precision power supplies), it rarely is possible to identify a hum "signa-ture" — primarily since nearly all hum is produced at 60 Hz and is a sinusoid or nearly so. Once in a great while, a hum will leak into the system which is unique enough with respect to its base frequency or harmonic partials that an identifica-tion can be made; occasionally, two hums will be present that are out of phase with each other. Ordinarily, however, conclusions based only on hum analysis can be a little hazardous.

The Signatures of Tape Recorders

Now that we have established the fact that there are hundreds—perhaps thousands—of mechanical and/or electronic devices that can, and do, leave a trail which reveals their previous use, let us concentrate on that system which is perhaps of greatest importance to the areas reviewed in this book. As you already are aware, this device is the tape recorder. Indeed, magnetic recorders are central to nearly all of the work associated with the field of forensic phonetics—primarily because they are the basic storage system we use. Of course, nearly all the materials retained by a tape recorder are in analog form, but even when digital processing is carried out, the signal can be, or is, stored magnetically.

Several questions can be asked here. First, do tape recorders have electronic signatures? Second, if so, are they unique to each specific machine and, third, are these observed patterns (if they exist) consistent under any and all recording and operating conditions? As stated above, current opinion would suggest that an affirmative answer can be given to all of these questions. Certainly many experts (and people who call themselves experts) have testified in court that there is little question about these relationships. I tend to agree with these "experts," to a limited extent anyway, and have gone so far as to conclude that a pair of electronic "signatures" I had analyzed probably were made by a single tape recorder. However, and as indicated earlier, when I went to validate this position, all I found was a brief letter report and a popular article suggesting that such a relationship exists. So where are all the oft-quoted data? I certainly do not know.

The Experiment

To fill the void, several of my colleagues and I are carrying out a research program which is focused on tape recorder signatures (5). Two experiments were structured; the first is complete and about to be published; the second is still underway. Each of them consists of several substudies. In the first, the basic relationships are explored and the effects of several of the more common operat-ing modes are evaluated. Over 50 tape recorders were evaluated. The second investigation was structured to replicate the first plus test the effects of adjacent speech and high noise levels on various electronic patterns. In all, the effect of different (1) modes of operation, (2) switch manipulation and (3) levels of noise were evaluated—as was machine wear and the potential relationships among serially numbered models.

Analysis

Two analysis systems were utilized for the research; both provide about the same type of data. Indeed, they were functionally interchangable and, thus, each could be utilized to validate the other. One of these systems was a Kay Elemetrics M7800 Digital Sonograph. In this case, the signal was digitized at 10 kHz per second and signal readouts generated for each of the experimental conditions. The second procedure involved digitalization of the signal on a PDP 11/23 computer by ILS software and then conversion to a trace by the IASCP DOER program (see Figure 14-1). Initially, we intended to employ only statistical analyses—rather than visually match patterns—as we expected to describe these relationships mathematically. However, once we discovered how little actually is known about these patterns, we were forced to approach the problem first by means of visual pattern matching.

The tape recorders utilized in the investigations involved both reel-to-reel and cassette systems. Included were 30 Wollensalk 2526-AV cassette units—all of which were purchased at the same time and most of which exhibited identification numbers in serial order. A smaller number of units were utilized in the second of the major experiments, but they were studied more intensively. The procedures employed in both experiments were straightforward. The tape recorders were operated under stringently controlled conditions and the resulting (recorded) signals were replayed into the analysis equipment from a "master"

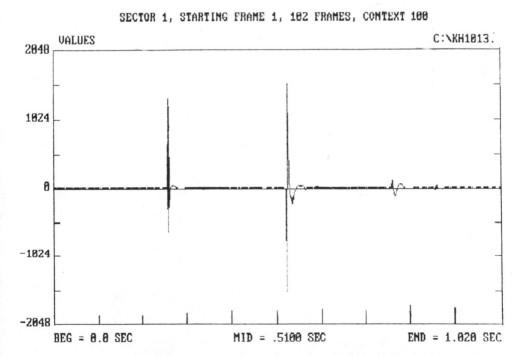

SECTOR 1, STARTING FRAME 1, 102 FRAMES, CONTEXT 100

Figure 14-1. Printout of a digitized click created when a tape recorder is turned first off and then on.

tape recorder. All recorders were calibrated and/or checked for constant speed, even though these factors were not thought to constitute a fundamental source of bias. The resulting traces were judged visually by three experimenters; they are now being quantified (by a mathematician) for statistical analysis.

Results

The primary results of the experiments described above can best be understood by consideration of Figures 14-2 through 14-5; they will provide at least some confirmation of the statements to be made. First, it can be said that, if conditions are held constant, different tape recorders appear to exhibit different signatures, and these signatures can be repeated at high reliability levels (see again Figure 14-1 plus Figure 14-2). However, if the tape recorder signatures are analyzed as a function of noise, the differences among the units appear to be somewhat obscured (Figure 14-3). As a matter of fact, noise level appears to correlate (at least mildly) with the reduction in observable differences among machines as we found that the stop-start characteristics provided more accurate

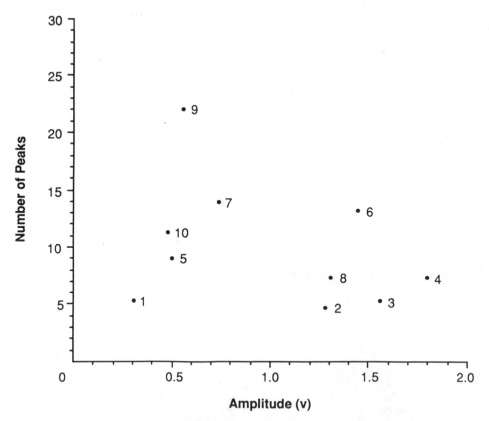

Figure 14-2. Two-way analysis of 10 tape recorders. The number of peaks in an off-on click are seen plotted as a function of the amplitude (in millivolts) of the major peaks. Note that none of the tape recorders show identical intersects (or signatures) for measurements of this type.

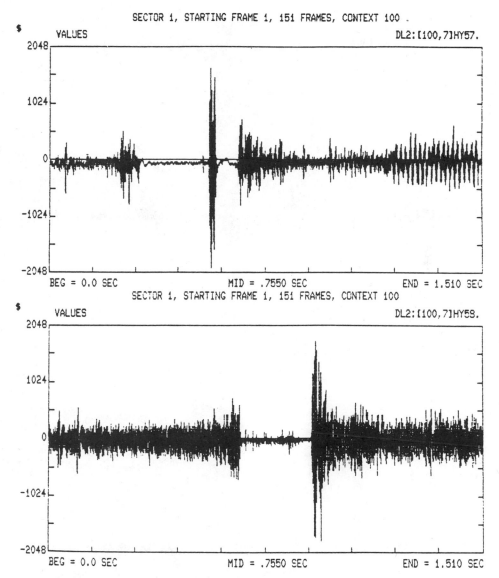

Figure 14-3. Patterns created by the same type recorder when operated under two sets of conditions. In the plot above, the "off-on" mechanism was activated during a relatively quiet recording, whereas high ambient noise was being recorded when the second (below) activation took place. Note how the differences in recording conditions tend to obscure some of the details necessary for identification.

tape recorder identification in quiet than they did in noise. Third, while it appears that an electronic signature can be associated with each tape recorder—especially if both wave form and event period are analyzed—related units may exhibit somewhat similar signatures (Figure 14-4). Nonetheless, it can be assumed that, if a known recorder "off-on" can be found on a tape recording, other instances where such activity takes place should be discernable, that is, if

SECTOR 1, STARTING FRAME 1, 102 FRAMES, CONTEXT 100

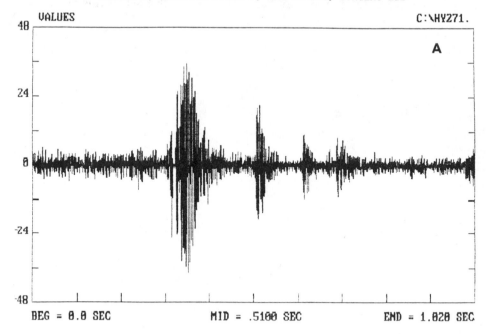

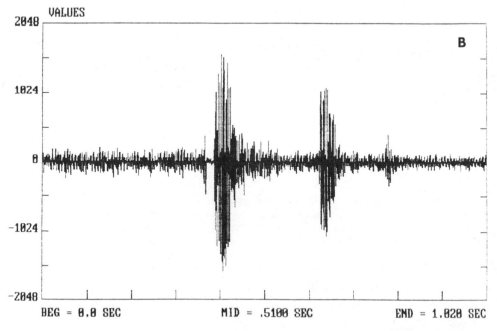

Figure 14-4. Off-on configurations obtained from two tape recorders of identical make—and exhibiting consecutive serial numbers.

they occur. As you will remember, techniques such as this are quite useful when attempts are made to authenticate tape recordings. The bad news is that such matches cannot be made as easily (or as validly) if high noise levels are present.

The data from the second experiment supplement the first. Here we attempted to determine if tape recorder signatures were changed as a function of time, use, and the way the recorder controls were handled. As may be seen from examination of Figure 14-5, the patterns serve to confirm the first conclusion— i.e., that tape recorder signatures tend to be discernable one from another. However, it can be seen that repeated operation, wear and noncontemporary use have at least a minor effect on these patterns. Moreover, it also was observed that variation in the strength used to manually operate the control switches had a modest effect on the patterns and especially on the length of the (signature) click. Worse yet, forceful switch manipulation sometimes added transients to the signal, with a resulting reduction in the idiosyncratic nature of the signature.

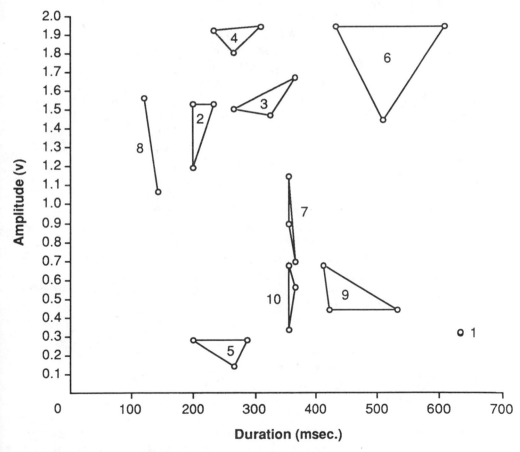

Figure 14-5. A plot of amplitude/duration data for 10 tape recorders operated in the "off-on" mode on three separate occasions. Amplitude data are obtained from the major peaks within a click; duration is the temporal length of the click. Note that even when the intersects for a given unit form a field, no overlaps are observed among the different machines.

Summary

What can be said about tape recorder signatures at this rather early stage in their evaluation? First, it is obvious that, while legends and misconceptions abound, only a very little "hard" evidence is available. About all which can be determined (and primarily from our research) is that tape recorders do appear to exhibit individual signatures, at least under "ideal" conditions. We also are pretty sure that it is possible to utilize data of this type to determine if a specific tape recorder was employed to make a particular recording or if an unannounced interruption on a recording was made by switching the unit "off" and then "on." Of course, the validity of these (and related) decisions is lowered if (1) substantial periods of time have occurred between the original and test recordings, (2) noise is present at any time, and (3) the tape recorder was operated in an inconsistent manner.

Telephone "Signatures"

Another place where electronic analysis for possible signatures may be useful relates to the switching that occurs when telephone calls are made. Permit me to provide you with but a single example. When a telephone is hung up, a rather complex click is produced. This disturbance is due in part to the coupling effect of the switch and in part to the voltage changes along the line. We have studied these clicks (primarily in pilot experiments) and, as yet, have not found any two (from different telephones) that are exactly the same. On the other hand, whenever we analyzed signals serially created by operation of a single (known) telephone, we found them to be virtually identical to each other. Consideration of Figure 14-6 should serve to illustrate this point. Note the differences between the patterns in frame C and those in frames A and B and, conversely, how well matched are the two patterns in figures A and B. Other illustrations could have been provided; all are consistent with the configurations found in the figure. Here, perhaps is a whole new identification area. Just imagine what would happen if the hang-up signature of an extortionist's telephone could be captured and identified. If the criminal made the call from his or her house (and was among the suspects), the telephone signature from an "exemplar" call then could be compared to that of the original. Admittedly, definitive relationships of this type are not yet available. However, the area appears to be a potentially promising one.

Other Examples

The issue of electronic signatures appears to be a much more complex one than has been thought. This position is supported by the data provided above plus relationships derived from "The Case of the Blue Box." Yet another example may be found in "The Case of the Devious Lawyer." Here we were able to determine that hand-held tape recording erasers (or degaussers) also appeared to exhibit unique signatures (see Figure 14-7). In this instance, a defense lawyer coerced an agent into his office in order "to make a copy" of a tape recording

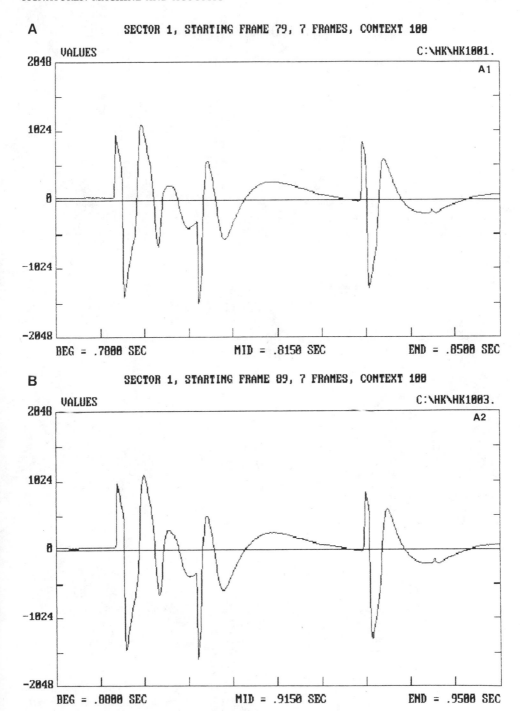

Figure 14-6. Plots of the disconnect clicks produced by two telephones. The first two curves (A, B) are from a single unit operated at different times (they are almost identical). The third configuration (C) was recorded when a second telephone was operated. As can be seen, the configuration in C is different from that produced by the first telephone.

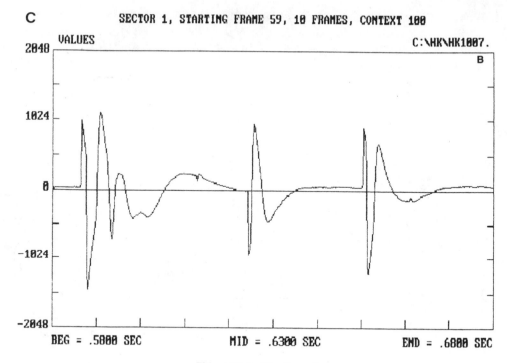

C

SECTOR 1, STARTING FRAME 59, 10 FRAMES, CONTEXT 100

VALUES

C:\HK\HK1007.

Figure 14-6. (Continued)

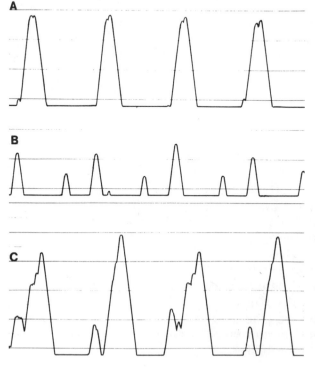

Figure 14-7. Output patterns of three magnetic tape degaussers. Although only a small number of these units have been evaluated, all produced consistent configurations for different trials—and none were similar to each other.

which was harmful to his client. He succeeded in briefly separating the agent from the tape and attempted to destroy it by erasing it with a hand-held degausser. The incriminating part of the tape survived and the attorney's client was tried and convicted. The agent, now angry, returned to the lawyers office with a search warrant and found the degausser. He requested that I attempt to determine if these units exhibited signatures, if they were unique and if the signature of the one he seized was on the damaged tape. A series of tests resulted in an affirmative answer (see again Figure 14-7). The attorney was convicted of destroying evidence and later disbarred. However, I stressed in my report that my conclusions were tentative because there was no general literature on the subject and I tested only a few devices of the type used by the attorney. Here is a good example where a position about a set of relationships might be formed prematurely and, while my opinion probably was correct, little solid evidence actually was available. Indeed, if you were to encounter a case or question of this general type, you undoubtedly would have to carry out your own experiments. Moreover, they should be thorough ones as a search of the literature probably would provide you with very little real evidence on the nature of, and discriminability among, the signatures of electronic devices you were evaluating.

SIGNATURES OF NOISES

Nearly all mechanical devices and machines make some sort of intermittent or continuous noise when operated and, often, the noise is created in such a manner that its pattern is continued or reoccurs. For example, a stamping machine in a factory will produce an impact noise (a banging or clanging) each time it is operated. In turn, many of these "noises" have acoustic characteristics that are identifiable and measurable. You can time the length of the clang or its repetition rate; alternatively, you can spectrally analyze its component frequencies. You also can study the noise made by automobile/aircraft engines—or air conditioning blowers. While many different systems and devices create noise that can be identified, there are so many of them that even a simple listing is far beyond the scope of this discussion. Thus, while I will cite a few examples, please remember that these are but a very few drawn from hundreds or even thousands. The first example involves the acoustic analysis of gunfire.

Questions about the acoustic characteristics of gunfire sometime occur in criminal investigations and courts of law; actually, the problem takes two forms. The first of the two, relates to what witnesses heard or think they heard and the second, directly to the signatures of gunshots that, for one reason or another, have been tape recorded. Specifically, it may be necessary to know if lay witnesses can identify the presence and nature of gunfire as well as the direction from which it came and/or the type of gun fired. The second area is focused on the ability of an expert to determine which of several guns were fired, the firing sequence, the direction or area from which the shots originated and/or the actual conditions under which the gun or guns in question were discharged.

At first glance, it would appear that issues such as these might not be suitable for inclusion in a book on forensic phonetics. Indeed, the first of the two appears to be more in the realm of forensic psychoacoustics and the latter in the areas of physical acoustics and/or engineering. These points are conceded. Nevertheless, I have been involved in nearly a dozen such cases and have found that the procedures phoneticians have developed for other types of (related) problems can be used quite effectively here also. As has been stated, the ability of a professional to identify an acoustic event would appear to be somewhat independent of the signal source. What does it matter if the comparisons to be made involve speech, music, clicks or impact noises? In short, the issues here parallel those discussed in previous chapters to a great degree. Moreover, you may find this section to be interesting in and of itself.

As would be expected, some research literature is available on the acoustics of gunfire. These reports take several forms; one involves the effects of impact noise on human hearing (8,9,11). In this case, scientists have attempted to evaluate how the very loud noise created by gunfire is perceived by humans—and how these impulses affect human hearing on both a short-term and a permanent basis. Temporary threshold shifts (TTS) occur with each exposure to loud sounds and permanent damage will result if the person is continually subjected to them. Indeed, a great deal of information is available about noise-induced hearing loss, as well as on how and where it starts neurologically and on how it develops. Studies such as those cited have led to the development of the acoustic ear muffs now used by individuals who spend even short periods of time around gunfire. Anyone operating in this area should become familiar with what is known about the interaction between gunfire and hearing.

The second class of literature (2,10,12) relates primarily to the acoustics of the gunfire itself. A number of issues appear to be of significance here. For one thing, it is important to know how much energy is present when different caliber guns are fired and it is even more useful to be able to determine the acoustic signature of a particular class of firearm. While only a small amount of data are available about the latter of these two questions, the procedures and techniques used by the engineers who have studied artillery (i.e., the acoustics of cannon fire) can be helpful to anyone attempting to decipher the cited relationships. These, and the references cited, provide at least a limited foundation upon which to base the analysis of the acoustics of gunshots.

The Psychoacoustics of Gunshots

The focus of the first of the two problems is on lay witnesses who have been called upon to testify about the gunfire they have heard. The questions asked usually concern their ability to determine the direction from which the shots originated and/or the nature of the gun or guns being fired. It also can be important to determine if a witness actually heard a gun being fired or rather perceived some other impact type of sound—such as a door being slammed, a firecracker or an automobile backfire. Here again are issues which are subject to much opinion but very little evidence. Some sources insist that individuals simply cannot discriminate among these sounds and that it is dangerous to place any reliance at all on earwitness testimony of this type. Other authorities will indicate that valid judgments can be made. Who should we believe? We do know that firing range officers are reputedly able to discriminate between gunfire and other like sounds, but can the average citizen do so also? To my knowledge, there are no experimental data available on this issue. Hence, court testimony of this type should be viewed with some caution. What really is needed is definitive study of the issues involved here.

On the other hand, there is a great deal of information available about how well people can determine the direction from which a sound originates. Indeed, psychoacousticians have been studying these relationships for years and have been able to establish that individuals with normal hearing ordinarily can specify the location of a sound source and do so with a reasonably high degree of accuracy. I am familiar with this literature, having studied it in order to design experiments by which I evaluated how well divers can make sound location judgments underwater. Basically, the direction of a sound can be determined by phase, or time-of-arrival, differences between the two ears for the lower frequencies (i.e. those in air below about 1,500 Hz) and by loudness or intensity differences (again between the two ears) for higher frequency sounds. Both of these localization "systems" can be utilized to assist an individual in determining the source of high-impact sounds also—and it can be expected that perception of their locale should be accomplished with some accuracy. Of course, no investigations have been carried out which bear directly on the specific issue of gunfire. Nevertheless, the wealth of appropriate data available on the sound localization capabilities of humans should permit understanding of these relationships also.

The last of the three issues—i.e., that related to the type of gun which was fired—is not as amenable to satisfactory resolution as are the others. To reiterate, a number of specialists agree that firing range officers usually can identify the type of gun being fired just by listening to the report it makes. While this capability has not been tested, both logic and experience suggest that at least some discriminations should be feasible here. For example, it should be possible to differentiate larger caliber guns from smaller ones simply by perceiving the energy fields they produce. To illustrate, in "The Case of the Husband-Wife Shootout," I was asked to testify if the sound of a .357-caliber magnum revolver would be heard as being "heavier and louder" than that produced by a .25-caliber automatic pistol, and if earwitnesses (i.e., neighbors) would be able to make appropriate judgments about these sounds. The guns had been fired serially and, as it turns out, the sequence was of substantial importance to the outcome of the trial. Superficially, the answer would be in the affirmative, as the two sounds should be perceived quite differently. Actually, however, a number of questions would have to be answered before a reasonable decision could be made. That is, it would be necessary to know (1) the relationship of the earwitnesses to the sound source (distance, angle, reflective surfaces, sound barriers, etc.), (2) their expectancy level and especially (3) the acoustic environment within which the firing took place (i.e., whether it was inside or outside a building, the position and type of furniture, the direction the guns were pointed, and so on).

In short, it appears that earwitness testimony about gunfire generally must be viewed with some caution. While it is possible that accurate information can be provided by such witnesses, it also is important that their testimony be weighed against the potential sources of error cited above. The most troublesome aspect of this situation is that a good many of the parameters that can affect the cited judgments/opinions will not be known. Of course, some of the relationships can be established by a replication of the events thought to have taken place. However, even if the physical relationships are known, the witnesses' judgments still will be variously biased by the behavioral states (arousal, motivation) they were experiencing at the time of the shooting.

Acoustic Analysis of Gunfire

Gunfire is tape recorded much more often than you would suspect. Indeed, sometimes people record it on purpose. As you will remember, such was the situation in "The Case of the Careful Killer" — the college student who was having trouble with his roommates and recorded the event when he shot one. You also will remember that the jury apparently did not believe him, as he was sent to prison. While the only "acoustics of gunfire" element in the events described above was the fact that a shot had been tape recorded, such was not

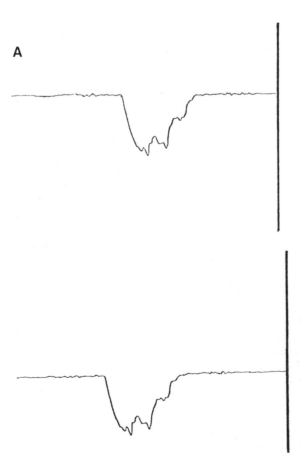

A

Figure 14-8. Comparison of the discharge patterns of several handguns. The first pair of traces (A) were produced at different times by the same revolver but under parallel firing conditions. The second pair (B) are from two different handguns. As can be seen, they are different from each other and from two sets produced by the first gun.

B

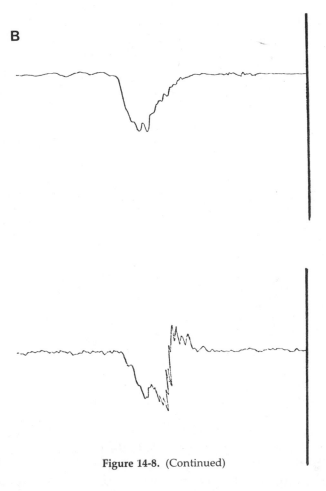

Figure 14-8. (Continued)

true in "The Jewelry Store Shootout." This case also was referenced in an earlier chapter; let me provide more details here. Its most relevant feature was that an individual in the building adjacent to the jewelry store in question was recording an employment interview and, thus, also (inadvertently) recorded the shootout through the separating wall. A "voiceprint" specialist was called in and indicated that his t-f-a spectrograms permitted him to determine the exact firing sequence of the three guns involved. The presiding judge was skeptical and allowed me to carry out a study using more efficient methods of analysis. A large number of handguns were studied; included were the three used in the gun battle. The issue investigated was: do handguns exhibit a signature when fired and, if so, is it unique to that gun in all instances? As can be seen from Figure 14-8A, a handgun apparently does exhibit an acoustic signature and its pattern is repeatable. Moreover, it appears to differ from those of other handguns (see Figure 14-8B). Of course, the study was substantially more extensive than Figure 14-8 would suggest, as numerous other parameters also had to be studied. They included such factors as: (1) gun type, (2) bullet weight, (3) load size, (4) barrel length, (5) shooter, (6) angle from microphone, (7) room acoustics, and so on. It was found that while the relationships seen in Figure 14-8 hold, they are overridden to some extent (often not critically, however) by various of the cited parameters. However, the one variable that has the most devastating effect on these signatures is that of "room acoustics." Specifically, the standing waves, echoes, absorption, reverberation-time and related conditions within a room differentially affect the acoustic signature of a pistol shot, and they do so depending on where the gun was fired, the direction it was pointed and the position of the pickup microphone. In short, it may be possible to determine if a particular gun was fired but, if you are to do so, all aspects of the environment must be exactly replicated during the tests.

Consider also the four panels in Figure 14-9, which contain a series of graphic readouts of the digital analyses of gunshots. Here, the top pair was made from the recordings of two of several firings of a police officer's service revolver during a shootout which followed a burglary; the second pair are test firings which were carried out at a police range. In both instances, the conditions under which the gun was fired were quite similar; however, the ammunition was different for the test firings (i.e., the lower two graphs). Note the difference between the two sets of patterns but the marked similarity within a pair. This figure provides further evidence that signatures often can be assigned to gunfire, that is, if conditions are relatively constant.

Of course, there are situations when the type of gun being fired and its position are very difficult to determine. An example of such is provided by the case I refer to as "The Commie-Klan Shootout." This event occurred some years ago between a group of communists and several members of the Ku Klux Klan. I will not reiterate the details of this very complex case to any great extent as they have been well publicized in the newspapers. However, the battle between these two groups resulted in three trials (re: murder, civil liberties and compensation); I was involved in the second two. In the first of the three, a government agent testified that he used the sounds of the gunfire (recorded by several television crews) and the known reflective surfaces of the environment to identify the source of the gunfire. From these data, it was concluded that the communists had shot first. The Klan members were acquitted of murder. However, during the second trial (involving violation of civil liberties), the agent indicated that he had recalculated his measurements and now believed that it was the Klan members who had first opened fire. Obviously, this reversal in position resulted in some confusion and it was requested that I reanalyze the data.

I was aware that, if you know the exact position of the pickup microphone and the source of all reflections, reverberations, and so on, it is theoretically possible to locate the physical source of a tape-recorded sound by signal analysis. However, I observed that several practical problems existed in this instance and I wondered if there was any possibility of applying accepted theory to this particular set of events. My reason for being concerned was that the neighborhood surrounding the shootout contained a large number of reflective surfaces in the nature of buildings, cars, people, trees and other structures, and many of them were moving. Indeed, could any major, yet stable, surfaces be found? Accordingly, I carried out a series of experiments at the local police range; all involved a much simpler set of reflective surfaces than those associated with this case. I found it almost impossible to locate the source of the gunfire from the great multitude of reverberations involved. Of course, when the experiment was carried out, we knew the exact position of the sound source as well as its distance/angle from the microphone. Hence, we could calculate where the source pulse should be on the recorded waveform and properly reconstruct all positions. However, when we worked backwards, reliable calculation of the gun's location was almost impossible to determine—even for the somewhat simpler model that we employed. Worse yet, we later discovered that the position of the microphone at the crime scene actually was unknown as it was on an 18-foot cord and, hence, only somewhere near the recorder. Fortunately, we were able to make a reasonable estimate of the general area from which the shots came by measuring their signal strength, roughly establishing the kinds of guns that were used (general classification only, of course) and combining these acoustic events with the behavior of the participants as seen on the video portion of the recording. From these data, it appeared quite obvious that the agent had been correct in his first assessment and that the communists had been the first to open fire. As best as I can tell, we were pretty much in agreement relative to the order of events by the time the third trial took place.

Many other examples could be cited, of course. One such instance involved the grisly task of determining how far away a criminal was from the police officer he murdered. The technique we utilized was to measure the time difference of a pair of recorded sounds: the explosion caused by the shot and the impact of the bullet striking the victim (both had been recorded). Since the speed of the bullet was essentially known, as is the speed of sound, comparison of the two times-of-arrival at the tape recorder (i.e., at the victim) provided the location of the shooter. This analysis certainly was in the nature of a service to the community but it was not a very pleasant one to carry out. I hope that I have been able to provide information about a number of the techniques that can be used to assist the courts and law enforcement agencies to answer at least some of the questions related to recorded gunfire. As you probably realize by now, only a limited number of these questions can be answered.

SUMMARY

How can this section on electronic/machine, impact noises and other signatures be summarized? First, it can be said that such patterns appear to exist but, currently anyway, it is not known if very many of them are so idiosyncratic that they can be correctly identified in all situations. For example, we now are pretty sure that the generally held opinions relative to the uniqueness of tape recorder signatures are roughly accurate. It can be assumed that the operation of a given tape recorder probably will result in an electronic signature which at least can be used to identify the further functioning of that unit if it (the pattern) appears again on the same tape recording. But whether a given configuration can be differentiated from those produced by all other tape recorders is not yet known. Nor do we know if a particular signature is idiosyncratic to a specific unit under any and all of the extensive number of operating conditions that can occur in real

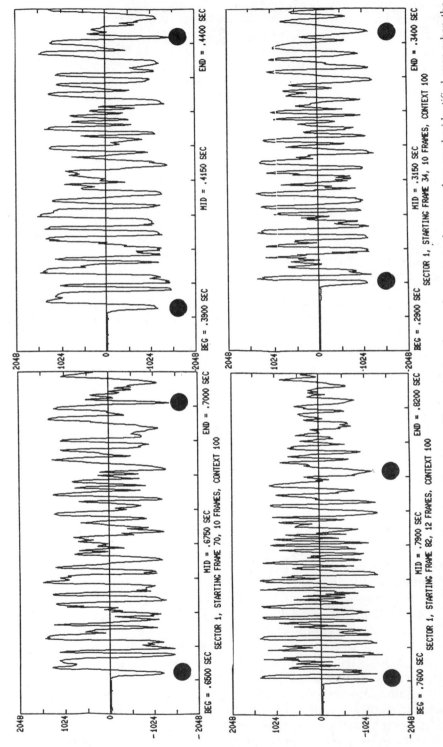

Figure 14-9. Plots of the discharge patterns of two handguns. The upper two frames demonstrate that a revolver can be identified even when the firing conditions are somewhat variable. The lower pair of frames resulted from the test firing of a second revolver. Here the pattern is different from the first and like itself—even though both ammunition and time analysis were different for the conditions depicted in the left and right frames. The dots indicate the initiation and end of the primary impulse.

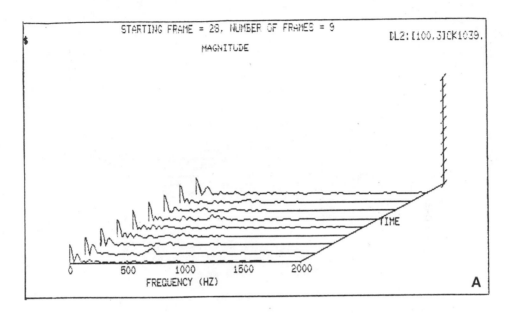

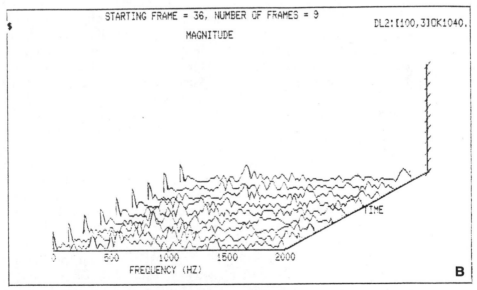

14-10. Plots of noise in an aircraft cockpit transmitted over a radio and tape recorded at a control tower. The first two spectra are from a specific aircraft operated with the main door closed (A) and then open (B) during flight. Spectrum (C) was made from the transmission received from a different plane just before it crashed.

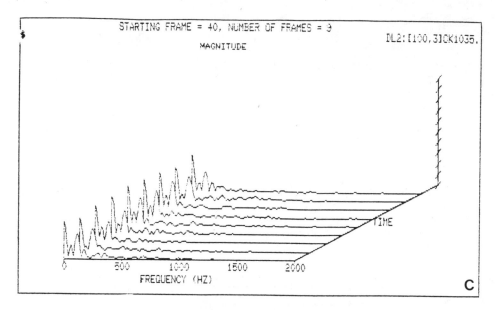

STARTING FRAME = 40, NUMBER OF FRAMES = 9

MAGNITUDE

DL2:[100,3]CK1035.

TIME

500   1000   1500   2000

FREQUENCY (HZ)

C

Figure 14-10. (Continued)

life. Factors such as different (1) operators, (2) times of operation, (3) modes of operation, (4) levels of noise, and so on may have an effect on the observed patterns. The same set of relationships holds for analysis of all types of mechanical devices as well as for the acoustic patterns of recorded gunfire and similar impact noises. If this discussion sounds a little familiar, you have but to turn back to the chapters on speaker identification for a similar one. In any case, we have just scratched the surface in this area. Much more research is needed on both class and individual signatures of electronic devices, mechanical systems, recorded gunfire and related events before we will be in a position to make firm postulations about their nature.

Finally, I cannot resist providing you with an additional example. It is based on one of a number of instances where the techniques described in this book have been used to shed light on the nature of aircraft disasters; that is, in those cases where recorded radio transmissions permitted signal analysis to be carried out. Please consider Figure 14-10. These three spectral displays are part of a series carried out during the investigation of an aircraft accident. The company which originally built the aircraft was alleged to be responsible for the disaster because the plane presumably was destabilized as a result of the sudden opening of a cargo door during flight. It was argued further that the failure of the door was caused by a defective latch; hence the aircraft manufacturer was at fault. These allegations might be true if, indeed, the latch actually had failed and the door opened. Review of the three frames found in Figure 14-10 should provide the answer. The last (C) of the three is a digital spectrum of the noise (engine plus movement) recorded from an open microphone and radio link just before the plane crashed. The first (A) frame contains the spectrum of the flight noise created by a similar plane over an analogous communication link, with the hatch in question firmly closed. The second slot (B) is a spectrum made of the sounds in the test cockpit under the same conditions; that is, with a single exception. Here the plane was being flown with the cargo hatch open. As is easily seen, the charge about an open door and, hence a defective latch, appears not to be true. In short, it is my opinion that the spectral measurements made by phoneticians can have many uses and not all of them have to relate to speech analysis.

Related Areas and Specialties

INTRODUCTION

Who knows how many areas within the extensive rubric of forensic communication relate functionally to forensic phonetics. Certainly, there are several; I do know that the four I have selected to review in this chapter overlap my specialty areas and do so to a substantial degree. They include (1) language analysis for forensic purposes (both spoken and written language are included), (2) psychoacoustics and the related area of audiology, (3) the pirating of audio- and videotape recordings and (4) the area of computer crime. These four topics will be discussed in the order of descending relevance to forensic phonetics. I will include a few references for each so you can read further if you find that particular topic to be of interest to you. Please note however, that my descriptions will be a little superficial. After all, the areas discussed are somewhat tangential to the basic focus of this book; moreover, each is worthy of its own text. However, I hope that I can provide you with some insight as to their dimensions and boundaries—and, especially, how they interface with forensic phonetics.

LINGUISTIC ANALYSIS

Semantic Analysis

This general area often is subtitled "conversational analysis" — at least when speech is being considered. It is a subarea within linguistics, but one (both with respect to theory and practice) which is organized for very specific purposes. Actually, either written or spoken dialogue can be analyzed; hence, transcripts, written accounts, autobiographies, newspaper stories, tape recordings, or similar materials can be used to provide the basic text for analysis. The question to be asked is what are the examinations that can be carried out in this area and how can they be useful in the forensic milieu?

People use language not just to communicate the denotative meaning inherent in the words and sentences they write or utter but also for connotative purposes. In linguistics, these terms—*denotation* and *connotation*—are used to distinguish the literal meaning of an utterance or passage from its subjective interpretation. An example used by Casagrande (8) involves the statement, "My house is your house." Denotatively, this sentence is rather unusual, as it only could be uttered by the co-owner of the house when speaking to its other owner. However, the phrase makes alot of sense connotatively; it is often used by a host when speaking to a preferred visitor (or to put a visitor at ease), even though he or she actually has no ownership claims on the house. In everyday interchange, connotation is known as "talking between the lines" or "the hidden agenda." Sometimes it is intentional, sometimes otherwise; it nearly always is revealing. In any case, denotation versus connotation analysis pits the literal meaning of some utterance or passage against its subjective interpretation.

Several interrelated techniques are employed in order to permit the contrasting or analysis of these classes of language use. They include evaluation of: (1) the inventory of elicitations, (2) specific topics (viz., those processes that focus on topic introduction, responses to them by the interlocutor, their reintroduction), (3) the cohesion and coherence in an utterance or passage, (4) the lexical choices made, (5) code switching and (6) the form or forms of address.

Elicitations

There are a number of ways that speakers (especially) invite or coax their interlocutors to participate in a specific conversation. These elicitations can be quite innocent or they can constitute an intentional effort to make the other speaker say something that will be incriminating. In this case, the linguist searches the questions and comments for bias and/or "leading" behavior on the part of the speaker (8, 22).

An interviewer or interrogator simply cannot let the nature of a case bias his or her efforts. An instance of such bias occurred in a case I refer to as "Did She or Didn't She?" Here, a woman was accused of sexually abusing a young boy. An analysis of the interview transcript led to the inescapable conclusion that the interrogator had made up his mind relative to her guilt prior to the interview, as he kept attempting to elicit responses from the child which were extremely biased. If the woman was guilty she should have been convicted, of course, as the damage to the child is serious and the problem, in general, is of substantial social consequence. Nevertheless, it also is important that she not be convicted, if innocent, solely on the basis of the skill of the interrogator to elicit specific (and misleading) responses.

Topic Analysis

Topic analysis is very important to any of the evaluations that might be conducted in this area. Naturally, before a topic can be evaluated, it must be identified. Usually its nature is obvious but, when it is not, there are technical procedures that can be applied for identification purposes. The primary approach is to establish the macrotopics first and then determine a hierarchy of subtopics (26). The resulting list then can be applied to the conversation (or passage) and combined with a topic introduction count. A procedure such as this one can document a speaker's attempt to direct the conversation into a given area.

Cohesion and Coherence

Cohesion is a term that refers to the appropriateness of linguistic usage, within a particular text, where it constitutes a body of language produced in written or spoken form by one or more individuals. Cohesion combines with coherence, a semantic concept, to represent the texturality of a body of data (10). Evaluations of this type can be used to identify what may be referred to as "irregularities" in the text. More specifically, they can suggest if the talker (or writer) is (1) lying, (2) being evasive or (3) attempting to change the subject in some manner. Analysis of this type also can be employed to identify those places where portions of the text may have been deleted or are missing.

Lexical Choice and Code Switching Analysis

These techniques are most useful when the person talking or writing is bilingual or bicultural. That is, the techniques involved are most effective when the individual in question ordinarily speaks or writes in a language other than your own—they are especially robust if you understand something about the bicultural person's "other" culture. These approaches ordinarily are designed to assess the cooperation of the speaker, with one such technique based on lexical choice (i.e., the speaker/writer's choice of words). For example, information about the informants intent can be gained by contrasting his or her use of English words with those from the foreign language (or from a subculture). Moreover, evaluation of code switching behavior may provide even more meaningful insights than do the bicultural analyses of the type cited above. To illustrate, it can be quite threatening if a speaker switches into the codes of a particular subculture—that is, unless you both are from that other culture. In any event, both lexical choice and code switching analyses can be useful for forensic linguistic purposes.

Form of Address

This type of analysis is primarily useful in the area of speaker discourse evaluation. It is employed to determine the interpersonal relationships among the informants or interlocutors. For example, failure to properly (or appropriately) address another person can reveal disdainful or even threatening behavior on the part of the speaker. Thus, analysis in this area can be helpful in evaluating spoken interchange. On the other hand, it cannot be adapted easily for the evaluation of transcripts.

A Summary

As can be seen, the analyses discussed above are quite intimately related to each other; indeed, several overlap to a considerable extent. An example of their combined or coordinated use can be found in "The Case of the Maligned Singer." The performer in question changed both his religion and lifestyle. As a consequence, he was the subject of a number of derogatory and slanderous news stories. Superficially, the situation (as I have described it anyway) would not appear to be serious enough to provoke a lawsuit but, in reality, it was—and it did. A colleage of mine (a linguist) was the primary examiner. Once his analyses had been carried out, it became quite obvious that the stories were far more derogatory than they appeared at first glance. They implied that the singer had become a fanatic, had lost his ability to tell right from wrong and had totally rejected his past, including his fans and supporters. It then became clear that the average reader would respond to the articles in a strongly negative manner. Suffice it to say that the case was settled out of court and to the singer's satisfaction.

Stylistic Analysis

A great deal more work has been carried out in the area of stylistic analysis than you would suspect. Either written texts or spoken speech (that is, if the utterances have been tape recorded and transcribed) can be evaluated by this method, and important concepts about the person who is writing or speaking can be established. For example, this type of analysis can be employed to establish the identity of a writer (including one long dead) who has not signed his work (11), determine how an orator adapts to his audience (5) or assess the personality of a president (7, 27). In the third instance, Carpenter and his associates predicted the passive aspect of the Carter presidency from his debates with Gerald Ford and his inaugural address. Perhaps, it is of far greater relevancy to our area of interest to point out that these approaches also can be employed to evaluate psychotics (15), predict suicides (18, 19) and, especially, assess the possibility that a given individual may be speaking either in a deceptive manner (or cautiously) in order to avoid self incrimination (6).

The major approach to stylistic analysis involved the development of an index referred to as the Type-Token-Ratio (TTR). A discourse TTR is obtained by counting the number of different words in a passage (or segment of a message) and dividing this value by the total number of words in that same passage. Carpenter (7) provides an example; he indicates that the process can be understood by consideration of a phrase uttered by Abraham Lincoln at Gettysburg; i.e., "government of the people, by the people, for the people." There are 10 tokens in this phrase but only six word types; hence, the TTR here is .60. Carpenter also points out that this TTR is a little unusual, as those for normal speech tend to be higher.

Can an index such as this one be of value in the forensic linguistics area? It can, if longer passages are analyzed (i.e., from 50-100 words or more). For example, a high TTR suggests that the person communicating employs a broad vocabulary, whereas a relatively low one reflects a communicator's preference for stereotypic language. This relationship is not one that can be easily, or consciously, manipulated. While subtle, it tends to reflect information about an individual's personality and/or emotional set. For one thing, the higher the motivation, the lower the TTR. A person with an active-type personality will reflect a heightened motivation and, hence, less diversity in language usage (i.e., lower TTR's) because his or her words will be chosen and articulated efficiently. To illustrate, the TTR for Theodore Roosevelt (an "active") was .454 when his inaugural address was analyzed, whereas Warren Harding (a passive) exhibited .528 for his. Of course, it is recognized that speech writers play an important role in the structuring of nearly any address presented by an important public figure; certainly they do so for an activity such as an inaugural address. Nevertheless, there is but little question that the person giving the speech makes a lot of the decisions relative to style and syntax; hence, his or her personality and preferences will be imbued in it and quite robustly so.

Perhaps more to the point here is that this technique possibly can be employed to analyze social discourse. First off, I must concede that approaches of this type still are in their infancy and that much more research needs to be carried out before they can be defended as stable and universally valid. Nonetheless, TTS has been found useful in discriminating between people that actually are going to commit suicide and those who only are threatening to do so (18, 19). Further, Carpenter (6) has suggested that this technique can reflect cautious and, perhaps, misleading or deceptive statements. He reports analyzing responses to questions given by a murder suspect. He hypothesized that a person who wishes to avoid incriminating himself will exhibit a high TTR, primarily because he will be cautious in his speech. In turn, this caution will lead to a greater than ordinary lexical diversity, as the talker will be much more careful in forming answers. That is, although not readily apparent to observers, the slightly longer times employed to construct answers will increase the likelihood that he or she will use a larger number of low-probability words. In any event, Carpenter found that the suspect in this case exhibited very high TTR's at critical points in the interrogation and, from the TTR patterning, concluded that the suspect actually was the murderer. That there was other evidence of the suspect's guilt (and that he was convicted) appeared to support this judgment—at least in a nonscientific way.

To summarize, a subarea that might be called stylistic analysis appears to be developing within forensic communication (if not forensic phonetics); it includes a number of basic issues fundamental to linguistics proper. At present, it is not known what techniques will grow out of the efforts of investigators in this area, nor how efficient they will be, once developed. It is fair to say, however, that a number of intriguing possibilities are apparent.

Psycholinguistics

The immediately preceding discussions have been skirting the area of psycholinguistics. Indeed, all of the approaches discussed markedly overlap with this component part of linguistics. Hence, a consideration of a few additional concepts within forensic psycholinguistics would appear warranted.

A number of methods and techniques have been proposed by professionals in this area. Some appear to be of good potential; others not. An approach that I will review, at least briefly, is one articulated by Miron and his associates (17). They have applied content analysis to coercive communications—those produced by terrorists, for example. In order to do so, they developed a technique that adheres to the following protocols; viz., they: (1) create a data-base from specific and relevant texts, (2) construct a special-purpose dictionary, (3) develop concept definitions specific to the task, (4) tabulate the observances of the identified concepts and (5) statistically analyze the resulting patterns. Their dictionary consists of 85 word classification categories. It has led them to a threat structure based on several dominant (and relevant) themes: (1) Impotence-Denial, (2) Destructive Reaction and (3) Affiliative Need. After completing some research (primarily on statements related to the Hearst kidnapping, an attempted skyjacking, and a set of serial murders), these investigators have indicated that they can accurately describe (and predict) the psychodynamics involved in cases such as those they studied. They also suggest that their procedure can be applied to a "wide range of communicative behavior" — apparently including the characterization of terrorists' acts, the illegitimate use of coercion, and so on. In my estimation, the cited approach appears to be one of reasonably good promise. Insights into the nature and intent of criminals by analysis of their statements (both oral and written) should permit more effective on-scene decisions to be made and better long-term countermeasures developed.

AUDITION

The three major areas (or subareas) in hearing or audition are psychoacoustics, otology and audiology. Psychoacoustics pretty much subsumes such areas as the fundamental nature of hearing and perception, the effects of acoustical events on people, the physiological and neurophysiological characteristics of hearing, and so on. However, the other two subareas also are concerned with these issues—at least, in a sense they are. Otology is focused to a great extent on the diagnosis and treatment of diseases of the ear and hearing, whereas audiology concentrates on the nonmedical but clinical interpretation of hearing levels and impairment as well as the rehabilitation and training of the deaf and hard of hearing. Thus, you can see that some of the tasks carried out by these specialists are encompassed by forensic communication and are closely related to, and/or overlap, forensic phonetics. Indeed, it is very difficult to carry out the analysis of any aural-perceptual behavior without a functional knowledge of psychoacoustics.

A case in point (I call it "Of Greed within a Family") was one of the very first investigations with which I was associated. Nearly 30 years ago, I was employed by an institution which required that I spend a half-day per week dealing with problems in the area of audition. My particular background permitted me to serve as a kind of troubleshooter in psychoacoustics/audiology and it was because of these responsibilities that I became involved in a rather strange series of cases. First, it seems that, sometime previously, a woman had slipped on ice and fallen while exiting a taxi. She claimed that, due to the laxity of the driver, her head was slammed in the door and, subsequently, she sustained a hearing loss of substantial proportions. She sued the taxi company and was awarded damages. As you would expect, these damages were paid by an insurance company. No one at the company was particularly concerned when this same type of accident occurred the very next winter, but one of their investigators finally became interested when it happened yet twice more. He noted immediately that all four people involved not only were from the same city but also were related, and that all of the accidents had occurred in close proximity to one another. I was asked to carry out a series of hearing tests—primarily those designed to identify malingerers—on these four individuals. To no one's surprise, I found that they all enjoyed normal hearing. While this scam was an interesting one, the people who perpetrated it appeared not to be very imaginative. In retrospect, it seems incredible that the members of this family actually believed they could keep repeating this strange accident but, then, greed can sometimes overcome intellect.

The question as to whether or not a person's hearing has been damaged by some sort of noise (impact or continuing, industrial or military, and so on) is the legitimate concern of almost any of the specialists in audition. Which subspecialist will be consulted relative to a particular case depends upon the nature of the suspected damage and the specific expertise of the professional. For example, many times otologists specializing in the damage-risk criteria related to the effects of long-term industrial noise will be asked to make diagnoses about individuals complaining of work-related hearing losses. However, some audiologists specialize in this area also. Certainly a physician (otologist) should be consulted if the case involves any type of disease or pathology.

Audiologists and psychoacousticians more often tend to be consulted about existing levels of sound energy and how they interact with humans. For example, a colleague of mine was asked to determine if a tugboat captain could hear a foghorn (located on a bridge) under a rather specific set of operational circumstances. It seems that the night was foggy when this captain ran his tug into the bridge, destroying a section of it. The controversy related to whether or not he "should" have heard the foghorn and taken evasive action. You can well imagine the dilemma faced by my friend. What was the tugboat's route to the bridge, how loud was the horn, how good was the captain's hearing, how loud would the horn's signal be: (1) in the tug's cabin, (2) through the fog, (3) at various distances from the bridge? It takes but little imagination to understand just how many questions must be answered (or researched) before a reasonable statement could be made relative to the case I call "The Captain and the Foghorn."

You should understand also, that many of the issues encompassed by forensic phonetics intrude into, or overlap with, the legitimate domain of the psychoacoustician. A sampling includes (1) the decoding of speech, (2) aural-perceptual speaker identification, (3) locating the source of gunshots, (4) identification of the pulses and clicks on a tape recording, and so on. Indeed, the listing of all the potential relationships between these two forensic specialties would be rather time consuming. As a mater of fact, forensic audition is so large an area that it would be quite difficult to outline; certainly a monograph of substantial size would be needed to fully describe its nature. For now, this brief review, the section on hearing (in Chapter 3) and information about the several auditory-based processes described in previous chapters will have to suffice.

PIRATING TAPE RECORDINGS

One of the areas tangential to both tape recording techniques, in particular, and forensic phonetics, in general, is one which can be identified as the illegal reproduction of commercial tapes and video programs. What happens here is that someone buys a single copy of a tape recording (or a video) and then reproduces it in quantity. The copies are sold at reduced prices and artists' royalties are not paid—nor are the costs incurred by the original studio and/or producer. As a matter of fact, industry sources estimate that tape recording piracy results in losses (to legitimate companies) of 100 to 500 million dollars per year.

The cited crime is a difficult one to control. Currently, even good tape recorders are inexpensive, and the duplication of tapes is a fairly cheap and easy process; it may cost less than a dollar per tape. Moreover, techniques currently being utilized permit reproduction and packaging at a quality level which is so good, the final product hardly can be discerned from the genuine article. To duplicate a tape, you need only to acquire a single legitimate copy, blank tapes and some relatively inexpensive duplicating equipment. Since the master duplicating machine can feed up to 10 slave units, as many as 300,000 copies can be produced in a single week.

The legitimate recording companies argue that bootleg operations are virtually crippling their industry. The reason for this is that they make most of their money from a relatively small number of "hits" and for each of these successes, they produce hundreds of tapes that do poorly or only marginally well. Thus, if a tape recording which is a hit is immediately copied by bootleggers, the profits are split with these "pirates" who, of course, do not have to adsorb any of the losses from unsuccessful projects.

Another, somewhat less serious problem involves the music "underground." Most of the large-scale bootlegging operations focus on pop or rock music. Classical music, also, is fairly popular but the pirating here is not so widespread (9). In this case, tape recorders often are smuggled into operas and concerts so that the bootleggers can tape live performances. These copies are sold in the same manner as other fraudulently developed tapes. However, there is yet another group of people who "bootleg" classical music. These "tapists" tend to be amateurs making up an informal society referred to as "the underground." As a countermeasure, many theater managers instruct their ushers to bar audience members from making recordings during a performance and, even, confiscate the tape recorders if they refuse to shut them off. However, enforcement here tends to be lax and "tapists" often are left alone if their activities do not bother other patrons (1).

Unfortunately only partial legal redress is available to legitimate companies and artists who face this type of piracy. The first law specifically focused on their problem was the 1909 Federal Copyright Statute; it was only designed to protect the composer. No shelter was afforded the work itself or the manufacturer and, as a matter of fact, they were on their own. Indeed, it was not until 1971 that Congress passed the Sound Recording Act—a law which was somewhat more detailed and extended protection to manufacturers as well as the recordings themselves (12, 21). Even then, however, numerous exceptions existed. As a matter of fact, the burden of protecting legitimate recording companies and the artists fell to the individual states and by the early 1980s, at least 44 of them had enacted legislation of some type. However, there is no functionally uniform code among these statutes and currently the situation is but little better than chaos—especially when the illegal copying of videotapes is added to the picture. Stern warnings made by the legitimate recording agencies (or disclaimers by the pirates) do little to clarify the situation, as they are both misleading and lack a legitimate legal basis.

Can the forensic phonetician play a role in programs designed to reduce these problems? The answer is tentatively in the affirmative, as sometimes procedures can be applied which can aid in determining if a particular copy actually is an original or has been pirated. Of course, the status of a given tape is much more easily determined if the copy is not a good one. Poor signal quality, cheap tapes/cassettes, poor or inappropriate art work and low price suggest bootlegging, just as they did in the earlier days of tape piracy. Currently, however, many clones are so well made that the forgery is quite difficult to detect. Yet, a number of the procedures found in Chapter 8 ("Authentication of Tape Recordings") can be applied here. For example, evidence can be sought as to whether or not: (1) multiple tape recorders were used in the production of the duplicated tape, (2) unusual temporal patternings occur, (3) the recording is of a live performance (analysis of background or ambient noise is especially useful here) and (4) the tape recorder was turned off and then on at some juncture (see again Chapter 14). Finally, speaker (or electronic) identification procedures sometimes can aid in the investigation. A case in point is one that I refer to as "Is it Elvis or Not?" This case occurred after Presley's death. Several underground (rather than duplicated) recordings appeared to have been released illegally. Analysis demonstrated that these recordings, while somewhat different from those legitimately on the market, undoubtedly were made while Presley was under contract to a particular studio. Thus, they had been illegally copied and were the property of that studio. When confronted, the pirates claimed that their recordings had not been made by Elvis Presley at all but, rather, by an imitator. However, they capitulated when confronted with the data we made available to the legitimate studio.

To summarize, it is conceded that, just as with the two previous areas, a forensic phonetician can make but limited contributions to the countermeasures employed here. Often he or she can provide an assist or serve as a team member; however, sole responsibility for the investigation should not be assigned to professionals of this type. Nonetheless, problems related to the pirating of audio and videotape recordings are of some consequence; it is an area which closely relates to, overlaps and/or parallels many of those described in this book.

COMPUTERS

In one sense anyway, computers are but very large and very complex tape recorders. Both operate on somewhat analogous principles. That is, input is converted and stored magnetically on some sort of recording material; later it is retrieved and used in some manner. Thus, the basic nature of a computer should be clear to you—at least relative to the conversion/storage aspects of their operation. Of course, I must hasten to add that computers differ from simple tape recorders in a number of ways. For example, they operate primarily in the digital domain, and if the input is not in binary form, it must be appropriately transformed. However, it is not my intent to review even the basics of digital computing, as the architecture involved, the programming and the many operations they can perform with incredible rapidity are both quite complex and beyond the scope of this book.

On the other hand, the second of the three major types of crimes that are related to computer operation—i.e., the theft of data, the pirating of programs and the spreading of program viruses—appears to interface somewhat with forensic phonetics. True, we can only appreciate many of the problems here and but rarely actively participate in countermeasures. Yet, at least a cursory understanding of computer crimes should provide yet another dimension to our thinking. Indeed, knowledge in an area such as this one (even if somewhat tangential) can lead to a better understanding of the basic concepts with which we deal.

One of the perspectives to be presented relates to the crimes themselves (see below); the other, what computers are and how they can be used in support of the various tasks related to forensic phonetics. First off, it should be remembered that the digital computer is but a tool, albeit a very sophisticated one. It can be used for many purposes, mathematical/statistical analyses, word processing, data storage and demographic (processing) functions are but four. However, it also should be remembered that even the most advanced of the computer systems cannot carry out any function they are not programmed to accomplish. Indeed, while a hardware-software array may be capable of carrying out thousands of complex tasks in a time frame of but little more than a millisecond, these machines still have to be "told" (i.e., programmed) when and how to complete them. On the other hand, computers now are available to virtually anyone and their enlightened use by forensic phoneticians should permit future analyses that are of greater and greater sophistication. It should be remembered, however, that it is important for you to insist that the computer and its programs provide the answers to the questions *you* have asked rather than attempting to design projects which "fit" a particular machine or operating mode.

Types of Computer Crimes

Other than the use of computers in the actual conduct of criminal activity, the three major types of crimes involving computers are: (1) the unleashing and spreading of computer viruses, (2) the process of stealing stored data/information (from a computer) and (3) the pirating of computer programs. While the forensic phonetician functionally would not be involved in countermeasures related to the first two of these areas, he or she can obtain useful information from the study of how these crimes are committed and the procedures employed in countermeasures. As you might expect, it is the third of these problems that is of most interest to us—primarily due to the various relationships it bears to analysis of tape-recorded evidence and especially to the manipulation of tapes. However, before proceeding, let me briefly review the second specified class of computer crime in order to illustrate how problems of this type can be created.

Illegal Access to Information

In a sense, computers are inert, hence, they are vulnerable. If technically competent, an individual can approach one, log on and access information. Countermeasures involve placing the computer terminals in isolated and secure positions, and the use of passwords. On the other hand, many companies and organizations have computer systems that can be accessed by telephone. Thus, virtually anyone who has a computer and a modem can call and attempt penetration (3)—that is, if they can appropriately identify themselves and have the access password. Since this access code can be any set of characters that appear on the keyboard, the trick is to find them. This task may not be as difficult as it seems, as many passwords are selected because they are easy to remember. Included are birthdates, social security numbers or the names of the people who use the system. Taking these relationships into account, a person who wants to penetrate a computer's memory can simply guess a series of names or numbers until the correct password is found. However, this approach is a rather inefficient one. A better way is to write a program that "guesses" thousands of names or numbers in a very short period of time. This approach is one which will work with most computers.

Manipulating software is another way by which information can be stolen from a computer. Two of the many types of software juggling include the "Trapdoor" and the "Trojan horse" methods. To be specific, programmers often place a trapdoor (or access code) in the software as it is developed. This feature permits the user to enter the system no matter what security devices are added to it. In the case of the "Trojan horse," instructions are included in the software which direct the computer to carry out sets of specific functions. To have it send certain information to a specified terminal at a predetermined time is one example. Of course, there are many other ways that data can be intercepted or stolen from a computer's files. To illustrate, a wire tap may be installed on any telephone line that is coupled to the modem of the target computer. There are others, of course. However, I believe that the examples cited provide sufficient insight into the processes and techniques involved.

As you might suspect, there are numerous countermeasures that may be applied in order to insure the integrity of a computer. Physical isolation or limited physical access is one; blocking access by telephone is another. Passwords can be protected to some extent by programming a computer to prevent intruders from making a large series of guesses relative to their identity. For example, it can be programmed to permit only two attempts to enter the correct password. Once two incorrect attempts are made, the computer can then refuse the third or allow the perpetrator to go on line but only obtain insensitive or false information. Simultaneously, other security procedures would be activated to either trace the call or summon appropriate personnel. As can be seen, while the forensic phonetician would play a minor role here, the issues, investigations and cited countermeasures closely parallel much of our work.

Software Theft

One problem facing the software industry is that programs which are recorded on floppy disks can be copied easily. So can hard discs, but the problem here, while similar, is somewhat more complex. Incidentally, this illegal traffic is what makes the introduction, and spreading, of viruses so easy. However, I will confine most of my remarks to floppies and program theft.

Since many of the programs currently available to us are quite difficult to conceive, structure, transform into computer language and test, they tend to be relatively expensive. Moreover, the consequences of a theft sometimes can involve issues much more serious than financial loss, i.e., problems of proprietary information or national security. Indeed, programs of various types are used for many purposes: in research, by businesses and industry, by the military and law enforcement agencies, even for games; they already number in the millions and this total is growing by the minute. While the programs themselves can be very expensive, blank disks are cheap. Thus, many people who buy computer programs copy and distribute them to their friends or colleagues and, just as with audio- and videotapes, there are still others who bootleg programs. This practice penalizes both the programmers (by loss of income) and other users, because distributors have to charge higher prices for their (legal) software. Some years ago, several manufacturers thought they could solve the piracy problem by writing programs in nonstandard ways—for example, by writing it in blocks distributed in a spiral pattern along the disk or by writing between its "grooves." However, other programmers then developed and sold special programs which unscrambled these protective schemes. It was legal to sell this type of program because users of computer software are entitled to make backup copies for their own use.

The contest between individuals who try to prevent the pirating of computer programs and the unethical operators who attempt to crack the resulting codes, and thereby benefit financially from someone else's product, goes on and on. One recent scheme (14) involves the addition of "coupons" to the software so that each time the program is run, the coupons are reduced in value. Additionally, the program user cannot make copies of the coupons or modify them. How does this particular system work? The coupons are created by software manufacturers by modifying their disk drives so as to include some weak bits on the floppies or disks. Of course, weak bits sometimes occur by chance when floppies are produced, but, in that case, they are eliminated either by rerecording the data or by directly correcting the errors. With "coupons" however, a large number of weak bits are intentionally hidden in certain sectors of the disk. When an individual uses a program of this type, his computer also is programmed to identify these weak bits by reading over the coupon section several times. If they are there, they can be read. If they are not, or are misinterpreted, the program will not run. How well this system will work over time or how easy it will be to defeat has yet to be determined.

In Summary

But why are these discussions included in a book on forensic phonetics? For one thing, they substantially overlap the areas of primary interest. They also provide us with insight about the nature and growth of a sophisticated technology. To illustrate, if the coupon approach described above can be used to protect computer programs, it should be possible to utilize similar techniques to protect tape and video recordings (some already are in existence) as well as prevent the tampering of tape recordings used in forensic, legal and related situations. Another example: just as one can learn how to determine if an aircraft's door is open during flight by application of digital signal analysis procedures originally developed to study voice function, and just as one can learn to better identify speakers from knowledge about techniques designed to study the signatures of clicks, so too can one learn how to better authenticate tape recordings from the battles between programmers and computer pirates. Of course, as with the other three areas reviewed in this chapter, a full description of computer-related crime and appropriate countermeasures would be pretty involved; hence, only an introductory outline is provided here. Nonetheless, knowledge of this type overlaps many of the issues central to our discipline and, as such, much can be learned from its study.

CHAPTER 16

On Ethics and Responsibilities

INTRODUCTION

This chapter is being included for several reasons. First off, books such as this one (i.e., those that focus on content areas) rarely include descriptions of the various behaviors associated with, or required by, the practical application of the processes involved. Of course, when engaged to carry out an evaluative task, the professional forensic phonetician practically always will be asked for some sort of report and, in perhaps 20-30% of the cases, he or she will be requested or required to testify in a court of law. Hence, I feel some responsibility to review the dimensions of these activities—just as I touched on report writing on several occasions. Second, although the content of this book is but an introduction to the area of forensic phonetics and not designed to turn the reader into an operating professional, you may have some questions about the proper application of ethics as they relate to the forensic milieu, the process of testifying as an expert witness, and so on. The comments to follow and, especially, the references listed should either answer these questions or lead you to sources that do.

Third, legitimate questions can be asked relative to the use of experts: the effectiveness of their testimony, the relationships that limit their efforts and their personal ethics. Discussions of this type are practically always provided by attorneys, judges, criminal justice academics or managers/decision makers within the criminal justice or judicial systems (see, for example, 4, 6, 8, 12, 14, 18, 22). It is but rarely that they are addressed from the experts' perspective (7, 9). Thus, some of the comments to follow will (or should) disturb certain members of the legal and law enforcement professions. Nonetheless, they involve issues and events with which I have struggled. Moreover, few (if any) are the product of my singular experience, as many other experts have expressed similar concerns. But, first, how important are experts?

A Perspective on Expert Testimony

There is little doubt that scientific testimony will impress a jury. Indeed, it can be quite compelling if it is articulately and ethically presented by a person who is viewed as an expert in his or her field—and the work of the competent forensic phonetician is no exception to this rule of thumb. Of course, the many relationships between experts and the judicial system result in a body of litera-ture much too large to include here. Nevertheless, perspectives about these numerous interfaces can be found in the reference section associated with this chapter (see especially 4, 12, 18, 27).

To be somewhat more specific, the value of scientific testimony has led one distinguished attorney (B. L. Cook, Sr., personal communication, February, 1981) to state that "many trials are but a battle among the experts." Perhaps so, but he may be imparting greater importance to experts than they deserve—at least universally so. Moreover, there are other individuals who appear to feel somewhat more negatively about these relationships; still others are concerned about the ethics (or advocacy) displayed by at least an occasional expert (2, 9, 10, 11, 12, 13, 23). For example, Ahearne (1) suggests that the only "experts" who should be allowed to testify are those called by the court and that all other individuals placed on the witness stand during any litigation should be con-sidered advocates or consultants. Worse yet, some jurists have displayed nega-tive feelings toward experts. For example, one federal judge (29) included the following statement in his memorandum opinion relative to a civil suit: "Both parties called expert witnesses and, as one would expect, the hired guns did what they were hired to do." Perhaps this judge was expressing more a frustra-tion than distrust, because he also wrote: "The experts, in my opinion, did more to obfuscate the problem than they did to clarify it."

In any case, it should be understood that substantial disagreement exists as to the value of experts—as well as their ability to avoid becoming advocates or indulging in behaviors that are less than impeccably ethical. The reasons for this spread appear obvious. First, there is a long history associated with experts; their early use was primarily as witnesses for the prosecution. Second, experts are not systematically trained in either the correct procedures to follow or the ethics related to testimony. Third, even today the qualifications of experts vary wildly; some who are accepted by the courts are not really experts at all. Fourth, many direct and/or subtle pressures can be focused on an expert and, lastly, there are a number of conflicts they face which are unnatural to them.

While I have no intention of exploring all of the enigmas and conflicts facing experts, I will attempt to address the five listed above. Moreover, your attention is directed to some of the cautions included in the content chapters. Many of the proper behaviors and positions to which you should subscribe are included there.

PROBLEMS AND DILEMMAS

Legacies from the Past

It is a little difficult to provide a comprehensive review of the first issue cited, i.e., that of the history of expert witnessing. For one thing, only a fraction of what really occurred has been recorded; moreover, at least some of what has been documented is self-serving. Worse yet, the courts in various countries deal with experts in different ways. For example, in Germany, this type of witness is nearly always called by the court (28) and is paid from state funds. While this procedure is one which also has been suggested as potentially viable for use in the United States (1, 9), practically all experts called here are employed by one side or the other. Unfortunately, any such association (i.e., with lawyers and other advocates) tends to degrade an expert's veracity, even when it should not.

In early days, expert witnesses ordinarily were associated with the prosecution. Indeed, as Moenssens *et al.* point out (18), many of them were "full-time salaried employee(s) of some division of local, state or federal government. (Their) expert opinion (was) sometimes controlling on whether or not an arrested person would be prosecuted." Thus, "experts" of varying levels of bias or advocacy and of many levels of competency testified in the courts of yesteryear. Again, the effect—rightly or wrongly—was one which has tended to burden the modern expert with an aura of advocacy.

Currently, experts are being called both by the prosecution and the defense, as well as (occasionally) by the court, a situation that tends to somewhat upgrade technical quality and ethics. Yet signs of bias or advocacy still can be observed, at least, occasionally. To be specific, some expert witnesses are, or appear to become, advocates for the side they are "representing." While sometimes it is obvious they are doing so, other times they are quite subtle about it. Worse yet, they often err quite innocently—essentially entrapped by their secondary role as consultant rather than by any direct slippage of their ethics. Some of the more common signs of advocacy in an expert is that he or she: (1) is exclusively, or almost exclusively, a prosecution—or a defense—witness, (2) makes statements that they could not be wrong, (3) makes statements about their "won-lost" record, (4) does not describe the procedures utilized when on the stand (examples: "they are classified," "they are too complex to understand"), (5) does not bring the appropriate data, materials or test results to the trial and/or (6) makes unwarranted (often vague) personal attacks on opposing witnesses.

Please be assured that I am not implying that very many old-time expert witnesses were unethical or biased, any more than I am suggesting that this type of behavior is common among modern experts. The point being made here is that, formerly anyway, expert witnessing was so closely associated with the prosecution that biases about their behavior developed on the part of at least some members of the judiciary and general public. Ironically, that experts are— or should continue to be—primarily associated with the prosecution or the criminal justice system is an opinion that can be harbored even today (15, 20), and this belief continues to foster the cited skepticism. Thus, an awkward, and probably unfair, legacy has been handed down from the early experts, primarily due to the fact that: (1) many of them were part of the criminal justice system itself, (2) some exhibited biases and advocacy and (3) most were seen as individuals attempting to please their employees. Thus, the cumulative history of expert witnessing is one which leads to varying responses within the judicial system. It also results in some confusion and discomfort among the experts themselves.

Educating Experts

It would appear that the well-trained phonetician has a right to assume that he or she is competent to testify in court about data, theories and relationships relevant to this specialty. True—but only in part—because some sort of forensic-related training and/or experience also should be required. Yet, while a few universities offer courses in the content areas of forensic phonetics, I am not aware of any that address the issue of expert testimony or the ethics, responsibilities and techniques associated with it. This lack is one of several which discourages many competent professionals from participating in the judicial system. It also tends to permit the utilization of some witnesses of dubious competency.

What characteristics must an expert possess? The list of attributes to follow is one which is based on logic plus the specifications and implications of a number of authors (see, for example, 4, 12, 16, 18, 21, 28). It is contended that, to be considered qualified, an expert should exhibit: (1) undergraduate and graduate degrees directly related to the field of expertise, (2) specialized training in the subject area as it relates to forensics, (3) at least minimal training in forensics, (4) those professional licenses or certifications universally required by recognized professional groups in the experts' discipline, (5) evidence of experimentation, teaching and publication within the specialty and (6) prior disciplinary experience that is direct and relevant to the issues under consideration. Also desirable would be (1) postgraduate (and/or postdoctoral) training, (2) publications which appear in reviewed scientific journals, (3) the development of scientifically acceptable tests and/or procedures, (4) association with, and leadership in, appropriate professional and scientific societies and (5) experience as an expert witness. As you can see this list probably is not complete. It certainly suffers from the fact that I have attempted to describe the requisites for all specialties and levels. Indeed, while it can be seen that any competent phonetician would meet the professional criteria listed, there are yet other (forensic-related) training and experiences necessary before the term "forensic" can be ethically added to his or her disciplinary title.

But how can the professionally well-trained individual acquire the specialized experiences which are required if he or she is to become an expert witness? Unfortunately, they are often learned on an ad hoc basis. Of course, some experts also have training in criminal justice programs or as criminologists (8, 19, 26), but they tend to be individuals whose basic functions involve work associated with crime laboratories. So how can you obtain the necessary education relative to forensics and courtroom testimony? There are several useful approaches. First, appropriate courses, seminars and workshops should be sought out and attended. Even a single experience of this type will be helpful. Second, you can learn a great deal from books and articles written by attorneys as to how they deal with experts (see, for example, 4, 6, 7, 12, 14, 16, 18). Moreover, "how-to" publications aimed directly at the expert witness are useful, as are treatises on ethics (10, 11, 15, 23) and even materials focused on issues only tangentially related to the expert witness process itself (5, 17, 22, 27). Third, and perhaps most important, is the "training" that can be provided by practicing attorneys. They advise, brief and otherwise prepare professionals for their role as an expert witness. In doing so they provide valuable information relative to the proper, ethical and effective procedures to be used in the courtroom. Finally, it can be said that experience teaches. While this type of learning does you very little good if you are a beginner, any experiences in the courtroom will serve to educate you in those approaches which are both appropriate and ethical. Indeed, there is much to be learned about resistance to advocacy from the assaults of opposing attorneys, about the appropriate presentation of evidence from the reaction of juries, and the strict adherence to proper ethics from observing the behavior of attorneys, judges and other witnesses. However, most experts develop their skills and effectiveness in a rather haphazard manner and this is one of several reasons why competency can vary so dramatically from person to person. Perhaps some sort of structured training should be established. Most law schools ignore the problem or, at least, concentrate their programs here on the needs of their own students. Occasionally an attempt is made to solve this problem by individuals responsible for criminal justice programs. However, they usually focus their efforts on criminologists in training rather than on disciplinary experts. Training—the need is obvious; not so the solution.

Is the Phonetician Different?

As you would expect, the answer here is "no." Forensic phoneticians differ little from specialists in other disciplines—except for content area. Of course, we sometimes run into "experts" who address issues within our discipline. Some are qualified to do so, some are not. At issue here is how should forensic phoneticians function?

First off, any expert should be competent in his or her field—in this instance, in forensic phonetics. You do not have to be a national or world-class leader in this specialty, but you certainly have to demonstrate training that is both appropriate and advanced. The relevant and necessary background, in our case, includes a rigorous education in experimental phonetics, psychoacoustics, engineering, computer science, linguistics, statistics, physiology, and the like. Moreover, research and teaching in this specialty area are mandatory. Second, the tests and experiments you employ should be appropriate and they should have been well established scientifically. If you use a novel, adapted or unusual approach, you should be able to defend it by means of solid research and unimpeachable data. For example, if you incorporate power spectra as a vector in a speaker identification system, you should be conversant with the research that has been carried out here. Better yet, you should have completed some of it yourself!

Third, just as the attorney with whom you work will expect a detailed and thorough report (usually written), you should expect him or her to rigorously prepare you for testimony. This statement does *not* imply even the slightest shift toward advocacy or a reduction in ethics on your part. It simply specifies that you should work with the attorney in question so as to be properly qualified for testimony and so you will not have to be an advocate even on your own behalf.

It also will insure that the relevant attorney will become fully aware of the factors and relationships within phonetics (and your findings) to which you can and cannot testify. This point is an important one. Under no circumstances should you allow yourself to be drawn into a situation where you in any way bias the data you present.

Examples from the Courtroom

As I stated previously, it is not enough just to know your field and its relationships to forensics and the courts. You also need to know how to deal with the actual process of testifying. Let me provide you with a few hints. For one thing, you should not be put off by opposing attorneys who act deviously. For example, they may: (1) ask long, complex and/or hypothetical questions (request that they ask them one at a time or explain them), (2) insist that you respond "yes" or "no" when it is impossible to do so (indicate to the presiding judge that you must qualify your answer), (3) ask you about your fees (tell them), (4) ask if you have discussed the case with "others" (only with the appropriate individuals; further, no one has or could bias your testimony), (5) ask you if you could be wrong (of course you could), and so on. Behaviors such as these—and others which are even more bizarre—would seem to be counterproductive. Yet you will encounter them from time to time. An example of one such tactic can be referred to as the "fake book ploy." While it constitutes a challenge that can be handled easily and ethically, it also can be a little disconcerting—especially if you do not understand its nature. What happens is that the opposing lawyer will obtain a list, a long list, of *old* books in the phonetics and related areas (presumably from a consultant or phonetician with questionable ethics). Care usually will be taken to avoid the inclusion of modern books or relevant scientific articles. The attorney, then, will begin to ask if you have read the first of these books—usually one or two that you reasonably can be expected to know about. The entire list then will be read. After a little while, you will find yourself searching back in your memory to see if you have even heard of some of the books—much less read them. Consider the dynamics of this situation. You are under oath and should not indicate that you have read a particular book unless you actually know you have. As the list grows longer and longer, you will begin to realize that many obscure, very old and often nonrelevant books are being included—ones that you know you have not read, and for very good reason. Most are out-of-date and/or contribute little to nothing (anymore) to forensic phonetics. Yet, as the dialogue goes on and on, and the number of your negative responses increase, you will begin to realize that the jury may be wondering about your competency. To combat this change in their mood, you might start to take a chance or two on books you think you remember reading. It is at this juncture that the lawyer in question will start including authors and titles that do not exist (even though they sound reasonable/possible). The attorney, of course, is hoping that you will admit to having read one of these phantom books. If you do, the "game" is over and the judge, jury, courtroom personnel, press, spectators and everyone else within earshot will be informed that you have perjured yourself. A nasty happening, of course, but nasty things happen in the courtroom. Moreover, it should be remembered that lawyers are advocates, that they are *not* under oath and that, as competitive individuals, they do not like to lose—ever. When this ploy was first directed at me, I did not know what was in the offing. What happened was that I became irritated and kept insisting that books such as those being listed were archaic, trival and/or off the point. I further demanded that I be queried about modern research. After a while the opposing attorney gave up. I respond in a different manner now that I know what this nonsense is all about. I simply ask the presiding judge if he is going to let such unethical behavior to go on in his courtroom.

WHO IS AN EXPERT?

The third problem to be discussed also is a very serious one; it concerns the striking variations among the qualification levels and competencies encountered in the modern "expert." For example, one of the problems sometimes faced by scientists and advanced professionals, when they take the witness stand, is that they will have their testimony countered by individuals who, while not on their level, are offered as experts and so recognized by the court. Indeed, like many scientists and practitioners, I have had the unhappy experience of listening to "expert" witnesses, who were only policemen or agents (with only a few weeks of "special" training), expound on subjects that I had spent nearly a lifetime studying and developing. There even are some instances where private detectives have been permitted to testify as "experts" in areas in which they had little background, training or, for that matter, understanding. Since it clearly is unethical to make negative comments about "opposing" witnesses (other than on the content of his or her testimony, that is), most professionals dread those trials where they have to explain their findings and conclusions to a court that is unaware that the witnesses for the other side are only superficially competent and actually lack the scientific and/or professional expertise necessary to comment on the relevant issues. Small wonder that many scientists and practitioners simply refuse to testify or even offer their talents and expertise on a consulting basis. Forget that work of this type interrupts the flow of their regular research schedules—and perhaps their teaching, administrative or professional activities as well. Forget that they will be buffeted (no matter how outstanding they are) during the examination of their qualifications and during cross-examination. Forget that they often are pressured or inconvenienced by attorneys, the agency involved, the client (or clients' family), the court schedule, travel times and accommodations. To many of us, the source of greatest discomfort is to be "challenged" by an opposing witness who actually is not qualified to do so.

But what qualifications are necessary before a person can be considered an expert; are there levels of expertise? In my judgment, there are a number of criteria to be met and, even when they have been satisfied, it still is necessary to classify individuals both into types of experts and on the basis of level of expertise. Of course, the criteria for general competency and ethics have been discussed in the previous two sections. What is to be considered now can be referred to as technical competency (J. M. Russ, personal communication, April,

338

1973). That is, if experts of various types (and levels) are to be sorted out, some attempt must be made at structering a system that will permit their classification.

In response to this problem, I have developed the two-tiered model seen in Figure 16-1. You will notice that it permits us to divide "experts" of all types by level, on one continuum, and into several categories, on the other. From the terminology I have selected, the group which is common to both systems is that of technician (see area A of the figure). However, even this domain is one that has somewhat generous boundaries. On the one hand, technicians range from police officers who are trained in making radar readings of the speed of vehicular traffic to individuals who perform ballistic tests in a laboratory; from officers who carry out "breath-analyzer" tests of intoxication to laboratory technicians who compare fingerprints. The scientific bases for, as well as the equipment and procedures used in most of, these forensic tasks are provided by the specialists and scientists. Moreover, technicians usually work under some type of supervision.

The second classification level is one where the individual is a criminologist or criminalist first and a specialist second. Most of these professionals are criminologists who have had some training in a disciplinary specialty. They tend to be divided into the practitioner or scientist categories (see intersects B and C), but at the secondary level of criminologist rather than specialist. Some of them obtain additional training (usually a doctorate) in order to achieve the higher level of specialist. Their work often overlaps somewhat with that of technicians, especially with respect to task. These professionals tend to be the product of criminal justice programs, and while some of them gravitate to supervisory and administrative levels, many are investigators. The specialty areas possessed by criminologists are many and varied. They can range from ballistics to chemistry, from toxicology to electronics, from handwriting to mechanics. The specialties that could be included here are far too numerous to list.

Specialists populate the third level of this continuum. They are individuals who are trained first in a discipline and participate in forensics on a secondary

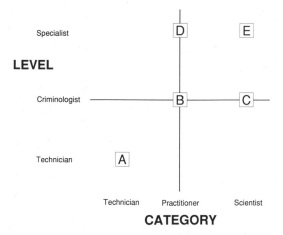

Figure 16-1. A proposed two-way classification model of the levels and categories of expert witnesses.

basis. Of course, they must be well versed in the forensic application of their field and competent to interface with the judicial system. Any discipline, or subdiscipline, can be included here. Specialists range from chemists to acousticians, from psychiatrists to engineers, from pathologists to social scientists, from phoneticians to computer scientists, and so on.

Once the three-way structuring relative to level is established, a second framework, which is based on category, can be organized. Of course, the first group (the technicians) is common to both continua. It is the other two of the three which would appear to require additional description. The second category is labeled practitioner; it includes many people drawn from the ranks of both the criminologist and the specialist levels. As a matter of fact, most criminologists (but not all of them) would be assigned to this category. But so too could many specialists such as physicians, chemists, psychiatrists, toxicologists and engineers (see area D). The test for membership in this category would be whether or not the individual in question spends the greatest portion of his or her time in performing tasks, administering tests or examinations and/or *practicing* the specialty. Thus, as you probably have deduced from the discussions about criminologists and specialists, level of education (i.e., the number of degrees) is not as important here as is the type of work activity being pursued. The third category in the classification triad is that of scientist; most of them would populate the specialty level (see area E of the figure). Here, the person spends most of his or her time in scholarly activity (experimenting, modeling, interpreting) and publishing much (or most) of the resulting work—especially in peer reviewed (scientific) journals. The individuals in this category virtually always represent well-defined and established disciplines.

As can be seen, these two continua place experts into a category-level paradigm: the first classifies the individual on the basis of task or focus; the second on level of activity. Taken together, five professional levels (A-E) result and at least a rough estimate of expected expertise can be generated by the judicious use of this model. Admittedly this structure is a rather crude one and the categories established best focus on activity than on level. Moreover, it probably is incomplete. However, it is necessary that individuals working in the judicial, forensic and criminal justice areas address the issue of an expert's levels/categories at some juncture.

As a matter of fact, this argument is validated by some authors who appear to be uncomfortable with the current lack of organization; however, they appear to offer no relief (4, 11, 12, 18). Other writers attempt to provide some structure (16) or contrast among types of training (25), and the final two groups either resist attempts at ranking (20, 23) or detail some of the negative reactions to (or about) experts without suggesting reorganization (2, 12, 13, 20, 23). Thus, the scheme reviewed above is provided as a point of embarkation. Hopefully it will lead to a more definitive model.

FUNCTIONAL CONFLICTS

The final two problem areas functionally overlap; hence, I should like to combine my remarks about them into a single section. Let me initiate the discussion by reminding you that even the expert who (1) represents an appropriate field, (2) has adequate training, (3) exhibits appropriate experience and (4) understands the forensic milieu will face a number of problems after agreeing to become an expert witness. They range (1) from the need to resist attorneys who desire opinions or testimony more supportive of their position than can be provided, to the fending off of panicked defendants (or their families), (2) from evaluations that prove disadvantageous to the side which has retained you, to the occasional insulting courtroom lawyer, (3) from attorneys who waste your time with long telephone consultations that interrupt your normal work schedule, to the necessary attempts to explain your results to individuals who do not understand the nature of your work. Even university scientists like me—for whom forensics constitutes an excellent practical forum for the application of my specialty research and teaching (as well as a stimulus which motivates new projects)—tend to find many of these situations debilitating. As I indicated previously, it is for these reasons, (and related ones) that many scientists and practitioners refuse to participate in the criminal justice system—or even in the civil courts.

Yet another important conflict of interest is added to the cited problems; it revolves around the ethical dilemma faced by the expert when approached for a combination of advice, evaluations and expert testimony. As with many judges and jurors, a prosecutor or defense attorney may not have a fundamental knowledge of the expert's field. Thus, there certainly are no ethical constraints in educating them—especially by providing them with reviews, reprints, interpretations and reference lists. Nor should requests that you carry out tests or evaluations result in conflict or discomfort. Thus, it should be of little concern if all you are requested to do is provide a simple education, evaluations of evidence and the presentations of your findings in court. Rather, the cited conflicts-of-interest occur as a result of other, but closely related, events.

To be specific, problems begin to arise when an expert is (1) invited to "strategy sessions," (2) asked to assist in the impeachment of experts testifying for the other side, (3) asked to sit with counsel and assist in the cross-examination of these (other) experts, and so on. Apparently, none of these events is considered to be in the least unethical at any level of the criminal justice system, as they occur quite openly and regularly; sometimes they even seem to be encouraged. Yet an expert can suffer substantial discomfort as a result of these requests. Indeed, it is quite difficult to participate in a long planning period designed to assist counsel in handling an opposing expert and then take the witness stand with total objectivity. Also seductive are the effects of extended sessions with a prosecution team organizing evidence for an important trial or spotting a fundamental error made by a prosecution witness in the middle of a defense strategy session. Further, it is just as interesting for a scientist to review data resulting from a forensic-type analysis as it is to observe the relationships which emerge upon the completion of a laboratory experiment. As you might expect, these events can subtly affect the expert in an undesirable fashion.

Problems can result even when the trial attorneys inappropriately attempt to shield the expert from conflicts associated with the consultant/expert dilemma. You think not? Consider the case I call "The Big Surprise." In this instance, I was sent a "body bug" tape recording of an agent-suspect interchange. It seems that the suspect, an enterprising public official, supplemented his regular income by issuing certain types of journeymen's licenses for a fee. The individuals who were granted these licenses were pleased, of course, because they were able to avoid all of the annoying classes, examinations and field evaluations required by the ordinary (and legal) licensing procedure. However, this little scam began to fall apart when someone noticed that the official had inadvertently issued a license to an applicant who was illiterate. The next "applicant" to approach the suspect was an undercover agent who was appropriately "wired." The recording I received was a good one. The conversations were clear and there was no evidence at all that the tape had been modified in any way. The only problem was that, after the interview, the official walked the "applicant" to his car which was parked near some heavy-grading equipment. Hence, the last 2-3 minutes of the tape recording were very noisy and it was difficult (but not impossible) to hear the two men bid each other fairwell.

After review, I returned the tape, indicating that it was a good one and that it exhibited no problems whatsoever. The prosecutor's puzzling response was a request that I attend the pretrial hearing and personally present the tape. While I could not understand the need for such action, I complied—playing the entire tape recording (on good-quality equipment) to the judge, the prosecutor, the agent and the defense attorney. The bribe came booming through and the recording ended with the noisy section. At that juncture, the judge ruled that the tape recording was "inaudible" and refused to admit it. I must confess that my head snapped around so fast that I nearly had whiplash. To be brief, the prosecutor had suspected all along that this was going to be the response, but did not warn me in order to avoid compromising my professional ethics. As it turns out, there actually was no conflict of interest on my part; given the chance I could have functioned far more effectively. That is, I could have made it difficult for the judge to rule improperly by (1) administering a hearing test to everyone present, (2) employing earphones instead of loudspeakers, (3) filtering the noisy section of the tape so that the speech there was also easily intelligible, (4) developing special tapes and transcripts of the bribe itself and (5) stopping the recording when the bribe was made and stressing what was said. It was only after the disaster had taken place that the individuals in question realized that they had incorrectly utilized my expertise.

The prosecutor, of course, was accurate in recognizing the potential conflict between consultation and testimony. Not so easy to understand was his confusion about when an ethical professional can be used as a consultant and when he must fill the role of a (protected) expert witness. On the one hand, no experience or event can be permitted to bias the expert once he or she takes the stand. The advocates are the attorneys, and the only courtroom "combat" in which the expert may participate is to insure that he or she is allowed to clearly present his or her findings and opinions, and/or to avoid being unfairly impeached in any way. On the other hand, no violence is done to the expert's ethics if he or she is employed either as a consultant (only) or warned ahead of time that there will be special problems with the presentation of evidence. This case simply provides another example to the many instances where confusions exist in the legal community about the consulting/witness roles to be carried out by experts. Worse yet, if members of the judicial system are this perplexed, imagine the expert's discomfort with these stressful events. Some of us respond to the problem by challenging the ethics involved in the process—especially in those instances where we are forced to alternate our consultant-expert roles back-and-forth in rapid succession. In any case, the question can be asked if there are any solutions to these dilemmas. Unfortunately, there do not seem to be many.

One potential among the few remedies available may be the categorization of the classes/levels of experts suggested above. A structuring of this type should provide some guidance as to which of the individuals considered would make the best consultant, which would be better utilized as an expert and, finally, who could be used in both categories.

The second, and perhaps most important, remedy is that the expert himself must be keenly aware of the cited bimodal situations and continually monitor his or her intent and behavior. That is, he should constantly assess the pertinent relationships so as to be keenly aware of the ethical boundaries faced. By this method, it should be possible to insure appropriate objectivity when on the witness stand. Third, the limits of the two cited functions should be stressed and restressed (by the expert) to the relevant attorneys and their clients. While attorneys will rarely exhibit unethical behavior, they do not always protect the expert (as was the case in the example given). Clients or the personnel at a particular agency often do not understand his dual responsibilities and can attempt to pressure him into becoming an advocate. Care must be taken to properly explain the expert's function and the very limited boundaries that exist relative to his or her contribution.

Yet another potential solution is to retain one expert as a consultant and another as the witness. This approach is one that can remove the professional from contact with those behaviors that could lead to bias on the witness stand; it is a method that has worked well in at least a few instances. Indeed, a remedy of this type has been suggested by several authors (1, 10, 15). However, the approach ordinarily interferes with the activities of too many professionals and the cost may be prohibitive—especially when many evaluations and/or tests are involved. Moreover, how can an expert testify about examinations he or she has not administered? Finally, the expert could limit himself only to those consultative tasks that result in no discomfort or ethical conflict. However, once retained, this course of action is a rather difficult one to pursue. Thus, while the dual role of consultant and expert witness appears not to contain elements that are inherently unethical, it can be potentially dangerous. If the two roles are not carefully controlled, they can lead to bias and a very real ethical dilemma.

CONCLUSION

The discussion above addresses some of the problems we face when we assume the role of expert witness. Many of these issues are of long standing; few have been addressed from our point of view. In any event, many confusions, conflicts and differences of opinion can be found among members of the judiciary, the legal profession and the experts themselves. Five of them have been reviewed and several remedies suggested. Few, if any, of these problems will be solved if they continue to be ignored and/or disavowed.

References

Chapter 1: Introduction

1. Hollien, H. (1978) Forensic Phonetics: A New Dimension to the Phonetic Sciences, *Phonetische Beiträge*, 25:157-190.
2. Hollien, H. (1983) Forensic Communication: An Emerging Specialty, *Criminal Defense*, 10:22-29.
3. Hollien, H. (1983) The Phonetician as a Speech Detective, in *The Linguistic Connection* (J. Casagrande, Ed.), New York, University Press of America, 101-132.
4. Hollien, Patricia A. and Huntley, R. (1986) *Admission of Tape Recorded Evidence: Case Law*, Gainesville, FL, Forensic Communication Associates.

Chapter 2: Simple Acoustics

1. Berg, R. E. and Stork, D. G. (1982) *The Physics of Sound*, Englewood Cliffs, NJ, Prentice-Hall.
2. Culver, C. A. (1956) *Musical Acoustics*, New York, McGraw-Hill.
3. Denes, P. B. and Pinson, E. N. (1963) *The Speech Chain*, Bell Telephone Laboratories, Baltimore, Waverly Press.
4. Pierce, J. R. and David, E. E., Jr. (1958) *Man's World of Sound*, New York, Doubleday.

Chapter 3: Speech Characteristics

1. Denes, P. B. and Pinson, E. N. (1963) *The Speech Chain*, Bell Telephone Laboratories, Baltimore, Waverly Press.
2. Dickson, D. R. and Dickson, W. M. (1982) *Anatomical and Physiological Bases of Speech*, Boston, Little, Brown.
3. Fant, G. (1973) *Speech Sounds and Features*, Cambridge, MA, The MIT Press.
4. Hirsh, Ira (1952) *Measurement of Hearing*, New York, McGraw-Hill.
5. Hollien, H. (1975) Neural Control of the Speech Mechanism, in *The Nervous System*, Vol. 3, *Human Communication and Its Disorders* (D.B. Tower, Ed.), New York, The Raven Press, 483-491.
6. Hollien, H. and Gould, W. J. (1990) A Neuro-Anatomical Model For Laryngeal Control, *J. of Voice*, 4 (in press).
7. Hultzen, L. S., Allen, J. H. D., Jr. and Miron, M.S. (1964) *Tables of Transitional Frequencies of English Phonemes*, Urbana, IL, University of Illinois Press.
8. Ladefoged, P. (1975) *A Course in Phonetics*, New York, Harcourt Brace Jovanovich.
9. Noback, C. R. (1967) *The Human Nervous System*, New York, McGraw-Hill.
10. Peterson, G. E. and Barney, H. L. (1952) Control Methods Used in the Study of Vowels, *J. Acoust. Soc. Amer.* 24:175-184.

11. Pick, T. P. and Howden, R. (1974) *Gray's Anatomy*, Philadelphia, Running Press (Reprinted and Revised).
12. Satalof, J. and Michael, P. (1973) *Hearing Conservation*, Springfield, IL, Charles C Thomas.
13. Shriberg, L. D. and Kent, R. D. (1982) *Clinical Phonetics*, New York, John Wiley and Sons.
14. Thomas, C. K. (1958) *An Introduction to the Phonetics of American English*, New York, The Ronald Press.
15. Tower, D. B. (Ed.) (1975) *The Nervous System* (Four Volumes), New York, Raven Press.
16. Wakita, H. (1977) Normalization of Vowels by Vocal Tract Length and Its Application to Vowel Identification, *Trans., Acoust., Speech, Signal Process, ASSP* 25:183-192.
17. Yost, W. A. and Neilson, D. W. (1977) *Fundamentals of Hearing*, New York, Holt, Rinehart, Winston.
18. Zemlin, W. (1968) *Speech and Hearing Science, Anatomy and Physiology*, Englewood Cliffs, NJ, Prentice-Hall.

Chapter 4: Basic Equipment

1. Begun, S. J. (1949) *Magnetic Recording*, New York, Rinehart and Co.
2. Boe, L-J and Rakotofiringa, H. (1971) Exinquences Realisation et Limites d'un Appareillage Destine' a l'Etudes de l'Intensite' et de la Hauteur d'un Signal Acoustique, *Rev. d'Acoust.* 4:103-113.
3. Brophy, J. J. (1966) *Basic Electronics for Scientists*, New York, McGraw-Hill.
4. Brown, P. B., Franz, G. N. and Moraff, H. (1982) *Electronics for the Modern Scientist*, New York, Elsevier Science.
5. Dempsey, M. E., Draegert, G. L., *et al.* (1950) The Purdue Pitch Meter—A Direct-Reading Fundamental Frequency Analyzer *J. Speech Hear. Dis.* 15:135-141.
6. Denes, P. B. and Pinson, E. N. (1970) *The Speech Chain*, Bell Telephone Laboratories, Baltimore, Waverly Press.
7. Engineering Department (1979) *Modern Instrumentation Tape Recording*, Second Ed., Atlanta, EMI Technology.
8. Fant, G. (1958) Modern Instruments and Methods for Acoustic Studies of Speech, *Acta Polytech Scan.* 1-81.
9. Gold, B. and Rabiner, L. R. (1969) Parallel Processing Techniques for Estimating Pitch Period of Speech in the Time Domain, *J. Acoust. Soc. Amer.* 46:442-446.
10. Harris, C. M. and Weiss, M. R. (1963) Pitch Extraction by Computer Processing of High-Resolution Fourier Analysis Data, *J. Acoust. Soc. Amer.* 35:339-343.
11. Hicks, J. W., Jr. (1979) An Acoustical/Temporal Analysis of Emotional Stress in Speech, Unpublished Ph.D. Dissertation, University of Florida.
12. Hollien, H. (1981) Analog Instrumentation for Acoustic Speech Analysis, in *Speech Evaluation and Psychiatry* (J. Darby, Ed.), New York, Grune and Stratton, 79-103.
13. Hollien, H. and Majewski, W. (1977) Speaker Identification by Long-Term Spectra Under Normal and Distorted Speech Conditions, *J. Acoust. Soc. Am.* 62:975-980.
14. Johnson, C. C., Hollien, H. and Hicks, J. W., Jr. (1984) Speaker Identification Utilizing Selected Temporal Speech Freatures, *J. Phonetics* 12:319-327.
15. Joos, M. (1948) Acoustic Phonetics, *Language* 24:1-136.
16. Keen, A. W. (1956) *Electronics*, New York, The Philosophical Library.
17. Liljencrants, J. (1968) A Filter Bank Speech Spectrum Analyzer, *Tech. Report, Speech Trans.*, Stockholm, Royal Institute of Technology, 37, (January 15).
18. Majewski, W, Rothman, H. B. and Hollien, H. (1977) Acoustic Comparisons of American English and Polish, *J. Phonetics* 5:247-251.
19. Markel, J. D. (1972) The SIFT Algorithm for Fundamental Frequency Estimation, *IEEE Trans. Audio Electroacoust.* 20:367-377.
20. McGonegal, C. A., Rabiner, L. R. and Rosenberg, A. E. (1975) A Semiautomatic Pitch Detector (SAPD), *IEEE Trans. Acoust. Speech, Signal Process.* 23:570-574.
21. McKinney, N. P. (1965) Laryngeal Frequency Analysis for Linguistic Research, *Rep. No. 14: NONR 1224-22*, Comm. Sciences Lab, University of Michigan.

22. Peterson, G. E. and Barney, H. L. (1952) Control Methods Used in the Study of Vowels, *J. Acoust. Soc. Amer.* 24:175-184.

23. Potter, R. K.(1945) Visible Patterns of Sound, *Science* (November).

24. Potter, R. K., Kopp, A. G. and Green, H. C. (1947) *Visible Speech*, New York, Van Norstrand.

25. Potter, R. K. and Steinberg, J. C. (1950) Toward the Specification of Speech, *J. Acoust. Soc. Amer.* 22:807-820.

26. Sondhi, M. M. (1968) New Methods of Pitch Extraction, *IEEE Trans. Audio Electroacoust.* 16:262-266.

27. Speliotis, D. E. and Johnson, C. E., Jr., (Eds.) (1972) *Advances in Magnetic Recording*, New York, New York Academy of Sciences.

28. Zahn, W. (1976) Preservation and Storage of Tape Recordings, *Phonographic Bull.* 15:5-6.

Chapter 5: Electronic Surveillance

1. Anonymous (1978) NILECS, *Standards for Personal FM Transmitters*, Washington, LEAA, Department of Justice.

2. Bloch, S. C., Lyons, P. W. and Ritterman, S. I. (1977) Enhancement of Speech Intelligibility by "Blind" Deconvolution, *Proceed. Carnahan Conf., Crime Countermeasures*, Lexington, KY, 167-174.

3. Buckwalter, A. (1983) *Surveillance and Undercover Investigation*, Boston, Butterworth Pubs.

4. Carrol, J. M. (1969) *The Third Listener*, New York, Dutton.

5. Dash, S., Schwartz, R. F. and Knowlton, R. E. (1971) *The Eavesdroppers*, New York, DaCapo Press.

6. Hartmann, H. P. (1979) Analog Scrambling vs. Digital Scrambling in Police Telecommunication Networks, *Proceed. Carnahan Conf., Crime Countermeasures*, Lexington, KY, 47-51.

7. Hong, S. T. and Kuebler, W. (1981) An Analysis of Time Segment Permutation Methods in Analog Voice Privacy Systems, *Proceed. Carnahan Conf., Crime Countermeasures*, Lexington, KY, 167-171.

8. Inocco, A. P. (1975) Investigative Recordings, *Law Enforcement Communications*, 20-21, 34-35.

9. Leitich, A. J. (1978) Scrambler Design Criteria, *Proceed. Carnahan Conf., Crime Countermeasures*, Lexington, KY, 5-9.

10. Lydon, K. (1982) Technical Surveillance Countermeasures, *Security World* 19:32-35.

11. Platt, E. and Bourbina, R. (1984) A Primer: Key Telephone Systems, *Sound and Video Contractor*, 50-57.

12. Pollack, D. A. (1973) *Methods of Electronic Audio Surveillance*, Springfield, IL, Charles C Thomas.

13. Salmon, V. (1986) Security By Masking, *J. Acoust. Soc. Amer.* 79:2077-2078.

14. Shapley, D. (1978) Pen Registers: The "Appropriate Technology" Approach to Bugging, *Science* 199:749-751.

15. Udalov, S. (1980) Analog Voice Privacy with a Microprocessor, *Proceed. Carnahan Conf., Crime Countermeasures*, Lexington, KY, 27-37.

16. Van Dewerker, J. S. (1976) State of the Art of Electronic Surveillance, *NWC Commission Studies*, 141-214.

17. Walker, C. P. (1980) Police Surveillance by Technical Devices, *Public Law*, 184-214.

Chapter 6: The Problem of Noisy Tape Recordings

1. Bekesey, G. V. (1960) *Experiments in Hearing*, New York, McGraw-Hill.

2. Blain, B. J. (1980) Tape Recording Enhancement, *Police Research Bulletin*, London, UK Home Office, 35:22-24.

3. Bloch, S. C., Lyons, P.W. and Ritterman, S.I. (1977) Enhancement of Speech Intelligibility by "Blind" Deconvolution, *Proceed. Carnahan Conf., Crime Countermeasures*, Lexington, KY, 167-174.

4. Carhart, R. (1967) Binaural Reception of Meaningful Material, in *Sensorineural Hearing Processes and Disorders* (A. B. Graham, Ed.), Boston, Little, Brown, 153-168.

5. Dean, J. D. (1980) The Work of the Home Office Tape Laboratory, *Police Research Bulletin*, London, UK Home Office 35:25-27.

6. Denes, P. B. and Pinson, E. N. (1963) *The Speech Chain*, Bell Telephones Laboratories, Baltimore, Waverly Press.
7. Egan, J. P. and Wake, H. W. (1950) On The Masking Pattern of a Simple Auditory Stimulus, *J. Acoust. Soc. Amer.* 22:622-630.
8. Hirsh, I. J. (1952) *The Measurement of Hearing*, New York, McGraw-Hill.
9. Hollien, H. and Fitzgerald, J. T. (1977) Speech Enhancement Techniques for Crime Lab Use, *Proceed. Internat. Conf. Crime Countermeasures*, Oxford, UK, 21-29.
10. Hollien, P. A. (1983) Utilization of Blind Decoders in Forensic Phonetics, *Abst., 10th Inter, Cong. Phonetic Sciences* (A. Cohen and M. Broeche, Eds.), Dordrecht, Holland, Foris Pub. 532.
11. Hollien, P. A. (1984) An Update On Speech Decoding, *Proceed. Inst. Acoustics, Part I: Police Applic. Speech and Tape Record. Analysis*, London, 33-40.
12. Lim, J. S. (1978) Evaluation of a Correlation Subtraction Method for Enhancing Speech Degraded By Additive White Noise, *IEEE Trans. ASSP* 26:471-472.
13. Lim, J. S. and Oppenheim, A. V. (1979) Enhancement and Bandwidth Compression of Noisy Speech, *Proceed. of IEEE* 67:1586-1604.
14. Lim, J. S. and Oppenheim, A. V. (1978) All-pole Modeling of Degraded Speech, *IEEE Trans. ASSP* 26:197-210.
15. Lim, J. S., Oppenheim, A. V. and Braida, L. D. (1978) Evaluation of an Adaptive Comb Filtering Method for Enhancing Speech Degraded by White Noise Addition, *IEEE Trans. ASSP* 26:354-358.
16. Paul, J. E., Reames, J. B. and Woods, R. C. (1984) Real-time Digital Laboratory Enhancement Tape Recordings, *Proceed. Inst. Acoustics, Part I: Police Applic. Speech and Tape Record. Analysis*, London, 6:1-11.
17. Rothman, H. B. (1977) Decoding Speech from Tape Recordings, *Proceed. Carnahan Conf., Crime Countermeasures*, Lexington, KY, 63-67.
18. Sanders, D. A. (1977) *Auditory Perception of Speech*, Englewood Cliffs, NJ, Prentice-Hall.
19. Wegel, R. L. and Lane, C. E. (1924) The Auditory Masking of One Pure Tone by Another and Its Probable Relation to the Dynamics of the Inner Ear, *Physics Rev.* 23:266-285.
20. Yost, W. A. and Nielsen, D. W. (1977) *Fundaments of Hearing*, New York, Holt, Rinehart and Winston.

Chapter 7: Speech Decoding and Transcripts

1. Aull, A. M. and Zue, V. W. (1985) Lexical Stress Determination and Its Application to Large Vocabulary Speech Recognition, *IEEE-ICASSP* CH218:1549-1552.
2. Bolinger, D. L. (1958) A Theory of Pitch Accent in English, *Word* 14:109-149.
3. Bolinger, D. and Sears, D. A. (1981) *Aspects of Language*, 3rd. ed., New York, Harcourt Brace Jovanovich.
4. Broadbent, D. E. (1954) The Role of Auditory Localization in Attention and Memory Span, *Psychology* 47:191-196.
5. Carhart, Raymond (1967) Binaural Reception of Meaningful Material, in *Sensorineural Hearing Processes and Disorders*, (A. B. Graham, Ed.), Boston, Little, Brown, 153-168.
6. Cutler, A. and Foss, D. J. (1977) On the Role of Sentence Stress in Sentence Processing, *Lang., Speech* 20:1-10.
7. Fonagy, I. (1966) Electrophysiological and Acoustic Correlates of Stress and Stress Perception, *J. Speech, Hear Res.* 9:231-244.
8. Francis, W. N. (1977) International Colloquium on Automatic Dialect Mapping: A Report, *Computers and the Humanities* 11:339-340.
9. Fry, D. B. (1955) Duration and Intensity as the Physical Correlates of Linguisitc Stress, *J. Acoust. Soc. Amer.* 27:765-768.
10. Fry, D. B. (1958) Experiments in the Perception of Stress *Lang., Speech* 1:126-152.
11. Hirsh, I. (1950) The Relation Between Localization and Intelligibility, *J. Acoust. Soc. Amer.* 22:196-200.
12. Hollien, H. (1980) Vocal Indicators of Psychological Stress, in *Forensic Psychology and Psychiatry* (F. Wright, C. Bahn and R. Rieber, Eds.), New York, New York Academy of Sciences, 47-72.
13. Hollien, H. and Fitzgerald, James T. (1977) Speech Enhancement Techniques for Crime Lab Use, *Proceed Internat. Confer. Crime Countermeasures*, Oxford, UK, 21-29.

14. Hollien, H., Geisson, L. and Hicks, J. W., Jr. (1987) Data on Psychological Stress Evaluators and Voice Lie Detection *J. Forensic Sciences* 32:405-418.
15. Hollien, P. A. (1983) Utilization of Blind Decoders in Phonetics, *Abst., 10th Inter. Cong. Phonetic Sciences* (A. Cohen and M. Broecke, Eds.), Dordrecht, Holland, Foris Publications, 532.
16. Hollien, P. A. (1984) An Update on Speech Decoding, *Proceed. Inst. Acoustics, Part I: Police Applic. Speech and Tape Record. Analysis*, London, 33-40.
17. Klatt, D. (1977) Review of the DARPA Speech Understanding Project, *J. Acoust. Soc. Amer.* 62:1345-1365.
18. Lea, W. (1980) *Trends in Speech Recognition*, Englewood Cliffs, NJ, Prentice-Hall.
19. Lehiste, I. and Peterson, G. E. (1959) Vowel Amplitude and Phonetic Stress in American Speech, *J. Acoust. Soc. Amer.* 31:428-435.
20. Mole, H. and Uhlenbeck, E. M. (1956) The Linguistic Relevance of Intensity in Stress, *Lingua* 5:205-213.
21. Osberger, M. J. (1979) A Comparison Between Procedures Used to Locate Speech Segment Boundaries, *J. Acoust. Soc. Amer.* 50:225-228.
22. Parsons, T. (1976) Seperation of Speech from Interfering Speech by Means of Harmonic Selection, *J. Acoust. Soc. Amer.* 60:911-919.
23. Peterson, G. E. and Lehiste, I. (1960) Duration of Syllable Nuclei in English, *J. Acoust. Soc. Amer.* 32:693-703.
24. Rothman, Howard B. (1977) Decoding Speech from Tape Recordings, *Proceed. Carnahan Conf., Crime Countermeasures*, Lexington, KY, 63-67.
25. Taylor, D. S. (1981) Non-Native Speakers and the Rhythm of English. *Internat. Rev. Applied Ling. in Language Teach.* 19:219-226.
26. Van Coestsem, F., Hendricks, R. and McCormick, S. (1981) Accent Typology and Sound Change, *Lingua* 53:293-315.
27. Warren, R. and Warren, P. (1970) Auditory Illusions and Confusions, *Scientific American* 223:30-36.

Chapter 8: Authentication of Tape Recordings

1. Aperman, A. (1982) Examination of Claims of Inauthenticity in Magnetic Tape Recording, *Proceed. Carnaham Conf. Crime Countermeasures*, Lexington, KY, 63-65.
2. Aschkenasy, E. (undated) The Authentication of Tape Recordings: A Brief Review of Basic Concepts and Techniques. Unpublished Manuscript.
3. Broad, W. (1979) Experts Debate Authenticity of "Shaw" Tape, *Science* 203:852-854.
4. Ford, H. D. (1974) The Legal Aspects of Magnetic Tape Recording, *J. Audio Eng. Soc.* 22:226-232.
5. Hollien, H. (1977) Authenticating Tape Recordings, *Proceed. Carnahan Conf. Crime Countermeasures*, Lexington, KY., 19-23.
6. Hollien, H. (1974-87) Procedures for Authenticating Tape Recordings, Unpublished testimony, lectures, classroom presentations and as Chair of the AFACS Committee on Authenticity of Tape Recorded Evidence.
7. Hollien, H., Holbrook, A. and Yamazawa, H. (1989) Electronic Signatures of Tape Recorder Operation, Unpublished Manuscript.
8. Hollien, P. A. (1989) New Approaches to Tape Authentication, Paper read at the Annual Meeting of the American Academy of Forensic Sciences, Las Vegas.
9. Klepper, B. (1984) The Authentication of Tape Recordings: Further Considerations, *Proceed., Inst. of Acoust: Police Applicat., Speech, Tape Recorded Analysis* 6:41-47.
10. McKnight, J. G. and Weiss, M. R. (1976) Flutter Analysis for Identifying Tape Recordings, *J. Audio Eng. Soc.* 24:728-734.
11. Ohio *vs* Haller (1986) Case No. 85CR071897, Court of Common Pleas, Franklin County, Ohio, November/December.
12. Speliotis, D. E. and Johnson, C. E. (1972) Advances in Magnetic Tape Recording, *Annals New York Academy of Sciences*, 189.
13. USA *vs* Guido *et al.* (1986) Case No. GCR8500034, Federal District Court of the Northern District of Florida, Gainesville, FL, May.
14. Wade, N. (1973) Watergate: Verification of Tapes May Be Electronic Standoff, *Science* 182:1108-1110.

15. Warriner, W. (1975) How to Falsify Evidence and Other Diversions, *High Fidelity Mag.* (Aug.) 48-53.

16. Weiss, M. R. and Hecker, M. H. L. (1976) The Authentication of Magnetic Tapes: Current Problems and Possible Solutions, *NWC Commission Studies*, Washington, DC, 216-240.

17. Yamazawa, H. (1989) A Study of Tape Recorder Signatures, Unpublished MA Thesis, University of Florida.

Chapter 9: Historical Issues and Perceptual Identification

1. Atwood, W. and Hollien, H. (1986) Stress Monitoring by Polygraph for Research Purposes, *Polygraph* 15:47-56.

2. Brandt, J. F. (1977) Can You Hear Me?, *Forensic Comm.* 2:9-11.

3. Bricker, P. and Pruzansky, S. (1966) Effects of Stimulus Content and Duration on Talker Identification, *J. Acoust. Soc. Amer.* 40:1441-1450.

4. Brown, R. (1979) Memory and Decision in Speaker Recognition, *Internat. Man-Machine Studies* ll:729-942.

5. Carbonell, J. R., Stevens, K. N., Williams, C. E. and Woods, B. (1965) Speaker Identification by a Matching-From-Samples Technique, *J. Acoust. Soc. Amer.* 40:1205-1206.

6. Compton, A. J. (1963) Effects of Filtering and Vocal Duration Upon the Identification of Speakers Aurally, *J. Acoust. Soc. Amer.* 35:1748-1752.

7. Cort, S. and Murry, T. (1972) Aural Identification of Children's Voices, *J. Acoust. Soc. Amer.* 51:131(A).

8. D'Angelo, F. G., Jr. (1979) Eyewitness Identification, *Social Action and the Law* 5:18-19.

9. Endress, W., Bambach, W. and Flosser, G. (1971) Voice Spectrograms as a Function of Age, Voice Disguise and Voice Imitation, *J. Acoust. Soc Amer.* 49:1842-1848.

10. Hecker, M. H. L. (1971) *Speaker Recognition: An Interpretive Survey of the Literature*, ASHA, Monograph #16, Washington, DC.

11. Hecker, M. H. L., Stevens, K. N., von Bismarck, G. and Williams, C. E. (1968) Manifestations of Task-Induced Stress in the Acoustic Speech Signal, *J. Acoust. Soc. Amer.* 44:993-1001.

12. Hollien, H. (1988) Voice Recognition, *Nonvelles Technologies et Justice Penale* (M. LeBlanc, P. Tremblay, A. Blumstein, Eds.), Montreal, 9:180-229.

13. Hollien, H., Bennett, G. T. and Gelfer, M. P. (1983) Criminal Identification Comparison: Aural vs. Visual Identifications Resulting from a Simulated Crime, *J. Forensic Sciences* 28:208-221.

14. Hollien, H., Majewski, W. and Doherty, E. T. (1982) Perceptual Identification of Voices Under Normal, Stress and Disguised Speaking Conditions, *J. Phonetics* 10:139-148.

15. Iles, M. (1972) Speaker Identification as a Function of Fundamental Frequency and Resonant Frequencies, Unpublished Ph.D. Dissertation, University of Florida.

16. Köster, J. P. (1981) Auditive Sprechererkennung bei Experten und Naiven, In *Festschrift Wangler*, Hamburg, Helmut Buske, AG, 52:171-180.

17. LaRiviere, C. L. (1971) Some Acoustic and Perceptual Correlates of Speaker Identification, Unpublished Ph.D. Dissertation, University of Florida.

18. LaRiviere, C. L. (1974) Speaker Identification from Turbulent Portions of Fricatives, *Phonetica* 29:246-252.

19. LaRiviere, C. L. (1975) Contributions of Fundamental Frequency and Formant Frequencies to Speaker Identification, *Phonetica* 31:185-197.

20. Mack vs. State of Florida, 54 Fla. 55, 44 So. 706 (1907), citing 5, *Howell's State Trials*, 1186.

21. McGehee, F. (1937) The Reliability of the Identification of the Human Voice, *J. Gen. Psychology* 17:249-271.

22. McGehee, F. (1944) An Experimental Study in Voice Recognition, *J. Gen. Psychology* 31:53-65.

23. McGlone, R. E., Hollien, P. A. and Hollien, H. (1977) Acoustic Analysis of Voice Disguise Related to Voice Identification, *Proceed. Intern. Conf., Crime Countermeasures*, Oxford, UK, 31-35.

24. Meltzer, D. and Lehiste, I. (1972) Vowel and Speaker Identification in Natural and Synthetic Speech, *J. Acoust. Soc. Amer.* 51:S131.

25. Michel, J. F. (1980) Use of a Voice Lineup, *Convention Abstracts*, American Academy of Forensic Sciences, 937.

26. Ohio vs. Trussell (1978) Montgomery County Court, Dayton, Ohio, February.

27. Pollack, I., Pickett, J. M. and Sumby, W. H. (1954) On the Identification of Speakers by Voice, *J. Acoust. Soc. Amer.* 26:403-412.

28. Reich, A. R. and Duke, J. E. (1979) Effects of Selected Vocal Disguise upon Speaker Identification by Listening, *J. Acoust. Soc. Amer.* 66:1023-1028.

29. Rosenberg, A. E. (1973) Listener Performance in Speaker Verification Tasks, *IEEE Trans. Audio Electroacoust.* AU-21:221-225.

30. Rothman, H. B. (1977) A Perceptual (Aural) and Spectrographic Identification of Talkers with Similar Sounding Voices, *Proceed. Intern. Conf., Crime Countermeasures,* Oxford, UK, 37-42.

31. Scherer, K. R. (1981) Vocal Indicator of Stress, in *Speech Evaluation in Psychiatry* (J. Darby, Ed.), New York, Grune and Stratton.

32. Shirt, M. (1984) An Auditory Speaker Recognition Experiment, *Proceed. 1st Conf. Police Appl. Speech, Tape Record. Analysis,* Inst. Acoust., London, 71-74.

33. Simonov, P. V. and Frolov, M. V. (1973) Utilization of Human Voice For Estimation of Man's Emotional Stress and State of Attention, *Aerospace Med.* 44:256-258.

34. Stevens, K. N. (1971) Sources of Inter- and Intra-Speaker Variability in the Acoustic Properties of Speech Sounds, *Proceed., Seventh Internat. Cong. Phonetic Sciences,* Montreal, 206-232.

35. Stuntz, A. E. (1963) Speech Intelligibility and Talker Recognition Tests of Air Force Communication Systems, *Report ESP-TDR-63-224,* Air Force Systems Command, Hanscom Field.

36. Stevens, K. N., Williams, C. E., Carbonell, J. R. and Woods, D. (1968) Speaker Authentication and Identification: A Comparison of Spectrographic and Auditory Presentation of Speech Materials, *J. Acoust. Soc. Amer.* 44:1596-1607.

37. Tosi, O., Oyer, H. J. Lashbrook, W., Pedrey, C., Nichol, J. and Nash, W. (1972) Experiment on Voice Identification, *J. Acoust. Soc. Amer.* 51:2030-2043.

38. Wilbur *vs.* Hubbard (1861) *New York Law J.* 35:303 (cited in McGehee, 1937).

39. Williams, C. E. (1964) The Effects of Selected Factors on the Aural Identification of Speakers, *Tech. Doc. Opt. ESD-TDR-65-153,* Electron. Syst. Div., USAF, Hanscom Field.

40. Williams, C. E. and Stevens, K. N. (1972) Emotions and Speech: Some Acoustical Correlates, *J. Acoust. Soc. Amer.* 52:1238-1250.

Chapter 10: The "Voiceprint" Problem

1. Albrecht, S. (1987) Electronic Investigation, *Police* 119:40-42.

2. Anonymous (1975) The Voiceprint Dilemna: Should Voices Be Seen and Not Heard, *Maryland Law Review* 35:267-296.

3. Black, J. W., Lashbrook, W., Nash, W., Oyer, H. J., Pedrey, C., Tosi, O. I. and Truby, H. (1973) Reply to Speaker Identification by Speech Spectrograms: Some Further Observations, *J. Acoust. Soc. Amer.* 54:535-537.

4. Bolt, R. H., Cooper, F. S., David, E. C., Denes, P. B., Pickett, J. M. and Stevens, K. N. (1970) Speaker Identification by Speech Spectrograms, *J. Acoust. Soc. Amer.* 47:597-613.

5. Bolt, R. H., Cooper, F. S., David, E. C., Denes, P. B., Pickett, J. M. and Stevens, K. N. (1973) Speaker Identification by Speech Spectrograms: Some Further Observations, *J. Acoust. Soc. Amer.* 54:531-534.

6. Bolt, R. H., Cooper, F. S., Green, D. M., Hamlet, S. L., Hogan, D. L., McKnight, J. G., Pickett, J. M., Tosi, O. and Underwood, B. D. (1979) *On the Theory and Practice of Voice Identification,* Washington, DC, National Academy of Sciences.

7. Burnham, D. (1971) Voiceprint Mistake Conceded in Tying Inspector to Gambler, *New York Times,* (March 27).

8. Carbonell, J. R., Stevens, K. N., Williams, C. E. and Woods, B. (1965) Speaker Identification by a Matching-From-Samples Technique, *J. Acoust. Soc. Amer.* 40:1205-1206.

9. Commonwealth (Pennsylvania) *vs* Topa (1977) No. 134 (appeal of No. 1465, 1972), *Opinion,* Supreme Court of Pennsylvania (February 28).

10. Crown *vs* Medvedew (1976) Provincial Judges Court (Criminal Division) Brandon, Manitoba, Canada (transcript of testimony).

11. Endress, W., Bambach, W. and Flossler, G. (1971) Voice Spectrograms as a Function of Age, Voice Disguise and Voice Imitation, *J. Acoust. Soc. Amer.* 49:1842-1848.

12. Frye *vs* United States (1923) 293 Fed. 1013, 1014, DC Cir.

13. Gray, C. and Kopp, G. (1944) Voiceprint Identification, *Report Presented to the Bell Telephone Labs*, 1-14.

14. Hall, M. (1975) Spectrographic Analysis of Interspeaker and Intraspeaker Variabilities of Professional Mimicry, Unpublished M.A. Thesis, Michigan State University.

15. Hazen, B. M. (1973) Effects of Differing Phonetic Contexts on Spectrographic Speaker Identification, *J. Acoust. Soc. Amer.* 54:650-660.

16. Hecker, M. H. L. (1971) Speaker Recognition: An Interpretive Survey of the Literature, *Amer. Speech Hear. Assoc. Mono.* 16.

17. Hennessy, J. J. (1970) An Analog of Voiceprint Identification, Unpublished MA Thesis, Michigan State University.

18. Hollien, H. (1971) The Peculiar Case of "Voiceprints," *J. Acoust. Soc. Amer.* 56:210-213.

19. Hollien, H. (1977) Status Report on "Voiceprint" Identification in the United States, *Proceed., Internat. Conf., Crime Countermeas.,* Oxford, UK, 9-20.

20. Hollien, H. and McGlone, R. E. (1976) An Evaluation of the "Voiceprint" Technique of Speaker Recognition, *Proceed. Carnahan Conf., Crime Countermeasures* , 30-45, 1976; reprinted in *Nat. J. Crim. Def.* 2:117-130, and in *Course Handbook.* The Institute of Continuing Legal Education, Ann Arbor, Michigan, 391-404.

21. Houlihan, K. (1979) The Effects of Disguise on Speaker Identification from Sound Spectrograms, in *Current Issues in the Phonetic Sciences* (H. and P.A. Hollien, Eds.), Amsterdam, J. Benjamins, B.V., 811-820.

22. Jassem, W. (1968) Formant Frequencies as Cues to Speaker Discrimination, in *Speech Analysis and Synthesis* (W. Jassem, Ed.), Warsaw, 1:9-41.

23. Kersta, L. G. (no date) Instruction Manual/Procedure for Voiceprint Examinations (with acknowledgment to F. H. East), Voiceprint Lab., Somerville, New Jersey.

24. Kersta, L. G. (1962) Voiceprint Identification, *Nature* 196:1253-1257.

25. Koenig, B. E. (1986) Spectrographic Voice Identification: A Forensic Survey, Letter to the Editor, *J. Acoust. Soc. Amer.* 79:2088-2090.

26. Koenig, B. E., Ritenour, D. V., Kohus, B. A. and Kelley, A. S. (1987) Reply to "Some Fundamental Considerations Regarding Voice Identification (JASA 82:687-688), *J. Acoust. Soc. Amer.* 82:688-689.

27. Kuenzel, H. (1987) *Sprechererkennung,* Heidelberg, Kriminalistik.

28. Ladefoged, P. and Vanderslice, R. (1967) The "Voiceprint" Mystique, *UCLA Working Papers in Phonetics,* 126-142.

29. Lundgren, F. A. *Message From the President,* International Association of Voice Identification, undated but presumably late 1976.

30. McGlone, R. E., Hollien, P. A. and Hollien, H. (1977) Acoustic Analysis of Voice Disguise Related to Voice Identification, *Proceed. Intern. Conf., Crime Countermeasures,* Oxford, UK, 31-35.

31. Michigan *vs* Chaisson (1974) Ingham County Circuit Court, East Lansing, MI., Case No. 73-246756-FY.

32. Mississippi *vs* Windham (1977) Circuit Court Atlata County, (March 17-19).

33. Obrecht, D. H. (1975) Fingerprints and Voiceprint Identification, *Abstracts, Eighth Internat. Cong. Phonetic Sciences,* Leeds, UK, 215.

34. Papcun, G. and Ladefoged, P. (1974) Two Voiceprint Cases, *J. Acoust. Soc. Amer.* 55:S463.

35. People (California) *vs* Chapter (1973) Case No. 4516, Superior Court., Marin County, *Findings and Decision* (July).

36. People (California) *vs* Kelly (1976) Crim 19028 (Super. Ct. No. C-29579), *Decision,* California Supreme Court (May 28).

37. People (California) *vs* Lawton, Gardener and Jackson (1973) Superior Court, Riverside County, Case No. Cr. 9138 (transcript of testimony).

38. Reich, A. R., Moll, K. L. and Curtis, J. F. (1976) Effects of Selected Vocal Disguises Upon Spectrographic Speaker Identification, *J. Acoust. Soc. Amer.* 60:919-925.

39. Rothman, H. B. (1975) Perceptual (Aural) and Spectrographic Investigation of Speaker Homogeneity, *J. Acoust. Soc. Amer.* 58:S107(A).

40. Shipp, T., Doherty, E. T. and Hollien, H. (1987) Some Fundamental Considerations Regarding Voice Identification, Letter to the Editor, *J. Acoust. Soc. Amer.* 82:687-688.

41. Siegel, D. M. (1976) Cross-Examination of a "Voiceprint" Expert, *J. Criminal Defense* 2:79-116.

42. Smrkovski, L. L. (1975) Collaborative Study of Speaker Identification by the Voiceprint Method, *J. of the AOAC* 48:453-456.

43. Stevens, K. N., Williams, C. E., Carbonnell, J. R. and Woods, D. (1968) Speaker Authentication and Identification: A Comparison of Spectrographic and Auditory Presentation of Speech Materials, *J. Acoust. Soc. Amer.* 44:1596-1607.

44. Tosi, O. (1979) *Voice Identification: Theory and Legal Applications*, Baltimore, University Park Press.

45. Tosi, O., Oyer, H. J., Lashbrook, W., Pedrey, C., Nichol, J. and Nash, W. (1972) Experiment on Voice Identification, *J. Acoust. Soc. Amer.* 51:2030-2043.

46. Truby, H. M. (1976) "Voiceprinting" A Critical Review, Brief presented to California Supreme Court (re: People *vs* Kelly) on behalf of the International Association of Voice Identification, 1-44.

47. Vanderslice, R. (1976) The "Voiceprint" Game, *UCLA Working Papers in Phonetics*.

48. Young, M. A. and Campbell, R. A. (1967) Effects of Context on Talker Identification, *J. Acoust. Soc. Amer.* 42:1250-1254.

Chapter 11: Machine/Computer Approaches

1. Atal, B. S. (1972) Automatic Speaker Recognition Based on Pitch Contours, *J. Acoust. Soc. Amer.* 52:1687-1697.

2. Atal, B. S. (1974) Effectiveness of Linear Prediction Characteristics of the Speech Wave for Automatic Speaker Identification and Verification, *J. Acoust. Soc. Amer.* 55:1304-1312.

3. Atal, B. S. (1976) Automatic Recognition of Speakers from Their Voices, *Proceed. IEEE* 64:460-475.

4. Bakis, R. and Dixon, N. R. (1982) Toward Speaker-Independent Recognition-by-Synthesis, *IEEE Proceed. ICASSP*, 566-569.

5. Basztura, C. S. and Majewski, W. (1978) The Application of Long-Term Analysis of the Zero-Crossing of a Speech Signal in Automatic Speaker Identification, *Arch. Acoust.* 3:3-15.

6. Becker, R. W., Clarke, F. R., Poza, F. and Young, J. R. (1973) A Semi-Automatic Speaker Recognition System, *Research*, LEAA, U.S. Dept of Justice, Washington, DC, 1-37.

7. Bobrow, D. C. and Klatt, D. H. (1968) A Limited Speech Recognition System, *AFIPS Conf. Proceed.* Thompson Book Co., Washington, DC, 33:305-318.

8. Bogner, R. E. (1981) On Talker Verification via Orthogonal Parameters, *IEEE Trans. Acoust. Speech Signal Process.* ASSP 29:1-12.

9. Bricker, P. D., Gnanadesikan, R., Mathews, M. V., Pruzansky, S., Tukey P. A., Wachter, K. W. and Warner, J. L. (1971) Statistical Techniques for Talker Identification, *Bell System Tech. J.* 50:1427-1450.

10. Bricker, P. D. and Pruzanski, S. (1966) Effects of Stimulus Content and Duration on Talker Identification, *J. Acoust. Soc. Amer.* 40:1441-1450.

11. Bunge, E. (1975) Automatic Speaker Recognition by Computers, *Proceed., 8th Internat. Cong. Phonetic Sci.*, Leeds, UK.

12. Bunge, E. (1977) Automatic Speaker Recognition System Auros for Security Systems and Forensic Voice Identification, *Proceed., Internat. Conf. Crime Countermeas.*, Oxford, UK, 1-8.

13. Calinski, T., Jassem, W. and Kaczmarck, Z. (1970) Investigation of Vowel Formant Frequencies as Personal Voice Characteristics by Means of Multivariate Analysis of Variance, in *Speech Analysis and Synthesis* (W. Jassem, Ed.), Warsaw, Poland, 2:7-40.

14. Carbonell, J. R., Stevens, K. N., Williams, C. E. and Woods, B. (1965) Speaker Identification by a Matching-From-Samples Technique, *J. Acoust. Soc. Amer.* 40:1205-1206.

15. Cheun, R. S. (1978) Feature Selection Using Adaptive Learning Network for Text-Independent Speaker Verification, *J. Acoust. Soc. Amer.* 64:S182.

16. Clarke, F. R. and Becker, R. W. (1969) Comparison of Techniques for Discriminating Among Talkers, *J. Speech Hear. Res.* 12:747-761.

17. Compton, A. J. (1963) Effects of Filtering and Vocal Duration Upon the Identification of Speakers Aurally, *J. Acoust. Soc. Amer.* 35:1748-1752.

18. Das, S. K. and Mohn, W. S. (1969) Pattern Recognition in Speaker Verification, *Proceed. Joint Comput. Conf., AFIPS Conf.*, Mondale, NY, 35:721-732.

19. Das, S. K. and Mohn, W. S. (1971) A Scheme for Speech Processing in Automatic Speaker Verification, *IEEE Trans. Audio Electroacoust.* AU-19:32-43.

20. Doddington, G. R. (1970) A Method of Speaker Verification, Unpublished Ph.D. Dissertation, University of Wisconsin.
21. Doddington, G. R. (1980) Whither Speech Recognition? in *Trends in Speech Recognition* (W. Lea, Ed.), NY, Prentice-Hall, 556-561.
22. Doddington, G. R., Hyrick, B. and Beek, B. (1974) Some Results on Speaker Verification Using Amplitude Spectra, *J. Acoust. Soc. Amer.* 55:S463.
23. Doherty, E. T. (1976) An Evaluation of Selected Acoustic Parameters for Use in Speaker Identification, *J. Phonetics* 4:321-326.
24. Doherty, E. T. and Hollien, H. (1978) Multiple Factor Speaker Identification of Normal and Distorted Speech, *J. Phonetics* 6:1-8.
25. Edie, J. and Sebestyen, G. S. (1972) Voice Identification General Criteria, *Report RADC-TDR-62-278* , Rome Air Develp. Ctr., Air Force Systems Command, Griffis AFB, NY.
26. Endres, W., Bambach, W. and Flosser, G. (1971) Voice Spectrograms as a Function of Age, Voice Disguise and Voice Imitation, *J. Acoust. Soc. Amer.* 49:1842-1848.
27. Everett, S. S. (1985) Automatic Speaker Recognition Using Vocoded Speech, *IEEE ICASSP* CH 2118:383-386.
28. Feiz, W. and DeGeorge, M. (1985) A Speaker Verification System for Access Control, *IEEE ICASSP*, CH 2118:399-402.
29. Floyd, W. (1964) Voice Identification Techniques, *Report RADC-TDR-64-312*, Rome Air Develp. Ctr., Air Force Systems Command, Griffis AFB, NY.
30. Foodman, M. J. (1981) Experiments in Automatic Speaker Verification, *Proceed., Carnahan Conf. Crime Countermeasures* , Lexington, KY, May.
31. Furui, S. (1974) An Analysis of Long-Term Variation of Feature Parameters of Speech and Its Application to Talker Recognition, *Electronic Comm. Japan* A57:880-887.
32. Furui, S. (1978) Effects of Long-Term Spectral Variability on Speaker Recognition, *J. Acoust. Soc. Amer.* 64:S183.
33. Goldstein, U. G. (1976) Speaker-Identifying Features Based on Formant Tracks, *J. Acoust. Soc. Amer.* 59:176-182.
34. Gubrynowicz, R. (1973) Application of a Statistical Spectrum Analysis to Automatic Voice Identification, in *Speech Analysis and Synthesis* (W. Jassem, Ed.), Warsaw, Poland, 3:171-180.
35. Hair, G. D. and Rekieta, T. W. (1973) Speaker Identification Research Final Report, *Research* , U.S. Dept. of Justice, LEAA, Washington, DC, 38-74.
36. Hall, M. (1975) Spectrographic Analysis of Interspeaker and Intraspeaker Variabilities of Professional Mimicry, Unpublished MA Thesis, Michigan State University.
37. Hargreaves, W. A. and Starkweather, J. A. (1963) Recognition of Speaker Identity, *Lang., Speech* 6:63-67.
38. Hazen, B. M. (1972) Speaker Identification Using Spectrograms Made on Different Sound Spectrographs, Unpublished MA Thesis, State University of New York, Buffalo.
39. Hazen, B. M. (1973) Effects of Differing Phonetic Contexts on Spectrographic Speaker Identification, *J. Acoust. Soc. Amer.* 54:650-660.
40. Hecker, M. H. L., Stevens, K. N., von Bismarck, G. and Williams, C. E. (1968) Manifestations of Task-Induced Stress in the Acoustic Speech Signal, *J. Acoust. Soc. Amer.* 44:993-1001.
41. Hennessey, J. J. (1970) An Analysis of Voiceprint Identification, Unpublished MA Thesis, Michigan State University.
42. Hollien, H. (1974) The Peculiar Case of "Voiceprints," *J. Acoust. Soc. Amer.* 56:210-213.
43. Hollien H. (1980) Vocal Indicators of Psychological Stress, in *Forensic Psychology and Psychiatry* (F. Wright, C. Bahn and R. Reiber, Eds.), New York Academy of Sciences, 47-72.
44. Hollien, H. (1985) Natural Speech Vectors in Speaker Identification, *Proceed., Speech Tech '85* , New York, Media Dimensions Inc., 331-334.
45. Hollien, H., Childers, D. G. and Doherty, E. T. (1977) Semi-Automatic Speaker Identification System (SAUSI), *Proceed., IEEE, ICASSP* 26:768-771.
46. Hollien, H., Gelfer, M. P. and Huntley, R. (1990) The Natural Speech Vector Concept in Speaker Identification, *Neue Tend. Amgerwandten, Phonetik III*, Hamburg, Helmut Buske, Verlag, 62:71–87.
47. Hollien, H., Hicks, J. W., Jr. and Oliver, L. H. (1990) A Semiautomatic System for Speaker Identification, *Neue Tend. Amgerwandten, Phonetik III*, Hamburg, Helmut Buske, Verlag, 62:88–106.

48. Hollien, H. and McGlone, R. E. (1976) An Evaluation of the "Voiceprint" Technique of Speaker Recognition, *Proceed., Carnahan Conf. Crime Countermeasures.*, 30-45; reprinted in *Nat. J. Crim. Def.* 2:117-130, 1976 and in *Course Handbook,* Institute Contin. Legal Ed., Ann Arbor, Michigan, 391-404.

49. Hollien, H. and Majewski, W. (1977) Speaker Identification by Long-Term Spectra Under Normal and Distorted Speech Conditions, *J. Acoust. Soc. Amer.* 62:975-980.

50. Hollien, H., Majewski, W. and Hollien, P. A. (1975) Analysis of F0 as a Speaker Identification Technique, *Eighth Internat. Cong. Phonetic Sci.,* Abstract of Papers, 337.

51. Hunt, M. (1983) Further Experiments in Text-Independent Speaker Recognition Over Communications Channels, *Proceed. ICASSP* , Boston, 563-566.

52. Ichikawa, A., Nakajima, A. and Nakata, K. (1979) Speaker Verification from Actual Telephone Voice, *J. Acoust. Soc. Japan* 35:63-69.

53. Iles, M. (1972) Speaker Identification as a Function of Fundamental Frequency and Resonant Frequencies, Unpublished Ph.D. Dissertation, University of Florida.

54. Jassem, W. (1968) Formant Frequencies as Cues to Speaker Discrimination, in *Speech Analysis and Synthesis* (W. Jassem, Ed.), Warsaw, Poland, 1:9-41.

55. Jassem, W., Steffen-Batog, M. and Czajka, S. (1973) Statistical Characteristics of Short-Term Average of Distribution as Personal Voice Features, in *Speech Analysis and Synthesis* (W. Jassem, Ed.), Warsaw, Poland, 3:209-228.

56. Jesorsky, P. (1977) Principles of Automatic Speaker Recognition in *Natural Lang. Comm. with Computers* (L. Bolc, Ed.), 1-15.

57. Johnson, C. C., Hollien, H. and Hicks, J. W., Jr. (1984) Speaker Identification Utilizing Selected Temporal Speech Features, *J. Phonetics* 12:319-327.

58. Kashyap, R. L. (1975) Speaker Recognition from an Unknown Utterance and Speaker Speech Interaction, *IEEE Trans. Acoust. Speech Sig. Process.* ASSP-24:481-488.

59. Kersta, L. G. (1962) Voiceprint Identification, *Nature* 196:1253-1257.

60. Kosiel, U. (1973) Statistical Analysis of Speaker-Dependent Differences in the Long-Term Average Spectrum of Polish Speech, in *Speech Analysis and Synthesis* (W. Jassem, Ed.), Warsaw, Poland, 3:180-208.

61. Ladefoged, P. and Broadbent, D. E. (1957) Information Conveyed by Vowels, *J. Acoust. Soc. Amer.* 29:98-104.

62. LaRiviere, C. L. (1971) Some Acoustic and Perceptual Correlates of Speaker Identification, Unpublished Ph.D. Dissertation, University of Florida.

63. LaRiviere, C. L. (1974) Speaker Identification for Turbulent Portions of Fricatives, *Phonetica* 29:98-104.

64. LaRiviere, C. L. (1975) Contributions of Fundamental Frequency and Formant Frequencies to Speaker Identification, *Phonetica* 31:185-197.

65. Li, K. P., Dammann, J. E. and Chapman, W. D. (1966) Experimental Studies in Speaker Verification Using an Adaptive System, *J. Acoust. Soc. Amer.* 40:966-978.

66. Li, K. P. and Wrench, E. H., Jr. (1983) An Approach to Text-Independent Speaker Recognition with Short Utterances, *Proceed. ICASSP*, Boston, MA, 555-558.

67. Luck, J. E. (1969) Automatic Speaker Verification Using Cepstral Measurements, *J. Acoust. Soc. Amer.* 46:1026-1032.

68. Lummis, R. C. (1972a) Implementation of an On-Line Speaker Verification Scheme, *J. Acoust. Soc. Amer.* 52:S181.

69. Lummis, R. C. (1972b) Speaker Verification: A Step Toward the 'Checkless' Society, *Bell Laboratories Record* 50:254-259.

70. Lummis, R. C. (1973) Speaker Verification by Computer Using Speech Intensity for Temporal Registration, *IEEE Trans. Audio. Electroacoust.* AU-21:50-59.

71. Majewski, W. and Hollien, H. (1974) Euclidean Distance Between Long-Term Speech Spectra and a Criterion for Speaker Identification *Proceed. Speech Comm. Seminar-74* , Stockholm, Sweden, 3:303-310.

72. Makhoul, J. and Wolf, J. (1973) The Use of a Two-Pole Linear Prediction Model in Speech Recognition, *Bolt, Beranek and Newman Report No. 2537*, 1-21.

73. Meeker, W. F. (1967) Speaker Authentication Techniques, *Tech. Report ECOM-02526-F*, U.S. Army Electronics Command, Ft. Monmouth, NJ.

74. Meltzer, D. and Lehiste, I. (1972) Vowel and Speaker Identification in Natural and Synthetic Speech, *J. Acoust. Soc. Amer.* 51:S131.

75. Ney, H. and Giercoff, R. (1982) Speaker Recognition Using a Feature Welding Technique, *Proceed. ICASSP*, Paris, 1645-1648.

76. Obrecht, D. H. (1975) Fingerprints and Voiceprint Identification, *Proceed., Eighth Internal. Cong. Phonetic Sci.*, Leeds, UK.

77. Preusse, J. W. (1971) Word Recognition and Speaker Authentication Using Amplitude Independent and Time Independent Word Features, *Tech. Report, ECOM-3439*, U.S. Army Electronics Command, Ft. Monmouth, NJ.

78. Pruzanski, S. (1963) Pattern Matching Procedure for Automatic Talker Recognition, *J. Acoust. Soc. Amer.* 35:354-358.

79. Pruzanski, S. and Mathews, M. W. (1964) Talker-Recognition Procedure Based on Analysis of Variance, *J. Acoust. Soc. Amer.* 36:2041-2047.

80. Ramishvili, G. S. (1965) Automatic Recognition of Speaking Persons, *Report FTG-TT-65-1079*, Air Force Systems Command, Wright-Patterson AFB.

81. Ramishvilli, G. S. (1966) Automatic Voice Recognition, *Engng. Cybernetics*, 5:84-90.

82. Ramishvili, G. S. (1974) Experiments on Automatic Verification of Speakers, *Proceed., Second Internal. Conf. Pattern Recognition*, Copenhagen, 389-393.

83. Rosenberg, A. E. (1973) Listener Performance in Speaker Verification Tasks, *IEEE Trans. Audio, Electroacoust.* AU-21:221-225.

84. Rosenberg, A. E. (1974) A Practical Implementation of an Automatic Speaker Verification System, *Proceed., Eighth Internal. Cong. Acoustics*, London, l:268.

85. Rosenberg, A. E. (1975) Evaluation of an Automatic Speaker Verification System Over Telephone Lines, *J. Acoust. Soc. Amer.* 57:S23.

86. Rosenberg, A. E. (1976) Automatic Speech Verification: A Review, *Proceed., IEEE* 64:475-487.

87. Rothman, H. B. (1975) Perceptual (Aural) and Spectrographic Investigation of Speaker Homogeneity, *J. Acoust. Soc. Amer.* 58:S107.

88. Sambur, M. R. (1973) Speaker Recognition and Verification Using Linear Prediction Analysis, *QPR No. 108*, Massachusetts Institute of Technology, 261-268.

89. Sambur, M. R. (1975) Selection of Acoustic Features for Speaker Identification, *IEEE Trans. on Acoustics, Speech and Signal Process.* ASSP-23:176-192.

90. Sambur, M. R. (1976a) Speaker Recognition Using Orthogonal Linear Prediction, *IEEE Trans. Acoust. Speech, Signal Process.* ASSP-24:283-287.

91. Sambur, M. R. (1976b) Text-Independent Speaker Recognition Using Orthogonal Linear Prediction, *Proceed., IEEE ICASSP*, Philadelphia, PA, 727-729.

92. Scarr, R. W. A. (1971) Speech Recognition by Machine—Art or Science? *Electronics and Power*, 302-307.

93. Schwartz, R., Roncos, S. and Berouti, M. (1982) The Application of Probability Density Estimation to Text-Independent Speaker Identification, *Proceed., ICASSP*, 1649-1652.

94. Smith, J. E. (1962) Decision-Theoretic Speaker Recognizer, *J. Acoust. Soc. Amer.* 34:1988.

95. Steffen-Batog. M., Jassem, W. and Gruszka-Koscielak, H. (1970) Statistical Distribution of Short-Term f0 Values as a Personal Voice Characteristic, in *Speech Analysis and Synthesis* (W. Jassem, Ed.), Warsaw, Poland, 2:197-208.

96. Stevens, K. N. (1971) Sources of Inter- and Intra-Speaker Variability in the Acoustic Properties of Speech Sounds, *Proceed., Seventh Inter. Cong. of Phonetic Sci.*, Montreal, 206-232.

97. Stevens, K. N., Williams, C. E., Carbonell, J. R. and Woods, D. (1968) Speaker Authentication and Identification: A Comparison of Spectrographic and Auditory Presentation of Speech Materials, *J. Acoust. Soc. Amer.* 44:1596-1607.

98. Tarnoczy, T. (1961) Uber Das Individuelle Sprach Spectrum, *Proceed, Fourth Inter. Cong. Phonetic Sciences*, 259-264.

99. Tosi, O., Oyer, H., Lashbrook, W., Pedrey, C., Nichol, J. and Nash, W. (1972) Experiment on Voice Identification, *J. Acoust. Soc. Amer.* 51:2030-2043.

100. Voiers, W. (1964) Perceptual Basis of Speaker Identity, *J. Acoust. Soc. Amer.* 36:1065-1073.

101. Waldrop, M. M. (1988) A Landmark in Speech Recognition, *Science* 240:1615.

102. Wolf, J. J. (1970) Simulation of the Measurement Phase of an Automatic Speaker Recognition System, *J. Acoust. Soc. Amer.* 47:S83.

103. Wolf, J. J. (1972) Efficient Acoustic Parameters for Speaker Recognition, *J. Acoust. Soc. Amer.* 51:2044-2055.
104. Wolf, J., Krasner, M., Karnofsky, K., Schwartz, R. and Roucos, S. (1983) Further Investigation of Probabilistic Methods For Text-Independent Speaker Identification, *Proceed. ICASSP,* 551-554.
105. Young, M. A. and Campbell, R. A. (1967) Effects of Context on Talker Identification, *J. Acoust. Soc. Amer.* 42:1250-1254.
106. Yang, M. C. K., Hollien, H. and Huntley, R. (1986) A Speaker Identification System for Field Use, *Speech Tech '86,* New York, Media Dimensions, 277-280.
107. Zalewski, J., Majewski, W. and Hollien, H. (1975) Cross-Correlation Between Long-Term Speech Spectra as a Criterion for Speaker Identification, *Acustica* 34:20-24.

Chapter 12: Psychological Stress and Psychosis

1. Almeida, A., Fleischmann, G., Heike, G., and Thormann, E. (1975) Short Time Statistics of the Fundamental Tone in Verbal Utterances, *Eighth Internat. Cong. Phonetic Sciences,* Leeds, UK.
2. American Psychiatric Association (1980) *Diagnostic and Statistical Manual of Mental Disorders: DSM-III,* Washington, DC.
3. Appley, M. H. and Trumbull, R. (1967) On the Concept of Psychological Stress, in *Psychological Stress: Issues in Research* (M. H. Appley and R. Trumbull, Eds.), New York, Meredith Publishing Co.
4. Arnold, M. B. (1967) Stress and Emotion, in *Psychological Stress: Issues in Research* (M. H. Appley and R. Trumbull, Eds.), New York, Meredith Publishing.
5. Atwood, W. and Hollien, H. (1986) Stress Monitoring By Polygraph for Research Purposes, *Polygraph* 15:47-56.
6. Bachrach, A. J. (1979) Speech and Its Potential for Stress Monitoring, *Proceed., Workshop on Monitoring Vital Signs in the Diver* (C. E. G. Lundgren, Ed.), Washington, DC, Undersea Med. Soc. and Office of Naval Research, 78-93.
7. Bannister, M. L. (1972) An Instrumental and Judgmental Analysis of Voice Samples from Psychiatrically Hospitalized and Non-Hospitalized Adolescents, Unpublished Ph.D. Dissertation, University of Kansas.
8. Basowitz, H., Persky, W., Korchin, J. T. and Grinter, R. R. (1955) *Anxiety and Stress,* New York, McGraw-Hill.
9. Bollinger, D.L. (1958) A Theory of Pitch Accent in English, *Word* 14:109-149.
10. Chevrie-Muller, C., Dodart, F., Sequier-Dermer, N. and Salmon, D. (1971) Etude des Parametres Acoustiques de la Parole au Cours de la Schizophrenia de L'Adolescent, *Folia Phoniat.* 23:401-428.
11. Costanzo, F. S., Markel, N. N. and Costanzo, P. R. (1969) Voice Quality Profile and Perceived Emotion, *J. Counsel Psychology* 16:267-270.
12. Darby, J. K. and Hollien, H. (1977) Vocal and Speech Patterns of Depressive Patients, *Folia Phoniat.* 29:279-291.
13. Davitz, J. R. and Davitz, L. J. (1959) The Communication of Feelings Through Content-Free Speech, *J. Communication* 9:6-13.
14. Denber, M. A. (1978) Sound Spectrum Analysis of the Mentally Ill, Unpublished MA Thesis, University of Rochester.
15. Eldred, S. H. and Price, D. B. (1958) A Linguistic Evaluation of Feeling States in Psychotherapy *Psychiatry* 21:115-121.
16. Fairbanks, G. and Hoaglin, L. W. (1941) An Experimental Study of the Durational Characteristics of the Voice During the Expression of Emotion, *Speech Mono.* 8:85-90.
17. Fairbanks, G. and Pronovost, W. (1939) An Experimental Study of the Pitch Characteristics of the Voice During the Expression of Emotion, *Speech Mono.* 6:87-104.
18. Fonagy, I. (1966) Electrophysiological and Acoustic Correlates of Stress and Stress Perception, *J. Speech Hear. Res.* 9:231-244.
19. Friedhoff, A. J., Alpert, M. and Kurtzberg, R. L. (1964) An Electroacoustical Analysis of the Effects of Stress on Voice, *J. Neuropsychiatry* 5:265-272.
20. Fry, D. B. (1955) Duration and Intensity as Physical Correlates of Linguistic Stress, *J. Accoust. Soc. Amer.* 27:765-768.

21. Fry, D. B. (1958) Experiments in the Perception of Stress, *Lang., Speech* 1:126-152.
22. Hargreaves, W. A., Starkweather, J. A. and Blacker, K. H. (1965) Voice Quality in Depression, *J. Abnormal Psychology* 70:218-220.
23. Hecker, M. H. L., Stevens, K. N., von Bismarck, G. and Williams, C. E. (1968) Manifestations of Task-Induced Stress in the Acoustic Speech Signal, *J. Acoust. Soc. Amer.* 44:993-1001.
24. Helfrich, H. and Scherer, K. R. (1977) Experimental Assessment of Antidepressant Drug Effects Using Spectral Analysis of Voice, *J. Acoust. Soc. Amer.* 62:S26(A).
25. Hicks, J. W., Jr. (1979) An Acoustical/Temporal Analysis of Emotional Stress in Speech. Unpublished Ph.D. Dissertation, University of Florida.
26. Hicks, J. W., Jr. and Hollien, H. (1981) The Reflection of Stress in Voice-1: Understanding the Basic Correlates, *Proceed. Carnahan Conf. Crime Countermeasures*, Lexington, KY, 189-194.
27. Hollien, H. (1980) Vocal Indicators of Psychological Stress, in *Forensic Psychology and Psychiatry* (F. Wright, C. Bahn and R. W. Rieber, Eds.), New York, New York Academy of Sciences, 47-72.
28. Hollien, H. (1981) Acoustic Correlates of Psychological Stress, *Trans. Tenth Symp. Care Professional Voice* (V. Lawrence, Ed.), New York, The Voice Foundation, 145-158.
29. Hollien, H. and Darby, J. K. (1979) Acoustic Comparisons of Psychotic and Non-Psychotic Voices, *Current Issues in the Phonetic Sciences* (H. and P. Hollien, Eds.), Amsterdam, J. Benjamin, B. V., 609-614.
30. Hollien, H., Geisson, L. and Hicks, J. W., Jr. (1987) Voice Stress Evaluators and Lie Detection, *J. Forensic Sciences* 32:405-418.
31. Huttar, G. L. (1968) Relations Between Prosodic Variables and Emotions in Normal American English Utterances, *J. Speech Hear. Res.* 11:481-487.
32. Kuroda, I., Fujiware, O., Okamura, N. and Utsukli, N. (1976) Method for Determining Pilot Stress Through Analysis of Voice Communication, *Aviat., Space Environ. Med.* 47:528-533.
33. Laver, J. (1975) Individual Features of Voice Quality, Unpublished Ph.D. Dissertation, University of Edinburgh.
34. Laver, J. (1980) *The Phonetic Description of Voice Quality*, Cambridge, The Cambridge University Press.
35. Lazarus, R. S. (1966) *Psychological Stress and the Coping Process*, New York, McGraw-Hill.
36. Lehiste, I. and Peterson, G. E. (1959) Vowel Amplitude and Phonetic Stress in American Speech, *J. Acoust. Soc. Amer.* 31:428-435.
37. Lieberman, P. and Michaels, S. B. (1962) Some Aspects of Fundamental Frequency and Envelope Amplitude as Related to Emotional Content of Speech, *J. Acoust. Soc. Amer.* 34:922-927.
38. Lykken, D. (1974) Psychology and the Lie Detector Industry, *Amer. Psychol.* 725-739.
39. Lykken, D. (1981) *A Tremor in the Blood*, New York, McGraw-Hill.
40. Markel, N. N., Bein, M. F. and Phillis, J. A. (1973) The Relationship Between Words and Tone of Voice, *Lang., Speech* 16:15-21.
41. Mol, H. and Uhlenbeck, E. M. (1956) The Linguistic Relevance of Instensity in Stress, *Lingua.* 5:205-213.
42. Moses, P. J. (1954) *The Voice of Neurosis*, New York, Grune and Stratton.
43. Moskowitz, E. (1951) Voice Quality in the Schizophrenic Reaction Type, Unpublished Ph.D. Dissertation, New York University.
44. Newman, S. S. and Mather, V. G. (1938) Analysis of Spoken Language of Patients with Affective Disorders, *Amer. J. Psychiatry* 91:912-942.
45. Ostwald, P. F. (1961) The Sounds of Emotional Disturbance, *Arch. Gen. Psychiatry* 5:587-592.
46. Ostwald, P. F. (1963) *Soundmaking: The Acoustic Communication of Emotion*, Springfield, Charles C Thomas.
47. Ostwald, P. F. (1964) Acoustic Manifestations of Emotional Disturbance, in *Disorders of Comm.*, XLII:Research Publications, A.R. .M.D.
48. Ostwald, P. F. and Skolnikoff, A. (1966) Speech Disturbances in a Schizophrenic Adolescent, *Postgraduate Med.* 12:40-49.
49. Rice, D. G., Abrams, G. M. and Saxman, J. H. (1969) Speech and Physiological Correlates of "Flat" Affect, *Arch. Gen. Psychiatry* 20:566-572.
50. Saxman, J. M. and Burk, K. W. (1968) Speaking Fundamental Frequency and Rate Characteristics of Adult Female Schizophrenics, *J. Speech Hear. Res.* 11:194-302.
51. Scherer, K. R. (1974) Acoustic Concomitants of Emotional Dimensions: Judging Affect from

Synthesized Tone Sequences, in *Nonverbal Communication*, (S. Weitz, Ed.), New York, Oxford University Press, 249-253.

52. Scherer, K. R. (1977) Effects of Stress on Fundamental Frequency of the Voice, *J. Acoust. Soc. Amer.* 62:S25-26(A).

53. Scherer, K. R. (1979) Personality Markers in Speech, in *Social Markers in Speech* (K. R. Scherer and H. Giles, Eds.), Cambridge, Cambridge University Press, 147-209.

54. Scherer, K. R. (1979) Non-Linguistic Vocal Indicators of Emotion and Psychopathology, in *Emotions and Psychopathology* (C. E. Izard, Ed.), New York, Plenum Press.

55. Scherer, K. R. (1981) Vocal Indicators of Stress, in *Speech Evaluation in Psychiatry* (J. Darby, Ed.), New York, Grune and Stratton, 171-187.

56. Scherer, K. R. (1986) Vocal Affect Expression: A Review and a Model for Future Research, *Psycholog. Bull.* 99:143-165.

57. Scherer, K. R. (1986) Voice, Stress and Emotion, in *Dynamics of Stress: Physiological, Psychological and Social Perspectives* (H. Appley and R. Trumbull, Eds.), New York, Plenum Press, 157-179.

58. Scherer, K. R. (1987) Vocal Assessment of Affective Disorders, in *Behavioral Assessment of Affective Disorders* (J. Maser, Ed.), Hillsdate, Erlbaum.

59. Scherer, K. R. and Oshinsky, J.S. (1977) Cue Utilization in Emotion Attribution from Auditory Stimuli, *Motivation and Emotion* 1:331-346.

60. Silverman, F. H. and Silverman, E. M. (1975) Effects of Threat of Shock for Being Disfulent on Fluency of Normal Speakers *Percep. Motor Skills* 41:353-354.

61. Spoerri, T. H. (1966) Speaking Voice of the Schizophrenic Patient, *Arch. Gen. Psychiatry* 14:581-585.

62. Starkweather, J. A. (1956) Content-Free Speech as a Source of Information About the Speaker, *J. Abnorm. Soc. Psychol.* 52:394-402.

63. Starkweather, J. A. (1961) Vocal Communications of Personality and Human Feelings, *J. Communication* 11:63-72.

64. Talevera, J. A., Hollien, H. and Tingle, D. (in press) Voice Analysis for Depression Assessment Through Dicotic Listening Tasks.

65. Talevera, J. A., Hollien, H. and Tingle, D. (1986) Computer Aided Diagnosis of Depression and Dichotic Listening, *IEEE Conf. Engineer. in Med.*, *Biology* CH 2368:789-791.

66. Williams, C. E. and Stevens, K. N. (1969) On Determining the Emotional State of Pilots During Flight: An Exploratory Study, *Aero. Med.* 40:1369-1372.

67. Williams, C. E. and Stevens, K. N. (1972) Emotions and Speech: Some Acoustical Correlates, *J. Acoust. Soc. Amer.* 52:1238-1250.

Chapter 13: Vocal Stress/Lie Detectors

1. Almeida, A., Fleischmann, G., Heike, G., and Thormann, E. (1975) Short Time Statistics of the Fundamental Tone in Verbal Utterances, *Eighth Internat. Cong. Phonetic Sciences*, Leeds, UK.

2. Andreassi, J. L. (1980) *Psychophysiology: Human Behavior and Physiological Response*, New York, Oxford University Press.

3. Anonymous (1975) Dallas: New Questions and Answers, *Newsweek*, 36-38 (April 28).

4. Bachrach, A. J. (1979) Speech and Its Potential for Stress Monitoring, *Proceed. Workshop on Monitoring Vital Signs in the Diver* (C. E. G. Lundgren, Ed.), Washington, DC, Undersea Med. Soc. and Office of Naval Research, 78-93.

5. Barland, G. (1973) Use of Voice Changes in Detection of Deception, *J. Acoust. Soc. Amer.* 54:63(A).

6. Bennett, R. H., Jr. (1977) *Hagoth: Fundamentals of Voice Stress Analysis*, Issaquah, WA, Hagoth Corp.

7. Board of Directors (1973) Resolution Concerning the Dektor Psychological Stress Evaluator (PSE 1), American Polygraph Association, Miami, Florida.

8. Brenner, M. (1974) Stagefright and Steven's Law (paper) Eastern Psychol. Assoc. Meetings (April).

9. Brenner, M. and Branscomb, H. H. (1979) The Psychological Stress Evaluator, Technical Limitations Affecting Lie Detection, *Polygraph* 8:127-132.

10. Brenner, M., Branscomb, H. H. and Schwartz, G. E. (1979) Psychological Stress Evaluator—Two Tests of a Vocal Measure, *Psychophysiology* 16:351-357.

11. Brockway, B. F., Plummer, O. B. and Lowe, B. M. (1976) The Effects of Two Types of Nursing Reassurance Upon Patient Vocal Stress Levels as Measured by a New Tool, the PSE, *Nursing. Res.* 25:440-446.
12. Brumlik, J. and Yap, C. (1970) *Normal Tremor: A Comparative Study,* Springfield, IL, C.C Thomas.
13. Cooke, J. (1981) Scientific Truth Detector Reveals: Sinatra Told the Truth When He Denied Mob Ties, *National Enquirer*, 7 (March 20).
14. Dick, W. (1975) Scientific Evidence Proves Ted Told the Truth About Chappaquidick, *National Enquirer*, 49 (July 1).
15. Dick, W. (1975) Sirhan Was Hypnotized to Kill Bobby Kennedy, *National Enquirer*, 50 (October 27).
16. Dworken, A. (1975) Patty Hearst Not Guilty, Voice Test Proves She Was Forced to Lie, *National Enquirer*, 50 (September 23).
17. Eisenberg, E. and Hill, T.L. (1985) Muscle Contraction and Free Energy Transduction in Biological Systems, *Science* 227:999-1006.
18. Ekman, P., Friesen, W. V. and Scherer, K. R. (1976) Body Movement and Voice Pitch in Deceptive Interaction, *Semiotica* 16:23-27.
19. Faaborg-Anderson, K. (1957) Electromyographic Investigation of Intrinsic Laryngeal Muscles in Humans, *Acta Physio. Scand.* 41 (Suppl.):140.
20. Geison, L. L. (1979) Evaluation of High Stress Lying by Voice Analysis, Unpublished MA Thesis, University of Florida.
21. Haines, R. (1976) Elizabeth Ray Told the Truth about the Washington Sex Scandal; Congressman Hayes Did Not, *National Enquirer*, 51 (April).
22. Hart, C. (1980) Scientific Truth Detector Reveals ... Laren Bacall is Lying in Her Ford TV Commercial, *National Enquirer*, 54 (July 29).
23. Heisse, J. W. (1976) Audio Stress Analysis—A Validation and Reliability Study of the Psychological Stress Evaluator (PSE), *Proceed. Carnahan Conf., Crime Countermeasures*, Lexington, KY, 5-18.
24. Hicks, J. W., Jr. (1979) An Acoustical/Temporal Analysis of Emotional Stress in Speech, Unpublished Ph.D. Dissertation, University of Florida.
25. Hocking, J. E. and Leathers, D. G. (1980) Nonverbal Indicators of Deception: A New Theoretical Perspective, *Commun. Monographs* 47:119-131.
26. Hollien, H. (1980) Vocal Indicators of Psychological Stress, in *Forensic Psychology and Psychiatry* (F. Wright, C. Bahm and R. Rieber, Eds.), New York Academy of Sciences, 47-72.
27. Hollien, H., Geison, L. L. and Hicks, J. W., Jr. (1980) Stress/Lie Studies Utilizing the PSE, paper read at the annual meeting of the American Academy of Forensic Sciences, New Orleans, LA.
28. Hollien, H., Geisson, L. L. and Hicks, J. W. Jr., (1986) Data on Psychological Stress Evaluators and Voice Lie Detection, *J. Forensic Sciences* 32:405-418.
29. Horvath, F. (1982) Detecting Deception: The Promise and Reality of Voice Stress Analysis, *J. Forensic Sciences* 27:340-352.
30. Inbar, G. F., Eden, G. and Kaplan, M. A. (1977) Frequency Modulation in the Human Voice and the Source of Its Mediation, *Proceed. Carnahan Conf., Crime Countermeasures* Lexington, KY, 213-219.
31. Krauss, R. M., Geller, V., Olson, C. and Appel, W. (1977) Pitch Changes During Attempted Deception, *J. Personality, Social Psychology* 35:345-350.
32. Kubis, J. (1973) Comparison of Voice Analysis and Polygraph as Lie Detection Procedures, *Technical Report LWL-CR-U3B70*, Aberdeen Proving Ground, MD, U.S. Army Land Warfare Laboratory.
33. Kupec, E. W. (1977) Truth or the Consequences, *Law Enforce. Comm.* 4:12-18/42-45.
34. Leith, W. R., Timmons, J. L. and Sugarman, M. D. (1977) The Use of the Psychological Stress Evaluator with Stutterers, Abstract, Conven. Amer. Speech Hearing Assoc.
35. Lippold, O. (1971) Physiological Tremor, *Scientific Amer.* 224:65-73.
36. Lykken, D. (1974) Psychology and the Lie Detector Industry, *Amer. Psychol.* 725-739.
37. Lykken, D. (1981) *A Tremor in the Blood*, New York, McGraw-Hill.
38. Matte, J. A. (1980) *The Art and Science of the Polygraph Technique*, Springfield, IL, Charles C Thomas.
39. McGlone, R. E. (1975) Tests of the Psychological Stress Evaluator (PSE) as a Lie and Stress Detector, *Proceed. Carnahan Conf., Crime Countermeasures*, Lexington, KY, 83-86.

40. McGlone, R. E. and Hollien, H. (1976) Partial Analysis of the Acoustic Signal of Stressed and Unstressed Speech, *Proceed. Carnahan Conf., Crime Countermeasures*, Lexington, KY, 19-21.
41. McGlone, R. E., Petrie, C. and Frye, J. (1974) Acoustic Analysis of Low-Risk Lies, *J. Acoust. Soc. Amer.* 55:S20(A).
42. Nachshon, I. and Feldman, B. (1980) Vocal Indices of Psychological Stress: A Validation Study of the Psychological Stress Evaluator, *J. Police Science, Admin.* 8:40-53.
43. Nagle, D. E. (1985) The Polygraph in Employment: Applications and Legal Considerations, *Polygraph* 14:1-33.
44. O'Toole, G. (1975) Lee Harvey Oswald was Innocent, *Penthouse*, 45-46:124-132.
45. Papcun, G. (1973) The Effects of Psychological Stress on Speech, paper presented to Convent. Acoust. Soc. Amer., Los Angeles, CA.
46. Reid, J. E. and Inbau, F. E. (1977) *Truth and Deception: The Polygraph ("Lie Detector") Technique* (2nd Ed.), Baltimore, MD, The Williams and Wilkins Co.
47. Sawyer, C. (1983) Detecting the Unspoken Deception, *Security World*, 50-51 (January).
48. Shipp, T. and McGlone, R. E. (1973) Physiologic Correlates of Acoustic Correlates of Psychological Stress, *J. Acoust. Soc. Amer.* 53:S63(A).
49. Shipp, T. and Izdebski, K. (1981) Current Evidence for the Existence of Laryngeal Macrotremor and Microtremor, *J. Forensic Sciences* 26:501-505.
50. Smith, G. A. (1977) Voice Analysis for the Measurement of Anxiety, *Brit. J. Med. Psychol.* 50:367-373.
51. VanderCar, D. H., Greaner, J., Hibler, N., Speelberger, C. D. and Bloch, S. (1980) A Description and Analysis of the Operation and Validity of the Psychological Stress Evaluator, *J. Forensic Sciences* 25:174-188.
52. Weir, R. J. and Atwood, W. F. (1981) Applicant Screening Polygraph Examinations, *Polygraph* 10:129-142.
53. Zuckerman, M.,. Lubin, B., Vogel, L. and Valeruis, E. (1964) Measurement of Experimentally Induced Affects, *J. Consult. Psychol.* 28:418-425.

Chapter 14: Signatures: Machine and Acoustic

1. Appendix to Hearings Before the Select Committee on Assassinations of the House of Representatives, Ninety-Fifth Congress, *Government Printing Office*, Washington DC, Vol 8.
2. Broner, N. (1987) Acoustic Characterestics of the Strait Line Starting Pistol, Unpublished Manuscript, Melborne, Australia.
3. Broner, N. (1987) Analysis of Tape Recorder Signatures. Unpublished Report. Melborne, Australia.
4. Committee on Ballistic Acoustics, NRC (1982) Reexamination of Acoustic Evidence in the Kennedy Assassination, *Science* 218:127-133.
5. Hollien, H., Holbrook, A. and Yamazawa, H. (1989) Electronic Signatures of Tape Recorder Operation, Unpublished Manuscript.
6. Koenig, B. E. (1983) Acoustic Gunshot Analysis, The Kennedy Assassination and Beyond (Part I), *FBI Law Enforcement Bulletin* 52:1-9.
7. Koenig, B. E. (1983) Acoustic Gunshot Analysis, The Kennedy Assassination and Beyond (Conclusion), *FBI Law Enforcement Bulletin* 52:1-9
8. Price, G. R., (1983) Relative Hazards of Weapon Inpulses, *J. Acoust. Soc. Amer.* 73:556-566
9. Rice, C. G. and Zepler, E. E. (1967) Loudness and Pitch Sensations of an Impulse Sound of Very Short Duration *J. Sound Vibration* 5:285-289
10. Schomer, P. D., Goff, R. J. and Little, L. M. (1978) Statistics of Amplitude and Spectrum of Blasts Propagated in the Atmosphere, *J. Acoust. Soc. Amer.* 63:1431-1443.
11. Ward, W. D., Selters, W. and Glorig, A. (1961) Exploratory Studies on Temporary Threshold Shift from Impulses, *J. Acoust. Soc. Amer.* 33:781-793.
12. Warren, C. H. E (1972) A Significant Single Quantity That Typifies a Sonic Bang, *J. Acoust. Soc. Amer.* 51:418-420.

Chapter 15: Related Areas and Specialties

1. Ampolsk, A. G. (1979) *Piracy on the High C's*, New York, 95-96.
2. Arens, R. and Meadow, A. (1956) Psycholinguistics and the Confession Dilemma, *Columbia Law Review* 56:19-46.
3. Ball, L. B. (1982) Computer Crime, *Technology Review*, April, 21-27.
4. Carpenter, R. H. (1969) The Essential Schemes of Syntax: An Analysis of Rhetorical Theory's Recommendations for Uncommon Word Orders, *Quart. J. Speech* 55:162-163.
5. Carpenter, R. H. (1977) Style in Discourse as an Index of Frederich Jackson Turner's Historical Creativity, *Huntington Library Quart.* 40:269-277.
6. Carpenter, R. H. (1981) Stylistic Analysis For Law Enforcement Purposes: A Case Study of a Language Variable as an Index of a Suspect's Caution in Phrasing Answers, *Comm. Quart.* (Winter), 32-39.
7. Carpenter, R. H. and Jordan, W. J. (1978) Style in Discourse as a Predictor of Political Personality for Mr. Carter and Other Twentieth Century Presidents: Testing the Barber Paradigm, *Presidential Stud. Quart.* 8:67-78.
8. Cassagrande, J. and Hollien, H. (1986) *Text Analysis*, Forensic Communication Associates, Gainesville, FL.
9. Davis, P. (1973) Piracy on the High C's, *Music and The Musician*, 38-40.
10. de Beaugrande, R. (1980) *Text Discourse and Process*, Norwood, NJ, Ablex Pub.
11. Francis, I. S. (1966) An Exposition of a Statistical Approach to the Federalist Dispute, in *Computer and Literary Style* (J. Leed, Ed.), Kent, OH, Kent State Univ. Press, 38-78.
12. Halpern, M. L. (1972) Sound Recording Act of 1971: An End to Piracy on the High C's, *George Washington Law Review* 40:964-994.
13. Johnson, W. (1944) Studies in Language Behavior: I. A Program of Research, *Psychol. Mono.* 56:1-2.
14. Kolata, G. (1983) Scheme to Foil Software Pirates, *Science* 232:1279.
15. Maher, B. A., McKean, K. O. and McLaughlin, B. (1966) Studies in Psychotic Language, in *Gen. Inquirer, Computer Appl. Content Analysis* (P. Stone, Ed.), Cambridge, MA, MIT Press, 469-503.
16. Miller, G. A. (1951) *Language and Communication*, New York, McGraw-Hill.
17. Miron, M. and Pasquale, T.A. (1978) Psycholinguistic Analysis of Coercive Communications, *J. Psycholing. Res.* 7:95-120.
18. Osgood, C. E. (1960) Some Effects of Motivational Style in Encoding, in *Style in Language* (T. Sebeok, Ed.), Cambridge, MA, MIT Press, 293-306.
19. Osgood, C. E. and Walker, E. (1959) A Content Analysis of Suicide Notes, *J. Abnormal Social Psych.* 59:58-67.
20. Parker, D. B. (1976) *Crime by Computer*, New York, Charles Scribner's and Sons.
21. Pesserilo, I. M. (1978) State Anti-Sound Piracy Laws and a Proposed State Model: A Time to Consolidate the Victories Against Sound Pirates, *Performing Arts Review*, New York, Law-Arts. Pubs. Inc., 8:1-49.
22. Prince, E. F. (1984) Language and the Law: Reference, Stress and Context, *GURT-84* (D. Schiffrin, Ed.), Washington, DC, Georgetown Univ. Press, 240-252.
23. Prince, E. F. (1985) On the Use of Social Conversation as Legal Evidence (paper), *Linguistics, Law Workshop*, Georgetown Univ., Washington (July).
24. Renshaw, B. and Kaplan, C. (1979) *Computer Security Techniques*, Washington, DC, U.S. Department of Justice.
25. Schrader, D. M. (1972) Sound Recordings: Protection Under State Law and Under the Recent Amendment to the Copyright Code, *Arizona Law Review* 14:689-715.
26. Shuy, R. (1981) Topic as the Unit of Analysis in a Criminal Law Case and Shuy, R. (1982) Entrapment and the Linguistic Analysis of Tapes. Referenced in Prince, E.F. (1985) On the Use of Social Conversation as Legal Evidence, *Linguistics, Law Workshop*, Georgetown Univ., Wash., DC.
27. Stone, P. and Glenn, E. (1966) A Content Analysis of Twenty Presidential Nomination Acceptance Speeches, in *The General Inquirer: A Computer Approach to Content Analysis* (P. Stone, D. Dunphy, M. Smith and D. Ogilvie, Eds.), Cambridge, MA, MIT Press, 359-400.

Chapter 16: On Ethics and Responsibilities

1. Ahearne, J. F. (1988) Addressing Public Concerns in Science, *Physics Today* 41:36-42.
2. Buckout, R. (1976) Nobody Likes a Smartass: Expert Testimony by Psychologists, *Social Action and The Law* 3:41-53.
3. Canton, B. J. (1986) Tips for Expert Witness, *The Expert and the Law* (M. J. Gorman, Ed.), Lawrenceville, NJ, 6:5-6.
4. Cederbaums, J. G. and Arnold, S. (1975) *Scientific and Expert Evidence in Criminal Advocacy*, New York, Practicing Law Institute.
5. Dean, D. J. (1984) The Presentation of Recorded Evidence, *Conf. Police Appl. Speech Tape Recording Analysis*, London, Institute of Acoustics, 49-55.
6. Fallis, S. M., Jr. (1981) Confronting the Expert Witness—The Prosecution Perspective, *Scientific and Expert Evidence* (E. J. Imwinkelried, Ed.), New York, Practicing Law Institute, 75-86.
7. Gench, W. J. (1987) Trial Success Linked to Meeting Expert Witnesses' Expectations, *The Expert and The Law* (J. J. Gorman, Ed.), Lawrenceville, NJ, 7:5-7 (reprinted from *The National Law Journal*).
8. Higgins, K. M. and Selavka, C. M. (1988) Do Forensic Science Graduate Programs Fulfill the Needs of the Forensic Science Community, *J. Forensic Sciences* 33:1015-1021.
9. Hollien, H. (1987) Consultant of Expert Witness? A Serious Problem for Scientists, paper presented at the Annual Meeting, American Academy of Forensic Sciences, February.
10. Hollien, H. (1988) Problems of Ethics. Symposium on the Use of the Language Scientist as Expert in the Legal Setting, New York, New York Academy of Sciences, April.
11. Howard, L. B. (1986) The Diochotomy of the Expert Witness, *J. Forensic Sciences* 31:337-341.
12. Imwinkelried, E. J. (1986) Evidence Law and Tactics for the Proponents of Scientific Evidence, in *Scientific and Expert Evidence*, (E. J. Imwinkelried, Ed.), New York, Practicing Law Institute, 33-74.
13. Imwinkelried, E. J. (1986) Science Takes the Stand: The Growing Misuse of Expert Testimony, *The Sciences*, November/December, 20-24.
14. Jenner, J. R. (1981) Meeting Expert Testimony—The Defense Perspective, *Scientific and Expert Evidence* (E. J. Imwinkelried, Ed.), New York, Practicing Law Institute, 87-97.
15. Kates, J. H. and Guttenplan, H. L. (1983) Ethical Considerations in Forensic Science Services, *J. Forensic Sciences* 28:972-976.
16. Liebenson, H. A. and Wepman, J. M. (1964) *The Psychologist as a Witness*, Mundelein, IL, Callaghan and Co.
17. Miller, T. H. (1983) Noverbal Communication in Expert Testimony, *J. Forensic Sciences* 28:523-527.
18. Moenssens, A. A., Moses, R. E. and Inbau, F. E. (1973). *Scientific Evidence in Criminal Cases*, New York, The Fountain Press.
19. Peterson, J. L. (1988) Teaching Ethics in a Forensic Sciences Curriculum, *J. Forensic Sciences* 33:1081-1085.
20. Phillps, K. A. (1977) The Nuts and Bolts of Testifying as a Forensic Scientist, *J. Forensic Sciences* 22:457-463.
21. Renshaw, B. and Kaplan, C. (1980) *Computer Crime: Expert Witness Manual*, Washington, DC, Department of Justice.
22. Rosenthal, P. (1983) Nature of Jury Response to the Expert Witness, *J. Forensic Sciences* 28:528-531.
23. Schroeder, O. C. (1984) Ethical and Moral Dilemmas Confronting Forensic Scientists, *J. Forensic Sciences* 29:966-986.
24. Sereno, K. K. (1983) Source Credibility, *J. Forensic Sciences* 28:532-536.
25. Siegel, J. A. (1988) The Appropriate Educational Background for Entry Level Forensic Sciences: A Survey of Practitioners, *J. Forensic Sciences* 33:1065-1068.
26. Smith, F. P., Lin, R. H. and Lindquist, C. A. (1988) Research Experience and Future Criminalists, *J. Forensic Sciences* 33:1074-1080.
27. Tanton, R. L. (1979) Jury Preconceptions and Their Effect on Expert Scientific Testimony, *J. Forensic Sciences* 24:681-691.
28. Undeutch, U. (1982) Statement Reality Analysis, in *Reconstructing the Past* (A. Trankel, Ed.), Deventer, The Netherlands, Kluver, Law and Taxation Pub.
29. Virginia Tech Foundation vs. Family Group Limited (1987) US District Court, Western District of Virginia. *Opinion*, March 18, 1987.

Index